After Calvin

OXFORD STUDIES IN HISTORICAL THEOLOGY

THE GOSPEL OF JOHN IN THE SIXTEENTH CENTURY
The Johannine Exegesis of Wolfgang Musculus
Craig S. Farmer

PRIMITIVISM, RADICALISM, AND THE LAMB'S WAR
The Baptist-Quaker Conflict in Seventeenth-Century England
T. L. Underwood

HUMAN FREEDOM, CHRISTIAN RIGHTEOUSNESS
Philip Melanchthon's Exegetical Dispute with Erasmus of Rotterdam
Timothy J. Wengert

CASSIAN THE MONK
Columba Stewart

IMAGES AND RELICS
Theological Perceptions and Visual Images in Sixteenth-Century Europe
John Dillenberger

THE BODY BROKEN
The Calvinist Doctrine of the Eucharist and the Symbolization of Power in Sixteenth-Century France
Christopher Elwood

WHAT PURE EYES COULD SEE
Calvin's Doctrine of Faith in Its Exegetical Context
Barbara Pitkin

THE UNACCOMMODATED CALVIN
Studies in the Foundation of a Theological Tradition
Richard A. Muller

THE CONFESSIONALIZATION OF HUMANISM IN REFORMATION GERMANY
Erika Rummell

THE PLEASURE OF DISCERNMENT
Marguerite de Navarre as Theologian
Carol Thysell

REFORMATION READINGS OF THE APOCALYPSE
Geneva, Zurich, and Wittenberg
Irena Backus

WRITING THE WRONGS
Women of the Old Testament among Biblical Commentators from Philo through the Reformation
John L. Thompson

THE HUNGRY ARE DYING
Beggars and Bishops in Roman Cappadocia
Susan R. Holman

RESCUE FOR THE DEAD
The Posthumous Salvation of Non-Christians in Early Christianity
Jeffrey A. Trumbower

AFTER CALVIN
Studies in the Development of a Theological Tradition
Richard A. Muller

After Calvin

Studies in the Development of a Theological Tradition

RICHARD A. MULLER

OXFORD
UNIVERSITY PRESS
2003

OXFORD
UNIVERSITY PRESS

Oxford New York
Auckland Bangkok Buenos Aires Cape Town Chennai
Dar es Salaam Delhi Hong Kong Istanbul Karachi Kolkata
Kuala Lumpur Madrid Melbourne Mexico City Mumbai Nairobi
São Paulo Shanghai Taipei Tokyo Toronto

Published by Oxford University Press, Inc.
198 Madison Avenue, New York, New York 10016

www.oup.com

Library of Congress Cataloging-in-Publication Data
Muller, Richard A. (Richard Alfred), 1948–
After Calvin : studies in the development of a theological tradition / Richard A. Muller.
p. cm.—(Oxford studies in historical theology)
Includes bibliographical references and index.
Contents: Approaches to post-Reformation Protestantism—Scholasticism and orthodoxy in the reformed tradition—Ad fontes argumentorum—Calvin and the "Calvinists," part I—Calvin and "Calvinists," part II—Calling, character, piety, and learning—Vera philosophia cum sacra theologia nusquam pugnat—Scholasticism Protestant and Catholic—The debate over the vowel-points and the crisis in Orthodox hermeneutics—Henry Ainsworth and the development of Protestant exegesis in the early seventeenth century—The covenant of works and the stability of divine law in seventeenth-century Reformed Orthodoxy.
ISBN 0-19-515701-X
1. Reformed Church—Doctrines—History—16th century. 2. Reformed Church—Doctrines—History—17th century. 3. Protestant Scholasticism. I. Title. II. Series.

BX9422.3 .M85 2002
230'.42'09—dc21 2002074899

2 4 6 8 9 7 5 3 1

Printed in the United States of America
on acid-free paper

Preface

The essays in this volume were researched and written in the course of some two decades of study on the subjects of the thought of the Reformers of the sixteenth century and their relationship to the later forms of Reformed thought identified by the terms "orthodoxy" and "scholasticism." With one exception beyond the new introduction and afterword, earlier versions of these essays have appeared previously—all of these older studies, however, have been reviewed, bibliographies updated, and arguments recast for the sake of the shape and direction of this book. The earliest of the group, "The Debate over the Vowel-Points and the Crisis in Orthodox Hermeneutics," dates from 1980, the most recent, "Protestant Scholasticism: Methodological Issues and Problems in the Study of Its Development," now a section of chapter 2, from 1999. Both in their subject matter and in their actual composition they parallel and supplement the research and writing that eventuated in a series of independent monographs, namely, *Christ and the Decree* (1986), *God, Creation, and Providence in the Thought of Jacob Arminius* (1991), *The Unaccommodated Calvin* (2000), and *Post-Reformation Reformed Dogmatics: The Rise and Development of Reformed Orthodoxy, ca. 1520 to ca. 1720*, volumes 1 (1987), 2 (1994), and 3–4 (2003). Although, moreover, the conclusions of these studies have consistently enlightened the research that contributed to the larger monographs, virtually none of the material found here was incorporated in full in any of the book-length studies.

Both in form and substance, the essays in this volume stand as a sequel to *The Unaccommodated Calvin: Studies in the Foundation of a Theological Tradition* and as a methodological statement in parallel with the *Post-Reformation Reformed Dogmatics* volumes. I have indicated the relationship to the book on Calvin in the subtitle, *Studies in the Development of a Theological Tradition*. Where *The Unaccommodated Calvin* attempts to look at Calvin's theological works in their historical context and to strip away various twentieth-century theological grids that have clouded our perceptions of the work of the Reformer, these essays carry the approach forward in an attempt to overcome a series of nineteenth- and twentieth-century theological grids characteristic of much of the scholarship on Reformed orthodoxy or what one might less accurately call "Calvinism after Calvin."

The opportunity to revise and edit these essays has enabled me not only to update the bibliography and, as that has proceeded, to work with the insights of more recent scholarship, it also has pressed me, particularly when recasting the older essays, to raise the question of method from the perspective of several decades spent learning the subject. I have been able to remind myself just how much my own approach to the material has changed, particularly with reference to the establishment of a context of interpretation. My earliest work, whether articles written between 1978 and 1987 or the initial monograph, *Christ and the Decree*, recognized the necessity of identifying medieval backgrounds, noting the relative lack of originality in many of the doctrinal statements of the Reformers and their successors, and examining a fairly broad spectrum of writers in a given era in order to begin to grasp the meaning of texts. From the outset, I saw the need to resist both nineteenth- and twentieth-century doctrinal constructs as keys to understanding sixteenth-century texts and the need to do more than simply read a basic text—such as Calvin's *Institutes* or Theodore Beza's *Tabula*—in order to find its meaning.

In several of the essays in this group, including in the monograph, I was consistently pressed to come to grips with what might be called collateral histories or intellectual contexts needed to interpret the religious or theological works: namely, the patterns of biblical interpretation brought about by the Renaissance and Reformation, including trajectories in the interpretation of particular biblical texts; and developments and changes in the study of philosophy, logic, and rhetoric, particularly as these impinged on issues of method and argument in theological works. Certainly some of these accents were brought to bear in the studies of theological prolegomena and of the doctrine of Scripture that appeared between 1987 and 1996, reaching some sort of a conclusion in the long essay on "Calvin and the Calvinists," found in this volume. There, I attempted to lay out a series of methodological issues standing in the way of much of the older scholarship on the subject of Protestant orthodoxy—many of those issues being directly related to the refusal of the scholarship to deal with the broader contexts in which the individual documents had been written, the international religious-theological-philosophical community of dialogue and debate within which the various documents were produced, the genre and intention of the documents themselves, and the simple fact that none of the documents was produced in order to set the terms of debate, whether positive or negative, for various twentieth-century theological movements.

Identification of the broader contexts from a methodological perspective has been a central concern of my more recent work, most clearly expressed in *The Unaccommodated Calvin* and in the methodological proposals found in the second chapter of this volume. This question of context is basic to the reappraisal of the course of Protestant thought in the sixteenth and seventeenth centuries both in view of the layers of bias, misrepresentation, and theologized readings of the era that have to be stripped away in order access the intellectual history of the Reformation and post-Reformation eras and in view of perhaps more fundamental question of the nature and viability of intellectual history as a field of inquiry. Specifically, the more recent studies have raised the question of what precisely frames the individual writings and teachings—is the context a contemporary polemic; is it the immediately intended audience whether in the classroom of an academy or university, in a service of worship, in a broader discussion or debate; is it a regional issue or debate, a national matter, or an international religious question; is it a trajectory of interpretation of a text of Scripture bounded less by issues in the immediate social or political context of the writer than by perennial questions of meaning—or does the seemingly perennial question receive an answer dictated by a particular moment; is the context identified by collateral questions arising from philosophy, political, or even the literary and editorial concerns of an author? Quite simply, the framework for understanding a theological point may not be entirely theological—just as the intention of an author in organizing a more systematic treatise may be academic, traditionary, or literary and editorial, relating more to the chosen genre of the document than to a highly specified dogmatic interest.

Finally, I would like to offer my sincere thanks to the colleagues and friends who have made this work possible and who, at various stages in its production, have offered both help and encouragement. Among those to whom the greatest thanks must go is David C. Steinmetz, first my doctoral mentor, more recently a most supportive colleague, always a friend, and by way of his lectures on the scholastic distinctions of late medieval theology, the *causa proxima et instrumentalis* of my abiding interest in things scholastic. To my colleagues at the University of Utrecht, in the *Onderzoeksgroep Oude Gereformeerde Theologie*, and in the conference that led to the volume on *Reformation and Scholasticism*, I express a profound appreciation, both for the ongoing dialogue that we have had concerning sixteenth- and seventeenth-century thought and for their consistent efforts to refine this field of investigation. I must mention here Willem van Asselt, Eef Dekker, and Anton Vos. My thanks also to Carl Trueman, with whom I have discussed many of the issues addressed in the following pages and who read through several of the chapters and offered sound critique and significant advice. To him go thanks not only for these direct efforts on behalf of the manuscript but also for an ongoing and fruitful dialogue that extends now over half a decade. My graduate assistant Gregory Schuringa read through the penultimate manuscript with great care and offered significant help in producing the final draft for publication.

Contents

After Calvin

1

Approaches to Post-Reformation Protestantism

Reframing the Historiographical Question

Scholarly perspectives on the phenomenon of post-Reformation Protestantism have altered dramatically in the last three decades. Studies of the Reformed or Calvinistic theology of the late sixteenth and seventeenth centuries written before 1970 or even 1975 tended to pose the Reformation against Protestant orthodoxy or, in the phraseology then common to the discussion, "Calvin against the Calvinists." This rather radical dichotomy between the thought of the great Reformer and even his most immediate successors—notably, Theodore Beza—was constructed around a particular set of highly theologized assumptions, concerning the Reformation and Protestant orthodoxy, humanism and scholasticism, piety and dogma. At the heart of the dichotomizing argument was a contrast between the "biblical humanism" and christological piety of John Calvin and the Aristotelian scholasticism and predestinarian dogmatizing of nearly all of the later Reformed theologians, the sole exceptions being those who followed out the humanistic patterns of Calvin's thought into fundamentally antischolastic modes of thought.[1]

Since that time, this view has been increasingly challenged and the attempt to offer a balanced, historically couched as distinct from theologically or even dogmatically-controlled account of the later Protestant development has proceeded on several fronts.[2] The essays in this volume provide a point of entry into the scholarship of reappraisal, whether from the perspective of the basic definitions of the terms and issues (such as "scholasticism" and "orthodoxy" in the Protestant context), from the perspective of the historiographical problems encountered by the study of post-Reformation Protestantism, or from the perspective of selected examples of Protestant thought as it developed into the era of orthodoxy.

There is, moreover, a similarity in method and approach between the scholarship that has begun to reappraise the transition from Reformation to post-Reformation era thought and the scholarship that, shortly before, had launched a reappraisal of the transition from the later Middle Ages to the Reformation. Specifically, the reappraisal of Protestant scholasticism has been attentive to studies of late medieval scholasticism, both in view of the definitions of the scholastic enterprise developed by scholars of the Middle Ages and Renaissance and in view of the more nuanced conception of "forerunners" of the Reformation arising out of studies of the thought of the fourteenth and fifteenth centuries. Thus, scholarship on medieval thought has consistently identified "scholasticism" as a method of discourse used in the schools and universities, applicable to nearly all disciplines. So, too, has scholarship identified humanism as fundamentally related to method and to philology rather than to a particular philosophical or theological perspective.[3] Given these definitions, moreover, the nature of the conflict between humanists and scholastics has been reassessed.[4] On the second point, concerning the identification of "forerunners of the Reformation," a newer scholarship has set aside the examination of reformist rebels, notably John Wyclif, Jan Hus, and Girolamo Savonarola, and sought out currents of thought, and series of issues and problems, that track from the later Middle Ages into the Reformation. The result of this investigation has been to identify a host of thinkers—such as Thomas Bradwardine, Gregory of Rimini, or Wessel Gansfort—virtually none of them rebels and nearly all of them belonging to identifiable traditions within medieval thought, whose positions and arguments led positively toward the Reformation.[5]

Applied to the study of the transition from Reformation to post-Reformation Protestantism, these conclusions concerning the later Middle Ages yield both a revision of the notion of scholasticism and a rethinking of the ways in which continuity and discontinuity of development ought to be charted. On the one hand, the scholasticism of the late sixteenth and of the seventeenth centuries, like the scholasticism of the medieval period, is understood more as a method than as a content. The claim of an intrinsic relationship between the rise of scholasticism among Protestants and the creation of a highly speculative and rigidly predestinarian theology can no longer be maintained. Understood as a method, scholasticism evidences an institutionalization of Protestant thought in its academies and universities, not the rise of a specific doctrinal perspective. On the other hand, the use of particular writers or documents as emblematic of a new theology—the most notable instance being Beza's *Tabula praedestinationis*—simply doesn't function as a method for approaching the diverse and varied materials of the developing Protestant theology.[6] In other words, leaping from Calvin's *Institutes* of 1559, to Beza's 1555 *Tabula*, to the Canons of the Synod of Dort (1618–1619), and thence to Francis Turretin's *Institutio theologiae elencticae* (1679–1685), merely for the sake of documenting the scholastic elaboration of the Reformed doctrine of predestination, overlooks different historical contexts, different issues addressed, contrasting literary genres, and vast numbers of intervening events. The result is a simplistic and flawed picture of post-Reformation thought.

The Course of Orthodoxy: A Brief Chronology

The "orthodox" or "scholastic" era of Protestantism extends for nearly two centuries past the Reformation—a phase of the intellectual development of Protestantism that stands some three times the length of the Reformation. Like the Reformation itself, the era of orthodoxy both drew on and worked to set aside its medieval heritage. Also like the Reformation it both participated in and confronted the shift in European consciousness that belonged to the early modern era.

For convenience of discussion, the span of the post-Reformation era can be divided into four somewhat vaguely defined periods: early orthodoxy, in two phases (ca. 1565–

1618–1640), one leading toward, the other following the Synod of Dort; high orthodoxy, also in two phases (ca. 1640–1685–1725), the former developing the orthodoxy of the confessions in considerable detail both positive and polemical, the latter phase characterized by deconfessionalization and transition; and late orthodoxy (ca. 1725–1770). These periods correspond with the initial framing and formulation of orthodoxy, the large-scale elaboration of the theology, and the decline of the movement in the eighteenth century. The beginnings of Protestant orthodoxy were, certainly, in the Reformation itself, both in normative confessions of the early Reformers, such as the Augsburg Confession and its Apology, the Tetrapolitan Confession, and the First Helvetic Confession, and in the major theological treatises of the great Reformers, particularly those who are counted as second-generation codifiers, works such as Philip Melanchthon's *Loci communes*, John Calvin's *Institutes*, Heinrich Bullinger's *Decades*, or Wolfgang Musculus's and Peter Martyr Vermigli's *Loci communes*. Largely in the seventh decade of the sixteenth century, a significant shift took place, however, marking the beginnings of the early orthodox era: at approximately the same time, the larger number of major national confessions appeared and the majority of the significant second-generation codifiers died. Thus, the Gallican Confession (1559), the Scots Confession (1560), the Belgic Confession (1561), the Thirty-Nine Articles of the Church of England (1563), the Heidelberg Catechism (1563), and the Second Helvetic Confession (1566)—and among the major codifiers, Philip Melanchthon (d. 1560), Jan à Lasco (d. 1560), Peter Martyr Vermigli (d. 1562), Wolfgang Musculus (d. 1563), John Calvin (d. 1564), Andreas Hyperius (d. 1564), Guillamme Farel (d. 1565), Pierre Viret (d. 1571), and Heinrich Bullinger (d. 1575). The transition to early orthodoxy occurred, therefore, not as a major shift in ethos or direction but as the transition from one generation to another and, specifically, as the transition from the work of a group of thinkers who produced the fundamental Reformed confessional and theological perspective to the work of another group of thinkers whose theology tended to develop within the confessional boundaries and along trajectories of argument set by the writers of the second generation.

The one slight exception in the roster of documents and names just noted is the Heidelberg Catechism, written in large part by Zacharias Ursinus. Although its date of composition places it among the major national confessional documents that together constitute the confessional codification of Reformed teaching, its primary author, together with various advisors such as Caspar Olevianus and Petrus Boquinus, belongs to the next generation of the Reformed. The catechism itself, and especially as augmented by Ursinus's catechetical lectures, stands as a founding document of the early orthodox era. The first phase of early orthodoxy comes to a close with the deaths of a significant series of third- and fourth-generation codifiers and the beginnings of the Arminian controversy: Franciscus Junius (d. 1602), William Perkins (d. 1602), Theodore Beza (d. 1605), Gulielmus Bucanus (d. 1603), Thomas Cartwright (d. 1603), the Lucas Trelcatius Jr. (d. 1607), Jacob Arminius (d. 1609), Bartholomaus Keckermann (d. 1609), and Amandus Polanus (d. 1610).

We can, therefore, mark a transition from the initial phase of early orthodoxy to the second phase at the time of the Arminian controversy—and the involvement in doctrinal debate of a largely new roster of theologians: Franciscus Gomarus, Antonius Walaeus, Johann Polyander, John Davenant, Johannes Maccovius, and others. In the Arminian controversy (ca. 1605–1619), the confessional settlement of the mid-sixteenth century, together with the various trajectories of Reformed thought emanating from the second generation and elaborated by the writers of the close of the sixteenth century, were defended and further institutionalized by the canons or theological definitions promulgated at the international Reformed Synod of Dort in 1618–1619.

After the promulgation of the Canons of Dort and the other Reformed confessional statements of the early seventeenth century,[7] there was a gradual transition to the high orthodox era, defined primarily by the passing of the larger number of Reformed writers who either sat at the Synod of Dort or whose thought matured in the early seventeenth century. This second phase of early orthodoxy (1618–1640) follows the publication of the significant later confessional documents—the Irish Articles (1615), the Confession of Sigismund (1614), the Brandenburg Confession (1615), the Canons of Dort (1619)—that marked out the confessional beginnings of the so-called Second Reformation in northern Europe. This phase of early orthodoxy also corresponds roughly with the religious phases of the Thirty Years' War. By the end of the second phase of early orthodoxy, all of the major theologians of the era of the Synod of Dort were dead or close to the end of their careers: Sibrandus Lubbertus (d. 1625), Matthias Martinius (d. 1630), Benedict Turretin (d. 1631), William Ames (d. 1633), Franciscus Gomarus (d. 1641), Antonius Walaeus (d. 1639), Johann Heinrich Alsted (d. 1638), John Davenant (d. 1641), Samuel Ward (d. 1643), Johannes Maccovius (d. 1644), and Johann Polyander (d. 1646). In addition, by 1640, other controversies, notably those over various teachings of the School of Saumur, were beginning to spread beyond France and to become major issues of debate in the broader Reformed community.

High orthodoxy (ca. 1640–1685–1725) can be defined as the era of post- and intraconfessional conflict as well as the time of the full development and codification of the Protestant orthodox theology in the face of various newer adversaries. The first phase of the high orthodox development was a time of theological development and of the framing of the full, confessional theology in its disputative and scholastic as well as positive, didactic, and catechetical forms. It also was an era of what can be called postconfessional or intraconfessional conflict, in which the process of fully formulating and then teaching the now detailed positions of Reformed orthodoxy brought new and highly defined internal conflicts to the movement: this is the era of the spread of the Amyraldian controversy and of debates with other theologians of the school of Saumur, of the controversy over Cocceian federalism and the eventual absorption of many elements of the federal perspective into the basic model of Reformed orthodoxy. In addition, in this era, the Reformed encountered the full implications of the Socinian challenge and faced questions concerning the development of theology in relation to the new rationalist philosophies, Cartesianism and Spinozism.

There is good reason to mark the end of one phase of high orthodoxy and the beginning of another circa 1685. Certainly, many of the major formulators of the fully developed Reformed orthodoxy had passed or were passing from the scene—Johannes Cocceius (d. 1669), Samuel Maresius (d. 1673), Gisbertus Voetius (d. 1676), Stephen Charnock (d. 1680), John Owen (d. 1683), and Francis Turretin (d. 1687). The revocation of the Edict of Nantes occurred in 1685, signaling a disastrous cultural and social moment for the continental Reformed communities and their theology—and 1685 also signaled the beginnings of the massive British trinitarian controversy that began in debate over Bishop Bull's *Defensio fidei nicaenae*, continued with Sherlock's attempt to restate orthodoxy, and moved through various stages, including the debate over Samuel Clarke's theology,[8] lingering on into the second decade of the eighteenth century.

Given the difficulty of identifying a clear ending to the high orthodox era and the fairly clear breakdown of the major confessional models both on the continent of Europe and in Britain around 1725, many of the older histories of Protestant thought have identified an era of transition and deconfessionalization (ca. 1685 to ca. 1725), prior to the beginnings of the late orthodox era.[9] One might reasonably include these several decades in the declining years of the high orthodox era, inasmuch as many of the major theologians who published and taught between 1685 and 1725, some as late as 1735, belong stylistically to the orthodox era—writers such as Petrus van Mastricht (d. 1706), Herman Witsius (d. 1708), Wilhelmus à Brakel (d. 1711), Salomon Van Til (d. 1713), Johannes Van der Kemp (d. 1718), Melchior Leydekker (d. 1721), Benedict Pictet (d. 1724), Jacob Leydekker (d. 1729), Johannes Marckius (d. 1731), Thomas Boston (d. 1732), and Thomas Ridgley (d. 1734). Still, the thought of these writers was, in the same era, balanced against an equal number of representative thinkers whose thought moved toward a less confessional and more latitudinarian perspective—notably Louis Tronchin (d. 1705), Gilbert Burnet (d. 1715), Pierre Poiret (d. 1719), Samuel Clarke (d. 1729), and the Jean Alphonse Turretin (d. 1737). The result is a time of a unique perspective, neither thoroughly shaped by the ethos of orthodoxy nor fully drawn into the era of a dominant rationalism.

Late orthodoxy (ca. 1725–1775) might be called the beginning of the afterlife for Protestant orthodoxy. The orthodox theology, as a system, had not disappeared and its descendants, particularly the doctrinally orthodox pietists of the *Nadere Reformatie*, still taught lively versions of the older Reformed confessional systems. By contrast, orthodoxy had all but lost its relationship to philosophy and its ties to the scholarly or academic methods of biblical exegesis had been all but broken. In addition, the scholastic method, which had been supported throughout the seventeenth century by the retention of Latin as the language of the classroom and by the use of traditional texts in logic and rhetoric, like those of Spencer and Burgersdijk, no longer was the standard method of the academy and university. Philosophically, logically, and rhetorically, the style of theology was changing, and not in a way that could support the older orthodoxy either in style or in substance.

The deaths of a series of representative writers—in whose work one witnesses both the attempt to carry forward the doctrinal substance of orthodoxy but also the changes brought on by the loss of traditional philosophy and logic, the decline of scholastic method, and the absence of broadly accepted confessional standards in international Reformed thought—mark the close of the late orthodox era: Bernhardus De Moor (d. 1765), John Gill (d. 1771), Alexander Comrie (d. 1774), Johann Friedrich Stapfer (d. 1775), Daniel Wyttenbach (d. 1779), and Herman Venema (d. 1787).

The Theological Tradition

The Reformed Tradition: Confessional Unity and Theological Diversity

What I have already begun to describe in this discussion of the successive generations of Reformed theologians and the rise of a scholastic orthodoxy is a single but variegated

Reformed tradition, bounded by a series of fairly uniform confessional concerns but quite diverse in patterns of formulation—not two or more traditions, as is sometimes claimed.[10] The identification of a single, variegated tradition as opposed to multiple traditions is not merely a matter of semantics. It is a major methodological point that influences the historiography of the movement of Reformed thought. The point is perhaps best understood when the history of the Reformed confessional documents is distinguished from the history of theological controversy in the Reformed churches—the former historical discussion serving to identify how the Reformed churches of the sixteenth and seventeenth centuries defined their own identity as Reformed and serving, also, to identify the boundaries of controversy between the Reformed and other confessions, whether Lutheran, Roman, Remonstrant, or Socinian; the latter history having both extraconfessional and intraconfessional dimensions, with the extraconfessional dimensions manifesting the differences between the Reformed and various other theological or confessional traditions and the intraconfessional dimensions evidencing the debates that occurred among the Reformed.

Problematic historiography resulting from failure to make the distinction can be easily exemplified. The most basic instance of the problem is the attempt to pose "Calvin" against "the Calvinists." Not only does this historiographical model fail to address the issues of context, literary genre, and development within a tradition, it also fails to recognize the nature and boundaries of the tradition itself. Calvin was not the sole arbiter of Reformed confessional identity in his own lifetime—and he ought not to be arbitrarily selected as the arbiter of what was Reformed in the generations following his death. Calvin himself recognized the need to balance his own particular theological views with those of his contemporaries in such confessional efforts as the *Consensus Tigurinus*, where the eucharistic teaching was a compromise between Geneva and Zurich.[11] Most of the major confessional documents of the Reformed churches produced in the mid-sixteenth century were conceived with a breadth of definition capable of including diverse individual theologies. Each of these individual theologies, moreover, left its mark on its time and on the writers of the early orthodox era, accounting for a series of trajectories of formulation, all within the boundaries set by the confessions. Given the diversity and the fact that the confessional boundaries were set by no single theologian, it is historically inaccurate to identify the later generations in a strict sense as "Calvinists" and it is quite useless to measure them against Calvin as if he were the standard of orthodoxy.

Confusion of confessional history with the history of theological controversies underlies the presentation of Reformed thought in Jan Rohls's recent *Reformed Confessions*, in which the theological chapters draw nearly exclusively on confessional documents and the historical introduction engages in juxtapositions of Calvin and Beza on predestination, comments on the impact of Ramism on Reformed dogmatics, poses the federal theology of Cocceius against the scholastic orthodoxy of Voetius, and notes the heated debates of the seventeenth century over the theology of Saumur.[12] None of these issues except the problem of the Saumur theologies affected any of the confessions and even the debate over Saumur occurred largely within confessional boundaries. Here, as in Brian Armstrong's study of Moyses Amyraut,[13] the result of a mistaken construal of the Reformed tradition is the assessment of the debates between Amyraut and thinkers such as Pierre Du Moulin, Friedrich Spanheim, and Francis Turretin or those between the Cocceian federalists and the Voetians as battles between opponents and proponents of "scholastic orthodoxy"—whereas the documents of the era indicate battles among the Reformed orthodox and, indeed, among thinkers, all of whom used the scholastic method.

A somewhat different, albeit related, problem is encountered in the efforts of various writers to argue multiple and rather divergent Reformed covenant traditions.[14] I will return to the question of covenant theology later and confine comment here to the issue of tradition or traditions. The core of the argument for distinct Reformed covenant traditions, indeed, in the case of J. Wayne Baker's version of the argument, two nearly inimical Reformed traditions, rests on the presence of unilateral and bilateral definitions of covenant in the Reformed tradition and the claim of these writers that the definitions are mutually exclusive and held by different thinkers, to the point that the unilateral definition belongs to a more "predestinarian" approach and the bilateral definition to an approach that verges on synergism in its emphasis on human responsibility. The problems with the theory are many: in the first place, many Reformed writers of the sixteenth and seventeenth centuries employ both definitions, the unilateral and the bilateral, in their identification of different aspects or stages in the covenant relationship between God and humanity.[15] In the second place, all of the writers, whether Bullinger and Calvin in the sixteenth century or Perkins and Cocceius in the seventeenth, are mongergistic in their soteriology and intent on defining covenant within the boundaries of the confessional tradition. There is, in other words, one variegated Reformed tradition in which there are several trajectories of thought. Ultimately, whatever differences may be identified between the individual formulations of various theologians, all stood within the Reformed confessional tradition and, more to the point of the present discussion, all stood within the pattern of a developing Reformed orthodoxy. It is only by breaking apart the actual tradition, as defined by its own confessions and by labeling one side of the debate as "orthodox" and the other as an opposition to "rigid orthodoxy," that the older scholarship has managed to produce its portrait of a rigidly monolithic or monochromatic orthodoxy.

The Theological Task Defined

The success of the Reformation left Protestant forces in command of large geographical areas. With this ground gained, Protestantism increasingly was defined in religious matters by confessional documents and, from an institutional perspective, proved capable not only of surviving but also developing. Such development, framed by confessional definition, in turn provided a context for the rise of educational issues somewhat different from those faced by the Reformers themselves. The Protestant universities now were pressed to formulate and teach theology in detail to generations of students and pastors who had been raised Protestant—and at the same time to identify Protestantism as not only a form but also the correct form of Christianity over against the claims of Rome.

From an educational or pedagogical perspective, the era of early orthodoxy was, for the Reformed churches, an era in which theologians had to concern themselves with methods of education, specifically with the heritage of logic and rhetoric, the practice of exegesis, and the proper identification and arrangement of theological *loci* or topics for the sake of teaching. Increasingly, the Reformed universities and, given the nature of the academic curriculum, the large-scale theological systems, were modeled on scholastic disputations. At the same time, the logical tools of the early Reformation, notably the Agricolan place-logic as modified by Melanchthon, and the later method known as Ramism, were used by Reformed thinkers to give form and structure to their theology. The formal and methodological result of this development was a Reformed scholasticism, a theology academic in its method, structured around the traditional method of disputation and definition, but altered from the medieval versions of scholastic method by its training in late Renaissance logic and rhetoric.

Some definition is necessary here: the place-logic of Agricola and Melanchthon emphasized the examination of the text of a document in order to identify the topics or central issues presented there. This approach led directly to a pattern of biblical interpretation and theological formulation that related the exegesis of the text of Scripture to the task of eliciting *loci communes*, "standard topics" or "places," from Scripture and then using these topics as the core of theology. This approach is found early on in the Reformation in Melanchthon's *Loci communes* (1521; final edition, 1560) and is evident also in Calvin's *Institutes* (1539; final edition, 1559).[16] It is also a significant methodological link between the Reformation and later Protestant orthodoxy, given the tendency of late-sixteenth- and seventeenth-century Reformed thinkers to continue the *locus* method both in their biblical exegesis and in their theological systems.

As is the case with much of the theological development that took place in the sixteenth century, the detailed presentation of rules for theological formulation—whether on the larger scale of methods for the whole of a theological system or on the smaller scale of definitions of theology as a discipline and finely grained arguments concerning the relationship of biblical interpretation to doctrinal formulation—during the rise of Reformed orthodoxy meant the explicit statement of norms and issues that had often been left unstated or barely sketched out by the Reformers. In true Renaissance fashion, however, the Reformers did produce a variety of treatises on theological pedagogy, indicating how theology ought to be studied. Melanchthon and Bullinger are noteworthy for their essays—and here again there is demonstrable continuity in development from the Reformation into the era of orthodoxy.[17]

Scripture and Exegetical Issues

One of the erroneous contrasts often made between the theology of the Reformers and that of their orthodox and scholastic successors presents the theology of the Reformation as a biblical and exegetical theology and that of the Reformed orthodox as a highly dogmatic and rational theology, largely negligent of exegetical issues. It is important to remove this fiction explicitly and entirely. Like the Reformers, the Protestant orthodox held Scripture to be the Word of God and understood the relationship between God as the primary author of the whole and the prophets and apostles as the human authors of each part on the analogy of "dictation." This identification of Scripture as the authoritative Word was the basis for the Reformers' insistence that Scripture alone is the final norm for theology and of the Reformed orthodox identification of Scripture as the "cognitive foundation" or *principium cognoscendi* of theology, in contrast to the fallible, albeit useful, standard of the church's tradition and the standards of contemporary teachers, councils, or philosophical argument.[18]

We can certainly speak of a development of the Reformed doctrine of Scripture from the Reformation into the era of orthodoxy: the later theologians, honed by debate with Roman Catholics, offer detailed discussions of the clarity and sufficiency of the text. Specifically, they argue that although all texts in Scripture are not equally clear, yet the truth that is necessary to salvation is clearly and sufficiently given. They also insisted that the difficult portions of text can be interpreted by properly trained clergy, in the light of the clear statements found in other places and on the basis of an understanding of the original languages. It is possible to identify, in other words, the development of a fairly refined doctrine of Scripture in the late sixteenth century—but it is quite incorrect to claim that the later writers depart from the basic teaching of the Reformation. It is certainly incorrect to assert that the Reformers understood Scripture as anything other than the infallible, inspired Word of God and the sole foundation for Christian teaching—or to assert that the later orthodox developed a mechanical form of the doctrine of Scripture that was insensitive to power of the preached Word.[19]

Far more interesting from a historiographical perspective than modern, dogmatically motivated attempts to read the Reformers' doctrine of inspiration out of context and sever the links between it and the later Reformed orthodox approach is the examination of shared hermeneutical and exegetical approaches and their trajectories of development from the later Middle Ages, through the Reformation, into the era of orthodoxy.[20] Underlying the doctrinal formulations of the Reformers and the orthodox is a common tradition of biblical interpretation. Not only do both the Reformers and the seventeenth-century orthodox writers belong to the precritical exegetical tradition, their exegetical results are more often than not in agreement.

Predestination and Covenant

It is one of the more curious errors of interpretation of the Reformed tradition to speak of "Calvin's doctrine of predestination" as if it were his own peculiar formulation and something new grafted on to an earlier, less predestinarian movement. Whereas it is true that there are several different formulations of the doctrine to be found in the Reformed tradition, all three of the basic forms have the same basic implication: some members of the human race are eternally chosen by God to be saved by grace through faith and the remainder are justly damned for their sins. Thus, from the beginnings of the Reformation, we can discern a double predestinarianism, a language of divine election and reprobation, similar to Calvin's in Bucer and probably in Zwingli. Although he included the Fall and human sin in the divine decree (which has led to the identification of his teaching as "supralapsarian"), Calvin quite clearly taught both election and reprobation of human beings, considered eternally by God as created and fallen (what would come to be called the "infralapsarian" view).[21] While Bullinger could define the doctrine as a double decree, as in his *Decades*, he could also, as in the Second Helvetic Confession, a work largely his, argue a single predestination consisting only in God's election of some, leaving the remainder of humanity to its own devices and, as a result, to its damnation (another form of infralapsarianism). Bullinger differed with Calvin specifically over the inclusion of the fall in the eternal divine decree and over the extent to which predestination ought to be preached—but he consistently assumed that only the elect would be saved and that election did not rest on divine foreknowledge of human choice. All in all, the differences between Calvin and Bullinger, albeit genuine, can be easily overestimated.[22] Rather than use the confession to argue a deep rift between Calvin and Bullinger, the difference between the confession and the *Decades* ought to alert us to the differing needs of personal formulation (as in the *Decades*) and public or corporate statement (as in the confession) and, again, to the relative breadth of the Reformed confessional tradition.

In the work of Calvin's associate and successor, Theodore Beza, we encounter a tendency to argue double predestination, election and reprobation, as defined in the mind of God prior to the will to create—a tendency, therefore, toward the so-called supralapsarian view. Beza's motive in arguing in this fashion was to exclude all possibility of understanding human merit as a ground of the divine choice of some for salvation.[23] Still, Beza's approach appealed only to a minority of the Reformed thinkers of the orthodox era, notably Perkins, Gomarus, and Maccovius, while the infralapsarian model was ensconced as the confessional norm in the Canons of Dort. The Reformed orthodox doctrine of predestination differs from the doctrine found in Calvin and his contemporaries only in its form of presentation and precision of definition: in the era of orthodoxy, it received closely defined scholastic elaboration and debates arose between proponents of the infra- and supralapsarian definitions—the substance of the doctrine, however, was unchanged. In other words, the basic premise of the doctrine, whether formulated as a single or double decree or in infra- or supralapsarian terms, is that salvation rests on the free and sovereign election of God and damnation results from human sin.

A similar issue arises in the development of the Reformed doctrine of the covenant: the doctrine was formulated differently by theologians of the generation of Calvin and Bullinger— with Bullinger providing the more significant doctrinal statement in various treatises and Calvin offering primarily exegetical and homiletical statements. In addition, the trajectory of the development of the doctrine between the time of Calvin and the era of orthodoxy remains somewhat unclear. Both Calvin and Bullinger wrote at length of the covenant of grace—Bullinger in several treatises and in his commentaries and Calvin in both commentaries and sermons, although not in his *Institutes*. Although there are some minor differences in formulation, both Calvin and Bullinger proposed a thoroughly gracious covenant given unilaterally by God as the basis of salvation and both used bilateral language in describing human responsibility in covenant with God. The Reformed doctrine of covenant is, therefore, neither opposed to nor in tension with the Reformed doctrine of predestination, which also declares a grace unilaterally bestowed by God and assumes human responsibility and obedience under and enabled by grace.[24]

Following 1560, both Musculus and Ursinus proposed, albeit very briefly, a concept of a covenant in creation that had certain affinities with medieval conceptions of creation as an order established and maintained by God. This concept, together with a view of unfallen human nature as capable of understanding God's law, was developed by thinkers such as Caspar Olevianus, Dudley Fenner, William Perkins, Franciscus Gomarus, Robert Rollock, and John Ball (1585–1640) into an elaborate doctrine of two covenants, the covenant of works or nature and the covenant of grace, with the covenant of grace following out a historical pattern of several Old Testament administrations followed by its fulfillment or complete revelation in the New Testament. This model became increasingly important in the Reformed theology of the seventeenth century, as exemplified in the works of Johannes Cocceius (1603–1669), Franz Burman (1632–1679), and Herman Witsius (1636–1708).[25]

It is clear that the early orthodox Reformed thinkers do not oblige the excessively neat categories of those modern historians who have claimed "tensions" in Reformed theology between a covenantal and a predestinarian model or between bilateral and unilateral definitions of covenant. Indeed, early synthesizers of covenantal theology such as Fenner, Rollock, and Perkins held to clearly enunciated doctrines of predestination and often were able to fold both unilateral and bilateral definitions of covenant into their theologies. By way of example, Perkins taught a doctrine of full, double predestination and taught a unilaterally bestowed covenant of grace and at the same time (without either apparent contradiction or internal tension) argued a bilateral character of covenant once bestowed, according to which human beings were called on to act responsibly before God. Even so, Cocceius, who is mistakenly described by Baker as teaching a "conditional" doctrine of covenant in "opposition" to the rigid predestinarianism of "Reformed scholasticism," actually combined the unilateral and bilateral definitions of covenant in a system that taught an orthodox doctrine of predestination.[26] Nor can Cocceius' federal theology be neatly set against the scholastic models of his contemporaries.[27]

Christology and Atonement

Reformed teaching concerning the Person of Christ was, from its beginnings, fundamentally orthodox and formulated in the context of the great ecumenical creeds, particularly the Chalcedonian Formula. Still, there are at least two highly significant features of the Reformed approach that distinguish it from other approaches to the Person of Christ, particularly that of the Lutherans. From its beginnings, Reformed Christology focused on the issue of the integrity of the divinity and humanity of Christ in his person, teaching what is technically called a *communicatio idiomatum in concreto* or "communication of proper qualities in the concrete." Reformed thinkers such as Zwingli, Bucer, Calvin, and Bullinger were intent on affirming the fullness of Christ's divinity and the genuineness of his humanity and consistently refused to allow a flow of divine attributes from the divine to the human. Thus, all of the attributes of each of the natures belong to the concrete "person" of the incarnate Word—the Person of Christ is omniscient and omnipotent, according to the divine nature; finite and subject to death, according to the human nature.

The doctrinal point has a series of very specific applications, all of which remain typical of Reformed theology into the era of orthodoxy: the Reformed insist that, in his ascension to heaven, Christ remained fully human, concluding that his humanity could not therefore be present bodily in the Lord's Supper. This teaching was posed not only against the Roman Catholic doctrine of transubstantiation (which claims that the eucharistic elements are transformed into Christ's body and blood) but also against the Lutheran understanding of a bodily presence of Christ with the bread and wine, by reason of the ubiquity of Christ's resurrected humanity. From the Reformed perspective, to claim that a human nature has the attribute of being everywhere constitutes a denial of humanity, which can only be in one place.

The other central emphasis of the Reformed Christology, one which it took directly from Calvin, is its understanding of Christ as Mediator in terms of his threefold office as prophet, priest, and king—namely, as the revealer and fulfillment of God's promise, as the sacrifice for sin, and as the ruler of God's kingdom. Calvin did not invent the concept, but he gave it a prominence in Reformed thought that continued into the era of orthodoxy. Whereas Calvin had used the threefold office primarily to describe distinct functions of Christ's work, later Reformed theology developed the doctrine historically as well, indicating that, although each office was eternal and had been revealed in the mediatorial work of the Word throughout history, the prophetic office was most prominent in revelatory work of the Word in the history of revelation, the priestly office in the sacrificial life and death of Christ, and the kingly office in the final reign of God. The significance of the doctrine is certainly to be found in the way in which it roots the understanding of Christ's person in his historical work and in its stress on the breadth of Christ's work, not only in his atoning death but also in his revelatory mission and in his rule and headship over the people of God. This latter issue relates directly to the covenantal emphasis of Reformed orthodoxy.

Reformed theology also presented, both in the Reformation and the era of orthodoxy, a doctrine of the mediatorial work of Christ that paralleled the Reformed emphases on salvation by grace alone and divine election. Whereas Calvin, Bullinger, and others of their generation did not make a major issue of the limitation of Christ's atoning work to the elect alone, later Reformed thinkers elaborated the point, particularly because of the controversies in which they became involved. There has been some scholarly disagreement on this issue—and sometimes a doctrinal wedge is driven between "Calvin" and the "Calvinists," as if Calvin taught a "universal atonement" and later Reformed writers taught a "limited atonement." Yet, when the terms and definitions are rightly sorted out, there is significant continuity in the Reformed tradition on this point.

The terms "universal" and "limited atonement" do not represent the sixteenth- and seventeenth-century Reformed view—or, for that matter, the view of its opponents. The issue was not over "atonement," broadly understood, but over the "satisfaction" made by Christ for sin—and the debate was never over whether or not Christ's satisfaction was limited: all held it to be utterly sufficient to pay the price for all sin and all held it to be effective or efficient only for those who were saved. The question concerned the identity of those saved and, therefore, the ground of the limitation—God's will or human choice. Thus, both Calvin and Bullinger taught that Christ's work made full and perfect satisfaction for all, both commended the universal preaching of the Gospel, both taught the efficacy of Christ's work for the faithful alone—and both taught that faith is the gift of God, made available to the elect only.[28] In other words, the inference of a limitation of the efficacy of Christ's satisfaction to the elect alone is found both in Bullinger and in Calvin, despite differences between their formulations of the doctrine of predestination. The Reformed orthodox did teach the doctrine more precisely. In response to Arminius, they brought the traditional formula of sufficiency for all sin and efficiency for the elect alone to the forefront of their definition, where Calvin and Bullinger hardly mentioned it at all. The orthodox also more clearly connected the doctrine of election to the language of the limitation of the efficacy of Christ's death, arguing that the divine intention in decreeing the death of Christ was to save only the elect. This solution is presented in the Canons of Dort in concise formulae.

It is well documented that some of the delegates at Dort held that the sufficiency of Christ's death reflected the divine will to save all people, if all would come to believe and therefore found the formulae restrictive.[29] As the seventeenth century progressed, Reformed theologians such as John Davenant in England or John Cameron and Moyses Amyraut in France offered various conceptions of a "hypothetical universalism," according to which the sufficiency of Christ's death was willed hypothetically or conditionally for all human beings—on condition of belief—prior to the divine decree to save the elect by grace. This view was considered problematic by the majority of the Reformed orthodox, given that it conceived of an unrealized (indeed, an intentionally unrealized) will in God.[30] Still, inasmuch as the doctrine never claimed to broaden the efficacy of Christ's death on the assumption that nonelect individuals might actually believe, it can hardly be identified as an actual alternative to the more typical Reformed teaching of the limitation, by the will of God, of the efficacy of Christ's death to the elect. If there is a difference between "Calvin" and the "Calvinists" (or between Bullinger or Musculus and the Reformed orthodox) on this point, it is simply that, in the case of the Reformers, one must make a little effort to "connect the dots," whereas the Reformed orthodox made sure, against various doctrinal adversaries, that the picture was presented in full. Arguably, in the confessional context of seventeenth-century orthodoxy, this full presentation included both the hypothetical universalism of Davenant, Cameron, and Amyraut and the more strictly divided sufficiency/efficiency formula of Turretin, Heidegger, and the other signatories of the *Formula Consensus Helvetica*; although, equally so, it may be argued that some of the forms of hypothetical universalism included speculative elements that fell outside of the main trajectory of Reformed theology.

Reframing the Historiographical Question

Several of the generalizations and conclusions made in the preceding comments on the theology of the Reformed tradition point directly toward the need to reframe the historiographical analysis of the transition from Reformation to orthodoxy. To begin with the last example: the development of Reformed atonement theory has, in the older literature, consistently pitted Calvin against the Calvinists and in one instance linked a "humanistic" Calvin and a "humanistic" Amyraut in opposition to "scholastic Calvinists." There is good reason to argue the point quite differently, given clarification of the trajectories of scholasticism and humanism through the Reformation and into the era of orthodoxy: inasmuch as scholasticism and humanism represent issues of method rather than issues of theological content, the doctrinal debate over hypothetical universalism hardly stemmed from a difference between humanistic and scholastic trajectories of Reformed theology. What is more, the debate over the question of whether or not the sufficiency of Christ's satisfaction might be construed as a hypothetical or conditional decree of God prior to knowledge that no human beings would choose to believe and his consequent decree to save only the elect is so rarified a notion, so imbedded in the mentality of close distinctions, that it can only be identified as indicative of scholastic method on both sides of the argument. In this view, the Amyraut controversy evidences not a debate between humanistic Calvinians and rigid, scholastic Calvinistic orthodoxy, but an internal debate of the Reformed orthodox and, therefore, the variety and breadth within confessional orthodoxy, indeed, among the Reformed scholastics.

By extension, the most obvious example of the relationship between the essays found in *The Unaccommodated Calvin* and those included in this volume is the discussion of humanism and scholasticism that runs through both. In *The Unaccommodated Calvin*, I specifically addressed the issue of Calvin and scholasticism, concluding that Calvin's polemics against scholastic theology were more varied and nuanced than sometimes thought and that they indicated neither a rejection of all scholastic theology nor a refusal on Calvin's own part to incorporate scholastic distinctions and arguments in his own thought. This conclusion not only provides a somewhat different perspective on the kind of continuity that exists between Calvin and his predecessors, it also alters one's perception of the relationship between Calvin and his more scholastic Reformed successors—the contrast is not a great as is sometimes supposed. The essays gathered in this volume address the same issue from the opposite side: analysis of the "scholasticism" of later Reformed theology not only manifests its character as a method rather than as a specific theological or philosophical content but also manifests its use as a methodological vehicle for maintaining, in new or changed contexts, the basic theological perspectives of the Reformation. What is more, the "scholasticism" of the late sixteenth and seventeenth centuries is shown to have been different from the scholasticism of the medieval centuries, given modifications in style and method brought about by the Renaissance and Reformation. Thus, the contrast between Calvin and the later Reformed is diminished from both perspectives, that of Calvin and that of the later writers, and the continuities between the sixteenth- and seventeenth-century expressions of Reformed thought are more clearly identified.

A similar point can be made concerning the continuities of humanism. Whereas in *The Unaccommodated Calvin* I attempted to illustrate both scholastic and humanistic elements in Calvin's thought rather than reduce him to the generalized notion of a "biblical humanist," in the essays gathered here I have identified humanistic elements in the work of the writers nominally identified as Reformed "scholastics." Most notable here are the methodological continuities of this later scholasticism with the *locus* method developed by Renaissance rhetors and logicians, and the later scholastic continuance of the Renaissance interest in philology and the use of ancient sources in the original languages. If, in other words, it is unsuitable to identify Calvin as a "biblical humanist" utterly opposed to the results of scholasticism, so also is it fundamentally unsuitable to identify the later Reformed writers as scholastics who discarded or scorned the humanistic methods of the Renaissance and Reformation.

The essays gathered together here also form a reasonably cohesive unit, divided into two basic categories. In the first part, "Reframing the Phenomenon—Definition, Method, and Assessment," all of the essays offer redefinitions or reappraisals of the phenomenon of Reformed orthodoxy and scholasticism. The first essay of this part (chapter 2 of the book),[31] "Scholasticism and Orthodoxy in the Reformed Tradition: Definition and Method," represents a programmatic attempt at the identification of the problem of much of the older scholarship in its reading of scholastic orthodoxy—from its tendency to ignore the fundamental identity of "scholasticism" as a method rather than a particular theological or philosophical content, to its unwillingness to recognize that the Reformation itself, as the primary antecedent of Protestant orthodoxy, had the reestablishment of Christian "orthodoxy" as one of its fundamental goals. The essay concludes with a discussion of methodological issues and problems that need to be addressed for the full reappraisal of the phenomenon of Protestant orthodoxy.

In the second essay (chapter 3),[32] "*Ad fontes argumentorum*: The Sources of Reformed Theology in thc Seventeenth Century," I move past the basic issue of definition and approach and raise the question of the actual sources and materials used by the Protestant scholastics of the seventeenth century in the fashioning of their theological world, noting the Renaissance and medieval backgrounds of Reformed orthodoxy, and arguing that the sources used and, moreover, the way in which they were used, support the redefinition and reappraisal proposed in the initial study.

The final two chapters in part I ("Calvin and the 'Calvinists': Assessing Continuities and Discontinuities Between Reformation and Orthodoxy," parts 1 and 2) turn to the issue of redefinition and reappraisal from a more strictly methodological perspective.[33] Underlying their arguments, in parallel with the critical thesis of *The Unaccommodated Calvin*, these essays note both the failure of a highly theologized historiography to provide a balanced and convincing analysis of the transition from the Reformation into the era of orthodoxy and the need for a more objective and balanced historiography to look beyond the purely dogmatic content of the materials in order to ascertain their implications in and for their historical context. In form, these essays examine the grounds and issues facing the study of post-Reformation Protestant thought in series of theses designed to identify problems and issues in the historiography and to serve as points of departure for more detailed arguments concerning the method necessary to the field. Specifically, they take up several of the threads of the more programmatic first chapter and indicate some of the components of the requisite bibliography—given the assumption that much of the problem underlying the older scholarship was its narrow appeal to sixteenth- and seventeenth-century Protestant theology in isolation from the medieval and Renaissance antecedents of the Reformation and in isolation from the study of collateral fields of investigation such as the history of biblical exegesis and the history of philosophy.

Part II, "Scholastic Protestantism—Foundational Perspectives," contains six essays that illustrate and develop the definitions and critiques of part one in the form of concrete example. Quite specifically, they take up lines of argument indicated in the preliminary study of the "Sources of Reformed Theology in the Seventeenth Century." The essays, moreover, reflect the contents of the initial topics of most Reformed theologies of the orthodox era, namely, the prolegomena and Scripture. The significance of this grouping, therefore, is that all of the essays reflect issues raised consistently by the Reformed orthodox at the presuppositional level of their thought and, therefore, issues the resolution or definition of which carry over into their theology as a whole.

The first essay in this part (chapter 6),[34] "Calling, Character, Piety, and Learning: Paradigms for Theological Education in the Era of Protestant Orthodoxy," moves beyond the basic presentation of sources, materials, and methods to the examination of the ethos of study in the seventeenth century. After a preliminary examination of some of the approaches to theological study published by Reformers, the essay looks both at the large-scale program of study and spiritual formation recommended by later Calvinists and at the personal result of that program as detailed by one of its chief exponents. Not only does the essay register a continuity in intention and ethos in the development of Reformed thought between the time of the Reformation and the era of scholastic orthodoxy, the essay also documents the strong sense of calling and piety that accompanied and enriched the educational programs of the Reformed orthodox. This is, moreover, a significant issue in the reappraisal of the theology of scholastic orthodoxy given the tendency of a fair amount of the older literature to assume the opposite, namely, that the theology of the Protestant scholastics was spiritually arid and quite discontinuous with the piety of the era. The implication of an examination of the curricula, curricular recommendations, and the spirituality of study is that discussions of the piety of the English Puritans or of the Dutch *Nadere Reformatie* that ignore the connection of these movements to the scholastic orthodoxy of the era present at best a partial picture of the era and at worst a rather distorted picture of piety of the seventeenth century.

Two brief examples will suffice. Among the English writers of the era, Richard Baxter is best known for his works on piety and spirituality. Several of his spiritual works—such as *The Reformed Pastor* and *The Saints' Everlasting Rest*—have remained in print fairly consistently since his own time and now belong to a small body of perennial classics of Christian piety that are studied in their own right as spiritual literature, apart from consideration of the broader scope of Baxter's thought. The problematic of such a procedure is evident when Baxter's own sense of his spiritual and theological legacy was bound to works such as his *Catholike Theology*, *Methodus theologiae*, and *Aphorismes of Justification*, none of which are found on the list of popular spiritual classics and that, in fact, belong to the category of seventeenth-century scholastic theology. What is more, a glance at the sources, whether ancient or contemporary, cited by Baxter in the composition of his works evidences a reliance on the older scholastic tradition and a detailed acquaintance with the works of the continental theologians of his time. If Baxter's practical works cannot be understood apart from the larger theological context provided by his more technical works, none of his thought can be understood apart from the broad international context of British Reformed thought in the seventeenth century.[35]

A second parallel example is the work of the Dutch theologian Gisbertus Voetius, whose approach to theological learning is the subject of one section of the chapter. From one perspective, Voetius is remembered as one of the preeminent scholastic thinkers of his day. He presented his theology in the form of academic or scholastic "disputations" in which the thetically stated doctrines of orthodoxy were defended against heresies, whether ancient or modern, and against various philosophical errors. To this task of defense, Voetius brought a vast bibliography of patristic, medieval, Renaissance, and Reformation sources and an enormous array of linguistic tools. His references evidence a massive knowledge of the Bible in its original languages, and an equally impressive grasp of medieval scholastic theology documented by examinations of Thomist, Scotist, and nominalist argumentation on fairly rarified points of argument. He was an angry opponent of the "federal" or Cocceian school of Reformed thought in the seventeenth century, and he engaged at length and in some depth with Cartesian philosophy, viewing it as a thoroughly problematic mode of thought and no ally of Christian theology. Voetius is remembered also, as it were, by another constituency—students of the piety and spirituality of the Dutch *Nadere Reformatie*: indeed, in his treatises on piety, his work as a catechist, and his assumption that the Reformation of the church must be continued in the ongoing inner reformation of the believer, Voetius is remembered as one of the founding fathers of the late-seventeenth-century spiritual revival. He and his orthodox colleagues and followers—Johannes Hoornbeeck, Brakel, Mastricht, and Simon Oomius—serve as significant examples of the interrelationship of scholastic orthodoxy with piety and spirituality in the seventeenth century, a point all too often ignored in the older scholarship.

The next two essays (chapters 7 and 8)—"*Vera Philosophia cum Sacra Theologia nusquam pugnat*: Keckermann on Philosophy, Theology, and the Problem of Double Truth"[36] and "Scholasticism Protestant and Catholic: Francis Turretin on the Object and Principles of Theology"[37]—examine presuppositional questions concerning the relationship of theology to philosophy and the nature of the theological task. The study of Keckermann not only addresses the issue of the late Reformation or early orthodox approach to philosophy as a necessary element in the academy or university curriculum, it also examines the issue of the Reformed reappropriation of aspects of the older tradition in the era of the institutionalization of Protestantism—what might be viewed as the intellectual analogue of what various social historians have called "confessionalization." The study of Turretin looks at another aspect of the same development from the vantage point of the late seventeenth century, notes the critical appropriation of categories from the older scholasticism and then, within the framework of the definitions examined, argues against the fairly standard claim in much twentieth-century scholarship that thinkers such as Turretin moved away from the perspectives of the Reformation into various forms of rationalism. Both essays approach definitional aspects of the theological task in the era of orthodoxy with respect to traditionary and institutional contexts—underlining the point that Protestants did not construct theology either entirely *de novo* or as a matter of pure abstraction, and revealing, conversely, how examination of these writers apart from their context and from theologized perspectives of later eras can entirely misunderstand the nature and character of their work.

The other essays in this section of the book, chapters 9 through 11—"The Debate over the Vowel Points and the Crisis in Orthodox Hermeneutics,"[38] "Henry Ainsworth and the Development of Protestant Exegesis in the Early Seventeenth Century,"[39] and "The Covenant of Works and the Stability of Divine Law in Seventeenth-Century Reformed Orthodoxy"[40]—look at understandings of Scripture and its interpretation in the seventeenth century. In all three essays, chief concerns are the relationship of later Reformed theology to its past and the contextual reading of the seventeenth-century materials.

Each of these three essays examines an aspect of the Reformed approach to Scripture—a confessional position, an exegetical perspective, and a doctrinal issue with significant hermeneutical and theological overtones—and all register, albeit in different ways, the continuities and discontinuities belonging to the movement from Reformation to orthodoxy. Chapter 10, "The Debate over the Vowel Points and the Crisis in Orthodox Hermeneutics," examines the materials of a famous but little-examined and much misunderstood seventeenth-century debate over the text of Scripture. At least one modern discussion of the debate pits an obscurantist scholastic defense of the Mosaic origins of the vowel-points against the more open views of the Reformation and, presumably, the forward march of critical exegesis,[41] but the materials, examined in the context of the exegetical and philological discussions as well as the doctrinal controversies of the mid-seventeenth century, indicate that the lines of debate cannot be drawn so neatly. One of the foremost Judaic scholars of the era, John Lightfoot, who is remembered for arguing the use of Judaica to establish the context and meaning of the New Testament, upheld the Mosaic origin of the vowel points.

Analysis of the debate over the vowel-points, which is often cited as an example of the mental rigidity of the Reformed orthodox and their discontinuity with the exegetical and hermeneutical approaches of the Reformers, demonstrates, in fact, a rather complex issue and a rather variegated development of Reformed thought rather than a simple movement from a "dynamic" view of Scripture attributed to the Reformers and a "static" view attributed to the orthodox. The debate was not between proponents of confessional orthodoxy and proponents of a heterodoxy. Unlike the debates between the Reformed and the Socinians or between the Reformed and Roman Catholics, the debate over the vowel points cannot be described in terms of the standard confessional boundaries. Of course, various Roman Catholic polemicists argued the postcanonical origin of the vocalizations for the sake of claiming the priority of the Vulgate over the Masoretic text—but most of the later controversy was carried on intraconfessionally, between confessionally orthodox proponents of the Mosaic origin of the vowel points and confessionally orthodox proponents of a late origin. Even the association of Cappel's theory of late origin with the school of Saumur, which produced other variant doctrines, such as the Amyraldian "hypothetical universalism," cannot be easily placed beyond the pale of the confessions. What the debate indicates, therefore, is the internal variety of Reformed orthodoxy.

The study of Henry Ainsworth's work as an exegete also underlines the broader currents of thought in which the British theologians of the seventeenth century were involved. His exegesis certainly had explicit doctrinal overtones but, in the line of Calvin and other sixteenth-century exegetes who emphasized the literal sense of the text, Ainsworth devoted less of his energy to allegorical and typological expression of doctrinal points than to an exposition of the more direct teaching of the text. Nor does Ainsworth's exegesis evidence the shift, supposed by many of the older scholarly discussions of seventeenth-century Protestantism, from an interpretation of the literal sense of the text to a dogmatizing model intended to provide "proof-texts," to the scholastic theologians of the era. Rather, Ainsworth insisted on examining the entire text, verse by verse, in order to ascertain the meaning of the whole text—with a primary emphasis on right translation, to the point of forcing English syntax into Hebraic patterns in order better to represent the meaning of the original text. Ainsworth also evidences the broad philological interests characteristic of biblical interpreters in the era of orthodoxy, in his particular case, what can be called the targumic pattern of textual analysis. In this approach to biblical interpretation, in which Ainsworth was hardly alone in his age, ancient Judaica, especially the Targums, were used as keys to interpreting the language of the Bible, precisely because they were paraphrases of Hebrew into an ancient cognate language and therefore offered lexical assistance to the exegete. From the perspective of the historiographical establishment of context, Ainsworth's work requires an international rather than an insular explanation, a broad philological rationale rather than limited dogmatic one. The identification of Ainsworth as an "independent" churchman, exiled to the Netherlands, also serves to underline this broader context, as, certainly does his personal encounter with Judaism, however polemical. The cultural context of the Netherlands, particularly of Amsterdam, yielded a direct contact and a resourcing then impossible in England.

The final essay, "The Covenant of Works and the Stability of Divine Law," addresses an issue that is both hermeneutical and doctrinal. It also has been one of the most consistently identified issues in the discussion of continuity and discontinuity between the Reformation and the era of orthodoxy and, moreover, of similarities and differences among the Reformers themselves. This makes it a nearly ideal topic for the illustration of suitable and unsuitable ways of comparing sixteenth- to seventeenth- century Reformed thought. Given, for example, that there are differences in emphasis and interpretation of the concept of covenant and rather different ecclesial applications of the doctrine among the Reformers, any attempt to single out one Reformer, whether Calvin or Bullinger, as offering the model by which continuities with the seventeenth-century thinkers are to be judged, is certainly methodologically unadvisable. In addition, over against other lines of argument in recent scholarship, analysis of Witsius and Brakel on the covenant of works demonstrates that, at least in their cases, the doctrine was not a matter of excessive legalism, or a matter or setting an absolute priority of law over grace, or part of working out the "tensions" in Reformed doctrine generated by a doctrine of predestination and an assumption of human responsibility for sin. Rather, the doctrine was the result of the examination of a series of issues raised by biblical texts—and resolved through a method of juxtaposition and collation for the sake of drawing conclusions. In other words, the doctrine did not arise out of an overarching dogmatic concern pressed on the extant materials of system, but out of the typical way in which the theologians of the era constructed theological *loci* in the wake of their exegesis and drew doctrinal conclusions from the collation and comparison of texts. In the writings of Witsius and Brakel, moreover, the exposition of the doctrine stood in the line of a century-long discussion of covenant, human nature, law and grace, and human responsibility, and the nuances found in their writings relate less to what might be called macrotheological questions than to the intricacies of exegesis and polemics in their time.

PART I

REFRAMING THE PHENOMENON–DEFINITION, METHOD, AND ASSESSMENT

2

Scholasticism and Orthodoxy in the Reformed Tradition

Definition and Method

Toward Definition

The Problem of Scholasticism and Orthodoxy—An Invitation to Discussion

In the last quarter century, the study of Protestant scholasticism has evolved from a neglected, almost nonexistent subject into a fairly broad and increasingly defined field of study. The evolution and development of the field have been shaped by revisionist approaches to the study of the Reformation and its medieval background, and by the development of a broader scholarly perspective on the history of the post-Reformation era. It can certainly be said that, in the last twenty years, there has been a shift from an almost entirely dogmatic study of the thought of the period to a more contextualized historical analysis—a movement that parallels, in considerably less detail and far fewer studies, the development of scholarship on the Reformation.[1] The parallels, moreover, between these two fields of study are methodologically significant—particularly inasmuch as comparable revisions in outlook have characterized both fields and inasmuch as the revisionist approach to Protestant orthodoxy or scholasticism has reflected revisionist approaches to the Reformation and, in fact, has been methodologically as well as substantively dependent on them. In what follows, I propose to offer definitions of the terms of discussion (scholasticism and orthodoxy in the post-Reformation context) and then to offer an overview of the methodological issues and problems involved in the study of the era.

To someone acquainted only with the older scholarship, the title "Scholasticism and Orthodoxy in the Reformed Tradition" might seem a bit strange or obscure; to others it might seem a reference to things better forgotten. The older scholarship, exemplified by the writings of Ernst Bizer, Walter Kickel, Brian Armstrong, Thomas Torrance, and others has typically modified the term "orthodoxy" with the pejorative terms "rigid" and "dead," and modified references to "scholasticism" with the equally pejorative terms "dry" or "arid." Such assessment bespeaks bias, but it also reflects a rather curious sequence of metaphors. The implied alternative to such a phenomenon as "scholastic orthodoxy" would, perhaps, be a flexible and lively methodological muddle of slightly damp heterodoxy. Less facetiously, it is worth asking why "orthodoxy," which means simply "right teaching" and was the theological goal of nearly two centuries of Reformed pastors and teachers (not to mention all of the fathers and doctors of the church from the time of the Apostle Paul down to the Reformation), should have been viewed as a less than desirable—or less than pious—result of or declension from the work of the Reformers of the sixteenth century. It is also a matter of some curiosity that purportedly objective historical analyses should assess the desirability or the piety of a particular form of long past theological expression. Perhaps we also should ask why this specific "right teaching," designed by the immediate heirs of the Reformation to stand within the confessional boundaries set by the Reformers themselves, has been declared by a fair number of dogmatically trained historians as a step *away* from the concerns of the Reformers of the sixteenth century. So, too, it is worth asking why the "scholasticism" of the late sixteenth and seventeenth centuries, namely the academic *method* used by the teachers of the era to elucidate difficult problems and settle debates in theology (as well as in all of the academic disciplines), should be seen as something problematic and undesirable in the aftermath of the Reformation. As in the matter of "orthodoxy," the historians themselves register the term "scholasticism" as a pejorative, involving the importation of problematic philosophical or theological *content*.

The problem that many writers have had with the idea of a "scholastic *Reformed* orthodoxy" arose, arguably, out of a profound and entrenched misunderstanding and misuse of the terms at issue. Nor is this merely a "popular" misunderstanding and misuse of terms: the problem appears, also, in works of a more scholarly nature in which theological considerations have intruded on the work of historical analysis and have rendered the neutral descriptor "scholasticism" and the positive term "orthodoxy" into pejoratives. The sense of a largely pejorative meaning of "scholasticism" together with the assumption that "scholasticism" is not primarily a method but an excessively speculative form of Aristotelian philosophy can be traced to the polemics of the Reformers, notably Luther and Calvin. Yet, there is more to the discussion than can be gathered on the face of the old polemic—at very least, the Reformers' attacks on scholastic theology cannot be construed as an antagonism to all things medieval, a distaste for all examples of scholastic method, or a blanket rejection of Aristotelian thought. Recent scholarship has shown clearly the positive scholastic background of the Reformation and the scholastic elements imbedded in the thought of the Reformers.[2] In addition, it is one of the methodological problems of the older scholarship that it consistently assimilated the "scholasticism" of seventeenth-century Protestants to the "scholasticism" of the Middle Ages, as if there had been virtually no development or change in method or content since the fourteenth century.

The pejorative understanding of "orthodoxy," a bit more of a puzzle, given the Reformers' own sensibility that the core of the Reformation was a concern for right teaching, probably rests on the negative understanding of "scholasticism" in a Protestant context and, somewhat more covertly, on the comparatively greater difficulty of reinterpreting a Protestant scholastic thinker, such as Turretin, as a forerunner of neoorthodoxy than of so interpreting Calvin.[3] Given the discursive style of Calvin's *Institutes* and, moreover, the tendency of many modern readers of the work to read it in translation only and through the glass of a grafted-on modern apparatus, it has become all too easy to read twentieth-century accents into Calvin's theology.[4] The style of the seventeenth-century theology and the absence of long-established grids through which to read it precludes the same error in the reading of Turretin. At the same time, a contextual reading of Turretin that places his patterns of interpreting scripture and of formulating Christian doctrine closer not only in temporal but also spiritual and confessional proximity to Calvin than the work of various twentieth-century theologians creates problem for the ahistorical doctrinal reception of Calvin's thought. The alternative is to sever the historical link between the Reformation and "orthodoxy."

If the approach indicated by the negative readings of scholasticism and orthodoxy cannot stand, how then, should we understand "scholasticism and orthodoxy in the Reformed tradition?" In the first place, the two terms do not indicate the same thing: the former indicates a particular method in teaching or writing, the latter a specific attitude toward the content or substance of teaching and writing. "Scholasticism" is, therefore, the narrower term: a discourse is "scholastic" only when it follows scholastic method—specifically, only when it concentrates on (1) identifying the order and pattern of argument suitable to technical academic discourse, (2) presenting an issue in the form of a thesis or question, (3) ordering the thesis or question suitably for discussion or debate, often identifying the "state of the question," (4) noting a series of objections to the assumed correct answer, and then (5) offering a formulation of an answer or an elaboration of the thesis with due respect to all known sources of information and to the rules of rational discourse, followed by a full response to all objections. When that form or its outlines are not observed in a work, that work is not scholastic. By way of example, Thomas Aquinas's *Summa theologiae* is certainly a scholastic work—but his commentary on the Gospel of John is not, even though its content stands in a strong and clear relationship to the content of the *Summa*. Another example, taken from a place somewhat closer to home: Ursinus's *Commentary on the Heidelberg Catechism* is, arguably, scholastic. The catechism itself is clearly not—even though the theological content of the catechism closely reflects that of the commentary written on it.

I am reminded here of the historical contortions that a former colleague engaged in for the sake of proving that the Westminster Confession was not a "scholastic" document: he tried to show that "scholasticism" had not entered English Protestantism until after the confession had been written, despite the use of scholastic method in English theology by a number of significant theologians (e.g., Perkins, Ames, Davenant) a full half century prior to the confession.[5] He might simply have noted that the Westminster Confession, although produced in an era of scholastic method, does not itself follow the method. As the theologians of the day would have noted, a confession is not "scholastic"; rather, it is positive or declarative and belongs to a genre parallel to that of a catechism. Even so, various commentaries on and systematic elaborations of the Westminster standards do reflect scholastic method.[6] And it is doubtless true that the architectonic vision and the pattern of definition found in the Westminster Assembly's confession and catechisms reflect the concerns for clarity, precise definition, and logically presented argument characteristic of a mind trained in scholastic forms, but the documents themselves are not strictly "scholastic."

Scholasticism and the Reformed Tradition

"Scholasticism" has been mistakenly understood as a particular philosophy or as engendering a particular philosophical or theological result. That result, moreover, has been dubbed "Aristotelian" and, by more than one writer, has been viewed as a form of rationalism that places reason prior to faith and, therefore, philosophy prior to Scripture in the list of criteria or *principia* for theology. So, too, has scholasticism been defined as by nature "decretal" and deterministic. The case, however, against such claims is so easily made that one wonders why they continue to be pressed in the face of abundant evidence. Note, for example, that "scholastic" theology and philosophy, from the twelfth through the seventeenth centuries, offers a highly varied profile. When we move from Anselm, to Lombard, Aquinas, Scotus, and Ockham, on to Protestant "scholastics" such as Beza, Jerome Zanchi, Martin Chemnitz, Johann Gerhard, Polanus, Arminius, Perkins, Francis Turretin, and Mastricht, we encounter *not* identity of theological result or philosophical perspective, but enormous diversity—Augustinians, Aristotelians, monergists, synergists, philosophical realists, nominalists, and so forth.

What unites these thinkers is not a common doctrine, but a common method—albeit one that developed and altered over time. All of them engage in the forms of academic disputation that attempt to make clear distinctions concerning the parts or divisions of topics. All of them establish the order or pattern of argument with such basic questions as "Does it exist (*An sit?*)," "What is it (*Quid sit?*)," and "Of what sort is it (*Qualis sit?*)"—and ask them consistently in that order, moving from existence, to essence and essential properties (the question of "what"), to the attributes or qualities more broadly considered and the doctrine of the Trinity (the question of "what sort"). The scholastic assumption here is both fundamentally methodological and quite simple: if you answer "No" to the first question—does it exist?—you need not bother with the other two. And that procedure seems eminently practical. In appealing, moreover, to this series of questions ("Does it exist"—"What is it?"—"Of what sort is it?"), scholastics were hardly inventing a procedure or claiming a peculiar property: the pattern and various elaborations of it belong to classical rhetoric and logic, thus, to Quintilian as well as to Aristotle. The pattern was, moreover, recommended highly in the fifteenth- and sixteenth-century humanistic rhetoric of Rudolf Agricola and Melanchthon.[7] And why not? It conduces to clarity of thought.

This dialectical or logical teaching procedure accounts, for example, for the typical movement of theological systems from the proofs of God's existence, to the doctrine of the divine essence, to the question of attributes, and to the Trinity. We are dealing, here, *not* with a philosophically laden approach to the doctrine of God or with the assumption that natural reason provides the best foundation for theological argument, but with a standard format of the classroom: does it exist, what is it, of what sort is it? All of the scholastic thinkers noted, whether medieval or Protestant, assumed the priority of Scripture over reason and philosophy.

So, also, although some of these scholastic thinkers (notably Aquinas, Beza, Zanchi, Polanus, Perkins, Turretin, and Mastricht) held to an eternal divine determination of all things, none interpreted this determination to the exclusion of human free choice and responsibility.[8] Application of scholastic method does not imply philosophical or theological determinism—and it never implies that a theological system can be deduced from a particular doctrinal principle or point, certainly not from the doctrine of the divine decrees. We can state categorically, that orthodox Reformed theology of the sixteenth and seventeenth centuries *never* proposed predestination or any other doctrine as a central dogma or deductive first principle.[9] The way in which the many generations of nominally scholastic theologians managed to hold both an overarching divine causality and human freedom, moreover, consisted in their use of clear distinctions, such as that between the positive will and the permissive will of God: God certainly causes all things or wills all things in one sense or another—but sometimes God acts as the immediate, efficient cause of a thing or event, and sometimes God stands as the indirect, permissive, or remote cause of a thing or event. Freedom belongs to those things or events in which the immediate and efficient cause is a finite, rational will, and the remote cause or ontic ground is the divine actuality.

What is scholastic about the solution to the problem of divine willing and human responsibility that I have just summarized is *not* the particular way in which the various levels of causality are thought to relate to one another, but the methodological application of a series of distinctions to the problem in order to facilitate a solution. Or, even more precisely, what is scholastic about the teaching is the basic assumption that the topic of divine willing can be divided into various subcategories, that distinctions can be made corresponding to the divisions, and that these distinctions can be used as part of an argument designed to define and clarify the doctrinal point. That assumption, moreover, as can easily be documented from Lombard's *Sentences*, rests not on some abstractly applied principles of logic but on a long tradition of meditation on the text of Scripture in which the word "will" is predicated of God not in one but in a whole series of ways.[10] Sometimes "will" indicates the revealed moral will of God, sometimes the ultimate eternal will. Will can indicate either an antecedent or a consequent willing or, alternatively, a positive or a permissive willing.[11]

The Protestant writers of the eras of the Reformation and of orthodoxy were quite aware both of their debt to the medieval tradition and of the limitations of and the dangers inherent in the application of scholastic method to theology. We see, for example, in the writings of Calvin, numerous tirades against the "scholastics" and their unbiblical theology often alongside of concerted use of distinctions developed by the very same scholastics. In fact, we often see a dual use of the term "scholastic" in Renaissance- and Reformation-era writings. On the one hand, "scholastic" could refer to "school-theology" in the worst sense, a theology invested in academic quibbles, divorced from the needs of the Christian community, arcane and, as the humanistic mind of the Renaissance would add, barbaric in its use of language. On the other hand, however, the term could be (and was) used in a neutral sense, referring to the life of the academy, its classroom work, and its honored methods in discourse and argument: in his rectoral address of 1559 to the new Academy of Geneva, given in the same year that Calvin's *Institutes* redoubled its attacks on the *scholastici*, Beza referred to the Academy as a "scholastic commonwealth" and reminded his young "scholastics" there that all true philosophy was a pursuit of virtue and true virtue renders all glory to God. In typical humanist fashion, Beza cites a maxim of Plato as rendered into Latin by Cicero, reminding his audience that knowledge must not be severed from justice.[12]

So, too, other Protestant writers of the era, such as Andreas Hyperius, could use the term "scholastic" with favor—or at least not pejoratively—simply indicating the academic exercise.[13] We see the same usage in the *Statutes of the Genevan Academy*, written most probably by Calvin, for its official establishment in 1559: the young scholars or *scholastici* are enjoined to study and then write out, every month, "positions that are neither curious nor sophistic, nor contain false doctrine."[14] Students in the Academy would study, in addition to their theological subjects, logic or dialectics, defined in the *Statutes* as "the classification of propositions," the identification of "figures" or rhetorical forms of "argument," and, more generally, as "the science of predications, categories, topics (or *loci*), and disputes (*elenchus*)." On the first Friday of each month, these budding Genevan *scholastici* would engage in formal theological disputation.[15]

The reason for this usage is not that Beza and others were subtly reintroducing medieval scholasticism under the noses of their antischolastic colleagues—or that the usually antischolastic and humanistic Calvin gave in to dark scholastic urges as he devised the course of study for the Genevan Academy. Rather, Beza's—and Calvin's—positive references to "scholastics" are indications of one of the fundamental efforts of Renaissance humanism. What is at issue here is that the Latin noun for "school," *schola*, had not changed—nor had the Latin adjective applied to the things, attitudes, and persons associated with the school, *scholasticus*. The Latin adjective *scholasticus* translates, quite simply, not as "scholastic" in any highly technical or restrictive sense but as "academic"—with all of the positive and negative connotations that we today find in the word. Thus, *scholasticus*, referring to "academic standards" or "academic method" has a positive sense; referring, for example, to "the merely academic theology that has no reference to faith and life" has a negative implication.

One aspect of the Renaissance humanist program, not without late medieval parallels, was the reform of the school and of student life, including a reform of the study of logic and disputation along classical lines.[16] So, too, the student dialogue or *colloquium scholasticum*, which had been a standard teaching form in the classical age and that had not entirely disappeared in the Middle Ages, experienced a major revival at the hands of Renaissance educators, notably in the *Colloquies* of Erasmus and Vives. Thus, Mathurin Cordier, Calvin's teacher in Latin at the Collège de la Marche and later one of the professors at the Academy in Geneva, published his own set of *Colloquia scholastica* in 1564.[17] Humanism was not posed against all things scholastic. It was posed against problems in scholasticism, notably the absence of a refined use of classical languages and rhetoric that was rooted in the absence of sound philological training.

This, too, is why the term "scholastic" gradually crept back into the prefaces and even titles of Protestant theologies: it was the term universally recognized as denoting, in a quite neutral sense, the academic enterprise, not only of the Middle Ages, but of the Renaissance and Reformation as well.[18] We ought, in fact, to reconsider our typical translation of the term *theologia scholastica* as it appears in the titles of sixteenth- and seventeenth-century Protestant works and render it not "scholastic theology" but "academic theology." The accuracy of these generalizations can easily be documented from the theological writings of Protestants in the late sixteenth and seventeenth centuries. The English theologian and biblical scholar Edward Leigh noted three methods or approaches to theology:

1. Succinct and brief, when Divine Truth is summarily explained and confirmed by Reasons, and this Divinity is called Catechetical, Systematical.
2. Prolix and large, when Theological matters are handled particularly and fully by Definitions, Divisions, Arguments, and Answers; and this is called handling of Common-Places, Scholastical and Controversial Divinity. . . .
3. Textual, *which consists in a diligent* Meditation of the Scriptures, the right understanding of which is the end of other instructions.[19]

A similar division of the subject of theology is found in the *Synopsis theologiae* of the mid-seventeenth-century theologian Franz Burman:

> Theology . . . is divided by some into didactic and polemical [*didacticam & polemicam*)] or, better, into positive and scholastic [*positivam & scholasticam*] theology: of which the former meditates on the analysis and interpretation of Holy Scripture: the latter on the synthesis of commonplaces [*synthesi locorum communium*] so that those "places" or "topics" [*loci*] that are spread here and there throughout Holy Scripture can be presented in a definite order.[20]

Not all Protestant orthodox theology, therefore, is scholastic. In fact, only a small portion is actually "scholastic" in the proper sense of the term—whether the sense found in the seventeenth-century documents or the nearly identical sense found in modern scholarship dealing with scholasticism.[21] In addition, as both Leigh's and Burman's definitions make clear, the scholastic method and form subserves the Protestant insistence on the biblical norm. For Leigh, the "right understanding" of Scripture is the goal of all forms of theological instruction; for Burman, the scholastic method serves primarily to order and arrange the theological topics elicited from Scripture by exegesis. Burman's "scholastic . . . synthesis of commonplaces" springs from an intention not unlike that behind Melanchthon's *Commonplaces* (*Loci communes*) and Calvin's *Institutes*.

As Leigh's definitions indicate, moreover, orthodox theology also took the form of confessions, catechisms, biblical commentaries, sermons, and treatises on piety. What is more, two of the orthodox Reformed theologians often remembered for their dexterity in the use of scholastic method, William Perkins and Gisbertus Voetius, also inspired the great development of Reformed piety in the seventeenth century. Wilhelmus à Brakel, the noted exponent of Dutch *Nadere Reformatie* or "Second Reformation" piety, was a student of Voetius and thoroughly orthodox in his teachings. Richard Baxter, remembered today only for his piety, was adept at scholastic argumentation. In the hands of the orthodox theologians of the late sixteenth and seventeenth centuries, scholastic method was used in the exposition and defense of orthodoxy. Of course, we also must remind ourselves that the method also was used for the exposition and defense by Arminius and his followers of a theology that, from the orthodox Reformed perspective, was heterrodox.

By the end of the sixteenth century, the irony of the language had pressed various Protestant writers carefully to distinguish between a right-minded and rightly constructed Protestant "school theology" and a problematic, which is to say, medieval or Roman Catholic one—recognizing, at the same time, that not all and perhaps not even most of what the medieval scholastics had said was problematic.[22] A useful summary of the points made is found in Burman:

> To be praised in this *theologia scholastica* are 1. the simple and concise kind of language, 2. the accurate and dialectical method, 3. the use or support of philosophy and of subjects concerned with the natural order [*disciplinarum naturalium*]. To be rejected, however, are 1. the obnoxious doctrine of Papal tyranny, false in many points, 2. the multitude of philosophical issues, 3. the curiosity over vain questions, 4. confusion of issues arising out of an ignorance of ancillary languages, 5. obscurity and barbarism.[23]

Leigh similarly noted the limits of human endeavor in matters theological: "We must not be too curious," he wrote, "in searching out the profound Mysteries of religion, as about the Trinity, predestination; we must be wise to sobriety, and not busy ourselves about perplexed and unprofitable questions, being content to know such things which are revealed to us for our Salvation."[24]

We see here, in both of these qualifications on the use of scholastic method in theology, a clear reflection of the Reformation era critique of medieval scholasticism—and in the case of Burman's explicit critique of problems in the older scholasticism, a reflection both of the objections leveled by the Reformers and of those leveled by Renaissance humanists. In the wake of the Reformation, Burman notes papal abuses, excessive philosophization of doctrinal points, and debate over vain or insignificant questions, while in the tradition of the humanistic critique of scholasticism, he faults the older school methods for ignorance of languages (by implication, Hebrew and Greek) and for "obscurity and barbarism" of expression. So, too, complaint over the intrusion of vain and insignificant questions into scholastic debate was also consistently heard from the humanists. Protestant scholasticism, thus, was intentionally different from medieval scholasticism, altered in its forms and approaches by both the Renaissance and the Reformation. The Protestant practitioners of scholastic method also recognized that it was a useful, even necessary, tool in debate with Roman Catholics—but that it was only a tool.

The positive elements of "scholastic theology" noted by Burman are not all the exclusive property of scholasticism, certainly not of medieval scholasticism. The use of "simple and concise . . . language," like the acceptance of an "accurate and dialectical method," is characteristic of much of the humanist endeavor of the fifteenth and sixteenth centuries as well. We should remind ourselves that Calvin's characterization of his exegesis with the terms "brevity" and "fluency" or "ease" (*brevitas* and *facilitas*) is usually credited to his humanistic training and that the use of logic, specifically, of logical forms such as the syllogism and enthymeme, was discussed at length in humanist as well as in scholastic manuals. And as for an interest in proper method, we can note the consistent refrain not only of nominally scholastic works but also of works by writers such as Erasmus, Melanchthon, and Calvin, each of whom was renowned for his mastery of Renaissance rhetoric and logic.

The positive or formative relationship between the logical developments of the Renaissance and the rise of a Reformed or Calvinist scholasticism is also illustrated by the impact of Ramism on Reformed theology. Petrus Ramus stands as one of the notable rebels of the Northern Renaissance against the older Aristotelian logic of the Middle Ages. His emphasis on "invention" and "disposition"—the former term indicating the investigation of a topic for the sake of discovering the substance or matter of an argument, the latter indicating a suitable arrangement of the materials discovered—places him in continuity with the emphasis of earlier Renaissance logicians like Agricola and Melanchthon. So, too, does his tendency to bifurcate arguments and topics and to follow out first one branch or member of the argument, then the other, look much like the method of his immediate predecessors.[25] Yet, it was precisely Ramus's bifurcatory method, taken perhaps to an extreme that he himself had not indicated, that became central to the architectonic task of the early Reformed scholastics. Theological systems such as Szegedinus's *Theologiae sincerae loci communes*, Polanus's *Partitiones theologicae* and *Syntagma theologiae*, and Ames's *Marrow of Theology*, DeLaune's influential *Institutio christianae religionis epitome*, or a treatise such as Perkins's *Golden Chaine* all offer evidence of the fundamental importance of the logic of bifurcation to the construction and ordering of theological systems during this era and, therefore, of the probable influence of Ramus. In other words, all evidence the formative influence of a Renaissance model on the rise of a renewed scholastic method.

Protestant scholastics such as Burman and Leigh approved of the simple and concise language of earlier scholasticism and of humanism as well but, following a humanistic inclination, frequently abhorred linguistic barbarism. The Protestant scholastic sought to infuse his theological efforts with philological expertise, not only in Greek and Hebrew but also in cognate languages like Aramaic and Syriac, a characteristic also resulting from humanism. The Protestant scholastic also, like his medieval counterpart, approved of logic and dialectic, but he learned his logical trade from handbooks that presented their subject with modifications brought on by the Renaissance. The *locus* method of the seventeenth century had as much, perhaps more, in common with Melanchthon's humanistic logic and rhetoric that it did with the medieval scholastic logic of Peter of Spain.[26] Much to the discomfiture of those who identify "scholasticism" and "humanism" as neatly designed and utterly separate pigeonholes into which to thrust recalcitrant historical subjects, "Renaissance humanism" appears to be one of the sources of "Protestant scholasticism."

Orthodoxy in the Reformed Tradition

The problem of "orthodoxy" is slightly different: it is not a problem of definition. At some level, even its critics recognize that orthodoxy indicates "right teaching" or the desire for "right teaching." The problem is not so much what the term is thought to mean as the attitude that has sometimes been found among the most zealous proponents of orthodoxy—and, in the case of "Protestant orthodoxy" the contrast created by a juxtaposition of stereotypes, a dynamic Reformation faith versus a rigidly defined and fundamentally inflexible system of dogmas. There is, certainly, a legitimate historical contrast that can be made between the teachings of the earliest Reformers in their struggle against the corruption and abuse of the late medieval or Renaissance church and the institutionalized forms of late-sixteenth- and seventeenth-century Protestantism working to maintain its confessionally codified teachings. But we must avoid the tendency to canonize the rebellion and demonize its result. The Reformers themselves were concerned with right teaching and it was they who produced the basic confessional documents of Protestantism. The institutionalized orthodoxy of the later generations labored to preserve the confessions of the Reformation as the foundational documents of the Protestant churches.

It is not a matter of accident that the era of Reformed orthodoxy begins in the decade of the deaths of Calvin, Vermigli, and Musculus, major second-generation codifiers of the Reformed tradition. Not only did this particular generation of Reformed theologians offer their church a fairly complete systematic expression of the chief teachings of the Reformation, they also oversaw the writing of the great confessions that define the shape and bounds of Protestant orthodoxy: the Gallican Confession, the Belgic Confession, the Heidelberg Catechism, the Thirty-Nine Articles, and the Second Helvetic Confession. The confessional position of the Reformed churches, unlike that of the Lutheran, was defined in the mid-sixteenth century and the orthodox theology that developed quite rapidly in the Reformed churches was able to rest on that relatively early confessional synthesis. Orthodoxy—a right teaching that represents the foundational teaching of the church catholic—was not a goal newly discovered in the post-Reformation era: it was the express intention of the Reformers themselves, brought to a confessional fruition in the work of Calvin and his contemporaries. We have to look no farther than Calvin's *Letter to Sadoletto* to see the intention to claim the banner of catholic orthodoxy for the Reformation.

If we ask the question of the origins of Reformed orthodoxy (as distinct from the question of the scholastic form taken by many of the orthodox theological systems of the Reformed), we will find it in the theological systems and the confessions wrought by the second-generation codifiers. In these works, not only are all of the distinctive doctrinal forms of the Reformed churches clearly defined but also the accepted spectrum of doctrinal opinion within the Reformed churches is presented: the doctrine of election can be found in the form of a double decree of election and reprobation in Calvin's works and in the form of a single decree of election in Bullinger's. So, too, can the doctrine of the sacraments be identified in two forms, occupying opposite sides of the Reformed spectrum: Calvin's identification of the sacraments as means and instruments of grace and Bullinger's teaching of a conjoint and parallel action of grace with the administration of the sacraments. In the era of orthodoxy, these differences of precise definition continued to be found among Reformed theologians: rather than claim a shift from dynamic or fluid understandings of the faith to rigid and inflexible standards, the far more accurate description of the contrast between Reformation and orthodoxy consists in a contrast between the movement toward confessional and institutional stability and the later development of religious forms within the established confessional and institutional boundaries.

Diversity of formulation within the confessional norms continued to be present—registered both by internal debate among the Reformed and by the noncontroversial diversity of expression consistently found among the documents. There is, in other words, a distinction to be made between the ongoing debates with adversaries representing other confessions (Socinian, Roman, Lutheran, Remonstrant, and Anabaptist) and the internal debates such as those that took place between the Cocceian federalists and the Voetians,[27] between Amyraut and the opponents of hypothetical universalism, and between supra- and infralapsarians. As recognized by the debaters themselves, these latter controversies had a different status. It is also quite easy to note significant differences in organization, method, definition, and emphasis among the orthodox theologians, all of which were debated but none of which was a matter of confessionally divisive controversy: is the first covenant a covenant of works or of nature; is a covenant to be defined as bilateral, unilateral, or in some sense as both bi- and unilateral?[28] Is theology a theoretical, a practical, or a mixed discipline with both theoretical and practical dimensions? Should arguments be organized according to a Ramist bifurcatory model or not? Should the method of theology be analytical, moving from effects to goals or causes—or synthetic, moving from causes to effects?[29] A host of other examples might be noted.

The relationship between orthodoxy and scholasticism is clearest in the context of controversy and debate: inasmuch as the Protestants of the late sixteenth century, like the medieval doctors, understood scholasticism as a method suited to the resolution of disputed questions, it was precisely in the detailed defense of orthodoxy that a renewed and modified scholastic method found its place in Protestantism. It was also at this point that philosophical issues of logic and coherence had to be raised. It is worth noting here that philosophy was consistently regarded as ancillary by the Reformed writers of the sixteenth and seventeenth centuries—with the result that the eclectic but largely Aristotelian perspective characteristic of the thought and worldview of both the Reformers and their orthodox successors was incidental both to their scholastic method and to their orthodox doctrine. If a modified Aristotelianism, akin to the Thomist modification, and filtered through the lens of late Renaissance logic and metaphysics, was the philosophical and logical tool used by many of the Reformed orthodox, particularly in their more scholastic moments, there can be no neat equation of Aristotelianism with orthodoxy—just as there was no neat equation of Aristotelianism with scholasticism.

There are, certainly, points at which method and content conjoin. The increasing adoption of scholastic method and its distinctions by Protestant theologians of the latter half of the sixteenth century did lead, if not to an alteration of the substance of Protestant theology, at least to an ability to indicate fine nuances of meaning within that substance. We see, for example, in the Canons of the Synod of Dort, a document that itself does not utilize scholastic method, a refinement of argument on the subjects of sin, free choice, and predestination seldom, if ever, found among the Reformers. On the one hand, this refinement of argument may well have brought on the debate over infra- and supralapsarian formulations of the doctrine of predestination and, therefore, a return to debate over such subtleties of doctrine as had been scorned by Reformer and humanist alike. On the other hand, it was certainly this ability to engage in subtle distinctions that resulted in the clarity of the Canons of Dort on the issue of the human origin of sin and evil and, therefore, a less stringent understanding of the relation between divine causality and sin than that found in Calvin's thought.[30] It remains the case, moreover, that the doctrinal position of the Canons, whether despite or because of the impact of scholastic distinctions, remained solidly within the spectrum of Reformed opinion established long before by Calvin and Bullinger.

It is true, on the one hand, that Protestant orthodoxy did, in large part, adopt a form of late classical, largely but not exclusively, Christian Aristotelian philosophy. The philosophy itself had been modified in so many ways during the Middle Ages and the sixteenth century that Aristotle himself would have blinked more than once at its conclusions, but it also had been rendered quite amenable to theological orthodoxy.[31] Particularly by way of contrast with various skeptical and rationalist philosophies—like that of Descartes or Spinoza—modified Aristotelianism or modified Thomism appeared useful to the Reformed orthodox and, therefore, retained its ancillary role in theology. On the other hand, the Protestant orthodox were far less invested in philosophical discussion and far more conscious of the priority and limiting character of exegetical categories in theology than their medieval scholastic predecessors. In addition, as the seventeenth century progressed, even this modified Aristotelianism lost its attraction to theologians—who saw it discredited particularly in its cosmology. Various Reformed theologians, not without controversy, absorbed elements of Cartesianism.[32] In short, the Aristotelian philosophical perspective was never raised to confessional status, and orthodox theological statement could and did occur, without reference to it, just as orthodox theological statement could and did occur in forms and patterns that were not scholastic—simply because the technical disputative academic forms do not carry over into all works of theology.

In summary, the term "orthodoxy" has a much wider application than the term "scholasticism": not only the formally "scholastic" works of the late-sixteenth- and seventeenth-century Reformed theologians but also their confessional, catechetical, exegetical, and practical essays strove for orthodoxy in theological expression. "Reformed orthodoxy" indicates both the confessionally defined teaching of the Reformed churches *and* the era, circa 1565 to circa 1725, during which Reformed theologians made their greatest effort in the definition and defense of that confessional teaching. This orthodoxy implies the confessional acceptance, the systematic elaboration, and polemical defense of such teachings as the famous "five points of Calvinism," but also the acceptance, elaboration, and defense of the doctrines of the Trinity, the two natures of Christ, and infant baptism. These doctrines were held and defended by Reformed orthodoxy, not because they could be deduced logically from a single concept or principle (like the divine decrees)–no theologian of the sixteenth and seventeenth centuries ever attempted to present Reformed theology in this way–but because, as the orthodox assumed, these doctrines are either taught directly by Scripture or follow as necessary or suitable conclusions from the work of exegesis.[33]

"Reformed scholasticism" indicates the method characteristic of the classroom and of the more detailed systems of theology developed by the confessionally Reformed branch of the Reformation during its era of orthodoxy. This method, moreover, differed from that of the medieval scholastics by reason of the incorporation of many of the changes in logic and rhetoric brought about by the Renaissance and the Reformation. Nor are orthodoxy and scholastic method radically distinct from the intention and the methods of the Reformers: the Reformers themselves stood adamantly for right teaching over against the errors and abuses that they believed had crept into the church. Their method, moreover, carried with it many elements of the older scholasticism, modified by developments in the Renaissance: scholastic distinctions and the basic style of the scholastic disputation can easily, for example, be discerned in the text of Calvin's *Institutes*, although the method of the *Institutes* is certainly not as overtly "scholastic" as the method of Voetius's *Disputationes* in the middle of the next century. If Reformed orthodox theology has emphasized such doctrines as grace and predestination, that is because of its confessional stance and because of the teachings of the Reformers themselves as embedded in the confessions, not because its scholastic method and certainly not because of Aristotle. This confessional stance rests on the tradition of Augustinian exegesis of the New Testament, specifically of crucial passages in Romans, Ephesians, and the Gospel of John, again, not on scholastic method and not on Aristotle. The doctrinal stance is prior to the method: the method elaborates on and defends the doctrinal stance.

Protestant Scholasticism: Methodological Issues and Problems in the Study of Its Development

Given the relative newness of the field, particularly of what can be identified as the revisionist approach or "new school," as some have called it, the method of approach to the era of Protestant orthodoxy and its historiographical problems has not been fully charted. In this portion of the essay, I would like to point toward some of the gaps as well as gains in our knowledge and to the problems they raise, both historiographical and methodological, for the study of Protestant scholasticism and its intellectual context. As will become evident, one of the underlying methodological issues that the study of this field has encountered is the need for interdisciplinary and what, for lack of a better term, might be called cross-topical dialogue—quite in contrast to the fundamentally theological or even dogmatic approach of the older scholarship.

What I propose to do here is to offer a bit of clarification on the general point of interdisciplinary and cross-topical dialogue; then, with that general point in mind, I will address a series of more specifically historical and topical issues with reference to their relationship to the study of late-sixteenth- and seventeenth-century Protestant thought. Although the list is not exhaustive, I propose the following six topics for examination: (1) Middle Ages, Reformation, and Orthodoxy, with emphasis on continuities and discontinuities in development; (2) Renaissance, Reformation, and Orthodoxy, also with emphasis on the issue of continuities and discontinuities; (3) Reformation and Reformations—the problem of multiple trajectories; (4) the history of biblical interpretation from the later Middle Ages through the seventeenth century; (5) rhetoric, logic, philosophy, and scholastic method during the same period; and (6) the institutionalization and the "popular" dimensions of Protestantism following the Reformation.

First, the general point—which is in fact implied in the list of topics, inasmuch as the examination of materials from such diverse historical "periods" or disciplinary units as the Middle Ages, Renaissance, Reformation, and later Orthodoxy implies the relative removal of boundaries of academic specialization. The same implication arises from identification of the history of biblical interpretation and from the development of rhetoric, logic, philosophy, and method from the later Middle Ages to the end of the seventeenth century as a necessary area of inquiry. For such a breadth and diversity of topics and disciplinary areas to be addressed, even from a methodological perspective, there must be academic interdisciplinary and cross-topical dialogue: we do not live in a world in which any single scholar can master all of these materials, particularly given the increasing narrowing of focus in nearly all fields of inquiry as we attempt to work out the methodological implications of the contemporary "information explosion."

One may ask why such an interdisciplinary approach is necessary. The answer is quite simple from a historiographical perspective: contrary to the tacit assumption of past generations of historical theologians and historians of Christian doctrine, the subjects of the inquiry—the Reformation and post-Reformation eras and their many representative leaders and writers—simply do not oblige the categories of modern academic disciplinary divisions or rather artificially constructed historical periods. Nor is it the case that the writings of the Reformation and post-Reformation theologians can be explained either solely on the basis of textual analyses of individual documents or of purely theological or doctrinal criteria.[34] It is virtually impossible to identify any Reformation- or post-Reformation-era theologian who was not touched in some way by both scholastic and humanistic patterns of thought and education; who was a pure academic thinker not involved in the daily life of the church and the social and political changes of the time, including the rise of an institutional Protestantism; who was a dogmatic or systematic theologian not trained in the changing patterns of rhetoric and logic, not engaged in biblical exegesis, and not aware of shifts and developments in the philosophical models of the era. In other words, if we do not engage in a dialogue that crosses our disciplinary boundaries, we must content ourselves with the study not of Protestant orthodoxy and its exponents, but with bits and pieces of Protestant orthodoxy, indeed, bits and pieces of sixteenth- and seventeenth-century people, divorced from the historical context that they inhabited.

This argument may seem a bit exaggerated until one examines either the theological or dogmatic studies of writers such as Luther, Calvin, and Beza or the highly theologized discussions of Protestant orthodoxy and scholasticism produced in the last hundred years. By way of example, until very recently, it was not unusual for studies of Calvin's interpretation of Scripture to omit entirely any reference to the history of medieval exegesis, the probable medieval background to Calvin's work in such exegetes as Nicholas of Lyra, and even any reference to Calvin's immediate predecessors and contemporaries. So also has it been common to describe the development of Protestant scholasticism solely in terms of supposed dogmatic tendencies inherent in the nature of "scholasticism," rather than in terms of continuity and change in academic culture of the seventeenth century or in the religious and ecclesial context, the development of late Renaissance rhetoric, philosophy, and method, or the actual historical context of a particular theologian.

Middle Ages, Reformation, and Orthodoxy: Continuities and Discontinuities in Development

Research into the continuities and discontinuities between the Middle Ages and the Reformation has been, certainly, the most significant and influential dialogue partner of the reexamination of Protestant orthodoxy—in fact, the scholarship of the last half of the twentieth century concerning the positive medieval roots of the Reformation has provided much of the model for the examination of the relationship of post-Reformation orthodoxy to the Reformation. The reason for this relationship is also quite clear: from the standpoint of method, the discussion of medieval roots of the Reformation, notably Oberman's recasting of the concept of the "forerunner," not only has broken down the neat division between medieval scholasticism and Reformation thought but also has altered the way in which the continuities are identified.[35]

From a purely methodological perspective, the fracturing of a neat periodization between the Middle Ages and the Reformation, as also between the Reformation and post-Reformation eras, has increasingly led intellectual historians of the sixteenth and seventeenth centuries to become medievalists. We now recognize that it is impossible to understand Luther and, indeed, Calvin, apart from an understanding of their medieval background—and, what is more important, we now recognize that this background was not entirely negative. The identification of medieval roots of the Reformation also demands, by extension, an examination of the way in which that rootage in medieval thought-forms led both to the continuance of a fundamental framework for theology through the Reformation into the era of orthodoxy and to the orthodox reappropriation of the medieval theological and philosophical tradition in the late sixteenth and seventeenth centuries.

The complexity of this pattern of continuity and discontinuity presents a major methodological problem for resolution. Not only has the basic bibliography for the study of sixteenth- and seventeenth-century Protestantism been drastically changed, it also has been reconstituted in a way that demands scholarly dialogue—between Reformation specialists, medievalists, scholars of Protestant orthodox thought, specialists in the history of logic, rhetoric, and philosophy, and, indeed, scholars of the transmission of scholastic theology in the Roman Catholic world during the sixteenth and seventeenth centuries.[36] The issue here is the sometimes very subtly nuanced conversation that took place between Protestant thinkers (who assumed their own catholicity) and the traditionary sources that they used, including the works of late medieval and sixteenth-century transmitters of the medieval tradition. Thus, we need to ask whether the Protestant reappropriation of elements of "Thomism" ought to be taken as a direct reading of Thomas, or as a reading of Thomas as understood by Johannes Capreolus or by Cajetan—or, indeed, as not precisely Thomist but, rather, as an appropriation of elements of the medieval *via antiqua* by way of thinkers such as Giles of Rome and Thomas of Strasbourg (whose works were read and cited by Protestant scholastics). So, too, when we identify "Scotist" or "Ockhamist" elements in Protestant thought, we ought perhaps to pause and ask whether these are the result of direct reading of Scotus and Ockham or of encounters with the numerous Franciscan theologies of the late fifteenth and sixteenth centuries.

Renaissance, Reformation, and Orthodoxy

Just as scholars have been pressed to recognize the later Middle Ages as the proper context for understanding the Reformation and have moved away from the rigid perception of older scholarship concerning the relationship of scholastic method to the thought of the Reformers, so, too, has there been a shift in the understanding of the relationship of Renaissance humanism to scholasticism. This shift in understanding is, of course, not new to scholars of the Renaissance but, rather, has been a central feature of scholarly discussion since the work of Kristeller.[37] We now recognize that neither humanism nor scholasticism stood for a particular philosophical system, that much of the debate was confined to the arts faculties as they restructured curricular models and understandings of language and philology, logic and rhetoric—and, more important, we are now in a position to identify humanistic elements in the methods and studies of later scholastics as well as scholastic elements in the work of some humanists. And, particularly, when we examine fields like philosophy and theology, we see humanistic and scholastic elements in the approaches of many of the writers of the era.

Still, the impact of the work of Kristeller and others who have followed out details of his insight has been slow to have its full effect on scholarship concerning the Reformation and still slower to affect the understanding of the movement from the Reformation to orthodoxy. From a methodological perspective, there is a need for scholars of the Reformation and of post-Reformation orthodoxy to adapt the understanding of "humanism" as primarily a philological method and of the debate between "humanists" and "scholastics" as a debate primarily over the relationship of logic and rhetoric and over the use of philological analysis to their sense of relationship between the Renaissance and both the Reformation and post-Reformation Protestantism. This revision of approach and method also implies, mirroring the preceding point, a broadening of bibliography and the development of a scholarly dialogue: we must cease to view "Renaissance" as a scholarly province isolated from "post-Reformation Protestantism."

Reformation and Reformations—The Problem of Multiple Trajectories

Twenty-five years ago, the phrase "Calvinist Thomism" was a sign of altered perspectives in the field of sixteenth-century Reformed theology and a harbinger of major changes to come.[38] The notion that Calvinism and a form of medieval, indeed, scholastic, theology might have proved compatible fairly early on in the progress of the Reformation altered the picture that scholarship had of the Reformed or Calvinist side of the magisterial Reformation and opened the way to an examination of Reformed theology similar to the reexamination of Luther and Lutheranism generated by the study of positive reflection of medieval thought in the teachings of the Wittenberg Reformer and by the beginnings of investigation of Calvin's own "Scotistic" medieval background. Given that one of the "Calvinist Thomists" was Peter Martyr Vermigli, who was Calvin's senior and who died two years before Calvin, it became quite difficult to pose a nonscholastic Calvin against *later* scholastic Calvinists. It also became evident that any analysis of so-called Calvinism would need to take into consideration not one but a series of theologies and theological trajectories through the sixteenth century. Later Reformed thought was a product not merely of the dominant influence of Calvin but of the interplay of the thought of rather different reformist allies: Calvin, indeed, but also Vermigli, Musculus, Bullinger, Hyperius, not to mention their rather diverse predecessors.

This sense of diversity and the issue of multiple trajectories raise a series of significant methodological problems: the study of Reformed orthodoxy now is responsible for the analysis not only of a broad series of thinkers and their potentially rather varied impact on a developing tradition—rather than posing the simplistic "Calvin against the Calvinists" question—but also responsible for an account of the diverse background and context of these developing patterns of thought. "Calvinist Thomism" is also a simplification: as would be the equally broad counter of a "Calvinist Scotism": we must now account not only for the medieval background of the early Reformers, a background already quite removed from the original thought of Thomas Aquinas or Duns Scotus, but for the relationship of the Reformers and their successors to variations in the theology of their living opponents as well and to the probable points of reference of their thought in a living tradition of discussion and debate.

In other words, we must raise the question of the way in which the sixteenth and seventeenth centuries appropriated the understood and past of the church, specifically, the patristic, medieval, and classical traditions, as offering materials for debate and for use in (i.e., not abstracted from) a context of living interpretation. Here, too, as in the previous category, there are extant fields of scholarship that can and must be brought to bear on the discussion.

One of the methodological tools available to us here is the library catalogues and published auction catalogues of the thinkers of the era, plus the various attempts of writers in the sixteenth and seventeenth centuries to offer either guides to study and method or bibliographies. In this latter category we have works such as Conrad Gesner's *Bibliotheca universalis, sive catalogus omnium scriptorum locupletissimus* (Zurich, 1545); Gisbertus Voetius's *Exercitia et bibliotheca studiosi theologiae* (Utrecht, 1651); and Johannes Buddeus's *Isagoge historico-theologica ad theologiam universam* (Leipzig, 1727)—in short, a sixteenth-, a seventeenth-, and early-eighteenth-century bibliography. The latter two works are specifically devoted to the various branches of theology, while the former work has significant theological and philosophical sections. In each case, we have broad lists of works that were deemed significant for the discipline at crucial points in its history and, therefore, potentially significant bases for examining the thought of an era.

We have, for example, a finely annotated version of the late-sixteenth-century library catalogue of the University of Geneva—hardly definitive for Calvin's library, but still providing a beginning sense of books that the Reformer might have had at hand as he prepared his lectures. Several auction catalogues, notably those of Scaliger, Arminius, and Gomarus have been reprinted; there is a modern version, with annotation, of Baxter's library catalogue, and the library of John Owen can be read on film. In each case, the modern scholar can begin to understand the place of a thinker on the varied intellectual trajectories of the seventeenth century by approaching his reading list. Such lists must, of course, be cross-checked against the written works of the author to see whether the ideas found in a particular book had any impact—and there are, of course, a variety of methodological issues raised any time that one speaks of "influence" in the absence of evidence of citation and direct quotation. Fortunately, some of the writers of the era offer footnotes to or direct citations of their authorities and opponents.

Nonetheless, the "bibliographies" of the era provided by library catalogues or by sixteenth- and seventeenth-century bibliographical essays offer a beginning point. We can certainly conclude from such compilations, for example, that there was significant intellectual commerce between Britain and the continent and that, quite specifically, British writers such as Owen and Baxter cannot rightly be examined in what is literally, an insular manner—nor, conversely, can writers on the continent be understood apart from the impact of many of the British writers. Voetius cited numerous British writers. This assumption of an intellectual commerce is, moreover, confirmed by study of specialized book catalogues such as the Pollard-Redgrave and Wing catalogues, covering all books published in England or in English from 1475 to 1700: the number of editions and translations of continental works is noteworthy, and a consistent sign of the international character of the theological community.

The History of Biblical Interpretation

This is also one of the approaches to the sixteenth and seventeenth centuries that represents a broadening of the modern field of inquiry for the sake of beginning to approach the sixteenth and seventeenth centuries more contextually—and, again, broadening the bibliography of the field in order to engage in dialogue with other historical subdisciplines. The history of biblical interpretation is, moreover, a comparatively new field: it is really only in the last twenty years that we have seen examinations of the biblical interpretation of sixteenth and seventeenth centuries that do justice, historically and contextually, to the exegesis of the era—and the study of the seventeenth century still lags behind.[39]

From the perspective, moreover, of the study of Protestant orthodoxy, this inquiry supplies a major gap in method of the older scholarship. Older examinations of Protestant scholasticism and orthodoxy did not examine the history of exegesis in the era, but rested content with the generalization that exegesis after the Reformation and prior to the beginnings of modern criticism was a largely dogmatic enterprise. The dimensions of this aspect of the methodological problem become clear when we recognize, first, that this older scholarship never attempted to examine the hermeneutical and exegetical assumptions of the sixteenth and seventeenth centuries and, second, never took the time to identify precisely who were the exegetes of the era, what books of the Bible they interpreted, and what kinds textual criticism were developed or used during the period.

The results of the newer scholarship on the history of exegesis need to be increasingly integrated with the study of Protestant orthodoxy, particularly inasmuch as the individual thinkers who contributed to the history of post-Reformation Protestant theology are also the individual thinkers who contributed to the exegetical work of the sixteenth and seventeenth centuries. The point may be almost self-evident in the cases of Luther and Calvin, but it is clearly in need of discussion in the cases of Piscator, Polanus, Witsius, and Marckius—all discussed as representing various dimensions of Protestant orthodoxy, but also known in their own times as significant exegetes.

What is more—and specifically to the fundamental methodological point—the examination of larger tradition so-called precritical exegesis offers a clear indication of continuities and developments spanning the eras: there is, in other words, continuity in method and in the interpretation of particular passages of Scripture between the Middle Ages and the Reformation, between the Reformation and orthodoxy. We no longer can simply (or, indeed, dismissively) class the Middle Ages as practicing allegorical exegesis, the Renaissance as introducing philology and text criticism, the Reformation as pioneering genuine literal and historical readings of the text, and Protestant orthodoxy as following a dogmatic pattern of exegesis. Rather, we now have been pressed to see a genuine concern for the literal sense as well as some philological and text critical interest among the medieval exegetes, a continuance and enhancement of those developments in the Renaissance and Reformation, a flowering of philology and text criticism augmented by the study of Judaica in the era of orthodoxy, and, in addition, a rhetorical refinement of various figurative and allegorical understandings in the Reformation and orthodoxy. There is, in short, a gradual development and change in interpretive patterns. What is more, we have clear evidence of the continuing interest throughout the sixteenth century in the work of medieval exegetes such as Nicholas of Lyra, and the continuing interest in the seventeenth century in the writings of sixteenth-century exegetes.

Rhetoric, Logic, Philosophy, and Scholastic Method in the Late Sixteenth and Seventeenth Centuries

Just as we have had to overcome the tendency to identify "scholasticism" and "humanism" as neat philosophical packages directly opposed to one another, and to characterize the philosophy of the scholastic teachers as "Aristotelian," so also do we need to overcome a simple association of changes in logic and rhetoric in the sixteenth century with a return to classical norms, as if there were no issue of the way in which these classical models were interpreted and appropriated in the sixteenth and seventeenth centuries: in other words, unmodified reference to "Aristotelian logic" or "Ciceronian rhetoric" misses the highly contextualized use of logic and rhetoric in the Renaissance, Reformation, and post-Reformation eras and the long tradition out of which these uses developed.[40] Nor is there any historical validity in the kind of contemporary discussion that approaches sixteenth- or seventeenth-century thinkers as having a "theology of rhetoric" or, indeed, a "rhetorical context" as if "rhetoric" were a matter of literary strategy,[41] rather than a disciplined approach to figures of speech, forms of argument, patterns of amplification and ornamentation, and other tools of oratorical and discursive persuasion.

There is, certainly, a highly developed scholarship on the history of philosophy, just as there is a highly developed scholarship on the history of logic and rhetoric. But the methodological problem that must be overcome here—by interdisciplinary dialogue and broadening of the scholars' working bibliographies—is perhaps best illustrated by the absence of overlap between the bibliographies on theology and church, philosophy, and rhetoric. We have the problem that, particularly in the study of sixteenth- and seventeenth-century intellectual history (although not entirely absent from the study of the Middle Ages as well), many of the historical figures that we examine appear in all three of these rather distinct bibliographies: the topics that have been rendered separate by modern academic specialization were not so radically separate in the minds of their sixteenth- and seventeenth-century practitioners.

Here, too, examination of the collateral subject—namely, the rhetoric and logic—alters our perspective on the Reformation and orthodoxy. The claim, often heard in older analyses of Protestant scholasticism, that its use of syllogistic logic set it apart, as scholastic, from the more humanistic approaches of the Reformers is not only undermined by the clearer sense of the meaning and relationship of "scholasticism" and "humanism" noted above, it is also (hopefully, finally) set aside by a twofold recognition concerning the nature of logical and rhetorical developments from the fifteenth century onward: first, the rhetorical manuals of the Renaissance consistently taught syllogistic logic and second, the logical and methodological models of the seventeenth-century scholastics are explicable only in terms of the developments of logic and rhetoric during the Renaissance. The continuity between Reformation and orthodoxy is seen, perhaps most notably in the dominance of the *locus* method, developed in the fifteenth century by dialecticians such as Rudolf Agricola, adapted to the needs of Protestant theology by Melanchthon, refined for Roman Catholicism by Melchior Cano, and then used quite consistently as the method of Protestant dogmatics through the seventeenth century, specifically, as the basis of moving from the exegetically examined sources of theology to a topical and systematic model. There is also the fact that the *locus* was conjoined with the classroom method of disputation—with the result that this Renaissance development also marks and defines the survival of a fundamental aspect of scholasticism.

The Institutionalization and the "Popular" Dimensions of Protestantism Following the Reformation

Among the significant underlying factors in the development of Protestant orthodoxy and scholasticism is the institutionalization of the Reformation in the century after its successful establishment. Social historians, notably Heinz Schilling,[42] have used the term "confessionalization" to describe the sociopolitical process that took place in the later sixteenth century as the Protestant religion increasingly developed and imposed forms and standards on the daily or common life of society. We mistake the nature of Protestant orthodoxy, including its more academic forms, such as its scholastic method, if we abstract it from the social process. Two clearly identifiable symptoms of this problem in the older scholarship have been its willingness to abstract and absolutize theological ideas—on the one hand, ignoring the cultural and historical context in which the ideas were generated and, on the other, assuming that the primary context for the interpretation of the theology of the past is the theology of the present. One of the results of this older method was the interpretation of Reformed orthodox theology as a deductive system based on a single central dogma—rather than understanding it as the product of a tradition of debate and formulation, shaped by a late Renaissance academic culture, by the ongoing religious, social, and political encounter between Protestants and Catholics, and by the daily life of religion and piety of which even the most "academic" of its professors were a part. In the case of the central dogma theory, the purported coherence of a reified "Calvinistic system" becomes the primary criterion for evaluating a particular document or issue at a particular moment in time: and that is not only a theological and historical but also a methodological error.[43]

The point is not, of course, for intellectual history to be dissolved into social history—rather, the issue is for the historian of ideas to recognize consistently that the ideas belong to a particular historical context and that the context may be defined socially or politically within a very narrow geographical or chronological frame, just as it may be defined by a particular debate that was little informed or influenced by immediate social issues. Context may also be defined in part by participation in broader traditions. Given, for example, that the large-scale content and method of Reformed theology (or, indeed, Roman Catholic and Lutheran theology) changed but little during the post-Reformation era, individual theological statements in particular historical contexts cannot be reduced either to ephemera or to ideological statements masked in theological or philosophical terminology. The tradition of belief and discourse concerning belief must be recognized as an element—a major element, indeed—of the context of a particular theological statement.

Nonetheless, the specific nuances of a theological stance and the alterations both in form and content that did occur are best explained in a more closely defined context. We certainly can explain much of the phenomenon of Protestant scholasticism in terms of the adaptation of Reformation theology to the needs of a church that had to defend its theology and piety against a highly elaborate Roman Catholic theology. But we also must explain theological statements in terms of the adjustment of Protestant teaching models to the academic culture of the late sixteenth and seventeenth centuries—and there, in that academic culture, we have to deal with currents in philosophy and method broader than the stream of theology, but also with the social and political pressures of particular states and cities, the pressures of which often spilled over into the classroom, not to mention the pulpit.

Mention of the pulpit points, moreover, toward the interrelationship between the so-called academic theology and popular religion. Perhaps the best model here is the work done in recent years by Robert M. Kingdon and others in examining the life of the city of Geneva as recorded in the registers of the Company of Pastors and the minutes of the Consistory.[44] We are now in a position, thanks to these efforts, to examine the ways in which Calvin's ecclesiotheological program was worked out in fairly minute daily social detail, both in matters of public morality and in matters of doctrine. We can, for example, examine the popular effects of controversies over doctrine—notably the Bolsec controversy is recorded both in an ecclesiastical process in the Company of Pastors and a civil process before the magistrates, and is detailed in its popular dimensions in the Consistory records. What emerges is that although there was little popular support for Bolsec, there was, nonetheless a worry, at a very popular level, without any detailed or nuanced understanding, over the implications of the doctrine of predestination for personal piety. This kind of examination of the sociopolitical context needs to be brought to bear on the study of later developments in Reformed theology as well. Dialogue between historians of ideas and historians of society and culture must take place—and perhaps, what is most important, on both sides of the discussion there needs to be a willingness to break down the barriers between the disciplines, recognizing, on the one hand, the social context of the ideas and, on the other, the impact of ideas on the social developments.

Some Concluding Remarks

A methodological proposal such as this one, for the contextual examination of the documents, may appear quite self-evident and perhaps not in need of declaration. Yet, a critical review of the many studies of the theology of the Reformation and of post-Reformation Protestantism reveals that much of the older scholarship has not followed the simple rule of establishing historical context, and that much of the headway made by revisionist scholarship in the last twenty years has been grounded in the alteration of the field by means of a broadening and redefinition of the bibliography necessary to the discussion—and, with the redefinition of the bibliography, the clarification of the context or frame of reference necessary for the analysis of the subject of Protestant orthodoxy. The frame of reference can then be reconstructed with attention to such issues as the interplay of traditionary usages, whether dogmatic, exegetical, or philosophical, with such other determiners of meaning as the genre and intention of the specific document, the social or political context of the writer, and the implications of the forms of logic and rhetoric employed. And, of course, not all of these disciplinary dialogue partners need be engaged at all points: in the examination of an academic or scholastic document, the tradition of theological discourse and perhaps of philosophy will play a larger role than in a sermon or popular tract, in which immediate contemporary concerns, social and political issues, may play a greater role. In both cases, the history of biblical interpretation may provide an index to the relative originality or immediate contextual relationships of the document. In other words, the historian of theology or intellectual historian need not become a polymath—but the progress of our study of late-sixteenth- and seventeenth-century theology must be more sensitive than it was in the past to the varied issues and influences, some of them not at all theological, some contemporary, some traditionary, that impinge on the development of Reformed thought in the era after the Reformation.

This approach to the development of Reformation and post-Reformation Protestantism offers a substantive alternative to an older scholarship that consistently read major theologians such as Calvin as if review of their major writings was a sufficient context for understanding the thought of the Reformation, that has persistently judged the materials on the basis of nineteenth- and twentieth-century theological models, and that has all but ignored the context of the intellectual history of the sixteenth and seventeenth centuries. It has juxtaposed a "dynamic" theology of the Reformation with the "rigid scholasticism" of subsequent generations—a contrast given emblematic status in the juxtaposition of Calvin's *Institutes* with Beza's *Tabula praedestinationis*, both documents having been read out of context, with no attention having been paid either to the time frame, the original context of debate, the actual appropriation and/or use of the documents by contemporaries, or the broader frame of reference of Calvin's or Beza's work in general.[45]

In addition to its methodological failings, the older scholarship was also historically inaccurate, grounded in a set of mistaken ideas and definitions. Its proposal to give us the Reformation without orthodoxy must fail, if only because the intention to identify, present, and preserve Christian orthodoxy in and for the church lay at the very heart of the Reformation. The proposal to give us piety without the niceties of dogmatic development and debate must also fail inasmuch as it falsely bifurcates the life of faith into things of the heart and things of the head—as if the Christian intellect cannot be faithful or, to borrow from Augustine, faith ought not to go in search of understanding. The severing of piety from the debates of the era is also untrue to the historical case. The authors of scholastic theological systems were frequently persons of considerable piety and, more important, for the historical record, also wrote works intended to develop and support piety. So, too, the severing of biblical theology from scholasticism: the irony of this aspect of the proposal is that the Protestant scholastic dogmaticians were, more often than not, trained in the biblical languages and in exegesis and wrote commentaries on the text. What is more, their application of the *locus*-method to dogmatics served to bring both the text of Scripture and the best exegetical results of the time into direct relationship with the dogmatic task—a point that cannot be made about most of the systematic theology of the twentieth century. Finally, the severing of Calvin (or of aspects of Calvin's thought) from Beza is also historically unsupportable inasmuch as it claims to find a pious and nonscholastic Calvin (or part of Calvin!) to contrast with a scholastic and nonpious Beza: in both cases, Calvin's and Beza's, the picture is a gross caricature.

In short, what is wrong, desperately wrong, with the older project is that it offered, largely on the basis of nineteenth- and twentieth-century theological programs, a mythical Reformation as the foundation of the Reformed tradition rather than the historical Reformation—and, in order to justify the myth, it obscured the historical bridge that connects modern Protestantism to its genuine past. Both scholasticism and orthodoxy are found in the historical Reformed tradition. That is an established point of history. The scholastic method was used for nearly two centuries in a largely successful attempt to define and defend the faith of the Reformed churches. The result of that effort was a theology, grounded in the confessions of the church and defended at length against all adversaries. In no small measure, we have the nearly two hundred years of scholastic orthodoxy to thank for the preservation of the barely fifty years of theological achievement that was the Reformation. Without the establishment and successful defense of this confessional orthodoxy in the Reformed churches, the reform efforts of Bucer, Zwingli, Calvin, Bullinger, and their contemporaries would probably have registered in the pages of Western history as an evanescent movement long ago vanished from the face of the earth rather than as the foundation of an institutional form of Christianity.

3

Ad fontes argumentorum

The Sources of Reformed Theology in the Seventeenth Century

The theological development that we call Protestant orthodoxy is, from a historical perspective, the codification and institutionalization of the Reformation. This older dogmatics is the theological result of the interpretation of the Reformation (typically in terms of its confessional bounds) by its immediate heirs. Moreover, the broader phenomenon of successfully institutionalized Protestantism in the late sixteenth and the seventeenth century, consisting in the confessional character of its theology and piety, the scholastic method adopted in the universities and academies, the alteration of patterns of teaching and preaching—all in continuity but also discontinuity with strands in the religious past, all with elements of response and adaptation to the changing political, social, and intellectual contexts of Protestantism—is the historical link between the Reformation and modern Protestantism. Apart from an understanding of this, its immediate result, we will arguably be unable to understand the Reformation. Equally so, apart from an understanding of this nearly two hundred years of struggle, codification, and defense, we will be unable to understand the ways in which modern Protestantism has developed from its Reformation-era beginnings.

During the era of orthodoxy—namely, the late sixteenth and seventeenth centuries—Protestant theology was framed both positively and negatively against the background of both distant and recent theological tradition. The Reformed orthodox theology is characterized by a conscious catholicity. On the one hand, many of the exegetical insights, doctrinal formulae, polemical arguments, philosophical assumptions. and methodological directions of the Protestant orthodox arose out of positive elements in medieval and Renaissance thought that carried through the Reformation and were appropriated directly by late-sixteenth-century Reformed theologians. On the other hand, continuing protest against the ecclesiastical abuses and the exegetical and doctrinal problems of the later Middle Ages, together with continuing doctrinal strife with Counter-Reformation Roman Catholicism, bore fruit in large-scale theological systems such as the Reformers did not themselves produce.

Of course, much has been said in the last two centuries concerning the deficits of this orthodox theology. Protestant orthodoxy has, in general, been declared "rigid," "dry," and "dead." Reformed orthodoxy in particular has been accused of being "speculative" and "metaphysical," "decretal," "predestinarian," and "legalistic." It is said to deduce entire systems of theology from the central dogma of an eternal divine decree—and to draw its principles entirely from Aristotle. It is called by turns "biblicistic" and "proof-texting," or "rationalistic" and "philosophical." Now, certainly, no theology can be all of these things at the same time, in the same place, and in the same way. In fact, a closer look at the literature of the critique makes clear that much of the recourse to history and, specifically, to the examination of late-sixteenth- and seventeenth-century intellectual history on the part of modern theologians has been part of an attempt to detach the theology of the immediate heirs of the Reformers from the theology of the Reformation and, then, once the rift is assumed, to claim the Reformers as the forerunners of modernity. This approach has been typical of neoorthodox theologies, particularly among the followers of Karl Barth, and it has been typical of studies of the history of biblical interpretation.[1] This approach also has tended to stress issues such as the theological meaning of systematic structures—such as the placement of the doctrine of predestination in relation to other doctrines, or the placement of the topic of law prior to the topic of grace, or the identification of the original state of humanity as bounded by a covenant of works—instead of looking at the actual content of these doctrinal expositions in terms of their materials or sources and in terms of the ways in which the immediate intellectual, social, and political context of the documents in question has influenced their composition and argumentation.[2] The result of such work has been both the misinterpretation of the seventeenth century and the misappropriation of the Reformation.

Recent historical reappraisals of the "scholastic" or "orthodox" Reformed theology of the seventeenth century have concluded that this was *not* a theology deduced from or dominated by central dogmas and that its so-called scholasticism was a matter of theological method rather than of dogmatic content. We have even come to recognize that the distinctive element of seventeenth-century scholastic method, the theological *locus*, arose as a result *not* of the return of medieval dialectic to the Protestant classroom but of the impact of Renaissance rhetoric and logic on Protestant thought. This essay builds on these conclusions and, in an examination of the sources, namely, the biblical, traditionary, and philosophical materials used by the Reformed scholastics, offers a view of the composition or construction of the orthodox theological compendia as gatherings of *loci* or topics rather than as integrally argued a priori or a posteriori "systems."

During the past two decades, historians have reexamined the Reformed orthodox materials from several perspectives: notably, from the perspective of the problem of "central dogmas" in theology, from the perspective of the declared "grounds" or *principia* of the older orthodoxy, and from the perspective of its theological method (namely, the "scholasticism" of the late Renaissance).[3] When examined in terms of the problem of central dogmas (and, I might add, so-called formal and material principles of Protestantism) the older orthodoxy simply does not oblige the categories, which are largely nineteenth-century in origin.[4] When examined from the perspective of its own stated *principia*—namely, Scripture (the cognitive *principium*) and God (the essential *principium*)—the older orthodoxy evidences patterns that are, again, not sympathetic to the claims of its modern theological critics: specifically, it is not primarily philosophical or rationalistic; it is not fundamentally deductive (whether one looks to predestination, justification, or the Person of Christ as the central pivot); nor is it biblicistic and proof-texting in the sense alleged (i.e., it does not arbitrarily extract texts from the Bible for use as the basis of propositional claims unrelated to the original context of the verse in Scripture); nor, indeed, does its "scholasticism" imply either a return to medieval models or a particular theological or philosophical content.[5] The claims made by the modern theologians are either utterly wrong and undocumentable or they are simplistic in the extreme.[6]

What I propose to do here is to add another dimension to the discussion—the dimension of the sources, the very rich and diverse sources of Reformed orthodoxy—and the very specific manner in which those sources were used in the formation of theological system, namely, the use of these sources or materials in the elicitation and construction of theological *loci* or topics. When we move past the problems of central dogmas, *principia*, and the method of this theology to the issue of its actual sources, we come to a conclusion similar to those reached in the other just mentioned revisionist analyses: simply stated, the Reformed orthodoxy theology of the late sixteenth and seventeenth centuries is far too rich and variegated in its sources and in their use to oblige the rather simplistic and often reductionistic claims of the modern theological critics—namely, that it is dry, rigid, dead, deductive, speculative, metaphysical, decretal, predestinarian, legalistic, Aristotelian, biblicistic, proof-texting, rationalistic, and philosophical. The underlying point of the reappraisal of this theology has been and must continue to be the removal of modern theological grids from the analysis of historical materials and the examination of those materials in terms of their own historical antecedents and context. For the sake of clarity, I will examine a series of sources in an order that relates to their relative level of normativity and, with each source, comment on how it was used and integrated into the larger whole of theological thought: thus, (1) Scripture, exegesis, and ancillary disciplines; (2) the ancient creeds and the confessions of the Reformed churches; (3) the Church Fathers; (4) the theological tradition generally, including the medieval doctors and the Reformers: and (5) the philosophical tradition and reason, specified as logic, rhetoric, and their methodological applications. As a final issue—I hesitate to call it a "source" for both historical and theological reasons—I will note the relationship between systematic or dogmatic theology and practice in the era of Reformed orthodoxy.

The Sources of Reformed Orthodoxy

Scripture, Exegesis, and Ancillary Disciplines

Contrary to much of the "received wisdom" concerning the seventeenth century,[7] the era of orthodoxy was a time of great exegetical, textual, and linguistic development in Protestantism—and, indeed, it was the orthodox exegetes who were responsible for the major monuments to biblical scholarship. One need only mention such vast efforts as Buxtorf's *Tiberias*; the translations of Tremellius, Junius, and Polanus; Weemse's *Christian Synagogue*; Walton's London Polyglot Bible; Castell's *Lexicon heptaglotton*, Pearson's *Critici sacri*, and Poole's *Synopsis criticorum* to gain a sense of the magnitude of seventeenth-century efforts to analyze both the text and language of Scripture and the tradition of biblical exegesis.[8] Beyond this, it is no difficult matter to show the intimate relationship between the most detailed exegesis of the age and the development of Reformed orthodox theological systems.

Several specific illustrations of the scope of orthodox era exegesis are in order. First, the *Annotationes in Novum Testamentum* of the much-maligned and misunderstood Theodore Beza: from the perspective of the age and, most probably from Beza's own perspective, this was his chief work. The *Annotationes* evidence that Beza was as much a proponent of the philological methods of Renaissance humanism as he was an heir of the Reformed theology of Calvin, Vermigli, and others: for, on the one hand, the *Annotationes* are by far the most sophisticated effort of the age to establish the text of the New Testament and to translate it accurately—while, on the other hand, they are a remarkably finely tooled statement of the exegetical basis of Reformed theology. Beza examined the best codices of the day and then proceeded to analyze the critically emended Greek text over against extant translations—notably the Vulgate, Erasmus, and even Calvin—in order to argue his own conclusions and produce a superior Latin translation. Then, on the basis of his philological and exegetical conclusions, he offered a running annotation on the text.[9] One can get a partial glimpse of both of these aspects of the work by examining the New Testament of the Geneva Bible, which combines accurate translation of the Greek text and marginal interpretations, based largely on Beza's efforts.[10] One can also see the effects of his exegetical work in both the exegesis and the theology of the next several generations of Reformed orthodoxy.

Second, attention can be drawn to the exegetical model proposed by Andrew Willet.[11] Willet's method, identified in the titles of nearly all of his commentaries as "hexapla," was distinguished by its "sixfold" approach to a text.[12] Willet began with an "Analysis," "Method," or "Logicall resolution," corresponding to the "argument" placed by many sixteenth- and seventeenth-century commentators at the beginning of chapters. This he followed with "the Genesis or Grammaticall construction where the translations differ," namely, a verse-by-verse synopsis of the differences between extant translations, noting all of the variant renderings of the Hebrew together with additions found in the ancient versions. Willet's third section, "the Exegesis, or theologicall explication of doubtfull questions and obscure places," is constructed as a series of questions and answers, sometimes quite lengthy. Here, Willet resolves issues of textual variants, and various translations by comparison with other biblical texts, citations found in the Church Fathers, in rabbinic commentators, and in various ancient and modern translators. The fourth section, "the didactica" or "places of doctrine observed out of [the] chapter" follows the *locus* method of exegesis found in the works of earlier Reformed exegetes such as Bucer, Musculus, and Zanchi by offering positive theological statement of the topics related to the text: Willet thus not only understands doctrinal theology to be grounded in exegesis, he also models for his readers the movement from exegesis to doctrinal statement. The fifth section, "places of confutation," handles theological debates relating to these *loci*. Willet's sixth and final section, "the places of exhortation and comfort," moves his exposition from exegesis of text to homiletical application in a series of moral and spiritual observations on the text.

It is at this point that the criticism of "proof-texting" also falls flat: the theologians of the seventeenth century certainly did accompany virtually all of their doctrinal formulations, even at the level of finely grained propositions on minute points of doctrine, with a battery of citations from Scripture. Yet, when one follows out their citations to the biblical commentaries of the day, one finds that their citations do not represent texts torn out of context but, rather, their citations point toward what one can only call the "assured results" of the best exegetical methods of the age. Indeed, what the reader finds is a close cooperation between the theologian and the exegete, with the theological affirmation of Scripture as final norm of theology worked out in practice as a use not merely of biblical texts but of detailed exegesis in the original languages of Scripture as the basis for doctrinal formulation.[13]

Of course, we must remember that none of the theologians of the sixteenth or seventeenth centuries built (or even intended to build) new theologies on the basis of their own exegesis. From its very beginnings, the Reformation assumed its catholicity over against the abuses and dogmatic accretions of late medieval Roman Christianity. In other words, the Reformers and their successors understood their theology to stand in continuity with the great tradition of the church, particularly with the theology of the ecumenical councils, the Church Fathers, and the "sounder" of the medieval doctors.[14] Scripture was certainly the prior norm for theology on the basis of which all other norms were to be judged, including the ecumenical creeds and the Fathers. Nonetheless, the orthodox theologies of the Reformation and post-Reformation eras accepted the larger part of the Christian exegetical and dogmatic tradition—and rather than reinvent theological system, they reshaped it in terms of the Reformation insights. We therefore pass on to the subordinate norms and sources of Protestant theology.

The Ancient Creeds and the Confessions of the Reformed Churches

The ancient creeds, namely, the Apostles', the Nicene, and the Athanasian Creed, plus the decision of the Council of Ephesus and the formula of Chalcedon, are consistent guides for the Reformed orthodox in their identification of fundamental teachings of the faith, in the establishment of a foundation for catechesis (here the Apostle's Creed is of course most prominent), and in their formulation of the doctrines of the Trinity and the Person of Christ.[15] As theologians of both the great Protestant confessions recognized in their less-polemical moments, these boundaries were consistently observed on both sides, Reformed and Lutheran, and their differences, however substantial, went beyond the basic definitions: in virtually all of their colloquies, the dogmatic standards of the ancient doctrinal norms provided a point of initial agreement,[16] just as they provide touchstones for the statement of the orthodox Reformed teaching on these subjects,[17] and, indeed, just as the mutual recriminations of the Reformed and Lutherans also demonstrate. The claims of the Reformed that the Lutherans were "Eutychian" and of the Lutherans that the Reformed were "Nestorian" illustrate that error (whether accurately or inaccurately identified) was understood in terms of the creedal boundaries.

Beyond the creeds and marking the specific doctrinal boundaries are the confessions of the Reformed churches. The Reformed confessions took on, early in the sixteenth century, the appearance of systematic overviews of the faith: unlike the Lutheran confessions, which tended to be organized around the main points of Reformation era dispute, the Reformed confessional documents tended to begin with a doctrine of Scripture, to proceed through the basic body of theological topics, and to conclude with the doctrines of church, sacraments, and the Last Things. Nor are the Reformed confessions less than forthcoming in identifying adversaries of the faith. The relatively irenic Second Helvetic Confession condemns the "peculiar opinions" of the Anabaptists as "against the Word of God," noting specifically the "Jewish dreams" of Anabaptist millennialism.[18]

The Heidelberg Catechism identifies the Mass as "nothing else than a denial of the one sacrifice and passion of Jesus Christ and an accursed idolatry."[19] The Belgic Confession indicates that "we detest the error of the Anabaptists . . . who reject the higher powers and magistrates."[20] And the Gallican Confession condemns "the papal assemblies, inasmuch as the pure Word of God is banished from them, their sacraments are corrupted, . . . and all superstitions and idolatries are in them."[21] And, of course, the confessions uniformly uphold the ancient orthodoxy of the ecumenical creeds in their condemnation of the archetypal heresies–Arianism, Manicheism, Marcionism, Nestorianism, Eutychianism, and so forth.

The creeds and confessions, therefore, provide by way of affirmation and condemnation both a positive and a negative background for Reformed dogmatics–and the polemics of orthodoxy reflect in detail the polemics of the confessions.[22] There are, of course, numerous theological systems or synopses of doctrine (some in the form of sermons) from the era of orthodoxy that take either the Apostles' Creed or one of the confessions or catechisms as their point of departure: thus, Perkins's *Exposition of the Symbole or Creede of the Apostles*, Witsius's *Exercitationes sacrae in Symbolum*, Du Moulin's *Boucler de la foi*, Ursinus's, Bastingius's, Voetius's, Groenewegen's, Leydekker's, and Van der Kemp's expositions of the Heidelberg Catechism, and Ridgley's commentary on the Westminster Larger Catechism, just to name a few. Beyond these overtly confessional efforts, moreover, the large-scale dogmatic projects of the day were consistently conceived within the creedal and confessional boundaries–not out of undue deference to these secondary authorities but on the assumption that these churchly standards had been framed and tested by the study of Scripture and were, therefore, sound guides to the limits of theological formulation.

The Church Fathers

Although in the past it was a little studied field, an increasing number of scholars are beginning to examine the ways in which the Protestant theologians of the sixteenth and seventeenth centuries appropriated the patristic materials as sources for their theology.[23] These sources were of a profound importance to the Protestant orthodox–as witnessed, among other things, by the numerous gatherings of patristic materials and editions of Church Fathers printed during the period and, indeed, by the invention of the term "patrology" by the eminent Lutheran theologian Johann Gerhard.[24] On the Reformed side, Gerhard's work was preceded by the *Medulla theologiae patrum* of Abraham Scultetus.[25] In form, Scultetus and Gerhard adumbrated the modern patrology: they offer a brief explanatory prologue on the life of an author, a list of his works, and an analysis of their contents. It is worth dwelling on the fact that Gerhard was able to identify and name the specific discipline of "patrology" and to write a massive study of the Fathers that was organized very much like modern patrologies not because he was a uniquely creative individual in this field but rather because this field of study had so prospered among Protestants that it could, by Gerhard's time, be perspicuously organized and named as a distinct field of study.

This interest in the Fathers does not mean, of course, that the heirs of the Reformation yielded under the pressure of Roman Catholic polemic and accepted tradition as a norm of faith alongside of Scripture. Rather, they followed the lead of the Reformers themselves (and, in fact, of a host of medieval predecessors) in identifying Scripture as the sole absolute norm for theology and the Church Fathers as a subordinate norm or guide, continually to be measured against the results of biblical exegesis.[26] The Protestant orthodox use of the Church Fathers must be understood as the direct outgrowth of the great Reformers' assumption that the Reformation was the catholic church, that Rome had fallen away, and that the best of the tradition not only could be appropriated by, but belonged by right to, the Reformation and its descendants.

It was characteristic of the Reformed scholastics that they framed their respective christologies and their doctrine of the Trinity over against the clearly heretical theories of the Socinians—and, in so doing, identified their own positive relationship to the normative development of patristic christological and trinitarian thinking beyond a simple affirmation of the ecumenical creeds. We see massive dogmatic use of the Church Fathers throughout the seventeenth century—and we see, also, the beginnings of a detailed analysis of the variations of trinitarian and christological language in the patristic era, in part generated by the use of pre-Nicene resources by the antitrinitarians—among others, in the works of John Forbes and George Bull.[27] In the seventeenth-century polemics of orthodoxy, the Socinians, those exegetically grounded ancestors of the Unitarians, were consistently paired with the "Arians," both ancient and modern, and, at the same time, the use of the Fathers as models and secondary norms was discussed in detail by Reformed writers.[28] And it must be added that analysis of the Fathers in the seventeenth century also produced variations in trinitarianism that echoed not only the patristic heretics but also the non-Nicene elements of the churchly tradition from Origen to Cyril of Jerusalem.[29] The positive doctrine of the orthodox—I note Francis Turretin and van Mastricht as clear examples—was framed over against these opponents with consistent and detailed reference to the works of the Church Fathers.[30] It was quite typical of the Reformed to identify their synergistic opponents, whether Roman Catholic or Arminian as "Pelagians" or, if precise terminology was necessary, "Neo-Pelagians." Here, too, it was typical of the age to examine the controversies of the past in detail: we note James Ussher's analysis of the Gottschalk controversy and the debate it produced, as well as the significant Protestant interest in the Jansenist study of Augustine.[31]

The Theological Tradition Generally, Including the Medieval Doctors and the Reformers

It also was characteristic of the era of Protestant orthodoxy that the theologians, whether of the Reformed or of the Lutheran confessions, became masters of the great tradition of the Western church. They were not, in other words, sectarian theologians who blindly grasped onto Scripture as an exclusive basis for all theological insight and then proceeded to trust their own exegetical intuitions—nor were they blind followers and slavish imitators, *epigoni*, as they are often called, of the great Reformers. Rather, in the tradition of the Reformers, these successor theologians took the catholicity of Protestantism seriously, claimed for themselves and their churches the best of the Christian tradition, and appropriated it critically, for the clarification and for the defense of the faith.

Modern critics of seventeenth-century Reformed theology often point out how seldom Calvin's name is cited as an authority. Of course, a careful perusal of the writings of seventeenth-century Reformed orthodox writers does in fact yield a fair number of citations of the writings of Calvin, not only of the *Institutes*, which continued to be printed in multiple editions throughout the century, but also citations of the commentaries and of the many tracts and treatises.[32] So, too, do the seventeenth-century writers cite other Reformed predecessors, notably writers such as Vermigli, Zanchi, and Beza. Nonetheless, it is true that the citations of these significant forbearers are not found in the density that twentieth-century theological hagiographers might hope for. Reformed orthodoxy was, after all, a living movement reflective of its own contexts and not merely a carbon copy of the thought of the Reformers: but what we can declare, with some confidence, is that the developing tradition of Reformed theology in the seventeenth century paid close attention to its roots in the Reformation and was concerned as it encountered new adversaries and new problems–such as the detailed antitrinitarian exegesis of the Socinians, the denials of divine simplicity and eternity by Vorstius and the Socinians, and the pelagianizing "middle knowledge" theory of the Jesuits and Arminians–to maintain the tenets of the Reformation in increasingly detailed forms and to affirm the catholicity of Protestantism.[33]

To this end, the Reformed orthodox also drew on the medieval tradition as well as on the Church Fathers and the Reformers. Exemplifying the positive use of medieval materials, the Genevan-trained Lambert Daneau wrote a Reformed commentary on the first book of Lombard's *Sententiarum libri quatuor*. Daneau also drew on the thinkers identified by Calvin and other Reformers as *saniores scholastici*,[34] sounder or more trustworthy scholastics, such as Lombard, Aquinas, Bonaventure, and Durandus, to build his own system of theology.[35] Franciscus Junius of Leiden wrote the first major prolegomenon to theology, adapting the categories of the medieval scholastics (such as the distinctions between *theologia in se* and *theologia nostra* or *theologia in patria* and *theologia in via*) to Reformed doctrine in order to identify the meaning of the term theology, the genus of the discipline, its proper object, its divisions, and its goal or direction.[36] (Of course, here is a significant intersection of the history of the printed book with the history of theology–for just as the book fueled the Reformation, so also did it serve to assure the future of scholastic theology by making available works of scholastic theology in fine printed editions: Altenstaig's *Vocabularius theologiae*, in which scholastic theology was reviewed in definitions that cited the texts of Bonaventure, Aquinas, Scotus, and other major medieval theologians; printed editions of the theological works of Thomas Aquinas, Gregory of Rimini, Henry of Ghent, Pierre D'Ailly, and Thomas of Strasbourg, among others.[37])

Proofs of God's existence also entered the Reformed systems, probably by way of the later editions of Melanchthon's influential *Loci communes theologici*. What is important to note here is the development of patterns of argument: while the Reformed theologians of the orthodox era often drew on the causal, cosmological, and teleological models of Thomas Aquinas's "five ways," they also tended to follow patterns of Renaissance logic, and to develop discursive rhetorical arguments for the existence of God–as much for the purpose of persuading so-called practical atheists as for the sake of a rational demonstration of the existence of God.[38] It is typical, in other words, for the Reformed orthodox to blend the logical or demonstrative with the rhetorical or persuasive forms of the arguments and to use the proofs in order to persuade atheists of the truth of Christian theism as well as to show the limits of the natural knowledge of God. Specifically, they drew on rhetorical forms such as the argument *e consensu gentium* (used by Calvin in a similar way),[39] rather than design the proofs as a foundation for theological system.[40]

By way of example of the defensive and polemical use of the past, in the face of Jesuit, Arminian, and Socinian advocacy of a so-called divine middle knowledge, a divine knowledge of future contingents and counterfactuals prior to and outside of the divine willing, Reformed theologians drew on the medieval and late Renaissance scholasticism of various Thomist, Scotist, and Augustinian thinkers, noting the traditional distinction of God's knowledge into the necessary knowledge of God's self and of all possibilities and the free or voluntary knowledge that God had concerning all actuality. This division of the topic, noted the Reformed orthodox, was exhaustive and necessarily the only division. One may sense here an element of discontinuity in form and detail with the Reformation, but one ought also to recognize a substantive continuity in teaching, elaborated now in forms relevant to the context of philosophical development and theological debate in the early seventeenth century.[41]

The Philosophical Tradition and Reason, Specified as Logic, Rhetoric, and Their Methodological Applications

In the era of orthodoxy, albeit to a lesser extent than in the early stages of the Reformation, Reformed theologians remained wary of the wholesale adoption of any particular philosophy. In their prolegomena, the Reformed scholastics detailed the proper use and the limits of rational argumentation and of philosophy. Thus, reason or rational argument was consistently used for the sake of drawing conclusions on the basis or within the bounds of Christian doctrine but, equally consistently, denied principial status. Philosophy, understood as a rational form of knowing, was identified by the Protestant scholastics (just as it had been by the medievals) as an ancillary discipline, the handmaid and not the master of theological *scientia*.[42] An indication of this relationship between revealed, churchly theology and the exercise of reason can be seen in the very limited role accorded to so-called natural theology by the Reformed: they assumed the availability of truths about God in the natural order, particularly to the regenerate Christian, but always cautioned that such truths did not relate to salvation.[43]

Thus, the rather eclectic Christian Aristotelianism of the Protestant orthodox drew on rules of logic and devices like the fourfold causality in order to explain and develop doctrinal formulae—and only seldom, if ever, to import a full-scale rational metaphysics or physics into theology.[44] Contrary to what is sometimes claimed, the fourfold causality (i.e., first, formal, material, and final causes) does not imply a particular metaphysic. Specifically, it is not by nature "deterministic." One can use the model to delineate the soteriological patterns of the eternal decree of God and its execution in time; one also can use the model to describe the sources and effects of human sinfulness and human moral conduct; or one can use the model to explain how a carpenter makes a table. The large-scale result of Christian Aristotelianism was not, in other words, a fundamentally Aristotelian Christianity: Aristotle would have disowned this hybrid philosophy with its infinite God who created the world out of nothing![45] There was, certainly, less imposition of rational metaphysics on theology in the seventeenth-century orthodox affirmations of divine eternity, omniscience, and immutability than there is in the twentieth-century claims of a changing God whose very being is in flux and who lacks foreknowledge of future contingency!

The same must be said of the Reformed encounter with the philosophies of the late Renaissance and the seventeenth century. Rather, for example, than a wholesale adoption of the metaphysics of Francis Suárez, there was a critical appropriation and a revision of Renaissance Aristotelianism in the works of Reformed philosophers and theologians in the early seventeenth century. Protestants, as well as Roman Catholics, moreover, were aware of the various adaptations of older philosophical models—with the result that the Jesuit development of the theory of "middle knowledge" as a way of dealing with the divine foreknowledge of future contingents was received and debated in Protestant circles,[46] as was the transmission and adaptation of nominalist epistemology.[47] So, too, did Suárez's adoption of a concept of the univocity of being draw major discussion among Protestant thinkers as well as Roman Catholics.[48] In all of these instances, moreover, the philosophical discussion had immediate and significant ramifications for theology—and Reformed thinkers remained wary of the easy acceptance both of the conclusions of the older scholastic philosophical tradition and of the philosophical arguments of thinkers such as Suárez and Molina, even as they recognized the necessity of dealing with philosophical conclusions and of developing philosophical positions consistent with Reformed doctrine.

This wariness extended especially to the new philosophies of the day, most notably the philosophies of Descartes and Spinoza.[49] The Reformed orthodox worried that Descartes's principle of radical doubt and his subsequent deduction of an entire philosophy (including the existence of God and the interaction of body and soul in the pineal gland) from his own self-consciousness were contrary to their biblical and confessional norms—a rationalism that could not be accepted *in toto*. Spinoza's philosophical monism was condemned as a dangerous form of atheism. Descartes's philosophy was thus used eclectically and there were significant debates over its use and appropriation among the Reformed—and Spinoza's was utterly rejected by the large majority of Reformed writers.[50] It is perhaps worth noting one specific instance of debate: the Cartesian division of substance into thought and extension raised considerable concern among the Reformed over the traditional understanding of "spirit" as a substantial, but nonextended reality, not merely identical with thought.[51] The extended, substantive wrestling with the implications of Cartesian thought among the Reformed remains a subject for investigation.[52]

The Relationship between Systematic or Dogmatic Theology and Practice

At the outset, I noted that this issue could not properly be included among the "sources" of Reformed orthodox theology. After all, every one of the stated norms and grounds for the formulation of orthodox Protestant dogmatics are objectively given doctrinal or methodological principles, whether Scripture as the ultimate norm, or the confessions and tradition as subordinate norms, or philosophy and logic as ancillary and methodological tools. Nonetheless, the life, piety, and practice of the church did relate directly to dogmatic theology in the era of orthodoxy. Virtually all of the theologians of the era understood the discipline of theology either as a mixed "speculative" and "practical" discipline or, indeed, as a purely "practical" discipline.[53] What they meant by the inclusion of the term *praxis* in their definitions was that the entire discipline of theology was goal directed: theology, understood as a *praxis* or practical discipline, was directed toward the goal of human salvation. More specifically, each doctrine taught in the theological systems of the day (not merely, for example, the doctrine of God, but each individual divine attribute; not merely the doctrine of the last things, but each subcategory of the doctrine) was to be known both for itself as a truth of God and for the sake of the goal of salvation toward which it directed the human knower. Each rightly understood (i.e., orthodox!) doctrine would have a direct impact on piety, on the shaping of faith, on the shaping of Christian life: we see this movement from doctrine to practical "use" quite consistently in Puritan sermons and it stood as a formal aspect of theological system in the major works of Wilhelmus à Brakel and Petrus van Mastricht.[54] The "practice of piety," to borrow the title of a great treatise of the era, was not an objective source of theological system; yet, it was certainly a rule for the right conduct of theological system. In other words, it was very clear to the Reformed orthodox that rightly formulated Christian doctrine would relate directly to the life of the church and the individual believer and, conversely, poorly or wrongly formulated doctrine would not.

Not only, therefore, do we see in the era of orthodoxy a direct and profound relationship between the formulation of doctrine and the basic exegesis of the text of Scripture, but we also see a direct relationship between the formulation of doctrine and the life of the church. If, in the normative pattern of theological work, exegesis was intended to lead directly to the production of sermons, commentaries, and theological formulations, so, too, were the commentaries and the theological formulae of the full-scale systems intended to lead the exegetical result, through a rigorous process of interpretation and formulation, back to the life of the church both as a guide to right preaching and, like preaching itself, as a guide to Christian life. In this sense, Christian life or "practice" did function among the sources of orthodox theology—at very least, it was an index to the success or failure of the work of the theologian.

The Sources and the *Loci*

Our survey of the sources of Reformed orthodox theology also points toward the methodological issue, but at perhaps a more profound level and with a clearer insight into the nature of the *locus* method taken up by Reformed orthodoxy in the wake of the Renaissance recasting of the relationship of logic and rhetoric. A significant clue to this methodological issue can be found in the so-called commonplace books published during the sixteenth century: the books begin each section with a word identifying a significant or "standard" topic—and then proceed to the next section by way of blank pages. The purpose of the book was to give its purchaser a standard series of topics or *loci communes* for study, discussion, or debate, together with the blank paper on which to amass notes drawn from one's readings, literally, a gathering of the materials of the *loci* from sources not in themselves topically arranged. The Reformed orthodox theologians came to their theological task with a similar volume of collected topics, either as inherited from writers of the previous generation—such as Melanchthon, Calvin, and Musculus—or drawn form the earlier tradition, or, alternatively, identified by the highly topical model of the Ramist dialectic, which, at the end of its process of bifurcations (and occasional trifurcations!), concluded with a set of basic *loci* divided out of the larger topics of theology.

The very nature of this approach to the topics and materials of theology stood in the way of a neatly *a priori* approach to theology and, equally so, of a neatly *a posteriori* approach. There is, of course, a nominally *a priori* order in those theologies that begin with God and creation and proceed by way of the work of salvation to the last things—but this is also the order of Scripture itself, and it does not indicate a deductive process for identifying the topics and developing their contents. Similarly, as one works through a Protestant scholastic discussion of the divine attributes, one is struck by the number of arguments that are determined not by speculative or metaphysical concerns but, rather, by soteriological debate with such adversaries as Arminians and Socinians—thus introducing a distinctly *a posteriori* class of argument into the *locus*, without of course implying that either the *locus* itself or its contents were derived by an *a posteriori* logic in the strictest sense. Indeed, the intellectual work taken toward the development of the individual topics included many efforts that were not of a strictly logical nature but, rather, were related to the biblical, traditionary, polemical, and what might be called academic concerns (viz., concerns that were "scholastic" in the *methodological sense*) for gathering together the optimal sources for the exposition of a given topic.

Perhaps two examples are in order. First, we note the structure of the *locus* in Van Mastricht's *Theoretico-practica theologia*: each *locus* begins with an exegesis of a biblical text or texts, selected as *loci classici* or *sedes doctrinae*, in the original languages, proceeds to a dogmatic discussion of the *locus* or *topos* elicited from the biblical text (often making reference to historical or traditionary materials), then moves to an elenctic or disputative section in which various errors are refuted (whether ancient or modern), and concludes with a practical discussion. The model is neither purely or even primarily deductive or inductive, but, rather, is designed to move through the gathered materials of the *locus* in an order that respects the priority of Scripture as a norm of doctrine, presents the doctrinal concerns of the church, and then reflects on the concerns of piety.

Second, the example of Turretin's *Institutio theologiae elencticae*: here is an argumentative model that is primarily elenctical or disputative, and is designed to present a positive doctrinal result over against error. The basic shape of Turretin's theology, like that of Van Mastricht, moves from prolegomena and principia, by way of creation and the work of salvation to the last things—the nominally *a priori* order. But the construction of each *locus*, as we have been led to expect from our understanding of the *loci* and their sources, proceeds quite differently. Turretin never begins with a set of logical or theological principles: rather, he identifies the problem. His pattern is to pose a theological question and then either to offer a discussion of the "state of the question" and a brief positive definition of the Reformed view or, if he feels the historical background of the problem needs explanation, he will provide a discussion of the "origin" of the question prior to the "state of the question." Turretin invariably moves on to identify a series of "sources of explanation," typically beginning with a series of references to biblical texts and then presenting rational or traditionary materials, offered at some length—exemplifying the *locus* method.[55] The order of the discussion follows the assumption of the priority of Scripture and of the proper use of reason and tradition within the boundaries set by Scripture.

We ought also to take Turretin at his word that he is presenting "sources of explanation" and not a full exposition of the contents of all of the sources! In other words, he presents a ranked series of materials, biblical, rational, and traditionary, that he and others have gathered out of a broader study of the subject and its resources, a study that was, itself, not topically arranged in the same sense. He has, in the precise sense of Renaissance rhetoric and logic, constructed a *locus* that both presents the "sources" or *fontes* of explanation and also points his readers back to the sources—points them *ad fontes* in the more technical sense of the Renaissance motto. We should no more expect a full exegesis of the various biblical "proofs" at this point than we ought to expect a full historical examination of the patristic or other traditionary materials cited. As was true in the case of Melanchthon's and Calvin's theologies (in which this method was inaugurated for Protestants), the *loci communes* or *institutio* were not intended to stand independent of the other forms of theological inquiry and statement: the "proof texts" cited in the theological *locus*, for example, do not stand independent or even isolated from the work of the commentator—this is implied as the background of the doctrinal or elenctical exercise and it is assumed that the reader of the gathered *fontes* will also be a reader of commentaries, histories, and so forth. In short, the *locus* method of a Turretin or of a Van Mastricht was designed to display the varied sources of Reformed orthodox theology and to bring them to bear on a series of positive and polemical *loci* or *topoi*. In both cases, the *principia* of theology were identified as Scripture and God—and the grounds of each specific *locus* were made clear, by Mastricht in his exegetical and dogmatic expositions and by Turretin in his presentation of the *status quaestionis*.

Comparison of the work of Turretin and Mastricht also offers evidence of several rather different genres of theological discussion. Mastricht in fact identifies four—the exegetical, the dogmatic, the polemical or disputative, and the practical. Turretin, in the title to his work, indicates that his purpose is primarily elenctical or disputative. His entire work, therefore, takes the form of only one of the parts of Mastricht's system. Even so, many of the Reformed orthodox prolegomena make distinctions between textual or exegetical study, preaching, catechetical theology, positive or doctrinal exposition, polemical or elenctical theology, and the detailed or "scholastic" form of theology in the academy.[56] A given seventeenth-century theologian was, therefore, by his own definitions, not always engaged in scholastic theology—some of his work, the most academic, would qualify as scholastic, other of his works would be exegetical, catechetical, or homiletical. What is more, the Reformed scholastics distinguished between their scholasticism or "school method" and what they saw as the more speculative scholasticism of the Middle Ages—and certainly, given its characteristic *locus* method, their scholastic approach was distinct from that of the medieval scholastics.[57]

Our examination of the *locus* method, moreover, demands that we avoid the theological tendency to absolute these documents (or those of the Reformation) and make them emblematic of great dogmatic paradigms and "isms"—rather, the documents need to be historically contextualized and read as products of the academic culture of the late Renaissance and the seventeenth century, a varied culture in which scholastic models inherited from the Middle Ages, which had already been critically reexamined and revised in the context of Renaissance and Reformation, were further adapted and revised to serve the needs of newly Protestant universities and new Protestant academies. The contents of the *locus* and the specific directions of argument were not, after all, guided by central dogmas or necessarily controlled by century-old concerns of the Reformers, but by the debates of a particular era, perhaps of a particular university or church setting.

The basic *loci* remained largely the same: much of their content was biblical or traditionary, but the content is also quite contemporary in nuance, adapted to such alterations of the academic or churchly context as the shift at the beginning of the seventeenth century to a late Renaissance Aristotelianism and to the debate over Suarezian metaphysics—or, after 1640, to the debate over the newer philosophies of Descartes and his disciples—or, again, to the shifts in polemic and eschatological thought caused by the fortunes of the Thirty Years' War or the new intellectual and exegetical drive of Socinianism signaled (academically, at least) by the publication of the *Bibliotheca fratrum polonorum* in 1656—or, further, by the ejection of Puritan pastors and professors from their pulpits and university fellowships after the Restoration. Thus, by way of example, the Suarezian metaphysics generated a debate over whether God and finite creature ought to be identified univocally as "being" (with many of the Reformed responding in the negative). The Thirty Years' War inspired alterations in Reformed eschatology. Socinianism generated, as already noted, an increasingly historical examination of the Church Fathers. The ejection and disestablishment of the Puritans altered English Reformed ecclesiology. Events such as these, therefore, as linked to the use of very specific sources brought by Protestant authors to the formulation of their theologies, must be considered as far more fundamental to our understanding of development and change of Reformed orthodoxy than various theories of the abstract movement, relationship, and structure of dogmas—particularly given that such theories tend to be modern theological grids imposed on the historical materials.

Concluding Remarks

Examination of the sources of Reformed orthodox, particularly in connection with discussion of the topical method used in the construction or formulation of theology in the seventeenth century adds yet another dimension to the ongoing historical reappraisal of this theology. At very least, such examination shows that the claims, typical of older scholarship concerning central dogmas, deductive systems of theology, and rationalism fail because they do not at all reflect the actual methods of this theology. The theology of the Reformed scholastics was not developed by neat processes of deduction from single ideas or by recourse to a philosophical system, whether Aristotelian or Cartesian. The actual construction of the *loci* from their biblical, traditionary, polemical, and rational or argumentative sources appears as a highly complex process and, moreover, as a process rooted in a series of particular, identifiable historical contexts.

Finally, some comment needs be made concerning the relationship of the present examination of the sources, materials, and method of Reformed orthodox theology to the larger work of examining, analyzing, and reappraising Reformed thought in the seventeenth century. It is apparent that not only has a work of historical reappraisal of Reformed scholasticism has been effectively undertaken during the past two decades—it is also apparent that the reappraisal has itself altered in shape and developed new patterns of approach to the materials. I would suggest, in the first place, that we have seen a shift from a pattern of reappraisal that was in part determined by the underlying problematic of the older scholarship to a pattern that more closely respects the methods and approaches of the seventeenth century. Thus, the older quest to identify and analyze "central dogmas" was a nineteenth-century quest to find the roots of the nineteenth-century theological enterprise in the past—and it was, of course, anachronistic. Its transformation, in the hands of theologians such as H. E. Weber and J. H. Scholten,[58] into a highly negative assessment of the older dogmatics failed to escape the trap of anachronistic theological analysis: in fact, their work stands as curious polemic not against the actual theology of the seventeenth century but against an erroneous nineteenth-century reconstruction of that theology. Even so, the effort of Paul Althaus to identify the *principia* of Reformed orthodox dogmatics took a nineteenth- (or early twentieth-) century view of *principia* and pressed it on the older materials—ironically, without ever asking what the seventeenth-century writers identified as their own *principia*.

In addition, these older patterns of scholarship seldom looked beyond theological systems and dogmatic tracts for their documentation. What has become apparent as research into this era has progressed, is that the larger intellectual and spiritual enterprise of the seventeenth-century theologian must be examined. Even the materials examined in the present essay indicate that the thought of the Reformed orthodox will never be understood until we also have a clearer picture of biblical exegesis and patristic study in the seventeenth century—and, of course, a clearer picture as well of the relationship of the seventeenth-century version of these theological disciplines to doctrinal formulation. So, too, is it highly important that we examine more carefully the individual thinkers, who were frequently not merely university professors but also pastors and pastoral advisors: by way of example, the eminent Gisbertus Voetius who was not only one of the most adept scholastic thinkers of the seventeenth century, but also (in his pastoral and spiritual labors) he was a significant preacher, a catechist, and one of the founding fathers of the *Nadere Reformatie*. Although Voetius was certainly an exceptional intellect and an exceptionally energetic churchman, his engagement in diverse areas of theological and religious endeavor in fact echoes the patterns of his time. Other lesser-known professors and pastors also crossed what appear to us as disciplinary boundaries (but were not actually such in the sevententh century) and conjoined a methodologically scholastic theology with biblical exegesis and piety. We must cease to dichotomize scholasticism and piety in our examination of the period when these aspects of churchly existence cannot be separated out of the individual thinkers of the era. And we must study more of these individual thinkers to fill out our knowledge of the period.

Despite some very significant individual essays, moreover, there remains an unacceptable division in seventeenth-century studies between historians of church and theology and historians of philosophy: studies of the history of philosophy in the seventeenth century have so concentrated on what, from the perspective of the present, appear to be the major movements—and studies of the history of theology have so focused on dogmatic problems—that the profound interrelationship between the two disciplines has been largely overlooked. Just as we must identify the specific trajectories of biblical exegesis in the seventeenth century in order to understand the patterns of theological formulation, so also must we be aware of the trajectories of seventeenth-century philosophy, particularly as they represent modifications and adaptations of the older tradition.

In sum, this brief presentation and analysis of the sources of Reformed theology in the seventeenth century has pointed in two basic directions. First, it offers evidence of the nature and character of the theology of the seventeenth century, specifically, of its method. In so doing, it promises to provide a more historical and genuinely contextual understanding of this theology as we increasingly set aside the dogmatic and ideological analyses of older scholarship, such as the "central dogma" theory or the equally anachronistic and antihistorical "Calvin against the Calvinists" approach. In other words, analysis of the actual sources of seventeenth-century Reformed thought, the actual methods used to appropriate these sources, and the historical contexts in which the formulation was accomplished increasingly take us away from the notion that one thinker was the source or norm or that a single idea was the foundation.

Second, identification of these sources and methods offers some indication of the way in which the seventeenth century must be approached if we are ever to understand its patterns of thought. The *locus* method is crucial here. It represents the confluence of Renaissance logic and rhetoric with the scholastic or academic process and, in addition, it marks the movement or, indeed, the means and pattern of movement, of academic theology from classroom exercise to literary genre—much as the *quaestio* did for the Middle Ages. More than this, however, both in the form of classroom disputation and in the form of written theological texts, the *locus* method illustrates the relationship between the theological result and its sources. This conclusion applies, moreover, not only to the biblical sources that since the time of Melanchthon had been analyzed and interpreted with a view to the extraction or elicitation of theological topics or *loci*: the conclusion applies to all of the sources of the theology of scholastic orthodoxy and it therefore demands from us a historical, contextual, nondogmatic, and increasingly cross-disciplinary study of the period.

4

Calvin and the "Calvinists"

Assessing Continuities and Discontinuities between the Reformation and Orthodoxy, Part 1

The Problem of Protestant Orthodoxy

The study of Protestant orthodoxy has received more attention in the last two decades than it received in the entire earlier part of the twentieth century. For much of that century, scholarship was content to repeat, with minor modification, the generalizations and arguments of nineteenth- and early twentieth-century German historians and theologians such as Alexander Schweizer,[1] Heinrich Heppe,[2] Paul Althaus,[3] and Hans Emil Weber.[4] Variations on these generalizations and arguments have continued to be expressed but also have been significantly challenged in the past two decades.[5]

For the sake of convenience, we can identify five basic albeit sometimes interrelated approaches to the issue of Reformation and orthodoxy that belong to the history of scholarship—in roughly chronological order.[6] First and earliest, there is the nineteenth-century dogmatic approach that discussed the history of Reformed theology in terms of the development of predestination as a central dogma, represented in the works of Schweizer, Heppe, Althaus, Weber, and Ernest Bizer. Within this initial grouping, however, there is a disagreement over the nature of the development: Schweizer viewed it positively, the others tended to see predestinarianism as a problematic turn in theology. Second, there is a line of reappraisal of Calvin's relationship to the varieties of Reformed theology that resting primarily on purportedly significant differences between Calvin and Bullinger or, alternatively, between a "Genevan" and a "Rhineland" approach on the topic of covenant and arguing that covenant theology acted as a counterpoise to "rigid" predestinarianism in the seventeenth century: the main contributors to this paradigm are Leonard Trinterud, Jens Moeller, Charles McCoy, and J. Wayne Baker. Third, an approach, characterized by an almost polemical pitting of "Calvin against the Calvinists," draws on the arguments of Schweizer, Heppe, Weber, and Bizer that later Reformed theology is a predestinarian system, but argues that this development of predestination is a "departure" from the thought of Calvin. This approach typically accepts the results of the second model and is consistently grounded in a series of neoorthodox theological assumptions concerning revelation, Scripture, the relation of law and gospel, and the principial function of Christ in theology. It is also characterized by a negative, theologized understanding of "scholasticism"—found in the monographs of Walter Kickel, Brian Armstrong, Basil Hall, Thomas F. Torrance, Cornelis Graafland, Philip Holtrop, Cornelis van Sliedregt, and others.

Fourth, there is an approach based in a more limited way on Heinrich Heppe, Hans Emil Weber, and Ernst Bizer, conditioned by twentieth-century reappraisals of Calvin's views on predestination and Christology. Although these authors (John Bray, Joseph McClelland, John Patrick Donnelly, Robert Godfrey, Ian McPhee, Robert Letham) tend to look for the beginnings of Reformed scholasticism in writers other than Calvin—notably Theodore Beza and Peter Martyr Vermigli—they also find the documentation of a "predestinarian system" less than convincing and look to other sources for the development of Reformed orthodoxy than single central dogmas. This research has, typically, served as the basis of a transition to the fifth and final of the research models. Fifth, and most recent, there is a pattern of reappraisal (Willem van Asselt, Olivier Fatio, Richard A. Muller, Eef Dekker, Anton Vos, Carl Trueman, Martin Klauber, Lyle Bierma, and others) that contests the central dogma theory of the nineteenth century, continues the line of the early-twentieth-century reappraisal of Calvin into the theology of later Reformed theologians, examines more closely the medieval background of the Reformation, and rejects the theological premises of neoorthodox historiography. This fifth pattern, moreover, argues a degree of continuity in development that echoes aspects of the work of Schweizer and Heppe, but without its theological *tendenz* and its assumption of a method founded on "central dogmas"—and it engages in dialogue with arguments and definitions found in the fourth group of writers, specifically with reference to the beginnings of contemporary reinterpretation of figures such as Beza and Vermigli.

Of course, the extant body of literature on the topic of Reformation and orthodoxy evidences somewhat more diversity than this brief paradigm can indicate. The current discussion, moreover, has often failed to recognize either the internal divergences or the persistent and problematic theological *tendenz* of the first and fourth approaches. Thus, Schweizer, Heppe, and Althaus assumed the solidification of Protestant theological systems around central dogmas and viewed the Reformed dogmatics of the sixteenth and seventeenth centuries as resting on the doctrine of predestination. They argued both a high degree of continuity in development between Zwingli and Calvin and between Calvin and his contemporaries on the one hand and the Reformed orthodox on the other. Beyond this basic agreement, however, there are theological differences between these writers that influenced their views of the history—differences particularly evident in a comparison of Schweizer, Heppe, and Weber.[7]

Schweizer viewed the development of a predestinarian system in a highly positive light inasmuch as it could be seen as a development leading to Schleiermacher's theology and, specifically, to his own version of the Schleiermacherian system. He also assumed that the deterministic implications of predestination could be balanced against an understanding of human freedom.[8] Heppe, by way of contrast, had argued that the more predestinarian form of Reformed theology, associated with Calvin and Beza, and outlined in his *Reformed Dogmatics*, could be distinguished from a nonpredestinarian, fundamentally Melanchthonian, German Reformed dogmatics. The predestinarian system, according to Heppe, tended to reduce human beings to the status of marionettes. The German Reformed theology, with its nonpredestinarian, "*biblisch-soteriologische Princip*," was the most suitable confessional approach for the Evangelical-Reformed union project of his time.[9] (Over against these views, particularly in opposition to Schweizer, Schneckenburger denied the purely deductive model even in the more predestinarian systems—the eternal decree, he insisted, supplied neither the method nor the material of the older Reformed dogmatics.[10])

The more recent discussion of Reformed theology as constructed around central dogmas, typical of the writers that we will examine under the fourth paradigm of research, does not, typically, follow Schweizer in viewing this as a positive development in theology—nor does it generally follow Schweizer, Heppe, and Althaus in their perception of continuity between Calvin and later Reformed theologians. And, with few exceptions, it has ignored Schneckenburger's well-documented responses to Schweizer. This negative understanding of the central dogma theory follows out the line of argument initiated by Heppe and developed from a Lutheran perspective by Hans Emil Weber. In addition to his association of Protestant orthodoxy in general with rationalism,[11] Weber accepted Schweizer and Heppe's understanding of predestination as the fundamental principle of Reformed theology, and described the creation of a predestinarian system as a rationalizing declension from the central emphasis of the earliest Reformers on justification by grace through faith as the *articulus stantis et cadentis ecclesiae*. It is, moreover, Weber's association of the doctrine of predestination with a rationalizing scholasticism that has carried over into the negative appraisal of Protestant orthodoxy characteristic of the more recent scholarship. Weber stood, however, with Schweizer, Heppe, and Althaus in understanding Calvin as standing in continuity with later Reformed theology.[12] Bizer accepts the Weberian central dogma theory and attempts to argue the increasingly rationalistic and necessitarian character of Reformed theology. His argument is called into question by his failure to focus on treatises of similar topic and genre as he attempts to trace a development toward orthodoxy. He also takes particular works as emblematic of shifts in emphasis with little regard to context and genre of the documents.[13]

In order for the next three categories of scholarship to emerge out of this trajectory of analysis, given the sense of continuity between Calvin and later Reformed thought presupposed by the earlier scholarship, several further alterations of perspective were necessary. In short, Calvin's theology itself needed to be reappraised in various ways and a series of dichotomies argued between Calvin's theology and later Reformed thought. Thus, much of the recent literature identifies Calvin as the proponent of a predominantly scriptural and christocentric opposed to a predominantly Aristotelian, rationalistic, and predestinarian system,[14] as a theologian of grace to be distinguished from the legalism of later "Calvinist" covenantal or federal theology,[15] or again as a thinker who strictly distinguished between Word and Scripture and who denied a dictation theory of inspiration—again to be distinguished from later Calvinists.[16] This development began with the work of Paul Jacobs and of neoorthodox interpreters of the theology of the Reformation such as Wilhelm Niesel, J. K. S. Reid, and Ronald Wallace.[17] As I have argued elsewhere, Jacobs's reappraisal of Calvin as thoroughly trinitarian in his theology, as christocentric in his soteriological teaching, and as balancing the doctrine of election with a concern for human responsibility was never carried forward into the era of orthodoxy. The result of this failure to see the same issues in later Reformed thought (and, indeed, to give proper consideration to Aristotelian and scholastic elements in Calvin's theology) has resulted in the claim that Reformed orthodoxy is discontinuous with the Reformation.[18] Similarly, on the issue of covenant, law, and grace, as in studies of the doctrine of Scripture, recent readings of Calvin's and other Reformers' thought have driven a wedge between the Reformation and orthodoxy—although in both of these instances the reappraisals of Calvin's thought are arguably less accurate than Jacobs's work.

This neoorthodox historiography not only shifted the discussion of Calvin away from the nineteenth-century models that had placed him in continuity with the Reformed orthodoxy, it also added to the discussion a series of highly debatable dogmatic premises that have served to cloud the understanding of the Reformation. Dogmatic obfuscation of the Reformation at the hands of writers such as T. F. Torrance, Reid, Niesel, as well as by dogmaticians of the mid-twentieth century such as Brunner, Barth, and H. E. Weber,[19] became the basis for several generations of writers, most belonging to the fourth approach in our paradigm, to argue a radical distinction between the thought of the Reformation and that of the post-Reformation era. It is certainly true that, if the Reformers' theology was neoorthodox, it stood in massive discontinuity with the medieval background to the Reformation and with the Protestant orthodoxy that followed! Any number of ahistorical conclusions can be drawn from such absurd premises.

The second approach noted earlier tends to argue a limited disjunction between Calvin and the "Calvinists," in its acceptance of Beza and others of his generation as a cause of the "rigid" scholastic predestinarianism of later Calvinism. It differs with the "Calvin against the Calvinists" approach, however, given its assumption of a governing concept of predestination in Calvin's thought and its assumption that Calvin, quite apart from Beza, undercut the conception of human responsibility and of the historicity of salvation intrinsic to covenant thought. Calvin's predestinarianism, according to this view, led to a radically monopleuric and monergistic conception of covenant, distinct from the less-predestinarian and dipleuric covenant theology of Bullinger and the Rhineland theologians. This approach rests on the work of Trinterud and Moeller and has recently been amplified by work of McCoy and Baker.[20] There is some divergence among writers taking this line of argument concerning the question of the interrelationship of predestination and covenant, election and law, grace and responsibility: thus, the development of covenant theology is sometimes seen as a counterbalance to the predestinarian tendencies of Reformed theology—while other scholars associate covenant language with an increasing legalism in Reformed thought over against the Calvinian emphasis on election and grace.[21] In addition, beginning with McCoy and carrying over into Baker, the influence of the third approach is felt, with its use of the central dogma theory and its tendency to understand "scholasticism" as a predestinarian theology rather than as a method. McCoy and Baker draw out these arguments in order to place the federal tradition, particularly the work of Cocceius, in opposition to "scholastic" Reformed theology.

The third approach, evident in studies by Kickel, Hall, Torrance, Rolston, Gründler, Poole, Holtrop, and Sliedregt, draws on the nineteenth-century scholarship and assumes many of the disjunctions between Calvin and later Reformed theology indicated in our second and third approaches (despite their fundamentally different orientations) but rests primarily on a neoorthodox reassessment of sixteenth- and seventeenth-century theology. The problematic aspect of the approach of these writers is seen in their juxtaposition of a misconstrual of Calvin's thought with a caricature of orthodoxy and, more fundamentally, in the barely concealed neoorthodox theological *tendenz* that underlies their work: typical here is the attempt to identify Calvin as the direct ancestor of neoorthodox Christocentrism and to discredit theologically the Reformed orthodox teaching as incompatible both with Calvin and with Barth.[22] Kickel, to whose arguments we will return later, reads Beza as the source of a theologically problematic predestinarianism in Reformed theology and as the primary mover in the development of the rigid, rationalistic scholasticism of later generations of Reformed thought. Hall, while distancing himself from neoorthodox understandings of Calvin's theology, still contrasts the christocentric aspects of Calvin's theology with the predestinarianism of Beza's *Tabula praedestinationis*.[23] This perspective is echoed by Toon.[24] Gründler applies the same model to Zanchi, albeit with some attention to Zanchi's scholastic training. Sliedregt virtually duplicates Kickel's arguments for Beza, adding the claim that Beza is Thomistic.[25] In variant of this pattern, Holtrop links Armstrong's definition of Protestant orthodoxy with an alternative perspective on what constitutes christocentricity and with a fundamentally neoorthodox view of biblical theology as personal and nonpropositional in order to argue a continuity of negative aspects of Calvin's thought and personality with later Reformed scholasticism and of positive aspects of Calvin's thought and personality with Holtrop's own theology. Ironically, Holtrop attempts to provide some sense of historical context through discussion of the thought of Bullinger and Viret, when in fact all he provides is further illustration of his own theological program and *tendenz*, now pressed as an interpretive grid over Calvin's Reformed contemporaries as well as Calvin himself.[26] The result of this direction in research has been the definition of Protestant orthodoxy or Protestant scholasticism in rather stark contrast to the theology and method of the Reformation.

The clearest and certainly most influential form of the definition is found in Brian Armstrong's groundbreaking work on *Calvinism and the Amyraut Heresy*. Armstrong drew on the work of H. E. Weber and Walter Kickel, among others, and suggested four basic characteristics of the phenomenon of a Protestant scholasticism:

> (1) Primarily it will have reference to that theological approach which asserts religious truth on the basis of deductive ratiocination from given assumptions or principles, thus providing a logically coherent and defensible system of belief. Generally this takes the form of syllogistic reasoning. It is an orientation, it seems, invariably based upon an Aristotelian philosophic commitment and so relates to medieval scholasticism. (2) The term will refer to the employment of reason in religious matters, so that reason assumes at least equal standing with faith in theology, thus jettisoning some of the authority of revelation. (3) It will comprehend the sentiment that the scriptural record contains a unified, rationally comprehensible account and thus may be used as a measuring stick to determine one's orthodoxy. (4) It will comprehend a pronounced interest in metaphysical matters, in abstract speculative thought, particularly with reference to the doctrine of God. The distinctive Protestant position is made to rest on a speculative formulation of the will of God.[27]

Armstrong also juxtaposed "French humanism" with "Protestant scholasticism," and although he conceded, with acknowledgment of Kristeller, that the two phenomena were not mutually exclusive, he persisted in the claim that scholasticism and humanism represent two "orientations fundamentally at odds."[28] It is important to recognize that the contrast of humanism and scholasticism in Armstrong's definition drew on his theological reading of the Amyraut controversy and therefore points both to the relatively tentative character of the definition and to the historical limitation of its scope: even if Armstrong's dichotomization of humanists and scholastics could be documented from the Amyraut controversy, there is no ground offered by Armstrong's research for the application of this language to the larger phenomenon of Reformed orthodoxy. This point is seldom noted by subsequent writers. Thus, for example, Holtrop presses the distinction between humanism and scholasticism to the point of arguing an internal conflict in Calvin between the humanistic and scholastic sides of his personality, never recognizing that the definition does not fit the "scholastic" qualities that he finds in Calvin or that the untenable dichotomization in Armstrong's definition provided no basis for the psychological bifurcation of Calvin's personality.[29]

In addition, despite his nod in the direction of Kristeller, Armstrong's definition not only maintains the strict dichotomy that Kristeller argued against, it also falls into the trap of the older, pre-Kristeller scholarship in assuming that humanism and scholasticism each implied a particular theological and philosophical content. Furthermore, the theological content indicated in Armstrong's definition of scholasticism precisely echoes the neoorthodox caricatures of post-Reformation intellectual development. In short, what was given concise definition by Armstrong was not the historical phenomenon but the theological caricature of Reformed orthodoxy.[30]

Related to Armstrong's first, second, and fourth points and resting on the older theorizations of Schweizer and Althaus is the view expressed by Kickel, Hall, McCoy, and Kendall, that the eternal decree of predestination served as a principle from which the entire Reformed scholastic theological system was deduced. McCoy and Hall assume that the orthodox began their theologies with the decree, or with the decree placed into the doctrine of God, and followed out the sequence of doctrine deductively.[31] Althaus and Kendall state somewhat more guardedly that predestination functioned as a "central principle,"[32] while Kickel goes so far as to argue that Beza so makes predestination the center of his theology that Christ is no longer the "*Realgrund*" and "*Erkenntnisgrund*" of theology. (This understanding of Christ as *Realgrund* and *Erkenntnisgrund* is a clear example of the neoorthodox re- and misinterpretation of Reformation theology.)[33] Merging Weber's with Jacob's thesis, Kickel argues that a "rational system of final causality" so removes theological emphasis from Christ and the Word that Beza's thought cannot be christocentric (as Calvin's had been)—and that the eternal decree governs the place given by Beza to doctrines such as the Trinity, the two natures, justification, and the sacraments.[34] In Armstrong's, as in Kickel's view, Calvin's "balanced" and biblical approach was replaced by a rationalizing, predestinarian approach to theology that became the norm for Reformed orthodoxy.[35] Holtrop, still farther out on the weakened limb of theological *tendenz* than Kickel, gathers (or should we say, "lumps") the predestinarian, scholastic "side" of Calvin together with the theology of Beza and the Reformed orthodox under the rubric of "decretal theology" and proposes the synergistic views of Jerome Bolsec as a model for theological renewal in the Reformed churches—at least in part because he credits the Reformed refusal to ground predestination on a divine foreknowledge of faith to a scholastic use of Aristotelian causality rather than to the Augustinian exegetical tradition.[36]

A similar set of assumptions can be discerned in the series of essays on the development Reformed scholasticism by Van der Linde, van 't Spijker, and Graafland, albeit distinctions need to be made between the approaches of Van der Linde and Graafland on the one hand and that of van 't Spijker on the other.[37] Armstrong's definition is cited as a point of departure, but more attention is given to continuities between the thought of the Reformers and the medieval scholastics and between the Reformers and their orthodox successors, with the issue of a theologically defined negative continuity being argued by Graafland on the basis of scholastic influences on the theology of the Reformers. Van der Linde's essay can be seen to determine the problematic cast of the essays by introducing a contrast between the "Greek" thinking inherent in scholastic models and the "Hebraic" modes of thought implied in the biblicism inaugurated by the Reformation. Graafland, in turn, draws on this claim in consistently setting scholastic predestinarianism against humanism, piety, and covenantal thought. Graafland consistently identifies Beza as causing the problems of later scholastic orthodoxy. Equally consistently, he drives an unconvincing wedge between scholastic thinking and Christian piety—despite the fact that the wedge must occasionally and rather unceremoniously bifurcate the psyches of individual theologians.[38] Van 't Spijker's essays are less invested in these dogmatic models and fall more properly into the fourth category of analysis.

A preliminary distinction must be made between the third approach and the line of argument found in fourth approach, given the strong neoorthodox theological *tendenz* of the former group and the greater objectivity of the latter. Although the studies by Bray, Donnelly, McPhee, McClelland, Anderson, Letham, and van 't Spijker tend to follow out the lines of argument from Schweizer to Heppe and Weber and construct their arguments with reference to Armstrong's definition, they also point toward reappraisal. Thus, Bray argues against the understanding of Calvin as invariably the primary influence on later Reformed theology and recognizes the difficulty of arguing a fully deductive use of predestination as a central dogma, while Donnelly confirms the continuity of scholastic method and of the positive use of Aristotelian philosophy during the era of the Reformation.[39] Indeed, given the conclusions offered by these two scholars, their work marks the transition of scholarship on Reformed orthodoxy to the fifth model, that of the current reappraisal. Even so, both Donnelly and Bray indicate the need to reject parts of Armstrong's original definition and modify others and Donnelly in particular recognizes the methodological nature of the scholastic element in the thought of Vermigli and Zanchi, as well as the continuity between their thought and later Reformed theology.[40]

The work of J. C. McClelland and Marvin W. Anderson fits well into this category of the scholarship, given their examination of issues other than predestination and their unwillingness to press Vermigli and Beza into the neat categories of the "Calvin against the Calvinists" model.[41] McPhee's work stepped past the argumentation found in Bray to argue contextually that Beza's *Tabula* could not be read out as a paradigm for the systematic implementation of the central dogma theory, without, however, removing the theory itself from discussion as an anachonism.[42] Van 't Spijker finds elements of scholastic theology among the Reformers and points, nonpolemically toward continuities with the later Reformed tradition.[43] The essays in this grouping all indicate a development of scholarship framed by dialogue with and modification of Armstrong's definition—and thereby move the discussion into the fifth category of appraisal or reappraisal.

Two initial observations can be made on behalf of the fifth model, namely, full reappraisal of the relationship between the Reformation and the subsequent era of Protestant orthodoxy.[44] First, it can be fairly easily argued on the basis of this survey of scholarship that the contemporary understanding of "Calvin against the Calvinists" rests on several misapprehensions of the nature and character of the history of scholarship itself as well as on misapprehensions concerning the origins and development of Protestantism in the sixteenth and seventeenth centuries. At the very least, there has been little or no recognition of the various theological biases or tendencies in the older scholarship: Schweizer's central dogma theory, for all the historical detail marshaled in his various works, was intended to demonstrate the continuity of a Schleiermacherian project with the history of Reformed doctrine—with little consideration of the difficulty of fashioning a deductive system like Schleiermacher's out of the methodological presuppositions embedded in the *locus* method of sixteenth- and seventeenth-century Protestant orthodoxy.[45] Nor has it often been recognized that Weber's presentation of the predestinarian system as a rationalistic scholasticism and, therefore, as a negative development was, at heart, an argument for the superiority of Lutheran dogmatics and for the rectitude of the claim originally made by its seventeenth-century orthodox writers that the Reformed faith was a form of rationalism.[46] Even so, the contemporary scholarship has not reckoned with the theological context of its own reappraisals of Calvin—a broadly neoorthodox context in which the christocentrism of the Reformers, particularly if pitted against the reputed scholastic dogmatism of their successors, yielded up a suitable Reformation antecedent for the christocentric neoorthodoxy of the twentieth century. The creation of a rift between Reformation and orthodoxy was necessary to the neoorthodox appropriation of the Reformers' theology, given that the scholastic clarity of the orthodox Reformed systems could not so easily be bent to contemporary purposes.

Second, and perhaps more important, the resolute pitting of Calvin against the Calvinists and of the Reformation against all things scholastic has tended to ignore collateral interests in the contemporary scholarship of the Reformation—notably, the work of Oberman and others analyzing the medieval background of the Reformation and the frequently related work of various scholars on the diversity and complexity of the intellectual life of the Reformation era. Thus, on the one hand, the rather strict separation of Calvin from scholastic successor theologians begins to look altogether too much like the now-superseded view of the Reformation as separated strictly from medieval scholasticism. And, on the other hand, the strict distinction between Calvin and later Reformed thought appears to ignore the diversity of the Reformation in Calvin's own day and the many currents and influences at work in the development of Protestant theology in the later sixteenth and the seventeenth century. On a related point, the scholarship that has argued a sharp discontinuity between the Reformers and the Protestant scholastics has also failed to draw into consideration scholarly discussion of the meaning and implication of scholasticism in general, particularly that of the Middle Ages, has all too frequently blended a theological distaste for scholastic thought with historical discussion, and has pressed Armstrong's definition far beyond its original intended scope as a hypothesis for the understanding of Amyraut's relationship to his adversaries, governed primarily by Amyraut's own perspective on Calvin.

In short, the vastly different results of the two investigations—the older scholarship together with its contemporary manifestation in the "Calvin against the Calvinists" genre and the recent work of reappraisal—can be traced to differing methodological premises. As noted above, the continuance of the older claim of central dogmas and of rationalistic, predestinarian scholasticism is possible, at least in part, because of a failure to come to terms with the historical roots of the claim itself—and this failure in turn points to a series of issues in method and approach to the sources and to issues of continuity and discontinuity in history. In the remaining pages of this essay, I propose to outline what I believe to be the principal premises of reappraisal with reference to the recent secondary literature and various works from collateral fields in which the premises have been argued on the basis of primary sources. In addition, I will indicate points at which the standard definition needs to be augmented or modified in view of the work of reappraisal. (By way of qualification, I must point clearly to the limitation of the following essay to the issue of approach to and definition of Reformed orthodoxy and Reformed scholasticism, inasmuch as the effort to reappraise the historical materials, outline an alternative approach, and recast the definition in no way diminishes other aspects of scholarly projects, like those of Schweizer, Heppe, Armstrong, Bray, and Donnelly. These works must remain part of an ongoing historical dialogue and need to be carefully distinguished from essays such as those of Kickel, Torrance, Rolston, and Holtrop in which the historical element has been largely negated by theological program.) The premises of reappraisal that I propose are as follows:

1. The question of continuity and discontinuity between Reformation and orthodoxy must set against the background of an examination continuities and discontinuities running through the history of thought from the Middle Ages into the sixteenth and seventeenth centuries.
2. "Scholasticism" and "Aristotelianism" must not be understood as static or as purely medieval phenomena, as if neither underwent a historical development that extended through the sixteenth into the seventeenth century.
3. Descriptions of "scholasticism" must consider the meaning of the term as found *both* in scholarly studies of the Christian tradition prior to the Reformation and in the writings of sixteenth- and seventeenth-century Protestant theologians.
4. Scholasticism and rationalism also must be clearly distinguished—on historical, philosophical, and theological grounds.
5. Method and content need to be distinguished, albeit not utterly separated.
6. Continuities and discontinuities in the interpretive or exegetical tradition must be given at least equal weight with developments in scholastic method and philosophical usage.
7. Individual Reformation thinkers or treatises ought not to be made a measure either of the whole Reformation era or of the Reformed character of individual orthodox era thinkers or treatises.
8. The diversity of post-Reformation theology must be examined with a view toward relativizing standard generalizations about the relationships between the Reformation and post-Reformation orthodoxy, scholasticism and humanism, pietism and rationalism.
9. Nineteenth- and twentieth-century theological assumptions must not be allowed to impinge on or become the basis of an assessment of the thought of the sixteenth and seventeenth centuries, particularly inasmuch as such assumptions have frequently become imbedded in older theological examinations of the Reformation and orthodoxy and have often transformed nominally historical studies into justifications of modern theological views.
10. The various forms of the "central dogma" theory, both those that indicate a continuity between Calvin and Reformed orthodoxy and those that indicate a disjunction, must be set aside.

11. Issues of form, structure, and content of sets of *loci communes*, *disputationes*, *institutiones*, "bodies of doctrine," or what may loosely be called "theological systems" in the sixteenth and seventeenth centuries, ought not invariably to be explained dogmatically as the results of use of doctrinal motifs or as responses to purported "tensions" in theology.

(The first four premises are discussed in this chapter, part 1 of this essay; the remaining seven premises appear, together with my concluding remarks, as part 2, in chapter 5.)

Premises of Reappraisal: A Discussion of Directions and Current Research

1. The question of continuity and discontinuity between Reformation and orthodoxy must be set against the background of an examination of continuities and discontinuities running through the history of thought from the Middle Ages into the sixteenth and seventeenth centuries. It is no longer sufficient to note that the post-Reformation orthodox used scholastic method and that some of their theological and philosophical views stand in contrast with those of the presumably nonscholastic and antischolastic Reformers. Scholarship such as that of Paul De Vooght, Heiko Oberman, Karl Reuter, David Steinmetz, and Susan Schreiner has pointed toward continuities between the Reformation and the Middle Ages and made it impossible for stark contrasts to be drawn between the theological results of medieval scholasticism and the theology of the Reformation.[47] Neither Calvin's own theology nor the theology of various significant predecessors, such as Luther, Zwingli, and Bucer, or Reformed contemporaries, such as Vermigli and Musculus, can be understood apart from the positive impact of elements of the medieval scholastic background.[48] Indeed, it can easily be argued that the presence of elements of scholastic method and of the theological distinctions and definitions it produced in the theology of the Reformers was one of the grounds of the later Protestant scholastic enterprise.[49]

By the same token, radical distinctions and dichotomies between "humanism" and "scholasticism" need to be abandoned, given recent studies of the early sixteenth century in which the distinctions between humanism and scholasticism are drawn far more subtly and the point is made that, early in the sixteenth century, the two categories were not incompatible and could indeed describe the same person in different aspects of his work.[50] Certainly, we can identify humanists, such as Erasmus, who evidenced little impact of scholasticism (and, if Luther's assessment is accepted at face value, little impact of any theological learning) and scholastics such as Gabriel Biel, who were little touched by humanism—but in general both the contrast and "the struggle between humanism and scholasticism" have been "wildly exaggerated."[51] Even so, the development of Renaissance Aristotelianism owed much to the work of humanist scholars who provided new and better editions and translations of Aristotle's works and who contributed much to the ridding from Aristotle of centuries of interpretive accretion. Humanism itself was not a philosophy but, rather, a method or, better, an approach to texts and sources—and although its proponents frequently criticized scholasticism, they also frequently (whether wittingly or unwittingly) espoused philosophical and theological perspectives that reflected the views of the medieval scholastics. And although humanists were, typically, less ready to absorb and use elements of scholastic theology and philosophy, the scholastics of the sixteenth century often were quite open to the insights of humanism.[52]

In the case of the Reformers themselves, where allegiance either to a traditional scholastic theology or to a humanistic return to the sources was secondary to the religious reform of the church, humanistic and scholastic tools could both be employed to the attainment of a theological goal. Thus, an early Reformer such as Melanchthon was both a humanistic proponent of rhetoric and linguistic study and, in his emphasis on the use of the *locus* method in theology and his advocacy of traditional proofs of the existence of God, a founder of Protestant scholasticism. (The use of the *locus* method itself indicated an interrelationship of humanism with scholasticism.) Similar observations can be made concerning Calvin.[53] Reformers of the mid- and late sixteenth century, like Beza, can be seen to immerse themselves in the techniques of humanist linguistic and textual study and also to adopt a scholastic method in their theological disputation—without any sense of a conflict or contradiction but, rather, with a view to using the best tools available to them in different genera of theological discussion.[54]

Given this development in the study of the Reformation and its antecedents, we must recognize also that the gradual development of a Protestant scholasticism after the Reformation not only looked to the thought and method of pre-Reformation thinkers for its inspiration but to the thought and method of the Reformers themselves insofar as it partook of the scholastic past and insofar as it criticized and modified scholasticism. Thus, the modifications both of scholastic method and of the doctrinal contents of theological system by the Protestant theologians of the late sixteenth and seventeenth centuries indicate the impact of the Reformation (and the Renaissance as well) on scholasticism and on the scholastic form of theology: the scholastic tradition itself was at once mediated and modified by Reformed theologians such as Musculus, Vermigli, Hyperius, Ursinus, Beza, and Zanchi. Granting, moreover, the training of the earliest Reformers in scholastic theology, the nature of Melanchthon's development of Aristotelian logic and the *locus* method, and the maintenance of the *disputatio* as a standard educational practice, it is something of a misapprehension of sixteenth-century thought to assume that scholastic method was ever fully lost or set aside—rather, it was revised and adapted.[55]

At the same time, apart from the consideration of method, the doctrinal content of Reformation thought stands in clear continuity with the Augustinian tradition of the later Middle Ages, just as the doctrine of the more synergistic thinkers of the age has its clear medieval antecedents. Any comparison, therefore, between the teaching of Calvin and his contemporaries on the doctrine of predestination and the teaching of the later Reformed orthodox theologians must take into consideration the fact that Calvin and other Reformers did not invent the doctrine and that their definitions and those of the Protestant orthodox stand within and responsive to a long tradition of biblical interpretation and dogmatic formulation including later medieval theologians such as Thomas Bradwardine, Gregory of Rimini, and Johannes Staupitz.[56] Similarly, discussion of a late-sixteenth-century reformulator of the Reformed doctrines of grace and election, like Arminius, must understand his relationship to trajectories of thought leading out of the late medieval synergism of a Gabriel Biel to the teachings of earlier sixteenth-century synergists such as Fonseca and Molina.[57]

These considerations point directly to an underlying ecclesial continuity between medieval, Reformation, and post-Reformation Protestant theology: the rise of Protestant orthodoxy and, with it, the acceptance of scholastic method, are indications both of the fundamental catholicity of Protestantism and of the institutionalization of the reform movement as church. As much recent scholarship has shown, the rise of scholastic, confessional orthodoxy in the Reformed and Lutheran churches related both to polemical and pedagogical needs and, in the specific development of large-scale theological systems, to the need for a detailed working-out of theological and philosophical problems raised or posed by the Reformation. These needs—polemics, pedagogy, and positive doctrinal development—all relate to the broader task of the full appropriation of the substance of the catholic tradition and the identification of an institutional Protestant church as the church catholic. The renewed use of the scholastic method served both the polemical and pedagogical needs, even as it opened a path to the reception of all the Protestants understood as the best of the medieval theological tradition, as modified through the scholasticism and revived Aristotelianism of the Italian Renaissance.[58]

A similar point must be made concerning the profound interest of Protestant theologians, both during the Reformation and during the era of orthodoxy, in patristic theology as a foundation for the development of a catholic orthodoxy within Protestantism and, accordingly, for the identification of Protestantism as the true church. The assertion of catholicity can be seen clearly in Calvin's letter to Sadoleto, his massive use of Augustine, Chrysostom, and indeed of Bernard of Clairvaux—as it can be seen in Melanchthon's interest in the Fathers.[59] In the era of orthodoxy, this concern for continuity with the best of the tradition continued and even grew, with the result that the first patrologies were written by Protestants and the analysis and appropriation of patristic theology was a major element in the development of Protestant orthodox theology.[60]

2. "Scholasticism" and "Aristotelianism" must not be understood as static or as purely medieval phenomena, as if neither underwent a historical development that extended through the sixteenth into the seventeenth century. Just as scholasticism—as evidenced by thinkers such as Anselm and Bonaventure in the Middle Ages and Daniel Wyttenbach and Johann Friedrich Stapfer in the eighteenth century—is not "invariably based upon an Aristotelian philosophic commitment,"[61] so also is the scholasticism and the Aristotelianism of the second half of the sixteenth century not to be related to or described as a medieval phenomenon except by way of a process of historical development that, for Protestantism, included the Reformation. Not only was a fundamentally Aristotelian worldview (evidenced, for example, by language of fourfold causality) shared by the Reformers and elements of the older Aristotelian logic and rhetoric drawn into the service of the Reformation early on by Melanchthon, it is also the case that the study of Aristotle and, consequently, the shape of Aristotelian philosophy underwent a development in the sixteenth century—yielding at the end of the century the revised metaphysics of Suarez and, in his wake, of Protestant metaphysicians like Timpler.[62] In addition, the Aristotelian logic inherited by the Reformation, already quite modified in the fifteenth century by Rudolf Agricola, was further recast in the sixteenth under the influence of Ramus.[63]

Given these several developments and changes, the logical base of late-sixteenth-century scholasticism and the philosophical patterns of late-sixteenth-century Aristotelianism hardly indicate the recrudescence of a medieval phenomenon. The rise of Ramism offers a particularly significant example of the complexity of late-sixteenth-century thought—for, contrary to the distinction made by Moltmann between humanistic (even covenantal!) Ramists and scholastic, predestinarian, Aristotelians,[64] Ramism marks a point of continuity with the Agricolan emphasis on *loci* or *topoi* that fed the Protestant scholastic enterprise—and the Ramist technique of bifurcation became an architectonic device for the construction of scholastic efforts such as Polanus's *Syntagma* and Perkins's *Golden Chaine*. The question raised by the historical evidence is not whether Perkins was a Reformed scholastic predestinarian *or* the "father of pietism,"[65] but *how* he filled *both* of these roles. Neither Ramism nor the piety of the *Nadere Reformatie*, nor, indeed, covenant theology, can be set in clear opposition to "scholasticism" or, more precisely, to scholastic method. Protestant scholasticism clearly marks a distinction in method between the theology of the Reformers and their successors, but the distinction was the product of a gradual development that had roots not only in the Middle Ages but also in the Renaissance and the Reformation.[66] This development, therefore, must be described not simply as a matter of discontinuity with the Reformation but also as a matter of both discontinuity and continuity with its medieval and Reformation antecedents and, in addition, as a complex process of development.

The post-Reformation Reformed orthodox, moreover, were conscious of these issues. It was virtually a truism among the Protestant scholastics that the earlier medieval scholasticism of Anselm and Lombard was more congenial to the Reformation and less troubled by philosophical and speculative questions than the scholasticism of the later Middle Ages, particularly from the time of Duns Scotus onward. The discussions of scholasticism in the doctrinal systems of the Protestant scholastics indicate both a sense of the generic meaning of the term as a disputative method of the schools, distinct from the methods of exegetical or catechetical theology, and the limitations placed on the appropriation of medieval scholastic theology by the Reformation critique of its results.[67] This latter issue is particularly evident in the relationship between scholastic method and the appropriation of philosophy into theological systems during the era of orthodoxy. Even in the doctrine of the divine essence and attributes, the Protestant scholastics were insistent on the primary focus of discourse on the results of exegesis: unlike Aquinas, who grounded his presentation in a foundational discussion of the divine simplicity, the Reformed orthodox quite frequently framed their discussions with a discourse on the divine names and virtually never approached the level of philosophical interest typical of medieval scholastics such as Aquinas, Duns Scotus, or Ockham. It also should be noted that the rise of scholastic method and the increased interest of the Reformed orthodox in the patristic and medieval tradition did not mean an absence of interest in the theology of the Reformation—or, specifically, in the theology of Calvin.[68]

3. Descriptions of "scholasticism" must consider the meaning of the term as found *both* in scholarly studies of the Christian tradition prior to the Reformation and in the writings of sixteenth- and seventeenth-century Protestant theologians. In the standard scholarly definitions, "scholasticism" does not refer to a particular theology or philosophy but to a *method* developed in the medieval schools in order to facilitate academic argument, specifically argument leading to the resolution of objections, the identification and use of distinctions, and the establishment of right conclusions. Although it is certainly legitimate to speak of "scholastic theology" or "scholastic philosophy," Maurer warns that "since there was no one theology or philosophy taught by all the university

masters, scholasticism does not designate one uniform doctrine."[69] It is, in Weisheipl's words, a "rational investigation" of issues and problems, specifically, the dialectical examination of "opposing points of view, in order to reach an intelligent, scientific solution that would be consistent with accepted authorities, known facts, human reason, and Christian faith."[70] And Knowles comments pointedly that "the term 'scholastic' cannot rightly be applied to the content, as opposed to the method, of medieval philosophy; it is essentially a term of method."[71]

Certainly, therefore, the Protestant scholasticism of the seventeenth century involved "ratiocination" in order to formulate "a logically coherent and defensible system of belief"[72]—but it could take inductive as well as deductive forms, it did not follow logic for the sake of logic, and it did not set reason above other criteria, such as Scripture, "accepted authorities, known facts, . . . and Christian faith." The fundamental characteristic of the approach to theology found in the system of a Reformed scholastic such as Francis Turretin is a movement from a basic doctrinal question to a statement of the "state" of the controversy, to a resolution of the debate using the authorities and tools at hand, with Scripture standing as the foremost authority, followed by tradition (principally the Fathers of the first five centuries),[73] classical, and philosophical sources, and supported by rational argumentation concerning the right understanding of the various authorities.[74] Thus, the Reformed scholastics—beginning in the time of the Reformation itself in the scholastic aspects of the theologies of Vermigli, Musculus, and Hyperius—certainly sought to formulate a logically or rationally defensible body of doctrine, but they sought also to formulate a body of doctrine defensible in the light of the best exegetical results of the time and in the light of the catholic tradition to which they laid claim. Rational argumentation never displaced exegetical interest—indeed, the most scholastic of seventeenth-century Protestant theologians would assume that the defensibility of their theology was grounded in its intimate relationship with exegesis.[75]

The strongly deductive element of Protestant scholastic argumentation, apart from the use of syllogisms in polemic, belonged to the practice of drawing conclusions from biblical texts—not to any attempt to deduce an entire theological system from a single principle or "central dogma."[76] Thus, in addition to the broader and fundamental definition of Scripture as *principium cognoscendi*, the Reformed orthodox understood the text of Scripture as providing *principia* or *axiomata* from which conclusions could be deduced, as indicated in the hermeneutical principle of the Westminster Confession, "The whole counsel of God, concerning all things necessary for his own glory, man's salvation, faith, and life, is either expressly set down in Scripture, or by good and necessary consequence may be deduced from Scripture."[77]

Even so, the method is ill described as generally taking "the form of syllogistic reasoning":[78] few of the orthodox or scholastic Protestants lapsed into constant or exclusive recourse to syllogism as a method of exposition. The definition must be modified to indicate an increased, but not constant, use of the syllogism, particularly in polemics, by the Protestant scholastics—and modified, as well, to recognize that syllogistic argumentation, when it did appear, was but one aspect of the broader phenomenon of the increasing adoption of the *disputatio* as the form for the exposition of controverted questions in theology. Thus, in some of his works, Zanchi used syllogisms with astounding frequency, but this style was neither characteristic of all of his writings nor of the works of his early orthodox contemporaries.[79] Ursinus's use of syllogistic argumentation is perhaps typical: it appears as method for the exposure of error in arguments stated by adversaries and far less frequently as a form of positive exposition. Wendelin's polemical, high orthodox *Systema maius* is the sole example of continuous syllogistic reasoning that I have found—and his use of syllogisms appears more as a *tour de force* in polemical refutation than as a model generally to be followed in theological formulation. Wendelin's own more positive system, *Christianae theologiae libri duo*, does not adopt the highly syllogistic style. Logical deduction did indeed belong to the methods of orthodox theology, as indicated by its principial use of the text of Scripture as its source for the identification of "consequent" articles of faith—but here, as in the case of the doctrine of the covenant of works, the deduction frequently took the form of a lengthy comparative analysis of topically related texts rather than as a clearly syllogistic argument bristling with major and minor propositions.[80]

As indicated above, the Protestant scholastics themselves discussed the issue of scholasticism and scholastic method—and, typically, associated the terms with the highly technical, disputative mode of teaching theology in the schools, not with a particular theological or philosophical position. Moreover, they distinguished in their own work between the technical and disputative "scholastic" theology and theology written in other forms, whether exegetical, catechetical, positive (i.e., nondisputative), or ascetic. Thus, not all of the works written by the Protestant scholastics are scholastic in method, and the identification of these writers as "scholastics" relates to the disputational form of their education and to their advocacy of the dialectical and disputative method as a form for the exposition and defense of theology at its more technical levels.[81] This generic use of the term "scholastic" in late-sixteenth- and seventeenth-century Reformed discussions of theological method corresponds quite precisely with the definitions offered by historians such as Weisheipl, Fritz, and Knowles.

Of course, elements of the method, particularly the use of fine distinctions, can be discerned in nondisputative and less technical works, but it remains the case that the *Disputationes* of Gomarus, Arminius, and Voetius are fully scholastic works while Gomarus's biblical commentaries and Voetius's *Exercitia pietatis* are less indicative of scholasticism. Even so, Cocceius's *Summa theologiae ex Scriptura repetita* and his several sets of *Aphorismi per universam theologiam* are scholastic, while his *Summa doctrinae de foedere et testamento Dei* is not. Similar reflection is applicable to the work of Beza, whose many sermons and whose lectures on Job and the Song of Songs are characterized not by scholastic argumentation but by the language and attitude of piety and whose literary exercises in Latin and Greek evidence not the style and methods of scholasticism but a participation in the humanist program of the Renaissance.[82] The term "Protestant orthodoxy" has, therefore, a broader and more encompassing usage, given that the intention of the Reformed and Lutheran theologians of the late sixteenth and the seventeenth century was to produce confessionally orthodox works in all genera—only the more technical of which followed a strictly scholastic method.

Given their identification of their own disputative method as "scholastic," the Protestant orthodox also were interested in distinguishing between their scholasticism and the medieval variety. In the first place, much like Luther and Hyperius, they understood the early scholastic enterprise, witnessed by Lombard's *Sententia* as a more positive effort than the more speculative systems of the later Middle Ages. And they typically drew a distinction between their own scholasticism and that of the medieval doctors from

Thomas Aquinas to Gabriel Biel, in which they found excessive interest in vain questions, little evidence of the use of biblical languages, and an excessive interest in purely philosophical issues.[83] Their appropriation of materials from medieval scholastic systems—as from contemporary Roman Catholic theology and philosophy—was done with considerable attention to points of theological and eccelsiological disagreement.

Even so, some distinction must be made, in the context of any attempt to describe the relationship between the Reformation and scholasticism or post-Reformation orthodoxy and scholasticism, between the nonpejorative identification of "scholasticism" as a method, found both in modern scholarship on the question of scholastic theology and philosophy and in the sixteenth- and seventeenth-century identification of the disputative, technical forms of theology as "scholastic," and the highly pejorative usage of the term "scholasticism," characteristic of polemic in the Renaissance, Reformation, and post-Reformation eras, to indicate a rejected theology overburdened with its own logic and speculation. In the era of the Reformation, many of the attacks on scholasticism found in the writings of Protestant theologians presuppose the positive use of nominally "scholastic" distinctions. And, as is easily documented from Calvin, such attacks on the errors of the "scholastics" seldom apply to scholastic theology in general.[84] Similarly, in the era of Protestant orthodoxy, the same writers who accuse their adversaries of being scholastic (in the pejorative sense) frequently evidence the use of scholastic method in their own writings.[85] In other words, Renaissance, Reformation, and post-Reformation attacks on scholasticism do not necessarily indicate either a rejection of scholastic method generally understood or a significant discontinuity on all (or even, indeed, any) points of theology or philosophy between the formulator of the polemic and various nominally "scholastic" thinkers.

Finally, once the understanding of "scholasticism" primarily as the identification of a method has been taken seriously, it also becomes apparent that this understanding must be attentive to changes in method between the time of Anselm and the time of Turretin. Thus, the introduction of the *quaestio* as a standardized literary form in the *summas* of the thirteenth century marked a development that rendered the scholasticism of the thirteenth century noticeably different from that of preceding eras. So, too, the rise of the Agricolan *locus* method in the fifteenth century had a profound impact on the form of theological works in the Reformation and, albeit a development usually credited to "Renaissance logic" and its rebellion against scholastic forms,[86] as mediated by the writings of Melanchthon, Vermigli, Musculus, Hyperius, and Calvin, became the standard pattern of dogmatic exposition during the era of Protestant scholasticism. Similarly, the relative shift in emphasis from *quaestio* to *locus* and the association of the *locus* with the strongly rhetorical thrust of Renaissance logic altered the character of academic disputation. Given, moreover, the adaptation of the *locus* method to theological exegesis in the hands of thinkers such as Melanchthon and Bullinger, the *locus* (as the "seat" or source of arguments) and the *disputatio* (as the presentation of an argument on a particular controverted point) were rooted in the biblical and traditionary grounds of theology—both for the Reformers and the Protestant orthodox.[87]

4. Scholasticism and rationalism also must be clearly distinguished—on historical, philosophical, and theological grounds. Although it is certainly true that the beginnings of modern rationalism are found in the seventeenth century, during the era of Protestant scholasticism, it is also the case that the orthodox or scholastic theology of the late

sixteenth and seventeenth centuries generally opposed rationalist philosophy. Nor, indeed, ought scholasticism itself—whether of the medieval or of the post-Reformation variety—be identified as rationalism. The rise of scholastic method in Protestant theology brought about a clarity in organization and argument reminiscent of the clarity of the medieval summas and commentaries on the *Sentences*. Nonetheless, the presentation of logical or rational arguments in the context of faith and the typically scholastic recognition of a series of authorities are not supportive of rationalism unless reason is established as the primary authority and used as the foundation and source of the content of thought rather than as an instrument in argumentation. Rationalism, broadly defined, indicates "the exclusive or at least predominant use of reason, which is to say, of rational speculation and criticism . . . in the study of religious, moral, or metaphysics"—and, more specifically, the claim "to resolve religious and moral questions solely on the basis of the natural light [of reason], excluding all recourse . . . to divine authority as manifest in revelation," as typified in the seventeenth century by the thought of Descartes, Lord Herbert of Cherbury, Blount, Spinoza, and Leibniz.[88] Rationalism of this sort became a force in theology only in the decline of Protestant orthodoxy in the eighteenth century. Thus, Beza's attempt to offer clearer and stricter definitions of Reformed doctrine than those found in Calvin's writings, given Beza's insistence on the authority of Scripture and his recourse to traditionary norms, was not an evidence of incipient rationalism—nor should the sometimes *rationalizing* character of theological system seeking argumentative clarity be confused with *rationalism*.[89] Of course, a medieval scholastic philosopher like Siger of Brabant and an eighteenth-century Reformed scholastic theologian like Wyttenbach can be described as a rationalists—but the description holds *not* because of the scholastic character of their methods *but* because of their view of the place and function of reason in their teaching.

Like most of their medieval predecessors and, arguably, in a certain degree of continuity with most of the Reformers as well, the Protestant scholastics assumed an instrumental rather than a principial function of reason.[90] The view that scholasticism gives reason "equal standing with faith in theology" and therefore leads to "jettisoning some of the authority of revelation"[91] is erroneous: proponents of the method, whether in the Middle Ages or in the sixteenth and seventeenth centuries, argued various relationships between faith and reason, but reason and philosophy invariably stand below the authority of the biblical revelation.[92] The majority of Reformed orthodox theologians for the greater part of the era of orthodoxy (ca. 1565–1725) opposed not only a principial use of reason but also the specific rationalist philosophies of the age, notably the philosophies of Descartes and Spinoza.[93] Perhaps even more important than this datum is the nature of the debate that went on between the Reformed and various Cartesians—and among the Reformed themselves over the issue of the appropriation of elements of Cartesian rationalism on the part of various theologically orthodox writers. Here, the picture becomes highly variegated and the simplistic claims of either a rationalistic orthodoxy absorbing the tendencies of rationalist philosophy or of a highly fideistic confessionalism set intransigently against current philosophical developments are rather swiftly set aside.[94] The relationship between Cartesianism and Cocceian federalism is particularly complex.[95]

It is certainly possible to note an increasing use of rationalist argumentation in the theology of Protestant orthodoxy, but only at the end of the seventeenth century—as can be seen in Geneva in the transition between the generation of Francis Turretin and the generation of his son, Jean Alphonse.[96] Only in the eighteenth century did the thinkers such as Venema, Wyttenbach, and Stapfer accord a clear principial function to reason in general, Wyttenbach in particular arguing in Wolffian fashion that natural theology was the foundation on which a system of revealed theology ought to rest, and even at this point, the rationalist line was hardly the majority or the norm for Reformed orthodox discussion of the problem of revelation and reason.[97]

5

Calvin and the "Calvinists"

Assessing Continuities and Discontinuities between the Reformation and Orthodoxy, Part 2

In the first portion of this essay, I offered an introduction to the historiography of Reformed orthodoxy, an analysis of its several trajectories and problems, and a series of ten premises reflecting what I believe to be the basic thrust of the current reappraisal of "orthodox" or "scholastic" Protestantism. The first premise was concerned with the basic issue of continuity and discontinuity between the Middle Ages and the Reformation and between the Reformation and the era of orthodoxy, and the last three premises discussed in the preceding portion of the essay elaborated that theme in terms of "scholasticism," "Aristotelianism," and "rationalism." The remaining seven premises for reappraisal deal with more specific issues and problems that arise out of the discussion of these general issues: thus, once "scholasticism" is rightly understood as primarily a term indicating method, some recognition must be given to the relationship between method and content (premise 5), to the methodologically nonscholastic works of nominally "scholastic" thinkers, notably works of biblical interpretation (premise 6), and to a set of issues relating to the intellectual and methodological diversity of the era of the Reformation and the era of orthodoxy (premises 7–8). Finally, attention must be paid, once again, to the theological problem underlying much of the secondary literature, but now from the vantage point of the current work of reappraisal (premises 9–11).

5. Method and content need to be distinguished albeit not utterly separated. Much of the older scholarship has assumed an intrinsic relationship between "scholasticism," "predestinarianism," and "rationalism" or "Aristotelianism." Nonetheless, there is no historical justification for these associations. Anselm, Peter Lombard, Bonaventure, Albert the Great, Thomas Aquinas, Duns Scotus, William of Ockham, and Gregory of Rimini have all been called, and rightly so, "scholastics." The term "scholasticism" applies to this entire group of thinkers because of a shared dialectical method, characteristic of the schools in which they taught.[1] Nonetheless, once the common ground of method is acknowledged, the overwhelming impression given by a comparison of these thinkers with one another is one of substantive philosophical and theological differences.[2] Anselm, Peter Lombard, and Bonaventure can hardly be called Aristotelians—nor does the term apply nearly as well to Scotus, Ockham, and Gregory of Rimini as it does to Albert and Aquinas. What is more, it is something of a distortion to identify Albert and Aquinas

as Aristotelians without qualification, given the profound impact of Dionysius the Pseudo-Areopagite and Augustine on their thought.[3]

These considerations in no way detract from the close relationship between scholasticism, theology, and philosophy: the scholastic enterprise assumed the necessity of drawing out, debating, and, as far as possible, resolving apparent disagreements between theology and philosophy. Several of the most important of the thirteenth-century scholastics, most notably Albert the Great and Thomas Aquinas, sought to interpret and modify Aristotelian philosophy in the service of Christianity and in positive relation to theology. Interest in the medieval tradition in the sixteenth century, guaranteed by the training of many of the Reformers in scholastic theology and indicated by the numerous editions of commentaries on the *Sentences* and other works of scholastic theology, brought to Protestantism, particularly the rising orthodoxy of the late sixteenth century, various models for understanding the relationship between philosophy (typically a modified Aristotelianism) with theology.[4] The scholastic method itself, however, does not determine the result of the inquiry: beginning with Melanchthon's curricular efforts in early-sixteenth-century Wittenberg, dialectic was merged with rhetoric in the service of theology not for the sake of imposing conclusions but in the interest of clarity in argument.[5]

By the same token, Protestant theologians of the sixteenth and seventeenth centuries evidence rather varied approaches to and degrees of appropriation of Aristotelian philosophy.[6] Thus, a Protestant scholastic such as Francis Turretin or his less scholastic successor, Benedict Pictet, can hardly be called thoroughgoing Aristotelians nor should they loosely be called Thomists: Turretin held to a series of basic premises that follow out Augustinian and Scotist as distinct from Thomist views and Pictet had absorbed Cartesian assumptions as well. Their contemporary, Louis Tronchin, presaging the beginnings of a genuinely rationalist Protestant theology, advocated a form of Cartesian philosophy[7]; Johann Heinrich Alsted, a somewhat earlier Reformed scholastic, was clearly eclectic in his philosophy, while Reformed scholastics of a later era, like Daniel Wyttenbach and Johann Friedrich Stapfer, were not Aristotelians at all, but Wolffians. If Wyttenbach and Stapfer can be called rationalists, it is quite apparent that their rationalism was a result not of their use of scholastic method but of their adoption of Wolffian philosophy, a form of continental rationalism. By way of contrast, Turretin, who was certainly scholastic in his method, argued pointedly that theology does not and cannot rest on the rational argument. The medieval parallel is obvious: differences in the understanding of the relationship between faith and reason and over the compatibility of philosophical truth with revealed truth abound. Indeed, the entire spectrum of possible relationships—from a union of faith and reason, to a distinction with cooperation, to a diastasis, to a possible utter contradiction—can be identified in thinkers such as Anselm, Bonaventure, Thomas Aquinas, Duns Scotus, William of Ockham, Siger of Brabant, and Peter Damian. Rationalism and scholasticism do not stand in any necessary relation: the former is a matter of philosophical conviction, the latter of methodology.[8]

Similarly, the association of scholasticism with rigid, predestinarianism is fraught with historical problems: diverse users of scholastic method such as Duns Scotus, Gabriel Biel, Jacob Arminius, and numerous orthodox Lutheran theologians of the late sixteenth and the seventeenth century did not hold the doctrine. In fact, Scotus, Biel, and Arminius grounded predestination in divine foreknowledge and argued a fundamentally synergistic relationship between grace and will. If Gregory of Rimini and the Reformed scholastics of the seventeenth century were predestinarian, it was not because of their scholastic method but because of their high Augustinian doctrinal conviction: this point can and must be made of Calvin, as indeed for Amandus Polanus, Gisbertus Voetius, Francis Turretin, and other Reformed scholastics who held to an Augustinian doctrine of predestination. An identical point must be made concerning the absence of any necessary relationship between strict predestinarianism and the adoption of an Aristotelian philosophical perspective: Augustine, Gottschalk, and Calvin were not exponents of a thoroughgoing Aristotelianism! There is, therefore, no intrinsic relationship between the use of scholastic method and of Aristotelian language of causality and the development of a more strict or supralapsarian language of predestination—indeed, the contrary transpired in the formulations of Molina, Arminius, and the Synod of Dort,[9] and it is arguable that the introduction of the precision of scholastic distinction produced a finely defined diversity of formulation.[10] Indeed, the recourse of Protestant scholastics to the fourfold Aristotelian causality does not indicate an interest in philosophical determinism but, rather, an interest in clarity of argument, with the causal model used as a heuristic device: this is particularly evident in the description of Scripture in terms of its efficient, formal, material, and final causes by both Reformed and Lutheran scholastics.[11]

The failure of the standard definitions of Protestant scholasticism to recognize that "scholasticism" is primarily indicative of method rather than content and that, in any case, the method, whether of medieval or of post-Reformation Protestant scholastics is neither determinative of doctrine nor determined by doctrine can probably be traced to its formulation in isolation from scholarship concerned with medieval scholasticism. Users of the definition have not learned from the work of historians such as Oberman and Steinmetz, who have examined the medieval background of the Reformation, have revised the notion of "forerunners" or predecessors of the Reformation, and have shown theological, exegetical, and methodological continuities between the Reformers and the theologians of the later Middle Ages. In addition, extended use of Armstrong's definition of Protestant scholasticism by later writers such as R. T. Kendall and David Poole has obscured both the varying degrees of scholastic method and the varying influences of late medieval theology on the Reformers—and as a result has led to insufficient recognition either of the continuities of scholasticism or of various doctrinal and philosophical trajectories (Augustinian, Thomist, Scotist, and so forth) that run from the later Middle Ages into the Reformation and on into post-Reformation Protestantism.

6. Continuities and discontinuities in the interpretive or exegetical tradition must be given at least equal weight with developments in scholastic method and philosophical usage. Granting that the Protestant orthodox did not uniformly or exclusively follow scholastic method, that the post-Reformation form of scholastic method was only one of their ties to the earlier tradition, and that it governed the pattern of exposition and debate not the content of the theology or philosophy debated, attention also must be paid to the continuities and discontinuities in theological content between the post-Reformation era and the preceding eras. Patterns and trajectories of biblical interpretation, particularly given the tendency of sixteenth- and seventeenth-century authors to formulate their theologies on the basis of *loci* drawn out of their exegetical labors,[12] offer evidence of relationships not always identifiable through the comparison of indi-

vidual works of theology. Thus, the essentialist reading of Exodus 3:14 typical of the doctrine of God in the Protestant orthodox systems will stand in apparent discontinuity with Calvin's thought if only the *Institutes* is examined, but in clear continuity when Calvin's exegesis of Exodus 3:14 is brought forward.[13]

So, too, many of the distinctions in the Protestant scholastic doctrine of God that appear to be so "abstract" and "speculative" to the modern reader, notably those related to the will of God,[14] actually belong to the exegetical tradition, which had long labored to understand the seemingly equivocal uses of the phrase "will of God" in Scripture. Indeed, as early as Lombard, the scholastic distinctions between the ultimate divine "good pleasure," and such other meanings of "will" as "precept," "prohibition," "counsel," "permission," and "operation," rested on the theological problems raised by the comparison of various biblical texts.[15] Given, moreover, the controversies over the meaning of precisely these texts generated by the soteriological views of Arminius and his followers, the Reformed orthodox were pressed toward rather elaborate discussion of distinctions in the divine will—but, clearly, not out of any intensely speculative interest and, typically, in continuity with the Reformation-era understanding of these texts.[16] Consequently, the use of distinctions, such as those between the ultimate divine good pleasure and the revealed will or between the antecedent and consequent will of God, was governed as much by soteriological interests like the priority of grace as by questions concerning the divine essence. There is, certainly, an element of truth in the point that, with the full development of Reformed orthodox theological system, the more metaphysical questions of theology did reappear—albeit not with as great a speculative interest as found among the medieval doctors and not with the intention of discovering a single metaphysical principle from which theological system might be deduced.

What is more, the practice of identifying theological topics in the work of exegesis, the theological or dogmatic elaboration of those topics, and the subsequent compilation of *loci theologici* or *loci communes* is not only typical of the work of many of the Reformers and of the Reformed orthodox, it is also a point of connection between the initial construction of theological systems as books of *Sententia* in the twelfth century, the biblicism of the Reformers, and the theological construction of Reformed orthodox system. Not only are the systematic efforts of Melanchthon, Musculus, Vermigli-Massonius, and Ursinus presented as *loci*; Calvin's *Institutes* itself is a compilation of theological *loci* and *disputationes*.[17] The *locus* method of the fifteenth and early sixteenth centuries carried over into the era of orthodoxy and became one of the points of continuity between Reformation and orthodoxy and one of the points of development, modification, and to a certain extent discontinuity inasmuch as the method served to support the integration of Protestant theology with scholastic method, and with philosophical and theological elements of the tradition to which Protestantism increasingly has recourse as it appropriated the more scholastic forms of discourse and debate.[18] Thus, although the *locus* method was used by Melanchthon, Calvin, Vermigli, Musculus, and Zanchi, it certainly furthered the positive relationship with medieval theology evidenced in the thought of Vermigli, Musculus, and Zanchi somewhat more than the relatively negative relationship evidenced in the work of Melanchthon and Calvin—at the same time, it also evidenced the impact of the Renaissance and humanism on scholastic method itself and places all of the Reformers who used it on the line of methodological development from the approaches of the late medieval scholastics and their humanist critics to the development and recasting of scholastic method that took place among Protestants in the late sixteenth century.[19]

Under this insistence on the importance of the exegetical tradition arises the question of the Protestant orthodox use of the Bible. In Armstrong's definition, Protestant scholasticism can be characterized by the assumption that "the scriptural record contains a unified, rationally comprehensible account and thus may be used as a measuring stick to determine one's orthodoxy."[20] This element of the definition simply needs some qualification of terms and some indication of a continuity between Protestant orthodoxy and the Reformation on the issue of the biblical foundation of theology. Granting that the Protestant orthodox were as well aware as their predecessors in the Christian tradition that not all texts in Scripture are equally clear and comprehensible and that the unity of the biblical message could be perceived only when the correct "foundation" or "scope" of the text has been recognized (typically Christ or God's covenant of salvation),[21] this point in the definition can be accepted as quite appropriate. This characteristic, however, does not identify a difference between Protestant scholasticism or orthodoxy and the Reformation—or, for that matter, between either the Protestant orthodox or the Reformers and the entire preceding tradition of the church. After all, the notion that the Scriptural record *does not* contain a unified and rationally comprehensible account and *cannot* be used as a criterion for orthodoxy is a modern notion quite discontinuous with the Christian tradition up to the eighteenth century.

More important, the biblicism of the seventeenth-century orthodox must not be read as an era of dogmatizing exegesis devoid of careful textual analysis and devoid of any variety in interpretation among those of an orthodox confessional persuasion.[22] Instead, the age ought to be viewed as the great age of Protestant linguistic study and Judaica, of the textual analysis that led to such monumental productions as the London Polyglot Bible.[23] Rather, moreover, than producing only a single form (i.e., a dogmatic one) of exegetical work, the Protestant orthodoxy must be recognized as producing highly varied and diverse exegetical works and commentaries, ranging from text-critical essays, to textual annotations, theological annotations, linguistic commentaries based on the study of cognate languages and Judaica, doctrinal and homiletical commentaries, and, indeed, all manner of permutations and combinations of these several types of effort.[24] In the light, moreover, of this vast and detailed work of exegesis and of the significant continuity between exegesis and dogmatics in the seventeenth century, the understanding of orthodox Protestant theology as biblical or biblicistic ought to become the basis for examining, in exegetical depth, the kinds of continuities and discontinuities that obtain between the Middle Ages and the Reformation and the Reformation and orthodoxy, given the gradually shifting patterns of exegesis and hermeneutics.[25]

7. Individual Reformation thinkers or treatises ought not to be made a measure either of the whole Reformation era or of the Reformed character of individual orthodox era thinkers or treatises. It is one of the fundamental problems of the "Calvin against the Calvinists" approach to the relationship of Reformation and orthodoxy that it views Calvin as index of all that followed him.[26] Calvin was not, after all, the sole progenitor of the Reformed faith—nor is it useful to characterize later Reformed theologians in general as "Calvinists," as if they derived (or should have derived) their teachings solely from

Calvin. It has become increasingly clear as scholars have investigated the thought of contemporaries of Calvin, such as Bullinger, Musculus, Vermigli, and Hyperius, that the forms, patterns, and contents of later Reformed theology cannot be traced solely or even primarily to Calvin in all cases. Thus, Calvin evinced a considerable distaste for the concept of divine permission or divine permissive willing, yet in the thought of Vermigli, Bullinger, Musculus, and even Calvin's own successor, Beza, and the scholastic Zanchi, the concept of divine permission was integral to the explanation of how God was not the cause of human sin. Inasmuch as this explanation is the standard one among the Reformed orthodox, we must recognize that Calvin exerted a less than formative influence on this aspect of the doctrines of providence and predestination. Similarly, the doctrine of covenant, so architectonically significant for later Reformed theology, derives much more of its substance from the thought of Bullinger, Musculus, Ursinus, and Olevian than it does from Calvin. Discontinuities between Calvin's thought and the theology of any particular theologian of the seventeenth century do not necessarily indicate discontinuities with the Reformation.

To offer an example from a particular theological work,[27] the presence of elements of the standard proofs of the existence of God and of traditional language of faculty psychology in Du Moulin's treatise on the knowledge of God cannot be understood as an indication of discontinuity with the Reformation on the ground that Calvin's introductory discussion of the knowledge of God in the *Institutes* refers to neither issue. For Calvin does rely on the Aristotelian faculty psychology in his description of human nature and in his understanding of faith—and he assumed that the less technical language of Scripture could and ought to be explained in terms of the faculty psychology[28]: he merely chose not to refer explicitly to this issue in the opening chapters of the *Institutes*, but to reserve them for discussion in book II, when he came to the problem of human nature. The proofs of God's existence, used in a manner parallel to that of Du Moulin, do in fact appear in Melanchthon's 1536 *Loci communes* and Ursinus's lectures from the late 1560s on the *Heidelberg Catechism*. The language of the proofs in Du Moulin's treatise serves to illustrate the remnants of the *imago Dei* in fallen humanity and the extent of the natural knowledge of God. The assumption of some positive natural knowledge of the divine is, again, somewhat discontinuous with Calvin: although Calvin, too, assumes a *semen religionis* remaining after the Fall, he allows virtually no positive knowledge of God to fallen humanity. But Calvin on this point differs from contemporaries such as Vermigli and Bullinger. Du Moulin also organizes his treatise around the theme of the twofold knowledge of God, a theme that he shares with Calvin.[29] If, then, Du Moulin's thought is somewhat discontinuous with Calvin's on the matter of the proofs, it nevertheless stands in a rather complex relationship of continuity with the differing perspectives resident in the Reformation itself. In the broader context of his theology, Du Moulin must clearly be recognized as a scholastic thinker: his method is logical, disputative, and grounded on fine distinctions and definitions.[30] Once that is seen, however, the issue of continuity and discontinuity rather than being resolved has in fact only been raised.

So, too, the genre of documents must be noted when comparisons of content are made. The comparison of Calvin's *Institutes*, for example, with the doctrinal systems of Protestant orthodox writers such as Polanus or Turretin must come to terms with the difference in genre between the *Institutes* and these later works: the *Institutes* was understood by Calvin as a basic instruction in issues related to the study of Scripture, initially governed by a catechetical arrangement of doctrine, and specifically as a repository for the various disputations and doctrinal *loci* that he chose not to include in his commentaries. The dogmatic works of Polanus and Turretin, by way of contrast, although constructed with the biblical *loci* in view, were intended from the outset as complete systems of theology based not on catechetical but on earlier dogmatic models. In addition, Turretin's *Institutio theologiae elencticae*, as its title indicates, was a polemical or disputative, not a primarily positive exposition of doctrine like Polanus's *Syntagma*. Such genre differences are, by themselves, not evidences of doctrinal discontinuity. For example, there is no formal doctrine of creation in Calvin's *Institutes* comparable to the treatments in Polanus's *Syntagma* or Turretin's *Institutio*: this is not, however, ground for an inference that Calvin objected either to a traditional formulation of the doctrine of creation or to its potential inclusion in theological system, given the extended discussions of creation at various points in Calvin's commentaries. Given, moreover, the presence of the doctrine in the theological systems of Musculus, Bullinger, Hyperius, and Vermigli, there is certainly no ground for the claim that inclusion of the doctrine by later orthodox writers marks a point of discontinuity with the Reformation. The same point can be made for the extended systematic discussion of divine attributes among the Reformed orthodox: Musculus's *Loci communes* offers a systematic precedent for later Reformed theology, and the exegetical tradition, including Calvin's commentaries, manifests a continuity of interest in these topics.

Scholarly discussion of the movement from Reformation to orthodoxy also must recognize that the diversity of Reformed theology in the time of Calvin was matched by a diversity of Reformed thought during the era of orthodoxy: the attempt to weigh "Calvin against the Calvinists" not only fails on the ground that Calvin was neither the sole progenitor nor, frequently, the primary influence on later Reformed theology but also on the ground that later "Calvinism" was not a dogmatic monolith. The pattern of development and therefore of continuity and discontinuity was complex. Thus, diversity in the definition of covenant and in formulations of the relationship of the covenant of grace to the covenant of works are not grounds for identifying several opposing Reformed traditions or a divergence between sixteenth- and seventeenth-century Reformed theology: the Reformed tradition is a diverse movement, evidencing many streams of development that share a fundamental confessional identity.[31] And it ought also to be quite evident, after broad reading of Calvin's sermons and Old Testament commentaries, that presumed differences between his teaching and that of Bullinger or that of the later Reformed federal tradition is not nearly as great as has sometimes been asserted.[32] By way of further example, recent examination and reappraisal of the Synod of Dort has demonstrated an enormous variety of opinion and definition within the confessionally identifiable bounds of Reformed orthodoxy on the issues of "limited atonement" and reprobation together with diversity of views on the extent and propriety of the Reformed adoption of scholastic method.[33] The methodological diversity of scholastic orthodoxy is also apparent in the varied reception of Ramism by the orthodox theologians.[34] To claim that later theologians lost the "balance" of Calvin's theology or that their systematic efforts "misplaced" or forgot Calvin's doctrinal emphases is to miss the point that Calvin was but one of several significant second generation codifiers of the Reformation and not at all the sole point of reference for later Reformed theological formulation.[35] Indeed, the further one moves beyond the confines of the sixteenth century, the less useful comparisons between Calvin and so-called Calvinists become—and the question of continuity and discontinuity in the ever-lengthening Reformed tradition must take into consideration an ever-lengthening list of predecessors.

8. The diversity of post-Reformation theology must be examined with a view toward relativizing standard generalizations about the relationships between the Reformation and post-Reformation orthodoxy, scholasticism and humanism, pietism and rationalism. Although, certainly, some level of generalization is necessary to the understanding of historical phenomena as broad as scholasticism, humanism, the Renaissance, the Reformation, post-Reformation orthodoxy, pietism, and rationalism, the standard generalizations about the post-Reformation era, the "rigidity" or "dryness" of its theology, and, therefore, its relationship to these era-encompassing categories and movements must be modified. The relationship between the Reformation and Protestant orthodoxy must be interpreted, in other words, not only with a view of the diversity in the thought of the Reformers and the Protestant orthodox, but also with a view of the diversity characteristic of "medieval scholasticism," "Renaissance humanism," the pietist protest, and European rationalism. The standard generalizations are clear enough, but the generalizations fail to do justice to the diversity of thought in the fifteenth, sixteenth, and seventeenth century and the consistent blurring of these categories in historical reality.

Few students of the Renaissance and Reformation can ever quite forget the drama of their first reading of Jacob Burckhardt's *Civilization of the Renaissance in Italy* with its vivid image of the veil of medieval ignorance being torn away—nor should they.[36] Burckhardt's vision still offers insight into the thought-world of the fifteenth century, and, even more important, into the problems of modern scholarship on the subject of the Renaissance. What is far less understandable is that scholarship dealing with the Reformation and with post-Reformation Protestantism should attempt to look in some detail at the thought-forms of Protestantism while at the same time creating altogether too neat boxes into which to place the thought forms belonging to the cultural background and context of the Reformation and Protestant orthodoxy. Burckhardt's vision of a vast intellectual and cultural rebirth has been largely set aside—replaced by a far more subtle sense of continuities and discontinuities in the history of the thirteenth through sixteenth centuuries.[37] So, too, the notion of a rebirth of classical learning has been equally well applied to the twelfth and thirteenth centuries, and the great scholastics themselves have been identified as participants in the humanist program before the "birth" of Renaissance humanism.[38]

Even so, Calvin ought not to be interpreted against a generalized background of humanism and as, therefore, antischolastic and antisystematic. "Humanism" in this generalized sense is nearly meaningless. One must ask the question, "Which humanism?"—Italian Ciceronian humanism, one or another of the humanisms of the Northern Renaissance, the Christian humanism of Erasmus and Reuchlin, or the classical philological humanism of Budaeus, Beroaldus, and others?[39] So, too, "scholasticism" ought not to be juxtaposed with "Renaissance humanism," and "Reformation theology" or paired with "Protestant orthodoxy" before one asks the question "Whose scholasticism?" Not only are humanism and scholasticism both rather diverse phenomena, they also do not necessarily stand in radical opposition to one another.[40] Humanism, moreover, in its many forms is better identified as an attitude and an approach to learning, specifically to the liberal arts or *studia humanitatis*, the study of classical languages and to the disciplines of philology, logic, and rhetoric, than as a particular philosophy or philosophical result.[41] Humanism surely did not oppose "scholasticism" by scorning logic in general or the syllogism in particular: one only need note the extended discussions of the syllogism in Agricola's or Melanchthon's works on rhetoric and dialectic! So, too, was the "humanist" academic program characterized by a desire not to abolish but to reform "scholastic" education: in other words, in their nonpolemical moments, humanists used the adjective *scholasticus* to indicate simply the methods and approaches of academic study.[42] The relationship of humanism to scholasticism and to the theology and philosophy of the later Middle Ages and the Reformation is, therefore, quite complex.[43] It becomes impossible to claim "that Calvin is to be seen more as a reforming Christian humanist than either a representative of late medieval thought or as a precursor of Protestant orthodoxy."[44] Indeed, it was precisely by being a "reforming Christian humanist" that Calvin was also a representative of late medieval thought and a precursor of Reformed orthodoxy as well!

Not only are these movements or phenomena diverse in themselves, but the boundaries between them are often unclear: even in the case of Erasmus, who perhaps only had positive recourse to scholastic themes when their use was absolutely necessary to his defense, there remains a lingering respect for the great scholastics and an imprint, however faint, of their ideas on his.[45] Nor did Erasmus ever intend to set aside the theology of the later Middle Ages or to destroy scholasticism when he argued against scholastic subtleties: his desire was for reform, both of its language and rhetoric and of its tendency toward excessive speculation.[46] There would be no purpose in denying the heated character of debate between the more traditional, scholastic thinkers of the early sixteenth century and those who advocated the *studia humanitatis* as an alternative to the "barbarisms" of scholastic usage. The humanist argument, whether posed by Pico della Mirandola, Agrippa von Nettlesheim, Melanchthon, or, indeed, Calvin, saw little value in the approach of the *scholastici* to learning—and the "scholastics," once under attack, were not unwilling to trade insult for insult and to echo the humanist claim that the future of coherent discourse lay with their method alone.[47] Once the depth and rancor of the controversy and its focus on issues of method, with specific reference to logic and rhetoric, has been noted, we must also remember that the dispute arose in large part on the ground of a common intellectual heritage, that many aspects of the debate, like the argument over the use of logic and rhetoric and over the use of a rhetorically conceived *locus*-method in theology, were arguments concerning different approaches to or construals of that common heritage. Particularly in the case of theologians such as Luther, Melanchthon, and Calvin, none of whom had much good to say concerning the *scholastici*, the unabated complaint against scholasticism must be juxtaposed with the numerous borrowings, both conscious and unconscious, from the scholastic past[48]—and balanced against the numerous points of contact between scholasticism and humanism in the developing traditions of exegesis, theology, philosophy, logic, and rhetoric that extend from the late twelfth through the seventeenth centuries. Thus, in the midst of Erika Rummel's extensive documentation of the debate between humanists and scholastics, recognition of continuities abound: "whatever the nature of [the humanists'] criticism . . . it is significant that their proposals for a humanist dialectic remained a modification of medieval Aristotelianism rather than an original construct."[49]

The aspects of humanism—notably the emphases on classical languages and rhetoric—present or, one might say, omnipresent, in the work of Calvin do not only stand alongside but merge with the elements of patristic and medieval scholastic theology that are also consistently present in his thought. For example, there ought to be no difficulty in recognizing how the radical theology of grace and election found in the thought of the patristic rhetor, Augustine, found a congenial home in the sixteenth-century humanist rhetoric of Calvin, and how, therefore, lines of continuity can appear between the theology of the rhetorically trained Calvin and the distinctly less rhetorical argumentation of the medieval Augustinian tradition. And the same must be said of his successors: if Beza, for example, can be credited with a more consistent use of scholastic theological distinctions than his mentor, he also must be credited for bringing to bear the resources of humanist philology on the understanding of the New Testament.[50] So, too, the practice of academic *disputatio* in Beza's Geneva represents a long line of development, to be understood both in continuity and discontinuity with medieval scholastic practice and Renaissance humanistic impulses—and, in addition, understood as an exercise in the evaluation and defence of long-standing lines of argument extending from the twelfth to the sixteenth centuries.[51] It ought not to surprise us that the topical logic or *locus* method and the bifurcatory architectonics of the Protestant scholastics owed as much to the development of Renaissance logic as to the structure of the medieval *quaestio*. Notable here is the influence of Renaissance dialecticians such as Ramus and Zabarella on the rise of Protestant scholasticism.[52] Rather than bifurcate personalities to explain this intermingling of varied influences and antecedents, we ought to reconsider the broad generalizations about "scholasticism," and "humanism" on which such bifurcations have been based: and when the particulars do not fit the generalization, it is not the particulars that should be set aside.

Similarly, it is certainly true that Spener and his pietist colleagues protested against the replacement of the Christian piety of the Reformation with a strict confessionalism and to the confusion of confessional adherence with a life of faith. Nonetheless, Spener's complaint against impiety and laxity among the clergy was hardly applicable to the larger number of the Lutheran orthodox theologians—and more important to this essay, cannot be transferred successfully to the Reformed orthodox. Thus, the generalization that the Reformers held a relational view of faith as trust or faithful apprehension of Christ while the orthodox reduced faith to an assent to propositions simply cannot hold: both the Reformers and the Protestant orthodox insisted that faith consists both in assent to teachings and in trust.[53] The claim, moreover, that the Reformed orthodox removed faith from its central place in Protestant religion and reduced it to the status of one doctrinal *locus* among others[54] can hardly rest on a reading of the *locus*—Alting writes that faith consists in "certain knowledge" and in "faithful apprehension,"

> whereby the promise of the gospel concerning Christ with all his benefits, made to all who repent and believe . . . is assigned to himself by each repentant believer as a seal, put into practice, sought, applied, appropriated as being addressed to himself, and he rests wholly upon it . . . and because of his firm conviction of the truth and power of Him that promiseth, he ventures to risk his life and soul and salvation in every kind of way.[55]

No dry, marginal concept this!

When, moreover, we recognize that Spener and his colleagues were trained in and did not intend to remove confessional theology from the church or the university, and that many of the Lutheran orthodox, like their Reformed orthodox contemporaries, emphasized the interrelationship between personal piety and dogmatic theology in the life of the church, the line between orthodoxy and pietism becomes somewhat blurred—without, however, diminishing either the intensity of the Pietist protest against dogmatism without piety or the strict orthodox polemic against perceived theological and ecclesiological errors perpetrated by the Pietists.[56] More important to the reappraisal of Reformed orthodoxy are the models of piety found by Spener in the literature of the Reformed church in which, particularly in England and the Netherlands, a rich literature of praxis accompanied the so-called scholastic theology. Among the Reformed, therefore, it is far less easy than among the Lutherans to draw a firm line between scholasticism and pietism. In the cases of Perkins, Ames, Voetius, and Baxter, works of piety and works of scholastic theology emanated from the same pens. Among the Dutch Reformed in particular there is no clear division between the practitioners of scholastic, disputative theology of scholastic orthodoxy and the warm piety of the *Nadere Reformatie*[57]—just as there is no clear division between Protestant scholasticism and federal theology. Theologians, such as Voetius and Hoornbeeck, who wrote works of piety that followed a "positive" or "catechetical" method also wrote more technical and academic works using the scholastic method. Conversely, Brakel and Oomius produced theology in the vernacular for the laity that was overtly rooted in their scholastic training. Many of the scholastic as well as "positive" works were covenantal in their theology and deeply aware of the need for practical piety, a notable example being the theology of Mastricht.[58] Thus, the tendency of some writers to pose the pietism of the *Nadere Reformatie* against scholastic orthodoxy and to argue an opposition of "scholastic" and "practical" theology fails to address the rootage of the late-seventeenth-century piety in the work of the very theologians and clergy who wrote, disputed, and trained in the scholastic method.[59]

Similarly, as noted previously, rationalism does not enter with Beza—indeed, there is no direct line from scholastic orthodoxy to rationalism in the sixteenth or the seventeenth century. Not only did the Reformed scholastics insist on the instrumental, nonprincipial function of reason, they also tended to oppose rationalist philosophy, particularly in its early Cartesian and Spinozistic forms, just as they consistently opposed the beginnings of Deism. In addition, as we have indicated, they held firmly to the biblical norm and the exegetical tradition and they continued to view faith as central to Christian teaching and Christian life. Of course, the diversity of theology in the era of orthodoxy must be respected, and the rise of rationalism did affect Reformed theology particularly as the eighteenth century dawned: several important Reformed theologians in the latter half of the seventeenth century did attempt to appropriate elements of Cartesian philosophy as the failure of the older Aristotelianism became apparent. But here, too, it is of paramount importance to recognize the diversity of philosophical approaches in the seventeenth century, with particular attention to thinkers such as Suárez, Timpler, or Burgersdijk, viewed as significant in their own time, rather than those such as Descartes, Spinoza, and Leibniz, understood as important from the perspective of the twentieth century but viewed as less than helpful by many theologians and philosophers of the seventeenth century.[60]

The connection between Cartesianism and the Cocceian or federal theology is significant, inasmuch as it discredits the frequent juxtaposition in the older scholarship of federal theology with a rationalizing scholasticism.[61] The scholastic opponents of the

Cocceian theology stood firmly against the inroads of Cartesian rationalism,[62] even as others of the orthodox proved more open to elements of Cartesian thought.[63] It is of course true that several nominally orthodox and methodologically scholastic theologians—for example, Wyttenbach and Stapfer—followed the path of Wolffian rationalism in the eighteenth century; but the contrast between their understanding of the use of reason and the view typical of the seventeenth-century orthodox proves the basic point that Reformed orthodoxy was not a form of rationalism. Indeed, the point of transition between confessional orthodoxy and more rationalist and confessionally indifferentistic forms of theology occurred at the very end of the seventeenth century and in the early decades of the eighteenth, as the generation of Francis Turretin, Benedict Pictet, and J. H. Heidegger ended its work and that of J. A. Turretin and Jean Osterwald entered the pulpit and the university.[64] The varieties of Reformed theology during this transition evidence no single pattern of the appropriation of philosophy and no uniform relationship between Reformed orthodoxy and rationalism: at the same time that various Reformed writers, such as Heidanus and Tronchin in the seventeenth century Wyttenbach and Stapfer in the eighteenth, attempted to frame a Reformed theology in alliance with the new rational philosophies, others such as Turretin, Heidegger, Mastricht, and De Moor retained the older more eclectic approach and strictly limited the use of reason in doctrinal formulation.

9. Nineteenth- and twentieth-century theological assumptions must not be allowed to impinge on or become the basis of an assessment of the thought of the sixteenth and seventeenth centuries, particularly inasmuch as such assumptions have frequently become imbedded in older theological examinations of the Reformation and orthodoxy and often have transformed nominally historical studies into justifications of modern theological views. The problem of tendentious and anachronistic readings of the thought of the Reformers and the Protestant orthodox is imbedded, as indicated earlier, in the history of scholarship—whether in Alexander Schweizer's Schleiermacherian version of the central dogma theory, or in Heppe's attempt to create a vision of a Melanchthonian German Reformed theology distinct both from the Lutheran and the Calvinist traditions, or in H. E. Weber's negative Lutheran assessment of Reformed theology. So also is the problem present in neoorthodox readings of the Reformation as the theological precursor of neoorthodoxy and, by extension, of the Reformation as standing in disjunction with its own immediate heirs, the theologians of the orthodox era. It should not be necessary to point out that, despite certain differences and discontinuities between the theology of the Reformers and that of the Protestant orthodox, the theology of the Reformation is far more akin to the theology of seventeenth-century orthodoxy than it is to that of Schleiermacher or Barth or Brunner.

This seemingly obvious point has not prevented numerous writers from examining the theology of the Reformers virtually apart from its historical context—as if one might learn the principles of Reformed theology from a rather abstract portrait of the thought of Calvin and then move from this portrait to the formulation of nineteenth or twentieth theology, in the tradition of Schleiermacher or of Barth, with no recognition either of the background and context of Calvin's own work or of the enormous changes in exegesis, doctrinal theology, and philosophy that have occurred since the mid-seventeenth century.[65] A similar stricture can and must be leveled against studies that compare and contrast major thinkers such as Calvin and Luther, with little or no regard to the immediate context of their formulations or to the (frequently indirect) ways in which the common features of their respective formulations were mediated to them.[66]

The antagonism of some contemporary writers to "scholasticism," to the Reformed doctrine of predestination, and to what has been labeled as "decretal theology" also can be derived from the use of modern theological views as criteria for the evaluation of the past.[67] It is not the task of the historian (nor is it within the scope of historical method) to determine "correct doctrine." Quite simply, churches determine orthodoxy or "correct doctrine" in their credal and confessional statements: historians report, analyze, and otherwise attempt to account for the content and meaning of the past, including ideas and doctrines of the past. The insertion of one's own theological premises into a historical analysis—often with polemical intention—only muddies the waters and obscures the meaning of the past.

Accordingly, the pejorative use of the term "scholasticism" both ignores the complexity of the historical problem of Protestantism both during the Reformation and in the era of orthodoxy and inserts into the discussion a biased premise. The bias can be seen in the apparent view of much of the older scholarship that the identification of scholastic method in the works of post-Reformation Protestants in itself indicates a distortion of the teachings of the Reformers and a decline in theology. Such an assumption is, surely, grounded in the long-standing view of the Reformation as an utter rejection of medieval theology and to the consequent Protestant impatience with medieval scholasticism: as Kristeller pointed out concerning the exaggerated juxtaposition of humanism and scholasticism in much older scholarship, we are dealing here with a "modern aversion to scholasticism" rather than with a balanced historical assessment.[68] This aversion is also related to the view that the use of scholastic method entails the acceptance of certain philosophical and theological views inimical to Protestantism—a problem discussed previously. In the form of the assumption found in Holtrop's work, a certain continuity between medieval scholastic theology and the theology of Calvin is rightly recognized, but then the continuity itself becomes the basis for arguing a theological problem.[69] The theologized result of such assumptions is an attempt to strip away elements of the tradition that are in fact integral to the Reformation and to the post-Reformation establishment of a normative, confessional Protestant dogmatics—an attempt, in short, to redefine the phenomenon of Protestantism in the image of a particular twentieth-century theological perspective by denying a major part of its history.

In addition, the pejorative use of the terms "scholastic" and "scholasticism" reflects the attempt of several generations of contemporary theologians to rid themselves of the shackles (real or imagined) of their own "scholastic" tradition as mediated by older manuals of doctrine such as Charles Hodge's or Louis Berkhof's *Systematic Theology* and, at times, a failure to distinguish between this nineteenth- and early twentieth-century manifestation of the orthodox and scholastic Reformed theology and the rather different theology of the seventeenth century or, indeed, between a theologically motivated caricature of "dry scholasticism" or "rigid," "dead orthodoxy" and the late sixteenth- and seventeenth-century mind that found the scholastic method necessary and congenial to its academic and disputative needs.[70] The antagonism to "decretal theology" likewise draws on a contemporary distaste for recent tradition and on the assumption of the accuracy of the nineteenth-century "central dogma" theory. Similar modern worries over the detrimental effects of scholasticism, the problematic character of decretal theology, or the inherent legalism of covenant theology do not belong to legitimate historiography—rather, they appear in theologized examinations of the past written in support of contemporary theories. Such essays tell their readers much more about the biases of their writers than about the theology of their supposed historical subject. And, of course, biased argumentation in the field of systematic or dogmatic theology that fails to do justice to historical sources will ultimately call into question the results of theological inquiry as well.

When, moreover, the antagonism to scholastic theology is framed in terms of contrasts between rationalistic or speculative thinking and nonspeculative, biblical, dynamic, personal, and relational thinking in theology,[71] it offers evidence of its own theological roots in neoorthodoxy and the Biblical Theology movement of the mid-twentieth century. It draws on the view, characteristic of much of that theology, that a strict distinction could be drawn between Hebraic and Greek mentalities and that the Hebraic view of truth was fundamentally one of "personal encounter" and relationship, while the Greek view of truth was fundamentally propositional, impersonal, and nonrelational. It would take an entire essay, longer than this one, to discuss the historical and linguistic fallacies involved in this and similar dichotomies.[72] Suffice it to say that the view of "truth" found in the wisdom literature of the Old Testament has little to do with twentieth-century notions of "personal encounter" and much to do with the rectitude of ideas, while the Aristotelian view of truth as the adequation of the mind to the thing is inherently relational. It is a considerable distortion of the historical record to impose a twentieth-century theological distinction (and one that has proved untenable, at that) on the materials of the sixteenth and seventeenth centuries.

10. The various forms of the "central dogma" theory, both those that indicate a continuity between Calvin and Reformed orthodoxy and those that indicate a disjunction must be set aside. As already indicated in the introductory survey of older scholarship, the central dogma theory of Reformed orthodoxy served several nineteenth- and early twentieth-century theological programs. Of course, we must avoid falling into the genetic fallacy and arguing that, inasmuch as the theory was developed for nineteenth-century theological purposes, it also must be incorrect. Nonetheless, the genesis of the theory does point directly to its problems: it rests on the notion of a basic principle on which the entirety of a system can be built, as was argued of the "principle of sufficient reason" by the proponents of Wolffian rationalism in the eighteenth century and then adapted to the use of theology by various Wolffians, such as Wyttenbach.[73] Such a model points away from the *locus* method of the sixteenth- and seventeenth-century orthodox theologians. Indeed, the theory presents a late-eighteenth- and nineteenth-century view of the organization of theological systems, what Bauke called a "systematic monism," that is ultimately quite incompatible with sixteenth- and seventeenth-century dogmatics.[74] Not only do the theological systems of the sixteenth and seventeenth centuries attempt to survey all points of Christian doctrine rather than to gather into a cohesive whole only those doctrines which relate to particular dogmatic premises, moreover, the locus-method and the arrangement of *loci* into a historical series—adopted by virtually

all of the theological systems of the sixteenth and seventeenth centuries—precludes the purely deductive patterning implied by the central dogma thesis.

The order and method of Reformed theological systems was governed, thus, by at least two distinct motives: the Reformed, unlike the Lutherans, tended with notable exceptions to accept the synthetic model (proceeding from causes to effects) proposed by Renaissance logicians like Zabarella, rather than the analytic model (proceeding from effects to causes)—although the exceptions themselves, whether purely analytic models or attempts to combine analytic and synthetic, serve to refute notions of a monolithic Reformed orthodoxy.[75] The synthetic model, by definition, began with first principles and then traced out its order through means or instrumentalities toward the ultimate goal: this model is reflected in the Reformed patterning of system to move from Scripture and God, the two *principia theologiae*, through the body of doctrine to the last things. Yet this model neither presses a central dogma on the Reformed system nor indicates a purely deductive approach: the topics of the system were elicited from Scripture, echoed centuries-old assumptions concerning the basic topics in theology, and were given their content on the basis of rather painstaking reflection on Scripture and tradition. In addition, the internal dynamics of the Reformed systems, between God and the last things, reflected an interest inherited from Melanchthon in a *historica series ordo*[76]—which accounts for the arrangement of the *loci* concerning human nature, the Fall, sin, covenant, law and gospel, Christ, salvation, and the church, none of which are strictly deducible either from one another or from the doctrine of God.[77] When there was a strictly deductive approach used, it related to the practice of drawing conclusions from scriptural *axiomata*, that is, texts understood as *principia* in argument, not to the whole of theological system.

Even so, examination of other doctrinal *loci* in the thought of purported sixteenth-century proponents of the "predestinarian system," such as Beza and Zanchi, have shown that the theory is inapplicable.[78] Even Bray, who rested much of his analysis on Armstrong's definition and its version of the central dogma theory, concluded against Kickel that Beza "warned specifically that one should not employ predestination as a metaphysical principle which should be used to explain all phenomena of belief and unbelief" and that "it was never Beza's intention to use predestination as an organizing principle for a total theological system."[79] It is simply not the case that Reformed orthodox theologians began their systems with the doctrine of the divine decrees: the systems nearly invariably move from prolegomena, to the doctrine of Scripture, to the doctrine of God, and then and only then to the doctrine of the decrees. In addition, the prolegomena identify Scripture and God as the *principia theologiae*. From a purely historical perspective, no Reformed theology of the sixteenth or seventeenth century understood the decree as one of the *principia theologiae*, none ever set aside the *locus* method, and certainly none ever assumed that any single doctrine could be used as a central dogma or deductive principle.[80] The point also has been made by Helm from a logical or philosophical perspective and with great clarity that Beza's (or, we add, Perkins's) detailed charts of the order of causes never implied the possibility of understanding the divine decree as one of the *principia theologiae* or of deducing an entire system of doctrine from the decree. Those who cite the *Tabula* as an example of a "logical sequence of human redemption," writes Helm,

> do not succeed in showing anything other than that in Beza's view each phase of the execution of the decree is intelligible only in the light of what is immediately temporally prior to it; they do not show, nor could they, that any stage in the execution in time is logically deducible from the immediately prior stage, nor even from the conjunction of all prior stages. In other words, they confuse a logically necessary condition, consistency, with a logically sufficient condition, deducibility.[81]

Even so, against the views expressed by Kickel, examination of Reformed scholastic systems indicates that they follow a traditional order of the *loci*—common to the theological systems of the medieval period—and not an order determined by any process of deduction from a particular principle. The order of theological system, moreover, beginning with Melanchthon and Hyperius, consciously recognized the historical series of the biblical witness, as clearly indicated by the movement of the typical "scholastic" Protestant system from Scripture, to God and God's purposes, to creation, human nature, the Fall and sin, redemption in Christ, the church and the sacraments, and the Last Things.[82]

Nor, indeed, can it be shown that predestinarian concerns override concerns for the development of other doctrines—not even in the theology of writers such as Beza, Zanchi, and Perkins, who are frequently singled out as following such a line of thought. All three, like many of their contemporaries, were particularly concerned to ground their theology in the doctrine of the Trinity.[83] And whereas it is true that their understanding of Christ as Mediator, of the limitation of the efficacy of Christ's work of salvation, and of justification by grace alone is supported by their understanding of election, there is no ground in the claim that the doctrine of predestination is the sole or even the primary determinant of those doctrinal interrelationships.[84] The *locus* method precludes purely deductive interrelationship of topics—and documents that have been used as examples of the "predestinarian system," like Beza's *Tabula praedestinationis* or Perkins's *Golden Chaine*, simply cannot bear that interpretation.[85] The methodological problem intrinsic to the older scholarship on this point is is purely emblematic, decontextualized reading of these documents, as if Beza's little *Tabula*, rooted as it was in the era of the Bolsec controversy, was ever conceived, either by its author or anyone else in the late sixteenth or seventeenth century, as a model for a full dogmatic system!

What is more, the development of the doctrine of predestination in the era of Reformed orthodoxy, despite the increased recourse to scholastic argumentation and the relatively greater interest in Aristotelian discussions of causality, did not yield definitions that were more strict than Calvin's own. In fact, the doctrine was modified in a variety of ways, including by emphasis on the divine permission, by later Reformed theologians, and in many cases rendered less strict than the definition offered by Calvin. Nor, indeed, should either Calvin or the Reformed orthodox be viewed as adding any terribly original concepts to the doctrine of predestination that they inherited from Augustine by way of the medieval scholastic and exegetical tradition.[86]

Of course, descriptions of theology as "christocentric" or "theocentric" are still useful to the discussion of Reformation and orthodoxy—inasmuch as the theologies of the Reformers and of their orthodox successors consistently place Christ at the center of their discussions of redemption, consistently understand Christ as the center and fulfillment of divine revelation, and equally consistently understand the causality of salvation as grounded in the divine purpose. Christ, as Mediator, must be subordinate to the divine purpose, even as Christ, considered as God, is the one who with the Father and the Spirit decrees salvation before the foundation of the world: causal theocentricity guarantees redemptive christocentricity. Neither the doctrine of God nor the doctrine of Christ, however, serves as the basis of a neatly deduced system: the *loci* themselves arise out of the interpretation of Scripture. A similar point must be made concerning the doctrine of the divine will: not only are the greater number of distinctions intended to describe the divine work *ad extra*, but they are, in view of their grounding in the discussion of the divine purpose as revealed in the work of creation and redemption, less a "speculative foundation"[87] than a result of considerations in the larger part of the theological system and the examination of the various biblical *loci* on which it was constructed.

Kickel's objection that Christ was the "*Realgrund*" and "*Erkenntnisgrund*" of Calvin's theology and was replaced by predestination in later Reformed thought utterly misses the point that the older Protestant theology, whether that of Calvin or of the orthodox, could never have understood Christ (or predestination) as the *Realgrund* or *principium essendi* of theology—that place could be given only to God, as the much discussed *duplex cognitio* of Calvin and others and, indeed, the orthodox Reformed prolegomena clearly indicate. Even so, the *Erkenntnisgrund* or *principium cognoscendi* is not Christ (or, indeed, predestination) but the entire biblical revelation of God in which not only the identity of Christ's person but also a wide spectrum of other doctrinal *loci* are treated. Christ, however, is the *fundamentum* and *scopus* of Scripture inasmuch as he is the redemptive center on which the entire *principium cognoscendi* or cognitive foundation rests and in whom it find its unity. Kickel's approach replaces the Schweizerian-Schleiermacherian central dogma with a Barthian central dogma and misinterprets both the Reformation and orthodoxy accordingly.[88] Significantly, Barth himself examined the historical materials and found the central dogma theory inapplicable to Reformed orthodox dogmatics.[89] (On this and other historical points, such as the relationship of the *syllogismus practicus* to Calvin's doctrine of assurance, it would be far more useful to argue "Barth against the Barthians" than "Calvin against the Calvinists"![90])

Even so, the application of the term "christocentric" to the Reformation and the era of orthodoxy must not take on shades of the central dogma theory, as if a Christ-center in theology excludes the fundamental focus of Christian theology on God as Trinity or as if a Christ-center is incompatible with the presence of other theological *foci* that together with Christology determine the character of the system. Such doctrines as God, predestination, Christ, and covenant provide not alternative but coordinate *foci*—and the presence of each and every one of these topics in theology rests not on a rational, deductive process but on their presence as *loci* in the exegetical or interpretive tradition of the church.[91] The central dogma thesis stands as a more or less suitable description of the theologies of Schleiermacher, Schweizer, Thomasius, Ritschl, and Barth—not of the theologies of the sixteenth and seventeenth centuries. In examining the historical differences between these nineteenth-century models for theological system and the theological models of past eras, it is necessary, therefore, to distinguish between the soteriological christocentrism of traditional Christian theology and what can be called the "principial" christocentrism of the nineteenth- and twentieth centuries. The former christocentrism consistently places Christ at the historical and at the soteriological center of the work of redemption. In the theology of Calvin and of the Reformed orthodox, such soteriological christocentrism opposes all synergistic and, therefore, anthropocentric approaches to salvation. The latter, a principial christocentrism, may include the monergistic view of salvation, but it will also assume that Christ is the *principium cognoscendi theologiae* or, in Kickel's phrase the *Erkenntnissgrund* of theology. This latter view, a descendant of the nineteenth-century central dogma theory, is as foreign to the older Reformed theology as the notion of a deductive system of doctrine based on predestination.

11. Issues of form, structure, and content of sets of *loci communes, disputationes, institutiones*, "bodies of doctrine," or what may loosely be called "theological systems" in the sixteenth and seventeenth centuries ought not invariably to be explained dogmatically as the results of use of doctrinal motifs or as responses to purported "tensions" or "problems" in theology. There are two issues to be addressed under this point—the nature of theological "system" in the eras of the Reformation and orthodoxy and the question of grounds and reasons for arranging or inserting topics into the system. First, there is the nature of theological system and, specifically, the relative continuity or discontinuity between what is called "systematic theology" in our own times and the ancestor-discipline found in the sixteenth and seventeenth centuries that is often referred to as systematic theology.[92] The theological works of the sixteenth and seventeenth centuries tended to gather their topics or *loci* as results of biblical exegesis and traditionary or confessional identification of issues, and then to assemble the *loci* according to patterns deemed suitable for explanation. They did not, in other words, infer *loci* logically from other *loci* or attempt to develop a large-scale logic of "system" in the modern sense of the term.

Second, once it has been recognized that the older "systems" of theology were not organically or logically developed systems in the modern sense, but bodies of doctrine that collated and ordered a series of topics gathered on the basis of traditionary and exegetical concerns, it needs also to be recognized that the order and arrangement of the topics often reflected concerns other than such as might be called "macrotheological." It is quite unlikely that Calvin offered a so-called a posteriori placement of predestination in the *Institutes* in order to point his readers away from the recognition that the decree is an eternal willing of God, prior to all times. His definition indicated that the decree is eternal and prior—and his own statements in the *Institutes* concerning the order of doctrine point not toward a distinction between an essential and a cognitive order but, rather, to a concern for the proper order of teaching. Beyond this, the movement of the discussion of providence out of the chapter on predestination and into the doctrine of God probably tells us more about Calvin's editorial process in refining the shape of the *Institutes* than about any over arching dogmatic interest.[93] Similarly, in later Reformed theology, various theologians discussed predestination immediately following the doctrine of God in their theological systems but in the doctrine of the church when the developed a body of doctrine on the basis of the Apostles' Creed or the Heidelberg Catechism—reflecting not a change of mind, or an alternative understanding of the doctrine, but a different pedagogical interest and a sense of the traditionary order of teaching.[94]

Having noted the presence of a series of potentially nontheological or nondogmatic issues that impinged on the writing of theology in the sixteenth and seventeenth centuries, we can pass on to the related issue of so-called tensions, antinomies, and problems in the thought of the past. It has been characteristic of much of the theologized historiography of the sixteenth and seventeenth centuries that it has worried over such issues as the "tension" or even the "antinomy" between predestination and covenant or divine will and human responsibility, the "problem" of the *Deus nudus absonditus*, the "tension" between "biblical" and "non-Christian" elements in the older Protestant doctrine of God,[95] and the "problem" of the absence of a proper notion of revelation among the Reformed orthodox.[96] These exercises, which usually take the form of a critique of the past for failing to deal with the "tensions" or misunderstanding the "problems," fall into the category of historiographical problem identified by Skinner as historical "mythology" or "conceptual parochialism."[97] The tension or problem, in other words, exists in the materials if the materials hold a series of premises and presuppositions that belong to the mind of the historian—but that have in fact little or nothing to do with the historical record.

By way of example: Reformed covenant theology was purportedly plagued by a tension between the determinism brought about by the doctrine of predestination and the stress on responsibility that belonged to the concept of a bilateral covenant. Various writers have claimed that the seventeenth-century Reformed relieved the tension by accommodating their doctrine of covenant to the doctrine of predestination, rendering covenant a unilateral declaration or "testament" rather than a true covenant, thereby destroying "the significance of history" and rendering "meaningless the interaction between God and man."[98] The federal theologians of the late seventeenth century, notably Cocceius and Witsius, are argued to have taken precisely the opposite tack and employed concepts of covenant theology in an attempt to soften the rigors of predestinarianism. McCoy even hypothesizes a thought process in Cocceius, in which an awareness of the "central dogma" problem led to an attempt to use covenant theology as a way of rescuing the Reformed tradition.[99] Unfortunately, none of this language is found anywhere in the writings of the seventeenth-century thinkers. As we have already seen, the notion of predestination as the central dogma or deductive center of older Reformed thought belongs to the historiographical mythology of a later era. Cocceius, the preeminent example of an attempt to overcome the "tension," held an infralapsarian doctrine of predestination that would have pleased the Synod of Dort and taught that in its inception the covenant was unilateral, by grace alone, whereas within covenant there was a necessary human response that provided the bilateral sense of relation between God and humanity in covenant.[100] Perkins, who is purported to have followed the opposite approach, removing the tension by developing a deterministic predestinarianism, much to the confusion of the theory also argued a unilateral promulgation and a bilateral historical enactment of the covenant.[101] The "tension," arguably, is in the mind of the modern theologian, not in the seventeenth-century sources.

A similar case is the so-called problem of the *Deus nudus absconditus*. Karl Barth's excursus on the history of the doctrine of predestination, in the course of which his meditation on the problem of the *Deus nudus absconditus* appears, is one of Barth's more detailed historical analyses.[102] Unlike many of his followers, Barth recognized that the Reformed orthodox did not produce a "predestinarian system" and did not deduce their theology from the divine decrees. Still, as Barth examines the relationship between Christ and the eternal decree of predestination, he poses the problem that if predestination is not entirely known in Christ and if Christ is only the "agent" and not the *fundamentum* of the decree, the God of the decree becomes the *Deus nudus absconditus*, the utterly absent and unknowable God. Barth summarizes the problem:

> How can we have assurance of our election except by the Word of God? And how can even the Word of God give us assurance at this point if this Word, if Jesus Christ, is not really the electing God . . . but only the elected means whereby the electing God . . . executed what He has decreed concerning those whom He has—elsewhere and in some other way—elected.[103]

Since Calvin did not offer such a formulation, his God is the *Deus nudus absconditus.* Toward the end of the sixteenth century, Barth avers, Amandus Polanus recognized the problem and attempted to resolve it by defining the decree as a trinitarian work, involving Father, Son, and Spirit, and by arguing that the Son is both electing God and elect mediator. This excursus belongs to the dogmatic argument leading Barth to his own solution to the problem, "Jesus Christ electing and elected."[104]

In my own early research, I found that Polanus was hardly alone in recognizing that Christ, the divine Son, was not merely the agent of election. What I did not immediately perceive is that there is a rather heavy-handed anachronism at the heart of Barth's analysis.[105] The sixteenth-century writers do not mention "the problem of the *Deus nudus absconditus.*" Indeed, given that the Reformed orthodox defined election as ordained "in Christ" but never understood the *doctrine* to be *revealed* in Christ, but rather in the text of Scripture—they never exclusively identified the Word of God, namely the revelation of God, as the person of Jesus—the problem that Barth encounters in the doctrine was not encountered by the sixteenth- and seventeenth-century writers. They were not, indeed, they *could not* have been trying to resolve a problem that only arose in a twentieth-century definition of divine revelation: Barth imposes his theology on the materials, identifies a problem that was not actually present, and then, remarkably, all in the course of a "historical excursus," finds that the orthodox dogmaticians hinted at a way out of the "problem" in anticipation of Barth's own theology!

Concluding Remarks

The relationship of the Reformation to Protestant orthodoxy deserves further detailed study, if only because scholarly interest in the field has not been proportionate to its importance to the development of Protestant theology and exegesis. Whatever may be said of the ongoing need of scholarly reappraisal and of the present need to examine the work of the numerous lesser Reformers, the half century of Reform has been studied in great depth, with numerous monographs devoted to aspects—sometimes very minute aspects—of the life and thought of its major thinkers. This has generally not been so for the nearly century and a half following the Reformation. Detailed monographs remain comparatively few and even the major thinkers of the late sixteenth and seventeenth centuries have received only little attention. The absence of a comparatively large body of scholarship has been rendered still more troublesome by the biases inherent in most of the older extant studies and in some of the newer works that have not cast off the spell of the older theories. Certainly, as evidenced by the essays and monographs cited under each suggested premise of reappraisal, the balance has begun to shift—but much work remains to be done before we have a thorough and balanced picture of post-Reformation Protestant thought.

The issue confronting the study of post-Reformation Protestantism is not Calvin "against" the Calvinists (or Calvin "for" the Calvinists) but, rather, the analysis of continuities and discontinuities in thought in the context of diversity and development in the Reformed tradition. The discussion ought to avoid partisanship and either the praise or blame of various theologians and theological views. And, above all, the theological biases that would remake either Reformation or post-Reformation theology for the sake of arguing a twentieth-century position should be avoided and the documents allowed to speak for themselves.

This chapter has pointed somewhat negatively at a large body of older scholarship and its linear descendants, their approaches and their definitions but, hopefully, quite positively toward the task of reappraisal and, beyond that, the task of detailed examination suitable to the detail and complexity of the subject. Reformed theologians who wrote after the time of Calvin—whether several decades or a century after, it matters very little—did not duplicate his theology. Neither, of course, did his Reformed contemporaries. What is problematic from a methodological perspective in the study of developing Protestant thought is not the absence of duplication but its expectation. One never reads that Gregory of Nyssa should have duplicated Irenaeus (or, contrawise, that he "misplaced" or "distorted" one of Irenaeus's thoughts)—that Aquinas distorted the thought of Anselm, or that Barth departed dangerously from the road indicated by Schleiermacher whether intentionally or because of a theological amnesia. Yet it is a commonplace to criticize writers of the late sixteenth, the seventeenth, and even the eighteenth centuries for departing from, misplacing, or distorting Calvin's thought—as if Calvin held the patent on particular doctrinal *loci* and was somehow a perpetual norm for Reformed theology to the exclusion of doctrinal development, and even of occasional difference of opinion, whether on the part of his contemporaries or of the theologians of subsequent generations. One of the great ironies of the older scholarship is that it has criticized later Reformed theologians for being epigones, slavish imitators, and then has criticized them still further for failing to imitate. There is a saying about having one's cake and eating it too that applies here.

Beyond the problem of theological bias, however, there is resident in this older scholarship a related problem of failure to learn from the forward movement of scholarship in collateral areas of research. Throughout this chapter, the reappraisal of Protestant orthodoxy and scholasticism has been argued in the larger context of scholarship on the later Middle Ages and the Renaissance—whereas the argument that pits "Calvin against the Calvinists" or the Reformers against the Protestant scholastics has been shown to draw on a negative and monolithic view of "scholasticism" as a particular theological and philosophical system and on a positive and equally monolithic view of "humanism" as a particular antischolastic theological and philosophical conclusion. In fact, the "Calvin against the Calvinists" argument looks entirely too much like a reprise, in reverse order of Burckhardt's famous but now nearly universally rejected thesis that the Renaissance tore away the veil of medieval ignorance: only slightly modified, the post-Reformation Burckhardianism reads, "the veil" that had "first melted into air" in the Reformation was replaced by the epigoni, with the result that in the era of orthodoxy "both sides of the human consciousness—that which was turned within as that which was turned without—lay dreaming or half awake beneath a common veil. The veil was woven of faith, illusion, and childish prepossession, through which the world and history were seen clad in strange hues."[106] Unless examination of the transition from Reformation to orthodoxy is placed into the context of the ongoing reappraisals of the later Middle

Ages, scholasticism, the Renaissance, and humanism, a Burckhardian veil, stitched together with various theological and dogmatizing threads, will continue to cover the study of late sixteenth- and seventeenth-century Protestantism.

In moving toward a clearer and more accurate definition of the phenomenon of Protestant orthodoxy and Protestant scholasticism, examination of post-Reformation theology must be sensitive to the large-scale continuities in doctrine, evidenced by commitment to the Reformed confessions, by the maintenance of fundamental theological perspectives found in the teaching of the several major theologians of the first and second stages of the Reformation, and by a consistent recourse to a fairly stable exegetical tradition. At the same time, investigation must be sensitive to elements of discontinuity brought on by differences in personal style, issues addressed, the institutionalization of Protestantism, the increased use of the scholastic method and of various theological and philosophical views of the older tradition, and to a certain extent by place and time. Not only the dogmatic theology but also its exegetical roots and its practical adjuncts need to be examined—particularly in view of the diversity of the theology itself. That definition will respect the distinction between the drive toward confessional orthodoxy and the increasing use of scholastic method: the former term refers to the goal of "right teaching," the latter to the use of a disputative style, of a technique of making fine distinctions, of the tools of exegesis and logic, and of the study and ranking of various authorities, notably, Scripture, tradition, and philosophy in the construction of defensible theological systems.[107]

PART II

SCHOLASTIC PROTESTANTISM–FOUNDATIONAL PERSPECTIVES

6

Calling, Character, Piety, and Learning

Paradigms for Theological Education in the Era of Protestant Orthodoxy

From Reformation to Orthodoxy: The Trajectory of Protestant Theological Education

It can easily be argued that one of the primary roots of the Reformation was curricular reform in the university, specifically the reform of the theological curriculum.[1] Of the early Reformers, Luther in particular was an academician. As Gordon Rupp commented,

> We shall never understand Luther unless we remember that he was by trade a Theological Professor, that year in, year out (the exceptions can be counted on the fingers), twice a week at the appointed hour, he walked into the lecture-room and addressed successive generations of students, and this for thirty years until he was old and feeble and could only croak his last lecture.[2]

Luther's insistence on the study of Scripture in the original languages, his attacks on late medieval scholastic theology, and his demand for the liberation of theology from Aristotle rested, of course, on theological premises, but their most immediate impact was on the reshaping of the theological curriculum at Wittenberg. So, too, were the efforts of Luther's close associate, Philip Melanchthon, in the areas of logic, rhetoric, and ethics, attempts to reframe the curriculum under the pressure of new theological and philosophical assumptions. This reframing of the theological curriculum first to meet the needs of the early Reformation protest and, subsequently, to meet the needs of an institutionally as well as theologically successful Protestantism occupied the minds of teachers of theology throughout the sixteenth and the seventeenth centuries. In the following chapter, I will briefly trace out the earlier development of methods and rules for the study of theology, emphasizing the Reformed side of the development, and then focus attention on the completed form of Protestant theological education offered in the works of the seventeenth-century Reformed writers Voetius and Witsius.[3]

The crisis of the Reformation brought new questioning of the grounds for theology and of the proper methods of study. Already at the beginning of the sixteenth century Erasmus had put his humanist sensibilities to work on these questions and, in the preface on theological study affixed to the 1519 edition of his Greek New Testament, he strongly encouraged the study of biblical languages, and collateral disciplines such as logic and rhetoric.[4] Erasmus counseled that Aristotelian and scholastic philosophy be studied but not overemphasized: doctrinal theology ought to be constructed by the orderly, topical collation of texts from the Scriptures and the Fathers. He also emphasized, quite strongly, the relationships between study of the materials of theology and the development of personal piety. Prayerful study should transform life and, ultimately, issue forth in public morality and piety.

Influenced both by Erasmus's humanistic piety and by the Reformation battle cry of *sola scriptura,* Melanchthon on the Lutheran side and Bullinger on the Reformed wrote treatises on the spirituality and methodology of theological study. Melanchthon's *Brevis ratio discendi theologiae* is only a few pages long. It emphasizes the centrality of faith and justification not only to theology but also to the shaping of the curriculum: the New Testament, Melanchthon asserts, ought to be studied before the Old Testament and the exegesis of Romans and the Gospel of John should frame the study as beginning and end in order to establish the doctrinal foundation. The Old Testament ought to be read in sequence, beginning with Genesis and concluding with the Psalms and the prophets.[5] Melanchthon also offered his students a series of brief works on the method of Christian preaching, notably, the section *De sacris concionibus* in his *De Rhetorica libri tres* (1519), *De officiis concionatoris* (1529), and *De modo et arte concionandi* (1540).[6] Beyond this, the prefaces to various editions of his *Loci communes* offered suggestions on the pattern and method of theological system. Here, Melanchthon emphasized the identification and arrangement of the fundamental theological topics and recommended a model in which causes preceded effects and in which the "historical series" of events in the plan of redemption be observed. Thus, discussion of God precedes the doctrine of creation, sin precedes redemption, law precedes gospel.[7] What we do not find in Melanchthon's work is an integrative approach to the study of theology as a whole or a discussion of the life and character of theological students, although Melanchthon did recommend study of the Church Fathers, particularly of Augustine, of the Greek and Latin classics, and of philosophy. Melanchthon warned of the dangers of worldly wisdom but nonetheless insisted, like Erasmus, that philosophy could not be ignored.

A more thoroughly integrative approach, written from a very practical standpoint and including both curricular and attitudinal insight, was, however, forthcoming from Heinrich Bullinger. His *Ratio studiorum* (1527) offered a basic approach to study followed by a presentation of philosophical and theological *loci communes* and a brief, axiomatic statement of Christian doctrine—in short, it provided a general approach to study followed by a basic pattern of instruction focused on theology.[8] Bullinger recommends a disciplined structuring of the hours of the day to avoid waste of time, particularly in the morning, and indicates that the day's study ought to begin with prayer. There can be no success in study unless God instills it (*nisi Deus aspiret*): Bullinger's prayer requests the ability to serve God in purity of life with wisdom, intelligence, and memory, under the law of God, with genuine reverence and erudition.[9] After further counsel about the conduct of the day, including comments about meals and the importance of evening study, Bullinger proposes a course of readings, beginning with "profane letters." Pagan authors, he notes, were read and used by the Apostle Paul and by fathers like Basil the Great; so, too, Quadratus, Aristides, Justin, Irenaeus, Tertullian, Clement of Alexandria, and Origen. Even so, the various divisions of philosophy—verbal, moral, and natural—ought to be studied and the works of the poets, orators, and ancient historians carefully perused.[10]

Bullinger introduces his discussion of the study of sacred letters with a citation from the Wisdom of Solomon: "The spirit of wisdom will not be sent into a wicked mind."[11] Here especially must iniquity be set aside and a love of God be fostered through prayer: in order for a right understanding, Bullinger notes, there must be sound belief, true worship, piety, and reverence to the end that all good results are dedicated to the glory of God.[12] Study in the ancient languages is necessary, Bullinger notes, for a right understanding of the text: he recommends Conrad Pellican's work on the Hebrew language, Sebastian Munster's and Elias Levita's Hebrew grammars; for Greek, the works of Conrad Pellican, Melanchthon, and Jacob Ceporinus.[13] Commentators, too, are to be consulted for the sake of understanding more clearly the "truth" of the Greek and Hebrew texts: he recommends Zwingli, Erasmus, Pellican, Johannes Oecolampadius, Melanchthon, Wolfgang Capito, and Munster.

Furthermore, although the basic linguistic techniques necessary to the understanding of Scripture do not differ from those necessary to the reading of classical literature,[14] the student of Scripture also must be aware of its unique center or *scopus* of meaning to which all the books of Scripture point, the covenant of God in which "God first binds himself to us . . . and then prescribes what is required of us." It is then in the light of this broader understanding that the tropes, analogies, and symbols in the text are to be understood. Bullinger concludes his discussion of Scripture with a lengthy examination of forms and patterns of interpretation.[15]

If the emphasis of Bullinger's treatise fell on the exposition of Scripture and on the identification of the theological topics or *loci communes* to be elicited from Scripture, he also clearly assumed both a breadth of general learning and a consistent exercise of piety on the part of the theological student—indeed, he viewed both as prerequisites to theological study. In addition, Bullinger's own experience of teaching in a Cistercian monastery surely appears in the treatise in the form of the ordering of the hours of the day, the planning of meals, and the intentional right ordering of the inward self through preparatory prayer.[16] This is a point of continuity in theological education that connects the later Middle Ages (and, in fact, the greater part of the Christian tradition) with the Reformation and, as will be evident in the discussion of Voetius, with post-Reformation Protestant orthodoxy as well.

The propaedeutic essays of Melanchthon and Bullinger were soon followed by lengthier essays on theological study by less-famous writers like David Chytraeus,[17] a pupil of Melanchthon, and Andreas Hyperius.[18] Chytraeus and Hyperius do not identify a strictly defined model for theological study such as the gathering of all subdisciplines into biblical, historical, systematic, and practical fields, but they do enumerate various aspects or elements of theological study that resemble this later and more elaborate "theological encyclopedia." Chytraeus presents ten rules for theological study, beginning with prayer and concluding with "cross and affliction": nothing in theology, he argues, can be learned apart from a right relationship with God and none of the subject matter can be divorced from personal piety. With these two rules of spiritual discipline framing his entire program, Chytraeus can go on to place the careful and continual study of Scripture second, the gathering of theological topics (*loci*) and the practice of logic and rhetoric in third, fourth, fifth place, and the study of languages, the reading of biblical commentaries and patristic study, history, and philosophy rounding out the list.[19]

Hyperius's far more detailed work, the *De theologo, seu de ratione studii theologiae,* may well be the most extended Protestant essay on the basic study of theology written in the sixteenth century.[20] In addition to this larger curricular essay, Hyperius also produced two treatises on preaching, *De formandis concionibus sacris* and *Topica theologica*,[21] and a treatise on the right method of reading and meditating on Scripture.[22] Quite characteristic of older Protestantism, Hyperius viewed theological study as an aid to piety and directed his readers to work prayerfully with due respect to their sources. He also, very clearly, draws on the medieval background of Protestantism in his identification of theology as a form of *sapientia* or wisdom as well as a form of knowledge or intellective discipline, a *scientia*. Indeed, the Apostle Paul himself, Hyperius argues, defines theology as "a wisdom not of this world . . . wisdom in a mystery . . . that was ordained by God before all worlds and revealed by his spirit."[23] This identification, moreover, provides him with the foundational assumption of his treatise, perhaps drawn from Bullinger, that the study of theology must be guided by the sapiential writings of the Old Testament: "the fear of God," he wrote, citing Proverbs 1:7, "is the beginning of knowledge (*scientia*)." The student of theology must therefore "prepare [his] soul for the diligent reading of sacred letters" by calling on God in prayer to purge him of "wicked affections," illuminate his darkness and render his soul calm, gentle, benevolent, and humble, to the exclusion of vanity and contentiousness.[24] Theological study, therefore, is not merely the learning of certain materials but the spiritual formation of the person. Again Hyperius has recourse to Proverbs: "He who walks with wisdom, is wise."[25]

Beyond piety and spiritual formation, Hyperius also assumes a rigorous course of study in various disciplines that are "necessary" to theological knowing: philosophy in its subdisciplines of grammar, logic, and rhetoric, as taught by the classical pagan writers and by the fathers of the church;[26] the mathematical arts of arithmetic, geometry, music, and astronomy;[27] physics;[28] ethics, politics, oeconomics, and metaphysics, again all resting on the classical models;[29] history, architecture, and agriculture;[30] and above all the classical languages, especially Hebrew and Greek.[31] In what is certainly a reflection both of the Melanchthonian roots of his thought and of the needs of curriculum in a time of the institutionalization of Protestantism, Hyperius argues the relevance and suitability of philosophical study on the ground that the "human" discipline of philosophy is a gift of God.[32] All of these subjects of study are, of course, recommended by way of preparation for theology–and reflect a humanistic revision of the medieval university curriculum that still respects the trivium and quadrivium but has broadened study particularly in the direction of languages and has insisted on the reading of sources in their original tongues.

Hyperius next divides the course theological study into three general topical areas that adumbrate the eventual division of theological study into a "fourfold encyclopedia"–Scripture and its interpretation,[33] doctrinal theology or the *loci communes*,[34] and practical consisting in the history and governance of the church, including polity, ritual, worship, and preaching.[35] The text of Hyperius's *De theologo*, extending to more than seven hundred pages, is far too detailed to examine here. Suffice it to say that, like Melanchthon, Hyperius understood doctrinal topics as following from exegesis, but he does not sever the study of the Old Testament from the study of the New Testament and he recognizes that theological works of the past, particularly the works of the Fathers, contribute to the identification of *loci*. It is also noteworthy that historical study, if not clearly distinguished from polemics as in the eighteenth- and nineteenth-century fourfold encyclopedia, is nonetheless understood by Hyperius as consisting in more than polemics.[36] His massive essay also continues to emphasize the importance of piety and prayer as it develops at its curriculum and, in much the same spirit as Bullinger's *Ratio studiorum*, assumes a vast bibliography of biblical texts and tools, patristic texts, classical works in the various areas of philosophy, theological works of the Reformers and, in Hyperius's case, a knowledge of the major scholastic theologians as well. As van 't Spijker has argued, the unifying characteristic of Hyperius' approach lies in its consistent union of learning and with religious life—of *ratio* and *oratio*, *eloquentia* and *pietas*—its stress on *pietas literata* and *literatura pia*.[37]

The orthodox or scholastic era of Protestantism was a time of further codification and institutionalization in the churches of the Reformation in which the initial efforts of Bullinger, Hyperius, and others in defining the shape of Protestant theology and at the same time of Protestant theological study were refined, elaborated, and adapted to new circumstances on the grand scale typical of the age of the baroque.[38] It is also one of the periods in the history of the church most subject to adverse comment and negative assessment in works of history and theology. The strict application of scholastic method by the Protestant thinkers of the period that has so often drawn anachronistic and theologically motivated critique from historians and theologians of the nineteenth and twentieth centuries not only aided this process of codification, it also provided one of the several crucial links between developing Protestantism and the ongoing Western intellectual and academic tradition. Indeed, the scholasticism of the late sixteenth and early seventeenth centuries ought not to be understood as a simple return to medieval methods: rather, it was the result of a developing tradition of logic, rhetoric, and learning that altered the patterns of scholastic education even as it preserved them.[39] Thus, also, the drive to enunciate and to maintain a churchly and confessional orthodoxy or "right teaching" that was characteristic of the era both reinforced the relationship of Protestantism to the great tradition of Christianity and encouraged Protestant teachers to examine theological training as one aspect of the ongoing codification and institutionalization of Reform.[40]

Even so, powerful continuities in doctrine, in biblical interpretation, and in the method and approach of theological study can be identified between the Protestantism of the sixteenth and that of the seventeenth century.[41] The institutionalization and codification of church and doctrine associated with scholastic orthodoxy entailed, in no small part, the institutionalization and codification of doctrinal and educational principles and concerns enunciated by the Reformers. In the seventeenth and early eighteenth century, even Hyperius's lengthy treatise was dwarfed by the introductory descriptions of theological study by Johann Gerhard, Abraham Calovius, and Johannes Buddeus among the Lutherans and Johann Alsted and Gisbertus Voetius among the Reformed.[42] In all of these works, the *sola Scriptura* of the Reformation is maintained while the exegetical study of Scripture is reinforced by intense study of ancient languages: the seventeenth century was the age of the great Protestant Hebraists and Orientalists—Buxtorf, Lightfoot, Walton—and of the great London Polyglot Bible. From exegesis, the authors move to doctrinal or systematic theology. Gerhard describes a five-year course of study, beginning with three years of biblical and doctrinal study. In the third year, students would study the great debated questions in polemic with Roman Catholics, Reformed and Anabaptist writers; in the fourth year, preaching would be added to the course; and, in the fifth year, church history.[43] Voetius presents a similar model, as do the other authors noted.[44] Here, too, as we noted in the work of Hyperius, the fourfold model of encyclopedia continues to emerge in the movement of the curriculum from biblical to dogmatic study and in understanding of ecclesiastical discussion as concerned with the history but also with the present practice of the church.[45]

The Theological Task: Gisbertus Voetius's Ideal for Theological Education

Gisbertus Voetius's *Exercitia et bibliotheca studiosi theologiae* or *Exercises and Library for the Student of Theology* (1651) is one of the academic and spiritual landmarks of the era of Reformed orthodoxy. Voetius himself was, by all testimony, one of the most adept of the Protestant scholastic theologians—adept at biblical languages and theological exegesis, adept at catechetical theology and intricate dogmatic argumentation, and adept above all at disputation and polemic. The greater part of his published output took the form of theological disputations on virtually all of the topics in dogmatics and against nearly all of the doctrinal adversaries of the Reformed faith.[46] He was not a specialist in polemics, like his colleague Johannes Hoornbeeck,[47] but he brought to the polemical task not only a mastery of style but also a mastery of materials for formal disputation that made him a dread opponent.[48] Granting that his reputation rests largely on his academic disputations, it is hardly surprising that he, together with the greater number of his scholastic contemporaries, is thought of as an unremitting logician rather than as a warm-hearted pietist and that historians have generally seen fit to remember with kindness not the sometimes stringent scholastic argumentation of Voetius but the covenantal biblicism of his chief adversary, Johannes Cocceius, the inherent problems and idiosyncrasies of Cocceius's exegesis and dogmatics notwithstanding.[49]

If Voetius was a scholastic and a logician, however, he was himself also a theologian who emphasized the covenantal theme of Reformed theology, who stressed the need for personal character and piety—indeed, of spiritual exercise—among his students, and whose teaching produced lights of the later seventeenth century, such as the covenant theologian Herman Witsius, and leading figures of the Dutch pietist movement known as the *Nadere Reformatie*, such as Jodocus van Lodenstein, Jacobus Koelman, and Wilhelmus à Brakel.[50] This other side of Voetius's teaching was presented at the very beginning of his academic career in his inaugural address at Utrecht, *De pietate cum scientia coniungenda* (*On the Conjunction of Piety with Learning*), developed in his *Exercitia pietatis in usum juventutis academicae* (*Exercises in Piety for Young Scholars*),[51] and subsequently documented on a grand scale in his *Exercises and Library for the Student of Theology.*

The *Exercises* begin with that perennial question of the church and its offices—how does one identify naturally gifted individuals who will, in Voetius's terms, be capable of the demanding course of "higher study" necessary for the understanding of theology? Such individuals, Voetius begins, are to be identified by professors in the university, by pastors, elders, and catechists of the church, in short, by those already chosen within the community to exercise such judgments. Gifted individuals may be identified either from among the uneducated or the educated—the former, he notes, will be as yet devoid of errors and delusions, the latter will at least have been able to demonstrate their ability and erudition. Personal character traits such as "piety, zeal, natural gifts, a capacity for remembering," a high theological eloquence, and a willingness to serve the cause of the gospel should be evident in the candidates.[52] Although he does not want to delimit unnecessarily the age of candidates, Voetius suggests that they be no younger than eighteen or twenty years and that they have completed their basic education in elementary Latin, philosophy, catechetical theology, and the lower curriculum or "trivium."

It is an unfortunate error, he adds, to secure candidates with promises of stipends before assessing fully their gifts. Even more problematic is the failure to identify the truly best candidates because of assumptions concerning social class; it is just as likely, Voetius indicates, for natural abilities to be found among the general populace as among the nobility. Natural abilities, piety, zeal, eloquence, modesty in behavior, prudence, serious demeanor, courtesy, and generosity are to be preferred to social rank![53] Beyond this, "it is a most grave error of epidemic proportion" to assume that an adolescent deemed studious and moral will necessarily retain and enrich these traits during his education with careful supervision of parents and mentors and to fall into the trap of equating the inception of theological study with "repentance and conversion from sin."[54]

This clear emphasis on piety and personal religion over social status and prior training in no way leads Voetius to deemphasize learning. After making the case for character and religiosity, he devotes three detailed chapters to the educational preparation for theological study, developing an ideal curriculum and a pattern of personal and spiritual formation designed to bring mastery in languages, rhetoric, logic, philosophy, general knowledge of diverse fields such as history, geography, politics, and astronomy, and, above all, a well-honed technique for and approach to the discipline of study. Thus, Voetius recommends a sevenfold pattern for study consisting of *lectio*, *meditatio*, *auditio*, *scriptio*, *collatio*, *collegia*, and *enotatio*, correlated with formal instruction in the various disciplines (*institutio*) and training in various lexical and linguistic tools (*apparatus*).[55] By *lectio* or reading, Voetius means a threefold pattern of studying basic disciplines: first, the student examines "synoptic or systematic" works that survey a field; second, he should read the foremost authors whose works both comment on all the significant topics and eludicate the relevant debates; and third, the student ought to study carefully the classic authors—"Aristotle, Euclid, Ptolemy, and so forth." This effort should be followed by a time of *meditatio* during which "definitions, distinctions, theorems, solutions related to necessary issues, especially to theology are inwardly grasped and committed to memory."[56] In addition to reading and meditation, there is also listening or hearing (*auditio*) consisting in the "delivery of expositions of Scripture and of the theological topics and in theological and philosophical disputation."[57]

As a fourth element in study, Voetius recommends *scriptio* or written composition, guided and organized according to the traditional categories of predication, on the basic themes of study, particularly those relevant to theology. Thus, a student ought to be able to formulate his thoughts in writing on the category of "substance" with specific attention to created substances such as human beings, animals, and things in the inanimate order, especially those identified in Scripture. "Quality" also ought to be discussed—with reference to issues such as physical, intellectual, or volitional qualities. In the category of "disposition" the student ought to be prepared to discourse on the intellectual dispositions of wisdom, prudence, art, superstition, and virtue, while, under the rubric of "action," he should understand such issues as creation, conservation, generation, action and reaction, and so forth. These and other categorical presentations should be accomplished with due attention to examples—again, often drawn from Scripture.[58] In support of his written exercises in the disciplines, a student ought to engage in *collatio* and *collegia*, the gathering and recapitulation of materials. Reading, meditation, hearing, composition, gathering, and recapitulation are finally sharpened by "enotation," by which Voetius understands a mental survey of the studied and memorized materials with a view to the inward systematization and summation of a discipline according to its "problems, arguments, objections, assumptions, distinctions, [and] examples."[59] *Enotatio*, thus, is the internalization of a scholastic method. Taken together in the context of a detailed curriculum, these seven aspects of disciplined study point toward a highly structured but also a carefully integrated pattern of education designed with a view toward mastery of the field both in theory and in practice. This full course of instruction (*institutio*), Voetius adds, ought, moreover, to embrace not only the life of intellect but also works of Christian love (*caritas*).[60]

The latter point—the connection between study and *caritas*—becomes the subject of an entire chapter in Voetius's *Exercises*. He indicates a series of "general adjuncts and special efforts and exercises" belonging to theological study. The "general adjuncts" that must accompany study are "the practice of piety," "academic devotion (*cura*) and scrutiny (*inspectio*)," and "examination." The "practice of piety," Voetius insists, ought to be "instilled and enriched" so that the student comes ever "closer to God through continual meditation on sacred things." This may be accomplished through "the frequent hearing of sermons, catechization, reading, and meditating on Scripture" followed by "private prayer," the "examination of one's conscience," renewals of faith and repentance—all under the care of church and school as represented by parents, mentors, counselors, and professors. Externally, piety ought to be further reinforced by regular evaluation by and conversation with professors in order that "deceit and spiritual cancers" (*fucos & carcinomata*) be cast out and that "by degrees" the student will advance in "piety, modesty, diligence, and gifts."[61] The piety and devotion of the faculty, all of whom should have passed through a similar training, is assumed by Voetius: the professors in the theological faculty serve, thus, as pastors within the institution and consistently engage in the spiritual formation and correction of their students. The second adjunct to formal study, "academic devotion and scrutiny" or, one might say, "management and inspection," takes place both privately and publicly, the former through the work of "ephors" or tutors and the latter through the oversight of classes and synods as well as that of the faculty. The third adjunct, examination, ought never to be perfunctory, but ought to be conducted with some gravity at the conclusion of semesters during the interval or period of theological study and at the end of the year during the second and third intervals.[62]

Having presented his basic pattern of discipline and piety, Voetius next describes the recommended three-part course of study in preparation for the ministry. In the first interval of study there are two basic tasks, a primary and a secondary. The primary task is the introduction to theological study and the secondary is the review and supplementation for the sake of theological learning of the student's previous studies in philosophy, language, and the arts.[63] The primary educational task itself Voetius divides into three parts, textual or biblical, systematic or dogmatic, and disputative (*elenctica*) and problematic theology. The first interval's biblical study stresses what Voetius, in accord with the Reformers and with his orthodox Protestant contemporaries, viewed as the books most central to the theological understanding of Scripture as a whole (Genesis, Isaiah, Psalms, Matthew, John, Romans, and Hebrews) and then takes up crucial texts in Scripture that are "the grounds (*sedes*) of the [theological] topics (*locorum communium*) . . . for example, Romans 3 and 4 on justification, Romans 9 and Ephesians 1 on predestination, Genesis 3 and Romans 5 on the first sin of Adam, 1 Corinthians 11 on the Lord's supper, 1 Timothy 3 on the office of ministry, and 1 Corinthians 5 on excommunication."[64] At the same time, the beginning student will be introduced to "systematic theology" not, Voetius adds, in the form of an epitome or summary but thoroughly and fully examined with a view to moral and ascetic theology and to ecclesiastical polity as well as to the more strictly dogmatic topics. And, finally, the student will be exposed to "disputative and problematic" theology with specific focus on "the controversies of the present day between the orthodox [Reformed faith] and the Socinians, Remonstrants, Papists, Anabaptists, Enthusiast, Libertines, Jews, Epicureans, [and] Atheists."[65] In this curriculum, Voetius indicates, it should be emphasized that the proper order of learning and of argument proceeds from the study of Scripture and of exegetically elaborated *loci communes* to "positive or systematic theology" and then, only on that foundation, to polemical topics. Also to be emphasized throughout this curriculum is the overarching identification of theology as the discipline concerned with "faith and practice," the latter term indicating both piety and the administration of the church.[66]

Study of each of the three portions of the curriculum ought to proceed according to the pattern of *lectio, meditatio, auditio, scriptio, collatio, collegia*, and *enotatio*. Thus, Scripture ought to be read using the original languages supplemented by Mercerus's and Drusius's annotations on the Old and by Beza's and Piscator's annotations on the New Testament. In the systematic field, students ought to engage in the "repeated reading" of Ames's *Medulla* and Maccovius's disputations, enriched, for good measure, by a reading of Gomarus's disputations as well. Problematic or polemical theology should survey Ames's refutation of Bellarmine, Hoornbeeck's exposition of the errors of Socinianism, and the relevant sections of the major dogmatic works of Polanus, Wendelin, and Alsted—and a host of other authors.[67] As for their meditation, students ought to study and memorize "select themes and sayings of Scripture" together with their analysis and exposition in the original languages. Similarly, the basic theological topics should be committed to memory following the outlines of Ames or Maccovius, with close attention to definitions and distinctions. Listening to and participating in disputations and the composition of suitable topical analysis will follow, succeeded by the final efforts of gathering, recapitulating, and annotating mentally the entire course of study.[68]

As their secondary task in their first part of theological study, future pastors and teachers review the course in philosophy with a view to engaging in disputation. They also study chronology, the history of the Old and New Testaments, they review Latin by reading various Church Fathers like Lactantius, Tertullian, Arnobius, and Prudentius and refresh their Greek through Plotinus, Proclus, Epictetus, and Fathers such as Athenagoras, Justin, Clement of Alexandria, Origen, and Athanasius. Voetius recommends specifically Origen's *Contra Celsum* and Athanasius *Contra Arianos*.[69] He concludes his discussion of the secondary areas of study by noting important editions of

Scripture and commentators to be consulted in attaining proficiency in Hebrew and by recommending the study of Aramaic, Syriac, and Arabic.[70] This linguistic emphasis in Voetius's curriculum underlines the positive connection between his methods and those of the humanists.

In the second stage of their study, theological students move forward from the basic exercises in their primary work of theological study and secondary work in the study of philosophical and ancillary disciplines to patterns of study more directly related to the work of the pastor. Voetius recommends that the secondary emphasis of study be medicine, jurisprudence, and their cognate disciplines, plus studies in history, antiquities, and the more practical areas of cases of conscience and counsel. At the same time, the primary theological work takes on a practical aspect and becomes considerably more diverse, now divided into textual or biblical study, the "practice of preaching," church polity, disputative or scholastic theology, patristics, and the later history of the church. In other words, the fundamental work of biblical study continues, systematic and polemical theology moves forward into the more technical areas of scholastic disputation, the historical concentration of earlier secondary study now passes over into the examination of church history, and what today would be called the more practical or pastoral disciplines appear both at the primary level in preaching and at the secondary in the areas of conscience and counsel.[71] As noted, moreover, in the discussion of Hyperius's *De theologo*, polemical and historical theology are not identical—indeed, in Voetius's model of study, they are quite distinct.

Here, too, study proceeds according to the model of *lectio*, *meditatio*, *auditio*, *scriptio*, *collatio*, *collegia*, and *enotatio*, correlated with *institutio* and the relevant *apparatus*. And, once again, the recommended bibliography is imposing. Scripture continues to be approached by way of the original languages and scholarly annotations with the pattern of reading emphasizing both central themes and the study of entire books from beginning to end with careful attention to annotations and marginalia. Theological reading, in view of the practical turn of the curriculum, now includes Calvin's *Institutes*, various works of English Puritan theology—notably by William Perkins, Robert Bolton, Paul Baynes, John Downham, Richard Sibbes, and John Reynolds—and the writings of Jean Taffin, William Teellinck, and Godefridus Udemans, associated with the *Nadere Reformatie*. Such works, comments Voetius, serve "as supplements to practical theology and to the development of sermons."[72] Polemical or disputative theology now also shifts its emphasis including not only works directed against the sects and heretics of the seventeenth century but also against Mohammedans. Voetius indicates that students ought to examine the Qur'an and he recommends Aquinas's *Summa contra gentiles* with the annotations of Francis de Sylvestris (Ferrariensis). Among the historical works added to the reading list are Scultetus's *Historia Reformationis* and the compendia of church history by Paraeus, Osiander, and Baronius. Voetius also recommends the reading of martyrologies—again because they provide both indications of style and content suitable to sermons.[73] The recommended time of meditation ought to concentrate, as before, on Scripture and theological themes, the latter specifically identified as "ascetic," "patristic," and "casuistic," as well as "natural and scholastic." "Hearing" in this phase of study consists in the public presentation of various didactic, historical, biblical, and philosophical topics.[74]

Voetius's fourth element of study, *scriptio*, is worked out in vast detail for this second phase of study: the work of writing annotations on difficult places, basic themes, and, indeed, the chapters of Scripture must be supplemented by analysis of the more "difficult problems related to the sacred history" and by "disquisitions concerning various literal and philological interpretations of Scripture." Here the student's use of grammatical and lexical tools and his ability to work in the cognate languages comes to bear. In addition, the student must begin to prepare sermons with attention to substance and form as well as to apparatus, at all times supported by practice in elocution and memory. Exercises in composition also should address issues of morality and conscience as well as current theological debate with Jews, pagans, Mohammedans, and enthusiasts. The subsequent exercises of *collatio* and *collegia* call for further topical reading and the careful study of issues through the bibliography—which, for Voetius, must range from biblical and lexical apparatus, to compendia and systems of theology written by medieval teachers, Protestant theologians, and recent Roman Catholic thinkers.[75] Through meditation and composition, the student integrates theological learning with personal piety and draws both inwardly to create a proper disposition for ministry. And, in addition to this more private pattern of study, Voetius details at length academic exercises in public disputation, preaching, and lecturing intended to solidify learning and churchly skills.[76]

The third interval or phase of theological study continues the patterns of the previous two parts but in greater detail and, Voetius indicates, extends into the several years of parish ministry.[77] No new subjects are presented at this point. Instead, Voetius's version of what might be called seventeenth-century Reformed "extended education" consists in the repetition and supplementation of what has already been learned. The burden placed on *lectio* becomes quite intense—students and new ministers are called on to read heavily in the theological and controversial literature of the day, with continued attention to the basic theological *loci*. Various works dealing with "the more sound (*sanior*) theology from the tenth century to the time of the Reformation" are recommended—including both the theology of those who "separated from popery," such as the Waldenses, Wycliffites, and Hussites, and the theology of those faithful who remained, as catalogued by Flacius Illyricus and Plessaeus. Here, Voetius specifically recommends the study of Aquinas's *Summa theologiae*.[78]

Meditatio during the third phase of theological education ought to be "occupied primarily with particular chapters and places in Scripture, both those that give the greatest difficulty either in the controversies of the present day or that appear to contradict one another, and to those that most properly and fully support practical and homiletical theology."[79] Voetius here recommends strongly the works of authors such as William Perkins, Robert Bolton, Paul Baynes, John Preston, and Thomas Hooker as supportive of piety and practice. Similarly, the continuing work of personal composition ought to emphasize the writing of sermons and the examination of the text of Scripture. The subsequent work of gathering, recapitulation, and final enotation reflects the earlier efforts to learn and reinforce materials, while the work of *institutio* or instruction now focuses on the process of preparation for "scholarly and ecclesiastical" examinations, both public and private—in short, for the final examination preparatory to full admission to ministry. Here again, Voetius offers rather daunting bibliographical advice.[80]

Throughout this course of theology, with its integration of piety and learning, Voetius insisted on the importance of piety in the life of Christians in general and on the ongoing relationship of piety to theology. To this issue he also devoted a separate treatise, his *Ta asketika, sive exercitia pietatis*, in which he emphasized the disciplined character of piety necessary to ministerial study—in his terms, the substance and subject of the discipline called *Ascetica*, ascetics. "Ascetics," he wrote, "is the theological teaching (*doctrina*) or division of theology that contains the method and description of exercises in piety." These exercises consist, specifically, in "the *praxis* of meditation, petition (*praecatio*), the renewal of repentance, faith, [and in] preparation for and participation in the Lord's supper, . . . the right ordering of thoughts, the *praxis* of the Sabbath day, spiritual warfare, inward trials, the control of the tongue, . . . [and] the excitement of love for the divine."[81] The fundamental relationship between this work of inward formation of spirituality and character and the study of theology proper lies in the fact, Voetius argues, that "theology is a practical science or discipline" and that practical uses can and must be "subjoined" to the various doctrinal topics. It is of course true, Voetius continues, that meditation on Scripture is sufficient for the formation and reinforcement of the piety of the unlearned—but training in piety in the academic context, specifically for "theological students and ministerial candidates," is another matter. Here, a variety of authors ought to be read: Voetius notes Daniel Tossanus's *L'exercice de l'ame fidele*, Johann Gerhard's *Exercitium pietatis quotidianum quadripartitum*, and the Dutch translation of Lewis Bayly's *The Practice of Pietie*, both for the sake of refining one's personal disciplines along well tried paths and for the sake of avoiding the errors of "pseudoexercises" like those of the Papists.[82] Understood rightly, the entire study of theology will be directed toward "the art [or technique] of applying theology to use and practice, to the edification of conscience, and to the direction of the will and its affections." In short, "saving doctrine" is always to be directed toward "the practice of piety, the art of worshiping God, affective theology, and the imitation of Christ."[83]

The Goal: Herman Witsius on the Character of a Theologian

Witsius's oration on the character of a theologian not only consciously bridges the gap between the study and the practice of theology, it also and more specifically provides an index to the goal and the real result of Voetius's teaching, inasmuch as Witsius had studied at Utrecht under Voetius.[84] His oration, moreover, was delivered as his inaugural address at the University of Franecker, as he prepared to assume the role of professor of theology for the first time. The oration is both retrospective and prospective. It looks back on Witsius's own theological education, clearly reflecting the model of Voetius's *Exercises* with its balance of personal, spiritual, and intellectual formation, and it looks forward toward Witsius's own appropriation of this educational approach in his career as a teacher.

For all Witsius's training in technical theology and incredible expertise in Hebrew, Greek, and Latin, the initial and certainly the strongest voice in his inaugural address is that of the *Nadere Reformatie*. He frames his discourse with three biblical texts, the Song of Hannah (1 Sam. 2:7–8), David's response to God's promise of an everlasting kingdom (2 Sam. 7:18, 20), and the Lord's promise of assistance to Joshua (Josh. 1:9). From the first text, Witsius draws a personal lesson of the divine providence that "makes poor and makes rich," that "brings low" and "also exalts," that "raises the poor from the dust . . . to make them sit with princes and inherit a seat of honor." It was the astonishing work of God, he writes, that first elicited this hymn from a "pious mother" and that now similarly presses him to review "the whole course of his life" and especially the divine assistance given to him throughout his work in the "sacred office" of Christian ministry: reflecting surely on the history of Samuel, Witsius indicates that his "pious parents" devoted him to the church at an early age and "took care to have [his] mind instilled with such doctrinal and practical teachings" as would train him up to do "no dishonor to the house of God." Granting all this, neither his parents nor he could have predicted his promotion to the professorship at Franecker—this "seat of honor."[85]

His reaction is both one of joy and amazement and one of fear: like David, he is constrained to ask himself, "Who am I, O Lord God, and what is my house that thou hast brought me thus far?" He has been brought from the daily task of catechizing and prayer and from the work of preaching a simple word of sound instruction "to the Christian common people" to be "a new teacher in this venerable seat of learning," a new participant in a "circle of erudite men." His consolation and his strength come not from himself, but from the Lord, who said to Joshua, "Have I not commanded thee? Be strong and of good courage . . . for the Lord thy God is with thee wherever thou goest."[86]

Once he has established his view of God's providential guidance over all life and, particularly, over his own, Witsius moves on to the main body of his discourse in which he proposes to examine the true theologian "as a student, as a teacher, and as a human being," because, he notes, "no one teaches well unless he has first learned well; and no one learns well unless he learns in order to teach; and both learning and teaching are in vain and unprofitable, unless accompanied by practice." Schooling, therefore, is important, but so also is personal manner and method, and beyond that, at the human level, "the habits of soul and outward walk" by which a teacher "may adorn his doctrine."[87]

As a first level of training, Witsius recommends "the lower school of nature" in which the student should examine not only "the wonders of divine providence" but also "the monuments of ancient as well as modern history," "the shrines of all the arts," and "the beauties of various tongues." Careful study ought to be made of grammar, logic, and rhetoric so that the student can learn "rules for definition, division, and arrangement" of his knowledge and also "the art of discoursing" about the topics learned "not only with purity and precision, but also with elegance and effect." So, too, should "moral precepts" be learned from the great philosophers and moral examples from "the monuments of history."[88] All these things ought to be recognized as divine gifts and to be memorized and treasured as a foundation for further learning. And if grammar, logic, and rhetoric are not immediately understood as divine, comments Witsius in a biblical echo of the scholastic identification of philosophy and its subdisciplines as the *ancilla theologiae*, they can surely be taken up into the service of religion and theology—and used "as the Israelites of old did the Gibeonites, whose work it was to cleave wood and to draw water for the use of the Sanctuary."[89]

What is significant here—as was also the case with Voetius—is the expectation of a breadth of culture and learning in the clergy. Indeed, this rather learned student, habituated to the reverent observation of nature, learned in history and languages, well versed in the arts and in the skills of communication, is only a beginner. Witsius comments that these studies cannot absorb all of the time of the student, who must devote the greater part of his intellectual energies to the study of Scripture: these initial studies were merely the prerequisite for theological education. Biblical study, moreover, while assuming the obvious attainments of the one who engages in it, ought nevertheless to bring humility. "Sitting humbly before God," Witsius continues, the theological student ought "to learn from [God's] mouth the hidden mysteries of salvation, which eye hath not seen, nor ear heard . . . which no power of reason, however well trained, could discover."[90]

Witsius quite clearly regards this course of study as a spiritual exercise conducive to building and cultivating personal character. Spiritual discipline is not something to be added to the curriculum so much as it is a fundamental aspect of the student's approach to the life of study and to the life of ministry for which it prepares him. The theologian or minister ought to so imbibe the teaching of Scripture as truly to meditate on it "day and night" and continually to "draw wisdom" from it. In words that reflect the earlier tradition of Protestant theological education, notably the sapiential approach of Hyperius, Witsius insists that the goal of this meditation is not a human, but a "divine faith" that rests "in God alone" and draws its strength from the "power" of God's Word.[91]

There is one character trait necessary to attaining such a goal. In a high rhetorical style, Witsius asks, "What will render the soul teachable and obedient when speaking of God?" His answer, "respect" or "propriety"–*modestia*. What, similarly, will enable a theologian to study the deep mysteries of religion without rashness? Again, "respect" or "obedience"–*modestia*. Or, again, what is required for a mind to be persuaded of the truth of the holiest teachings of the Christian religion? Again, he answers, "respect" or moderation of life–*modestia*.[92] No matter how learned the theologian or minister, he must retain the humility and modesty suitable both to the task of ministry and to the divine truths that he serves.

Even so, the true theologian is a "humble disciple of the Scriptures" who does not speak on his own authority and who recognizes that those who enter the study of theology enter into a knowledge of things hidden to the unaided human reason. This divinely given knowledge depends not merely on the reading of Scripture but also on attention to the inward witness of the Spirit. Spiritual things are not understood by "the blind eyes of nature": "in order to understand–spiritual things, we must have a spiritual mind," a mind conformed by God's gracious work to the mind of Christ. Witsius thus insists, as his teacher, Voetius, had argued so pointedly more than two decades earlier, that learning of a curriculum and graduation with a degree is not enough: "He who is a student in this heavenly school," Witsius writes, "not only knows and believes, but also has a sensible experience of the forgiveness of sins, the privilege of adoption and gracious communion with God, the grace of the indwelling Spirit, . . . and the sweet love of Christ."[93]

So, too, will the theologian or minister acquire, by the grace of God's Spirit, skills in the "art of teaching" and a profound desire to communicate what he has learned to others. Witsius, for all his mastery of the various theological disciplines and, in that time, his nearly unequaled skills in the ancient languages, scorns the "pedant from the schools" who has memorized a host of facts and is able to state them with facility but who is not genuinely schooled in his mind and heart. Such teachers can discourse on doctrine and even on "the Christian warfare" without ever reflecting on their own experience. The true theologian will teach out of the experience of a living faith and, Witsius adds, in a spirit of unfeigned love for God and God's children. His theology will consistently be placed in the service of the Gospel both to impart its truths and to fill its hearers with the Spirit of Christ.[94] Even so, the theologian or minister, guided by the love of God, will never act out of greed or covetousness, and will never seek his own glory, but only the glory of God. He will teach only "what is certain, sound, solid, and fitted to cherish faith, excite hope, promote piety, and preserve unity and peace." He will not "itch after innovation" but will rest on the deposit of biblical truth held within the Reformed churches and work to defend that truth against its adversaries.[95] Piety, for Witsius, excludes neither learning nor polemic! This portrait of the "true theologian," Witsius acknowledges in conclusion, is an ideal and a standard to which he himself has not attained—but he holds it forth nonetheless as the goal for all who train for the ministry. He asks for the aid of his colleagues, notably his elder colleague, Nicholas Arnold, renowned for his refutation of the *Racovian Catechism* of the Socinians, in leading him toward the consistent vindication of God's truth, the defeat of heresy, and the inculcation of piety as he attempts to lead his own students toward that goal.[96]

Concluding Reflection

The Reformed pastor of the sixteenth and seventeenth centuries was by all accounts a learned person. Even if the curricula set out by Hyperius and Voetius were ideals to be striven for rather than goals to be reached by all students, the standards they present were very high—and, given the presence of other disciplines like study of the classics, medicine, and jurisprudence at the edges of the curriculum, very broad indeed. Given also the high standards of character and piety set forth by Voetius and Witsius, there is little wonder that the clergy of the sixteenth and seventeenth centuries had such status in and impact on society. The model, if not classist—Voetius had held forth against this—was surely somewhat elitist. They excelled both in learning and in character, and they had a sense of purpose guided by an assumption of the unity and the unified goal of their knowledge and their ministerial task. Their education, whether in the academic pattern of *lectio*, *meditatio*, *auditio*, *scriptio*, *collatio*, *collegia*, and *enotatio*, or in the equally structured exercises in piety, was designed as a form of inward or spiritual discipline that balanced the issue of objective content with the concern for subjective reception and appropriation.

All of the writers noted, moreover, from the Reformers to the post-Reformation Protestant orthodox, despite the increasing identification of subdisciplines characteristic of the latter, viewed theology as a single united discipline. Whatever the tools and categories or modes of approach to the materials of theology, theological study was viewed as having a single object, God and the works of God, and as having a single goal, the glory of God in the salvation of believers; or, from another perspective, as having a single foundational source, the revelation of God in Scripture, and a single earthly purpose, the renewal of the life of human beings by God's grace in the church. Nonetheless, as we have seen, the basic structure that would become the fourfold encyclopedia was present—as, arguably, was the problem identified by Farley as the "diversified encyclopedia." The distinction between the canon of Scripture in the Old and New Testaments and churchly theology served to distinguish biblical or exegetical from dogmatic, polemical, and historical study. In addition, in Voetius's model, biblical studies were conjoined with their own ancillary linguistic fields and their own distinct apparatus, while dogmatic and polemical theology were quite naturally placed together. Historical study was distinguished from polemics, albeit placed as one discipline among others in a somewhat eclectic category. And the more pastoral studies, such as preaching, counsel, piety, and church polity, if not a precise grouping, were nonetheless associated by Voetius. Given, moreover, both the detail and the technical character of the various disciplines, the issue of specialization and of diversification was also present in the seventeenth-century curriculum—indeed, the intellectual demands placed on students were arguably more intense than in the present and the burden of integrating the various subject areas into a functional whole as heavy or heavier, even granting the greater incentive to conceiving the larger discipline of theology as a spiritual unity.

Perhaps the archetypal products of this understanding of the unity of theological study are Wilhelmus à Brakel's *Redelijke Godsdienst* or *Christian's Reasonable Service* (1700)[97] and Petrus van Mastricht's *Theoretico-practica theologia* (1682–1687),[98] in which exegetical, dogmatic, polemical, and practical elements are combined into single systematic expositions of the Christian faith. In Mastricht's work, the organization of each doctrinal topic manifests this precise fourfold division, whereas in à Brakel's treatise, the exegetical and dogmatic discussions are blended together, the polemic treated as "objections" to doctrinal formulation, and the practical application offered as a concluding pastoral reflection on the texts and doctrine.[99] It is important to recognize that in these, as in all of the works noted, "practical" does not indicate a tendency toward technique or the study of technique: instead, it indicates, as it did in the curricular projects of Bullinger, Hyperius, Voetius, and Witsius, knowledge oriented toward a goal, specifically, the goal of salvation. Technique, of course, had been instilled in the exercises in writing, meditation, speaking, and so forth, but it was viewed as a necessary adjunct, not as the central discipline. Homiletics or "Christian rhetoric," then, is a practical form of theology, not because it is a technique, but because it is learned for the sake of a goal external to it, the goal of the salvation of believers. Even so, à Brakel's and Mastricht's practical discussions deal primarily with the personal appropriation or application of doctrine.

According to the older model for the study of theology, the distinction between theory and praxis was not a distinction between a set of theoretical disciplines and a set of practical disciplines. More specifically, biblical, historical and doctrinal or systematic studies were not viewed as purely theoretical—and homiletical, ministerial study was not viewed as practical in the modern sense of the term. Theology as a whole was understood, particularly by the medieval Thomists and Augustinians and by later Roman Catholic and Reformed Protestant writers, to be a theoretical and a practical study in all of its aspects: theoretical because its contents deserve to be known as a goal of knowing and practical because its contents direct the human spirit toward its goal of eternal salvation. The modern loss of this understanding of theory and praxis has created problems for theology, not the least of which is a confusion over the character and use of the subdisciplines of theology and, because of this confusion, a failure to recognize the relationship of what, today, are called theoretical disciplines to the practice of Christianity. The older Protestant educational model inculcated both a rigorous engagement with the technical disciplines and a rigorous cultivation of personal and corporate piety—and, what is more, it assumed that each of these aspects of theological study reinforced the other and led to the spiritual formation of the whole person. At the beginning and at the end of the educational process, Witsius reminded his hearers that "Humility is the mother, and the root, and the nourisher, and the foundation, and the bond of all good: without it we are profane and detestable creatures."[100]

The beginnings of this change of perspective concerning theory and praxis were evident toward the very end of the era of orthodoxy in the Pietist critique of Protestant scholasticism.[101] (A significant distinction must be made, however, between the German Lutheran Pietism of Spener, with its sometimes pointed critique of scholastic orthodoxy, and the Reformed "Pietism" of the *Nadere Reformatie*, in which Voetius and many of the Reformed scholastics participated: on the Reformed side, there was far less tension between dogmatics and piety and Pietism did not press so pointedly against Protestant orthodox theology. It was, in fact, the model of the Reformed pastor as set forth by the English Puritans and the theologians of the *Nadere Reformatie* that framed much of the Pietist critique of German Lutheran ministry.) The German Pietists drew a line between the academic study of theology and the cultivation of the religion of the heart. Not that they either abandoned academics or failed to understand that academic study demanded inward, spiritual discipline: the Pietists were far more academic and, indeed, scholastic than contemporary evangelical critics of academic theology.[102] Rather, the Pietists made a sharp distinction between the theology of the regenerate and the theology of the unregenerate, potentially identical in intellectual content and distinguished only by the piety of the individual. At the same time, they emphasized not only the inward renewal of the individual but also its outward manifestation in personal lifestyle and in social programs. The effect of these two perspectives, taken together, was to disengage doctrinal theology, despite its traditionally practical thrust, from the various manifestations of Christian practice. This particular form of the Pietist critique, moreover, has had a greater impact on modern theology than the model presented by Reformed orthodoxy in association with the *Nadere Reformatie* because of the rootage of much of Schleiermacher's thought in German Pietism. As Farley has pointed out, in the wake of Schleiermacher's reinterpretation of religion, theology, and the curriculum, the practical emphasis, coupled with religion, can exist independently of theology as an exercise in ministerial practice, while the classical disciplines of theology can become increasingly purely theoretical enterprises.[103] In contrast to this bifurcation, the approach of the Reformers and, perhaps even more so, that of their orthodox or scholastic successors, points toward a unity of theory and practice, of learning and piety, and potentially toward a way out of our contemporary dilemma.

7

Vera Philosophia cum sacra Theologia nusquam pugnat

Keckermann on Philosophy, Theology, and the Problem of Double Truth

"Assuredly, no one can be a theologian except he become one without Aristotle." So wrote Martin Luther in his *Disputation against Scholastic Theology* of 1517.[1] According to Luther, philosophical knowledge was, at best, superficial: it discerned the one God but knew nothing of his identity as Trinity; it examined essences but failed to perceive either the present purpose or the end of man as ordained by God.[2] Calvin also was profoundly aware of the limitation of human reason and of the danger of placing too much confidence in the product of reason or philosophy: "one can read competent and apt statements about God here and there in the philosophers. . . . But they saw things in such a way that their seeing did not direct them to the truth, much less enable them to attain it."[3] Luther, Calvin, and the other early Reformers had little interest in elaborating a positive relationship between faith and philosophy. This is, of course, not to say that there was total antipathy to philosophical learning or, indeed, to the entirety of the scholastic past on the part of either Luther or Calvin.[4] On the Lutheran side, Melanchthon continued to teach Aristotelian logic and rhetoric, and among the Reformed, Vermigli maintained the outlines of his early Thomism, defining theology as both contemplative and practical.[5]

Melanchthon himself manifests the gradual rapprochement of revelation and reason in the theology of the Reformation. The first edition of his *Loci communes* (1521) contained a polemic against philosophy and scholasticism. Later editions omitted the polemic and treated natural reason as a preliminary source of truth, preparatory to revelation. Melanchthon could speak of a God-given "law of nature" implanted in the creature at creation and weakened, but not entirely extinguished, by sin. Again, the natural man, after the Fall, has an imperfect knowledge of God, which remains sufficient to induce obedience, although ultimately capable of leading the sinner only to an imperfect knowledge of the true God, a knowledge insufficient for salvation.[6] Without pressing the point as far as Hans Engelland—who argues that Melanchthon allowed scriptural revelation "only supplementary significance" in theology—we can conclude that Melanchthon's view of the relation of revelation and reason, theology and philosophy was fairly positive in comparison to that of Luther and, as frequently has been said, pointed the Reformation toward its scholastic formulation.[7] This is particularly apparent in Melanchthon's use of the proofs of God's existence.[8] (Also of significance here are the curricular shifts that took place at Wittenberg—after an initial demand in 1518 for better texts of Aristotle, the metaphysics, physics, and ethics were excluded from the curriculum, circa 1520—with the ethics returning in 1529.[9] The curricular loss of Aristotle's metaphysics, belongs, oddly, as much to the general tendency of the era as it does to the Reformation protest, given its deletion from the curriculum of Roman Catholic universities as well.)[10]

Reformed theology, in the person of Peter Martyr Vermigli, received much the same impetus toward the appropriation of philosophy that Lutheranism received from Melanchthon. The *Loci communes* collected out of Vermigli's writings by Robert Masson (1576) contain two discussions of this issue, the first on the natural knowledge of God,[11] and the second on the specific issue of the relation of philosophy to theology.[12] God's power, eternity, and divinity can be known to the natural man even though he be given over to unrighteousness. Like Melanchthon, Vermigli can speak of a *lumen naturale* according to which "divine things" are known—*anticipationes* and *informationes* implanted in the human spirit by God—which convey glimpses of the divine nature. This innate capacity, moreover, enables man to observe the created order and there find confirmation of inwardly known truths. This is, nevertheless, a knowledge of God quite apart from saving truth.[13] Philosophy, then, is a true wisdom, *sapientia*, a *habitus mentis*, a gift of God, a light and instruction to the soul. Paul intends no assault on *vera philosophia* when he attacks worldly wisdom but only a warning against the false inventions of ambitious men and the ineptitude of pagan thinkers. So far was Vermigli from condemning all philosophy that he commented on the *Nichomachean Ethics* of Aristotle—which, in point of fact, remained the text for the basic ethics course throughout the sixteenth century.[14]

When subsequent generations of Protestant theologians attempted to formulate more clearly and systematically the theological insights of the Reformation—in short, as they developed the academic and institutional forms of theology usually identified as "scholastic orthodoxy"—there was an increasing need to define the relationship of theology to the other academic disciplines.[15] The nature of this transition and whether the scholastic forms of Protestant thought remained in continuity with the teaching of the Reformers is the broader issue debated among historians of the era, with the older scholarship tending to view the thought of the Reformation as largely discontinuous with both the preceding and the subsequent scholastic theology and tending also to view "scholasticism" more as a content than a method,[16] the more recent scholarship tending to argue continuities extending from the later Middle Ages, through the Reformation into the era of orthodoxy, tending to understand scholasticism primarily as a method, and recognizing the alterations in scholastic method brought about by shifts in the understanding of logic and rhetoric during the Renaissance and Reformation.[17]

At issue here are both the development and change that took place in Protestant theology as it inherited and absorbed these problems and also the continuity that it sought to maintain with the principles of the Reformation.[18] For the Reformed orthodox, given both their rootage in the Reformation and its assumptions of *sola scriptura* and *sola fide* and their need, in the institutionalized context of the newly Protestant universities and academies struggling toward reestablishment of a full curriculum, the old questions concerning the relationship of philosophy to theology and of reason to faith were raised with some intensity.[19] Along with these fundamental questions, the nagging problem of double truth—can a statement be true *secundum rationem* but false *secundum fidem?*—also reared its head.[20] It is this question, in the context of the larger curricular development of the Protestant academy, that I now proceed to examine in the thought of Bartholomaus Keckermann Dantsicanus (1571–1609). The problem arose for Keckermann in his work as rector of the gymnasium at Danzig, where he had curricular and institutional responsibilities. In other words, the relationship between philosophy and theology was not merely an abstract issue but a concrete question of the reception of tradition, the creation of curriculum, and the conduct of the Protestant academy in the late sixteenth century.[21]

Philosophy and Theology: Problems and Definitions

In his brief career as teacher (1597–1609), Bartholomaus Keckermann belies the generalization made more than a half century ago by A. C. McGiffert that "Protestant scholasticism" did not attempt "to cover the whole field of human knowledge" but "confined" itself "strictly to the sphere of theology."[22] It is true, as McGiffert noted of the Protestant scholastics, that Keckermann made no concerted attempt "to bring science and philosophy and politics under the dominion of religion," but Keckermann did investigate and lecture on nearly all the topics in the range of academic discipline, and he did begin, in the last phase of his career, to draw some of the strands together.[23] Indeed, Keckermann's broad scope stands in clear continuity with the efforts of the next generation of Protestant thinkers, like the Herborn "encyclopedists," Bisterfeld and Alsted, to discuss and control a vast body of knowledge in the curriculum of the Protestant academy or university.[24] Keckermann's effort, moreover, did not pass unnoticed in his own day; Paraeus remarked that the rapid appearance in so short a time of such a vast sum of learning had the effect of "sibylline oracles publicly delivered," while several treatises against Keckermann's Aristotelian logic were written, for the most part out of Wittenberg.[25]

Among modern scholars, W. H. Zuylen took up the task of surveying Keckermann's encyclopedic project and argued that Keckermann envisioned a circle of the disciplines related, indeed, profoundly interconnected, by an interdisciplinary dynamic moving from the theoretical to the practical, from universal to individual and particular truths.[26] The theoretical and universal point of departure of academic study Zuylen characterizes as a "theosophy"—a theoretical science in which the doctrine of God given by revelation and the conception of God available from metaphysics would draw together into a unified body of knowledge. This science would, in turn, become the ground of the theoretical sciences (physics, mathematics, astronomy, geography, optics, and music) and of the practical sciences (ethics, economics, and politics). Finally, the whole series of disciplines would resolve into the practical science concerning the end, or goal, of life—theology.[27] The problem identified by the older scholarship as characteristic of early Protestant scholasticism in general is identified by Zuylen as belonging to Keckermann in particular: natural theology intrudes on the faith and governs the system of knowledge as a whole; rational knowledge of God, rather than the distinctively Christian view of God as revealed in Christ, becomes the dominant principle. Indeed, Zuylen declares, echoing the radical christocentrism of his era rather than attending to the more traditional accents of the sixteenth and seventeenth centuries, Keckermann has forgotten "that there can be no doctrine of God for Christians without Christ."[28]

Setting aside, momentarily, the heavy bias of Zuylen's judgment, it is worth noting some of the continuities between Keckermann's curricular project and what preceded his efforts in earlier sixteenth-century Protestantism. Keckermann's synoptic view of the presuppositions of philosophy, logic, physics, astronomy, geography, metaphysics, ethics, economics,[29] politics, rhetoric (both secular and Christian), and systematic theology covered topics not usually taught by a single person, adumbrating the encyclopedic efforts of his somewhat younger contemporaries, Johann Bisterfeld and Alsted.[30] Still, this list of disciplines has much in common with Hyperius's summary, published in 1556, of the Johann fields of study "necessary" as adjuncts for theological training—grammar, logic, and rhetoric (the *trivium*), arithmetic, geometry, music, and astronomy (the *quadrivium*), philosophy, physics, ethics, politics, oeconomics, metaphysics, history, architecture, and agriculture, and the study of languages, specifically, Latin, Greek, and Hebrew.[31] Indeed, except for geography and the course on specifically Christian rhetoric, all of Keckermann's subject areas were assumed to be necessary by a university theologian of the Reformation era. Zuylen may have been correct in registering surprise at a theologian daring to write manuals on such varied disciplines—but he was certainly incorrect in understanding Keckermann's curriculum as indicative of a massive intellectual shift in Protestantism.

Nor, I would argue, was Keckermann's concern for the relationship of philosophy to theology entirely discontinuous with the earlier Reformed tradition, as implied in the previous comments on Vermigli. Without engaging in excessive speculation concerning the reason for Keckermann's interest in the relation between theology and philosophy, it is well that we observe the coincidence of the chronology of his academic career with that of the great Lutheran controversy of his day, Daniel Hoffmann's attack on the harlot philosophy.[32] In 1592, Keckermann arrived in Heidelberg fresh from his university studies in Wittenberg and Leipzig. The following year, 1593, saw the beginning of the rupture between Hoffmann and his philosophical colleagues in the newly founded university of Helmstedt, barely seventy-five miles from Wittenberg. During the time of Keckermann's stay in Heidelberg (1592–1601), Hoffmann declared the absolute opposition of faith and reason, theology and philosophy, to the point of refusing philosophy any place in the Christian university—what is true according to philosophy is false according to theology. Indeed, the antagonism of the one for the other may be taken as a sign of the virtue and truth of theology—for philosophers, lost souls that they are, declare lies about the true God. Needless to say, Hoffmann became unpopular with the philosophical faculty at Helmstedt. By 1602, as Keckermann made his way home from Heidelberg to Danzig (perhaps by way of Wittenberg and Leipzig) to assume the post of rector in the gymnasium, the philosophers of Helmstedt had secured condemnation and deprivation of Hoffmann.[33] When Keckermann reached Danzig, he was ready to engage in the great issue of the day, the relation of philosophy to theology.

In the lectures on systematic theology that he had delivered privately at Heidelberg, Keckermann had laid the groundwork of definition for the theological side of his mature argument. Theology, he had argued, was *operatrix*, an "operative discipline," a "praxis," involving faith and life—not at all a *nuda notitia*, a mere or naked knowledge.[34] As such, it was distinct from those disciplines, like philosophy, that have a speculative or contemplative dimension. Theology, as a unified and practical discipline, must be classed as *prudentia* rather than *scientia*; whereas a metaphysician discusses God as Being, insofar as metaphysics is the science of Being, the theologian presents God the end, the *finis*, of all things. The end of theology is not the contemplation but the enjoyment of God, the *fruitio Dei*.[35]

Keckermann's use of the Augustinian motif of *fruitio Dei* in the context of his definition of theology as *operatrix disciplina* relates directly to the chief theological influence on his early systematizing effort–the theology of Zacharias Ursinus as embodied in that author's exposition of the Heidelberg Catechism. There the analytical method predominated. Beginning with the theme of comfort and pointing to the glory of God as chief end and the enjoyment of God as subsidiary end related directly to the problem of human existence, Ursinus developed a system teaching of the progress toward those ends. This practical focus and analytic (as opposed to synthetic) method impressed Keckermann deeply. His own system would be a modification of the analytical pattern.[36] Keckermann's direct and admitted reliance on Ursinus points us also to a continuity of development in Reformed and, to a certain extent, Lutheran theology. The great influences on Ursinus's intellectual development were Melanchthon, under whom he had studied in Wittenberg, and Vermigli, with whom he stayed and studied in Zurich.[37] We may point, therefore, to a fairly direct line connecting Keckermann with Vermigli and Melanchthon, the first major reformers to deal positively with the issue of the relation of philosophy to theology. Ursinus also had dealt with the issue briefly in a prolegomenon to theology belonging to his posthumous *Loci theologici* and published in several of the early editions of the catechetical lectures.[38]

At the very heart of Keckermann's thought, in the view of theology as practical and analytic rather than contemplative and synthetic, lay a methodological distinction designed to reduce the potential conflict of the disciplines. Whereas Vermigli had followed a Thomist pattern by defining both theology and philosophy as at once contemplative and practical, creating broad areas of correlation between disciplines, Keckermann followed a more Augustinian or perhaps Scotist view of theology, thereby reducing areas of correspondence.[39] Nevertheless, an interrelation and overlap remained. Keckermann accepted the Aristotelian view of philosophy as set forth in the *Metaphysics*. In Keckermann's words, philosophy is "a habit of mind through which we know divine, natural, and human things," and, therefore, broadly (*laté* as opposed to *stricté*) speaking, a *doctrina* or *eruditio* dealing with will as well as intellect, with *prudentia* as much as *scientia*.[40] Following the definition of the sixteenth-century metaphysician Fortunatus Crellius, Keckermann referred to philosophy also as "a habit of soul which consists in wisdom and prudence."[41]

Philosophy must be both theoretical and practical, both *contemplatrix* and *actrix* or *operatrix*, consisting in the subdisciplines of grammar, rhetoric, logic, physics, mathematics, metaphysics, ethics, economics, and politics.[42] Substantively, theology and philosophy both deal with divine things, human things, and modes of discourse; the study of God, of ethics, and of rhetoric belong to both. Since, moreover, ethics and rhetoric are "operative" in philosophy as well as in theology, there is methodological as well as substantive correlation.[43] Clearly, given this perspective and this sense of academic responsibility for the broad range of intellectual pursuit, Keckermann was pressed toward a formal answer to the question of faith and reason and toward a solution to the problem of double truth on a level unfamiliar to the reformers of the earlier part of the sixteenth century.

"Thesis: Vera Philosophia cum sacra Theologia nusquam pugnat"

"True philosophy in no way disputes sacred theology"—so Keckermann entitles the first thesis for discussion immediately following his two books of "philosophical presuppositions." He begins by declaring that there are no "universal principles" and no "conclusions or rules" of philosophy that are refuted or controverted by the principles, conclusions, or rules of theology: "the truth of theology and philosophy is but one and simple, so that it may not be construed that there is one philosophical truth and another theological truth."[44] Nor is it possible to have "something true in philosophy that is false in theology."[45] In the first place, there is no contradiction in form and method. Philosophy, as both speculative and practical, embraces both synthetic and analytic methods, concurring with theology in its use of the analytic method. The differences in material or subject between philosophy and theology provide no point of contention, since differences in terms and material do not necessarily lead to contradiction between fundamental propositions.[46]

In the syllogistic argument that follows, Keckermann asserts the priority of principle over conclusion, of presupposition over subsequent argumentation; if this assertion is accepted, then the absence of contradiction between the presuppositions of theology and philosophy provides a ground for the potential agreement of the disciplines themselves. Philosophical principles like "the whole is greater than the part" carry over into theology, while ethicophilosophical maxims as *honeste est vivendum* in no way contradict such theological presuppositions such as *Deus est justus, vindex peccatorum* or *Deus remittit peccata propter filium*, for the morals of good and honorable men can only reinforce piety. Since, moreover, the things of which theology and philosophy treat are not mutually repugnant—as, for example, God and his creatures—neither ought the disciplines to be mutually repugnant.[47] Deeper still than these reasons for agreement is the fact that all wisdom is a gift of God:

> The gifts of God do not conflict with one another,
> But philosophy is a gift of God; Exodus 31:3; Psalms 94:10; Sirach 1:1; 11 Chronicles 1:12; Daniel 2:21, "he gives wisdom to the wise"; Romans 1:19; James 1:17.
> Therefore it does not conflict with the gifts of God, which is to say, with theology.[48]

Only the lies of the devil are repugnant to the "word of God and sacred theology"; surely that philosophy that is the wisdom concerning natural things—the heavens, the elements, quantity and number, music and morality—is not from the devil but from the Creator himself. There will always be disagreement and strife, Keckermann avers, between errorists and heretics, but error ought no more to be confused with *vera philosophia* than heresy with *sacra theologia*.[49]

In his next series of syllogisms, Keckermann presents a more philosophically substantive argument, drawn from presuppositions concerning the unity and univocity of truth and the universal consonance of the good:

> VII. That which is one and simple cannot be contrary to itself.
> Truth is one and simple, whether conveyed by theology or by philosophy, and is true consistently wherever it is presented (for indeed the distinction of disciplines does not multiply truth).

> Therefore truth is not contrary to itself whether presented in theology or in philosophy.
> VIII. That which is one and simple is not multiplied.
> Truth is one and simple.
> Therefore truth is not multiplied, and by consequence not divided, as one thing in theology, another in philosophy.
> IX. Good does not conflict with good, but stands in perpetual concord
> Philosophy itself is good and deals with a double good, the natural and the moral.
> Therefore it does not conflict with sacred theology, which is itself good and which deals with spiritual good.[50]

As a teacher of theology and philosophy in an age preoccupied with syllogistic logic, Keckermann surely realized that his arguments would fall short of convincing a dedicated proponent of double truth; after all, he never proves the presupposition that truth is in fact one and simple. His arguments, like the subsequent mention of citations of the pagan philosophers Aratus and Menander by the Apostle Paul,[51] are important not so much for what they prove as for the presuppositions they state, the theological and philosophical milieu they represent, and the direction in Protestant thinking they adumbrate. Whereas Protestantism at the beginning of the sixteenth century was concerned to show its divergence from the sophisticated and barely biblical philosophizing of the late medieval scholastics, Protestantism at the end of the century was concerned to utilize as fully as possible the resources of tradition to buttress its newly erected system. Accordingly, Keckermann concludes that nothing truly known of God's power or divinity can be repugnant to theology: "In sum, the natural knowledge of God is not contrary to the supernatural, knowledge gained from nature is not repugnant to knowledge gained by grace, the book of nature does not overturn the book of scripture: therefore neither does philosophy conflict with theology."[52] In support of this opinion, he cites Augustine's *De trinitate*, Clement of Alexandria's *Stromata*, the Third Lateran Council (1180), Philip Mornay's preface to his *De veritate religionis Christianae*, and the prolegomena to Zacharias Ursinus's catechetical lectures.[53] If the positive epistemological relationship here established between nature and grace, natural reason and revelation were not enough to convince us of the distance traversed by Protestant thought since Luther's assault on the *theologia gloriae*, Keckermann's positive citation of the Third Lateran Council ought to make clear the issue—as should the authorities cited by Keckermann in his *Praecognitorum Philosophicorum* on the question of the inclusion of logic among the philosophical disciplines—the Stoics, the Academics, and "post hunc Boetius, Albertus Magnus & plerique Thomistae."[54]

Arguing in favor of this positive relation between the *liber naturae* and the *liber scripturae*, Keckermann next establishes the *termini* and *limites* of faith and reason, theology and philosophy and does so in a manner reminiscent of Thomas Aquinas's careful distinction between the two orders of knowing. There are four basic rules to be observed in defining the truth or falsity or the opposition of two propositions. First, both propositions must be free of ambiguity in both subject and predicate. Second, they also must be accurately opposed in the parts and character of the subject and must refer to the same issue and to the same time: there must be a violation of the law of noncontradiction. Keckermann does not debate just the assertion that a thing true in philosophy can be false in theology. The assertion needs to be clarified. Error and illogic occur when a statement true in philosophy is said to be false in the same respect and in the same manner when it is transferred to theology. Most so-called double truths can be ruled out of court by these first two rules of argument.[55] Beyond this simple logic, however, there lies the issue of the relationship of the two disciplines and the two orders of knowing and the third rule, namely, that subordination does not imply contradiction: "Human things are not opposed to divine, nor natural things to supernatural, rather they are subordinate. . . . [T]he creature depends upon the creator as an effect upon a cause; between causes and effects there is no conflict, but the fullest agreement."[56] As a fourth and final rule, touching the working relationship of the two distinct but not entirely separate orders, Keckermann asserts, "That which philosophy does not treat, neither does it refute, but concedes and even embraces or otherwise confirms it."[57] The dicta of philosophy have final negative authority only over matters belonging to the discipline of philosophy.

Against these arguments theologians cite the caveat of Saint Paul (Colossians 2:8) that Christians be not seduced by "philosophy and vain deceits." Here, we may fairly well assume that Keckermann has Daniel Hoffmann in mind. These writers, Keckermann continues, claim that philosophy is damned and ought to be eliminated from the church (*damnanda est & eliminanda ex Ecclesiis*) because it opposes the "word of God and the doctrine of the Gospel." Not content with his own arguments, Keckermann cites against the Lutheran Hoffmann other Lutheran authors; in Philip Melanchthon's commentary on Colossians we read that Paul does not condemn true philosophy but, rather, a false teaching and, indeed, the confused doctrine of crass Pelagians and monks—who erroneously conceive that man can satisfy the law of God, perfectly implement its demands, and merit remission of sins. Melanchthon's great pupil Victorinus Strigel argued similarly in his *Dialectica* that Paul condemns not philosophy itself but the corruption and imposture of sinful minds.[58]

It also might be argued that, since man is in conflict with God and since philosophy is a human invention, philosophy must naturally conflict with the divine gift, theology. Keckermann has already answered this question syllogistically, but he now elaborates, as if against an opposing syllogism. The argument is false both in the *major* and in the *minor*; it is not true in all respects that man is in conflict with God, nor is it true that philosophy is entirely a human invention.[59] A similar false antithesis occurs when it is argued that philosophy, as a function of human reason, must conflict with theology, which stands apart from reason. Again, a scholastic consideration enters—that which is above reason does not conflict with reason.[60]

Keckermann now comes to specifics. Since philosophy simply does not include within its purview such ideas as the redemption of mankind by the merit of Christ or the resurrection and its causes or the glorification of the body, it can no more refute these concepts than theology, which does not treat of the methods of healing the body, can refute or dismiss medicine. By the same token, philosophy does not really deny the doctrine of the virgin birth; for theology and philosophy agree that in the normal course of events virgins do not conceive and bear and remain virgins! And neither philosophy nor theology should deny that, in the extraordinary event recorded in the Bible, one virgin did conceive and bear a child by the supernatural power of the Most High.[61] More interesting from the point of view of logical argumentation are Keckermann's views on creation and the Trinity. It might appear that the dictum *ex nihilo nihil fit* is true in philosophy but false in theology. The problem here, however, is not contradiction but ambiguity of original statement. The philosopher in this statement correctly asserts *ex nihilo nihil generatur*, and no theologian would disagree. What theology teaches in its doctrine is not generation from nothing but creation from nothing, what it derides as false is the proposition *ex nihilo nihil creatur*. True philosophy recognizes both the error of the theory of the eternity of the world and the truth of the doctrine that a God infinite in power needs no preexistent material when he fashions his world.[62] A comparable imprecision in argument poses the simple dictum of philosophy "one is not three" against the mystery of the Trinity; yet no theologian claims that God is three in the same way that God is one—for God is one in respect of essence and three in respect, not of essence, but of person.[63]

Philosophy as Necessary to the Theological Enterprise

The development of scholastic Protestantism in the writings of Keckermann and his contemporaries meant not only the calling of a truce between Athens and Jerusalem but also the positive appropriation of philosophy by the authors of theological system.[64] If Luther did not entirely outgrow the thought-world of late medieval nominalism or Calvin ever fully set aside the Aristotelianism of his scholastic and "Sorbonnist" adversaries, they did, quite clearly, minimize the positive use of the older scholastic categories both theological and philosophical.[65] Even those writers of the mid-sixteenth century who adhered more closely to the categories of late medieval thought—such as the Thomist-trained Vermigli and Zanchi—cannot be called philosopher-theologians and cannot be fully separated from the powerful biblicism of the early Reformation.[66] With Keckermann's assertion of the agreement of philosophy and theology, however, a new dimension, a strongly metaphysical and philosophical component, is added to Protestantism. "Philosophy," wrote Keckermann, "is of the highest utility and greatest necessity to the study of theology: first, to the positive teaching or precepts of theology; second, to theological disputation or controversy, elenctical theology."[67]

Philosophy stands as an aid to the comprehension of things both "in Scriptura S. vel extra Scripturam in Systemate Theologico."[68] Many terms in Scripture itself relate directly to philosophy. The identification of God as existent and as good belongs to metaphysics, the teaching concerning creation and the order of creation to physics. Much in scripture—in the books of Moses, in Psalms, in Job, and in Isaiah—ought to be understood in the light of physics, geography, and astronomy. Philosophy also provides help in understanding fully the implications of the birth of Christ, the union and distinction of natures in his person, and his miracles. Similarly, in theological system philosophy identifies the *finis theologiae*, the *fruitio Dei*, as the *summum bonum*. The *principium* or foundation of theology, God, his essence, his existence, and his mode of existence "cannot be accurately explained by anyone without metaphysics."[69] Keckermann also distinguishes between "pure" and "mixed conclusions"; pure conclusions derive from one discipline alone, but mixed conclusions draw on terms common to more than one discipline. Theology, therefore, when it poses mixed conclusions on the theoretical level looks to metaphysics and when on the practical level to ethics, economics, and politics.[70] For Keckermann, faith and reason are inextricably linked at the point of understanding; indeed, in a truly Anselmic sense, his is a *fides quaerens intellectum*. For his theology is not *nuda notitia* neither is it *nuda fides*, but the faithful apprehension of a body of doctrine that must, if it is to be properly apprehended, also be understood.

This position on the relation of theology and philosophy, faith and reason, is a fully scholastic appreciation of and resolution to the problem and raises pointedly the question of the historical direction taken by Protestant orthodoxy and of the continuity or discontinuity of Protestant orthodoxy with the Reformation. As Paul Althaus has argued, Keckermann's work represents both a development and a compromise; metaphysical, indeed, ontological language quite absent from Reformed doctrine at the stage represented by Calvin's *Institutes* or Bullinger's *Compendium christianae religionis* now appears as essential to theology.[71] Aristotle, the philosophical elements of patristic theology, and the late patristic synthesis of John of Damascus together influenced Keckermann's formulation of the doctrine of God. This means that orthodoxy cannot be characterized simply as Aristotelian or Thomist or even Scotist; instead, we encounter in orthodoxy an accommodation to the philosophical aspect of the tradition analogous to the development of scholasticism in the thirteenth century. The accessibility of new tools, specifically the Aristotelian corpus and the philosophically oriented Damascene, alters and enriches the scope of theology. Althaus points to the scholastic identification of the *essentia* and the *ens Dei* by Keckermann, the qualification of this definition by recourse to the language of the Damascene—God as *huperousios*, supersubstantial—and the equation of essence and act in God.[72] The transcendence of God and the a priori character of our knowledge of God remain the primary emphases throughout these elaborations, but acknowledgment of the Aristotelian metaphysic as legitimate tempers this theological position with a sense of the indirect knowledge of God available a posteriori to philosophy.[73]

Zuylen differs strongly with Althaus on this point. Keckermann, he argues, did not develop a natural theology. From one point of view, Zuylen is correct. Keckermann did not predicate his doctrine of God, whether in its metaphysical or its theological aspect, on *a posteriori* proofs of the divine existence. If Keckermann had, as Zuylen assumes, impressed a primarily Thomist viewpoint on Reformed dogmatics, the absence of the *a posteriori* argumentation would be significant.[74] If, however, *theologia naturalis* indicates not only the five proofs from the created order but also the broader use of natural reason in theological matters, Keckermann does indeed develop natural theology. Thus, in his *locus de Dei essentia*, Keckermann discusses the "duplicita adminicula Deum cognoscendi"—the natural and the supernatural.[75] The latter he identifies with divine revelation, the former with the threefold pattern of argument set forth by Dionysius the Pseudo-Areopagite: the *via eminentiae*, *via negationis*, and *via causationis*. Althaus, I believe, is ultimately more accurate, since he both recognizes the presence of formative use of natural reason in Keckermann's system and, at the same time, sees a scholasticism not entirely Thomistic in origin in Keckermann's thought. Keckermann sees no need for theology to prove the existence of God, but he also allows reason to function within the bounds of theology.

Development and change such as this was neither unconscious nor unintentional. Keckermann and his contemporaries were nearly as sensitive to these issues as modern historians, although from a different perspective. This becomes immediately apparent in Keckermann's presentation of the elenctical or controversial use of philosophy. Philosophy supplements theology in those areas of terminological overlap where mixed conclusions must be drawn and provides a necessary aid against the "sophisms dreamed up by the adversaries" of true theology. Indeed, philosophy stands as a most necessary weapon in defense of the basic positions of Reformed theology.[76] Keckermann clearly recognized that a theology seeking to defend itself against the arsenal of sophisticated weapons—metaphysical, logical, rhetorical—possessed by Roman Catholic polemicists would have to develop equally competent weapons. Indeed, on the polemical side of its development, Protestant orthodoxy manifests all the characteristics of an arms race, albeit intellectual. He cites the great "injury" contemplated against "evangelical theology" by a polemicist like Melchior Cano, who accused the Lutherans (and with them all of the Reformation) of abdicating, after the manner of Epicureans and Saracens, all claim to rational doctrine. According to Cano, evangelical theology was a mass of error and absurdity incapable of discerning the order or connection of divine and human things, unable *adequately* to deal with "the causes, effects, antecedents and consequences of things."[77]

Against this assault, Keckermann posed a view of Protestantism as philosophically adequate, a view that manifests a desire for continuity with the early reformers but that also manifests a sense of development. Luther, comments Keckermann, was a "sound" (*sanè*) and Zwingi a superb (*optimi*) philosopher. After them Melanchthon, a "most excellent" philosopher, provided arguments both "admirable and formidable" against the "popish adversaries." But the truly great Protestant philosophers were Peter Martyr Vermigli and Jerome Zanchi—men eminent in dispute and of great acumen in philosophical matters: "Sed & magni Philosophi fuerunt Petrus Martyr & Hieronymous Zanchius, quorum scripta & disputationes egregia habent Philosophici acuminis specimina." That "perspicacious man" Zacharias Ursinus and others, such as Antonio Sadeel and Benedictus Aretius, also argued well and demonstrated in dispute the usefulness of philosophy to Protestant and evangelical theology.[78] The list, incidentally, is as significant for its exclusions as it is for its inclusions and its view of Protestantism; neither Calvin nor Beza are mentioned. With the exception of Sadeel, a Genevan thinker connected with the *Harmonia confessionum ecclesiae reformatae* (1580), the Germanic side of the Swiss Reformation—Zurich and Bern—and the Heidelberg theology provide the examples of sound argument. In these thinkers Keckermann seems to envision a continuity of validly philosophical theology that, presumably, testified consistently to the concord of philosophical with theological truth and the unity of truth itself, rejecting only error and heresy. This means also that Keckerman felt, apart from the errors of medieval speculation so powerfully rejected by the reform, a continuity between the theology of Reformation and of Protestant orthodoxy and the theology of the great medieval scholastics. With Flacius in the *Magdeburg Centuries*, he would have listed Aquinas among the seven thousand who refused to bow to Baal.[79] Whereas the mood of recent historiography has favored a theory of discontinuity between the Reformation and its orthodox or scholastic development, at least as great as that discontinuity traditionally seen between the Reformation and the Middle Ages, Keckermann and his contemporaries would have allowed only a minimal difference and that chiefly in style or organization of material; in Christian doctrine and in philosophical presuppositions they saw continuity.

The phenomenon to which Keckermann testifies is the continuity of Aristotelian scholasticism as the intellectual underpinning of theology and philosophy from the thirteenth to the seventeenth centuries.[80] He testifies also to the idea that, if this underpinning were dissolved or were suddenly acknowledged to be averse to theology, the possibility of intelligible discourse would also vanish. As Kristeller observes, "During the fifteenth and sixteenth centuries, university education in the philosophical disciplines continued everywhere to be based on the works of Aristotle . . . in spite of Luther's dislike for scholasticism, and thanks to the influence of Melanchthon."[81] Keckermann, we must remember, was not occupied with the establishment of an exegetical foundation for the theology of reform (that had been accomplished by Luther, Melanchthon, Bucer, Calvin, Vermigli, and their contemporaries), nor did he need to prove the need for a Protestant school-theology (that had been fully recognized by Ursinus, Zanchi, Beza, and others of the generation immediately preceding his own). What Keckermann attempted was the organization and development of a complete curriculum for a Protestant gymnasium. He could hardly foster an academy where two mutually hostile views of God and world opposed one another in daily lectures.

Keckermann's collected works, then, provide a picture of a coordinated, late-sixteenth-century, Protestant curriculum in which the Aristotelian corpus, augmented by geography, parallels and supplements the body of Christian knowledge. Metaphysics and physics aid in the analysis of God and his works, clarifying, for the sake of enriching finite minds, the higher truth of revelation. It was no accident that the Genevan-trained Lambert Daneau, in the same era, entitled his study of the six days of creation *Physica Christiana*. Philosophical ethics stood beside Christian ethics, even as classical rhetoric was, in Keckermann's curriculum, paralleled by Christian rhetoric.[82]

Conclusions

Throughout this chapter, I have posed the problem of continuity and discontinuity in sixteenth-century Protestant thought, or, if we accept the perspective of the early orthodox period, continuity with development, elaboration, and clarification. The perspective of the present sees somewhat more clearly the problem of altering method and of reintroducing or developing terminology without also affecting content.[83] In speaking of the Reformation as a partial departure from medieval theology and piety, we must not underestimate the Reformers' sense of true catholicity—as witnessed, for example, by the vast use of patristic sources in Calvin's *Institutes* and by the respect evinced, in the same place, for a medieval thinker like Bernard of Clairvaux.[84] Nor should we underestimate the profound continuities between the thought of the Reformers and main streams in the medieval tradition. Calvin's contemporary, Wolfgang Musculus, frequently cited Peter Lombard for standard theological definition.[85] The early orthodox phase of Protestant theology did bring about an important change in the forms and patterns of thought; indeed, what occurred at the hands of men like Bartholomaus Keckermann was a formalization, a strict patterning, even a rationalization of the Reformation. The protest had become established in its own normative expression that, by a virtual historical necessity, sought not only to maintain its continuity with the Reformation but that also sought to affirm the claim, resident in the protest itself, of a fundamental continuity with all that was truly Catholic and all that was universally true in the Western tradition.

This generalization, particularly the desire to maintain a twofold continuity, is borne out clearly in Keckermann's Reformed scholasticism and Christian philosophy, in a graphic way in his argument against double truth. On the one side lay the immediate problem posed for the late sixteenth century by Daniel Hoffmann; a rigid reprise of Luther's polemic against reason and philosophy threatened to produce a blind fideism narrow in its vision and little capable of rational defense. On the other side lay the memory of the antitheological theory of double truth set forth in the Middle Ages by the so-called Latin Averroists of Paris and more recently by Pietro Pomponazzi wherein philosophy effectually was set above theology or at the very least over against theology to the detriment of Christian doctrine.[86] Keckermann chose the pattern of his continuity carefully: theological continuity with the early reformers, Luther and Zwingli, by way of the more philosophically minded men of the second generation, Melanchthon, Vermigli, Zanchi, Ursinus; philosophical and, to a limited extent, methodological continuity with the older scholasticism by way of a modified Thomistic pattern that set faith and theology carefully in accord with but nevertheless above reason and philosophy. And on both sides of this pattern—for here we are dealing with *conclusiones mixtae*—Keckermann could affirm the oneness of God and of God's truth. The alliance here forged between philosophy and theology—between rational thought and Protestant orthodoxy—would hold for more than a century.

Without engaging in a lengthy examination of individual doctrinal topics, some mention must be made of the effect of this alteration of perspective and broadened use of philosophy and tradition. The most obvious point of comparison is the doctrine of God. Keckermann, in contrast to Calvin, concentrates on definition of the essence and attributes of God and calls on his knowledge of metaphysics to elaborate a full *locus de deo* in which Calvin had only pointed to those attributes revealed in Scripture.[87] The contrast is not so great, however, when Keckermann's doctrine is compared with that of Calvin's contemporary, Wolfgang Musculus of Bern, who developed at some length the doctrine of the divine attributes.[88] I also have, previously, noted the development of theology at the hands of Melanchthon and Vermigli. What has altered is the relative amount of emphasis on natural theology and, beyond that, on the use of reason. Keckermann places his doctrine of God prior to his doctrine of Scripture and makes little use of Scripture in the discussion of essence and attributes.[89]

Zuylen overstates his case for a major shift in Protestant thought evidenced by the Thomist or at least a medieval scholastic influence on Keckermann's view of the rational component of human nature. Keckermann does not, as Zuylen states, argue that human nature after the fall is "normal" and whole.[90] Where Calvin and, we add, Musculus and Vermigli postulated a nature so vitiated by sin that even the reason is corrupt and faith alone suffices as the ground of finding the true God in Scripture, Keckermann also can postulate a sinful human nature so fallen that reason fails to discern God rightly apart from the work of the Spirit—although he does not describe its faculties as quite as profoundly damaged as one might gather from a reading of Calvin's *Institutes*.[91] Yet, it is this reading of the *Institutes* and its use in establishing a trajectory of Reformed thought that creates the most significant problem for Zuylen's hypothesis: the intense noetic effect of sin indicated in Calvin's exposition in the *Institutes* and in his commentary on Romans 1:18ff does not carry over either into Calvin's commentaries on the Psalms or into the thought of contemporaries such as Vermigli and Musculus.[92] Calvin himself had declared a "knowledge of God the creator" accessible to human beings apart from Christ.[93] Vermigli, with less restriction than Calvin, declares that all things "the eternal power and divinity of God"—human nature, in particular, the soul, reflect the justice, and wisdom of God.[94] Nor is Zuylen's contrast between Keckermann's highly developed conception of the use of reason and a brief passage from the Heidelberg Catechism a suitable indication of contrasting views: Zuylen cites the twenty-sixth question and answer of the Heidelberg Catechism, arguing that even the "creator-God" is known only in Christ and for faith.[95] The passage reads, "Credo, aeternum Patrem domini nostri Iesu Christi, qui coelum & terram, cum omnibus, quae in iis sunt, ex nihilo creavit, quique eadem aeterno suo consilio & providentia sustenat ac gubernat: propter Christum, Deum meum & patrum meum esse"—"I believe that the eternal Father of our Lord Jesus Christ, who created out of nothing the heaven and the earth and all that is in them, and who sustains and governs them by his eternal counsel and providence, is my God and my Father on account of Christ." The identification here of the creator as the Father of Jesus Christ and therefore "our Father" does not in any way indicate the application of a Christological principle of knowledge to the doctrine of creation: the text indicates that we know the creator and ruler of the universe to be our Father because of Christ, but not that we need to know God as our Father in Christ in order to know that God is the creator and the sustainer of the universe! The catechism stands in accord with the notion of a *duplex cognitio Dei* found in Calvin and other early Reformed theologians: God is known generally as creator but only in Christ as Father and redeemer.[96] Keckermann, moreover, had read Ursinus' catechetical lectures, and Ursinus, coauthor of the catechism, not only implies no such principle in his exposition, but also includes reference to purely philosophical descriptions of God as creator, noting their value and limits.[97]

At the heart of the difference in emphasis between Keckermann and Calvin, moreover, is the significantly different context in which Keckermann lived and worked and the correspondingly different genres of the documents under comparison. Whereas Calvin's *Institutes* was a theological compendium designed for the training of candidates for ministry, in coordination with the study of Scripture, Keckermann's discourses on philosophy and the use of reason belong to the broader academic life of the Protestant academies and universities of the late sixteenth century. The issue for Keckermann was not the training of clergy but the development of a full curriculum for the Protestant school—and, more specifically, his context included the debate over double truth and the question of the validity of a philosophical component of the curriculum alongside of the theological component. His work, therefore, addressed more closely the relationship between the exercise of reason and value of conclusions drawn in both theology and philosophy.

In questions calling for "mixed conclusions" theology and philosophy can supplement one another because the *ratio* that stands as the fundamental principle in philosophy can come to an understanding, as a part of its normal function, of the contents of Scripture. If Keckermann's system seems to approach Scripture, in Zuylen's words, as the "wissenschaftliches Handbuch für die Erkenntnis Gottes,"[98] this view rests on Keckermann's denial of double truth and on his sense, shared by both medieval scholastics and the Reformers, that Scripture is the revelation of God presented in human words rather than on an unabated rationalism: human reason and the conclusions it draws from natural revelation cannot contradict the truth of the biblical revelation and in matters of salvation must be supplemented and transcended by it. There is, therefore, a point at which the rational initiative and natural theology fall short. If Keckermann was obliged to state a positive relationship of the elements of the academic curriculum and of the use of reason in the various disciplines, he was not obliged—indeed, he was prevented by his own principles—to allow the entrance of philosophy and purely rational enquiry into the specifically Christological and soteriological loci of his system. In these loci there are no *conclusiones mixtae*—discourse must be rational, but reason cannot govern discourse.

Zuylen's critique on this point arises out of a twentieth-century christocentric theology rather than out of an analysis of the sixteenth- and seventeenth-century materials. It would, in fact, be impossible to find a Reformation or post-Reformation era theologian claiming that Christ is the necessary focus of all God-language—for although doctrines in the older Reformed dogmatics such as the divine attributes, creation, and providence all recognized the trinitarian identity of God, none of them presumed a christological explanation. In effect, the rapprochement of Protestant theology with philosophy that took place in the writings of Keckermann and his contemporaries represents not a violation of Reformation principle but the elaboration of a positive, although nonsaving, knowledge of God within the bounds and under the terms of that very principle. This was not a knowledge of God that the reformers were inclined to emphasize, and its emphasis did bring about a more rationalistic theology, a different view of reason and its relation to certain components of theological system, and a stress on the knowledge component of faith, *notitia*, which although evident to the reformers had been greatly subordinated to *fiducia*. What we do not find is any great alteration of basic definition in Christology, in the *ordo salutis*, in the doctrines of church and sacraments.[99]

As Althaus, Zuylen, and Weber recognized, Keckermann must be counted as one of the pivotal thinkers in the development of scholastic Protestantism—we might add, in the development of the Protestant university. Where their verdict needs to be modified is in its generally negative appraisal of the impact of scholasticism and of Aristotelianism on the body of Protestant doctrine. For Keckermann's work, albeit more philosophical than that of his predecessors in the Reformed tradition and (despite the Danzig theologian's rationalization to the contrary) rather opposed to the views of Luther, did not bring about an unqualified intrusion of metaphysical categories into the nominally metaphysical topics of theological system, nor did it allow in any manner a priority of reason and philosophy over faith and theology.[100]

Keckermann's analysis of the problem of faith, reason, and double truth appears as an exercise not only in the positive appraisal but also in the delimitation of the bounds of philosophy. The result is different from the Reformation, but it cannot be called a triumph of rationalism. Indeed, if we look to the views of Luther cited at the outset, we find Keckermann in agreement but for one, albeit crucial, point: philosophy discerns God but cannot know the Trinity; it examines essences, but knows naught of the true meaning or end of human life—this Keckermann accepts; he refuses, however, to view the discussion of essences or of logic or of secular ethics and politics as superficial or as capable of being ignored by Christians in the academic context. "True philosophy" had regained its place as an adjunct to theological formulation.

8

Scholasticism Protestant and Catholic

Francis Turretin on the Object and Principles of Theology

Scholasticism Protestant and Catholic

During the past several decades, scholars have become more appreciatively aware of the medieval scholastic roots of Protestantism and have begun to gain some appreciation, albeit halting, of the scholastic form of Protestantism that dominated the Protestant universities in the seventeenth century. This awareness implies, in the first place, a development beyond the thesis advanced by Lortz and Bouyer that Protestantism was the effect of the decadent nominalist theology of the later Middle Ages.[1] Scholars such as Heiko Oberman, Bengt Hägglund, and David Steinmetz have acknowledged much of the continuity but have emphasized the positive character of late medieval thought.[2] Roman Catholic scholarship has produced positive readings of Scotist and nominalist theology,[3] and in the case of Donnelly's analysis of two sixteenth-century Protestant reformers, has noted—contra Lortz and Bouyer—the impact of Thomism on Protestant thought.[4] In the second place, more attention has been paid to the development of "scholastic" patterns in post-Reformation theology, and scholarship has moved considerably beyond the nineteenth- and early-twentieth-century thesis that Lutheranism developed into a "system of justification" while Calvinism moved toward a fully scholastic "predestinarian metaphysic."[5] Protestant scholasticism can now be represented as an attempt to produce not a restrictive system centered on a single doctrinal locus but, rather, a technically sophisticated school-theology. It was developed in part for the sake of debating Roman Catholic polemicists like the great Cardinal Bellarmine on the sophisticated level of his own scholasticism and in part for the sake of developing the implications of the Reformers' teaching for a full system of Christian doctrine.[6]

The positive side of this development is particularly apparent as Protestantism entered the seventeenth century, in the development of theological prolegomena or *loci* dealing with the topics of fundamental theology. This topic was not treated by Luther, Calvin, or their contemporaries. When the later generations of Protestant theologians approached the issue of theology as a discipline, they very naturally fell back on the theological prolegomena written by the great scholastics—Thomas Aquinas, Duns Scotus, Durandus, Thomas of Strasbourg.[7] Whereas we labor to detect the positive influences of such scholastics on the early Reformers and frequently find that antischolastic polemic makes difficult the identification of any specific positive use, we find that Protestant writers, beginning in the late sixteenth century, cite the medieval authors for opinion and even definition, without any polemical attack. Reformed systems, which developed prolegomena prior to the Lutherans, exhibit use not only of the typical distinction between *theologia in via* and *theologia in patria* but also of the Scotist distinction between *theologia in se* and *theologia nostra*.[8]

Turretin on the Nature and Genre of Theology

In Protestant circles, particularly among the Reformed, the name of Francis Turretin (1623–1687) is virtually synonymous with the term "Protestant scholasticism." Turretin's system, the *Institutio theologiae elencticae* (1679–1685), stands at the apex of the development of scholastic theology in the post-Reformation era, prior to the decline of Protestant system under the impact of rationalism, pietism, and the Enlightenment of the eighteenth century.[9] His thought is self- consciously scholastic and self-consciously Reformed, inasmuch as it echoes technical and methodological concerns parallel to those of the late Middle Ages and of the revived scholasticism of Zabarella and Suarez but also echoes the theological concerns of the Protestant reformers of the sixteenth century.[10] Because of his attempt (and the attempts of his contemporaries) to balance these two traditions, indeed, to utilize the former as a key to explicating and defending the latter, Turretin's theology has frequently been misunderstood, and, like the phenomenon of Protestant scholasticism in general, it has been viewed unsympathetically, particularly by Protestants.[11] In this chapter, I will examine the underlying principles of Turretin's theology and their historical roots, in an attempt to understand the phenomenon of Protestant scholasticism and its place in the history of Christian thought.

Determinative of Turretin's view of theology are his answers to two questions, whether theology is a science and whether theology is speculative or practical. These questions were crucial points argued in the prolegomena of theological systems of the scholastic age, from the early thirteenth century onward, but not specifically addressed in the theology of the Reformers. When Turretin asked the first of these questions, he meant much the same thing by *scientia* as did the medieval doctors. The rise of modern science was certainly evident in the seventeenth century, but the term *scientia* had not yet been restricted to the empirical and inductive disciplines. It still indicated a disciplined body of knowledge resting on evident principles. The widely used *Institutiones logicae* of the Leiden professor Franco Burgersdijk (1590–1635) indicates that "the word *scientia* is understood either as signifying any cognition or true assent; or, more strictly, a firm and infallible one; or lastly, as an assent to propositions made known by cause and effect."[12] A science is a discipline in which truth appears as rationally verifiable.

The dominance of this perspective led Turretin to deny to theology the status of science and to inquire, in some detail, into the precise "genus" of knowing to which theology belonged. Again, this issue was not addressed by the Protestant reformers of the sixteenth century. In search of an answer, Turretin was led first to Aristotle and classical philosophy and second to the medieval scholastics. His approach is critical but positive. Theology can be considered either systematically and objectively as a discipline or subjectively as a disposition resident in the intellect.[13] Systematically or objectively, the church can classify theology as doctrine (*doctrina*), but subjectively the types of mental "disposition" (*habitus*) need to be considered in order to develop the proper definition of the genus of theology. The subjective issue is how or according to which disposition of mind the *doctrina* of the church is appropriated to our salvation.

Turretin notes three mental dispositions: knowing (*habitus sciendi*), believing (*habitus crendendi*), and opining (*habitus opiniandi*). Each is identified by its own act of assent. If assent (*assensus mentis*) rests on "firm and certain reasoning," the disposition in question is *scientia*; if the basis of assent is "testimony," then *fides*; if "probable reason," then *opinio*. This language is of course fairly standard scholastic currency.[14] What is remarkable, however, is the normative use of such language in Protestant theology, given the Reformers' consistent repudiation of the medieval philosophical background and their refusal to describe faith as a habit or disposition of mind. Turretin's usage bears witness to a broadening of Protestant thought. It points to the transition of a protest movement of limited scope into an independent institution that could include a wide variety of philosophical and psychological categories. The Reformation did not need to develop its own version of faculty psychology to succeed as a theological protest.[15]

Turretin next asks whether the *habitus credendi*, which appears to be the proper subjective designation of theology, can be related analogically to the other ways of knowing, and whether theology thereby can be correlated with any recognized *genus* of academic discipline. The academic disciplines are intellectual dispositions (*habitus intellectuales*) that are included or embraced within the basic *habitus sciendi*. Aristotle enumerates, in the *Ethics*, five basic ways of knowing: *intelligentia*, *scientia*, *sapientia*, *prudentia*, and *ars*.[16] Any correlation, comments Turretin, will be only analogical, since theology cannot be one of these *habitus intellectuales* in a proper or strict sense. He gives three reasons for this view. First, theology is a *habitus credendi*, not a *habitus sciendi*. Second, all true intellectual dispositions are natural, while theology is supernatural, a result not of human *ratio* but of divine *revelatio*. Third, intellectual disciplines are either purely practical or purely theoretical, whereas theology can be shown to be a mixed *genus*, both theoretical and practical (which will be shown later).[17]

Theology is unlike *intelligentia*, since *intelligentia* is identified as knowledge of principles (*principia*) but not of conclusions; theology consists both in principles and in conclusions drawn from them. This argument is crucial to the scholastic Protestant definition of scripture as the cognitive principle (*principium cognoscendi*) of theology: the radical *sola scriptura* of the Reformers can be maintained only on the assumption that the theological system rests not only on statements drawn directly from scripture but also on logical conclusions resting on scriptural premises.[18] Nor is theology akin to *scientia*, "since it does not rest on rational evidence, but on testimony alone, nor does it repose in knowledge (*cognito*) but directs and orders knowledge toward activity (*operatio*)."[19] Similarly, theology stands apart from *prudentia*, because it treats of more than "things to be done" (*agenda*) and because it is spiritual rather than civil. Nor, finally, is theology like *ars*, for it is not a productive disposition (*habitus effectivus*) which intends to terminate in some external work."[20]

The Protestant scholastics were profoundly aware of the importance of the medieval debate over this issue, and even when they appear reluctant to cite the doctors of the thirteenth and fourteenth centuries directly, they draw substantively on the materials of the debate. Several of Turretin's contemporaries, in fact, had adopted a Thomistic view of theology as a subalternate science resting on the perfect science of God's self-knowledge.[21] Turretin's assertion of a radical distinction between theology and science most probably reflects the Scotist perspective, according to which God is truly knowable only to himself and known to us only in an operative (*operabilis*) sense as the goal of human existence. Scotus's distinction between *theologia in se*, the divine self- knowledge, and *theologia nostra*, "our theology" as determined by revelation, is mirrored in Turretin's use of a distinction between *theologia archetypa* and *theologia ectypa*, the former known only to God, the latter resting on God's self-revelation.[22] This does not mean that Turretin can be characterized neatly as a Scotist: he borrows from the medieval doctors when they contribute to his own theological efforts, but never for the sake of reproducing an earlier systematic pattern.

Although theology is not to be identified strictly with *sapientia*, there is greater analogy between theology and *sapientia* than between theology and the other disciplines. In the strict sense given the term by Aristotle, *sapientia* consists in the explanation of self-evident principles and of conclusions drawn from them. This definition, comments Turretin, separates theology from wisdom, since the principles of theology are not known in themselves.[23] Nevertheless, in the less strict definition of *sapientia* provided by the Stoics, as a gathering of speculative and moral dispositions or capacities, the term can be applied to theology. Similarly, the definition in Suidas—*sapientia* as the full understanding of skills, insights, knowledge, and intellect—corresponds with the biblical use of the term "wisdom" (Prov. 8–9; 1 Cor. 2:6–7) and with the needs of theology. Thus, theology may be viewed as the wisdom concerning the highest or most eminent things (*res praestantissima*). It is by nature a *disciplina Architectonia* that, like *sapientia*, governs lesser forms of knowledge and serves to direct them toward the highest or most eminent things that are its proper objects.[24]

These conclusions concerning the *genus* of theology predetermine the results of Turretin's next inquiry: whether theology is speculative or practical. Turretin believes the issue so crucial to the theological enterprise that he deals with it in considerable depth, drawing heavily and explicitly on the medieval tradition for his definitions. Henry of Ghent and Durandus, notes Turretin, viewed theology as utterly speculative. A similar view was put forth by Joannes Rada.[25] Against this perspective, Scotus and those who followed him claimed that theology is essentially practical. Still others—Bonaventure, Albert, and Aegidius Romanus—argued that theology is neither theoretical nor practical but affective (*affectiva*) or dilective (*dilectiva*), insofar as its goal is love (*caritas*). Beyond this, a number of theologians have declared the discipline to be both speculative and practical. Turretin notes two historical paradigms: the Thomist position, which declared theology to be both speculative and practical but that placed its emphasis on the speculative or contemplative side; and the position of Thomas of Strasburg, one of the doctors of the Augustinian order, which stressed the practical side of theology.[26]

This language is important to Turretin for two reasons. In the first place, he understands the terms speculative or contemplative and practical in the traditional scholastic sense in relation to the Augustinian language of "use" and "enjoyment." To know whether theology is speculative or practical is to recognize, in an ultimate sense, the place and purpose of theology in the divine order. A discipline is speculative or contemplative when its truths are grasped in and for themselves, when the knowledge it conveys is an end in itself; a discipline is practical when its knowledge does not end in itself but directs the knower toward an exercise or activity (*operatio*) and thereby toward a goal beyond the discipline itself.[27] In the second place, the language is a significant element in Turretin's polemic against several of his adversaries. Both the Socinians and the later Remonstrants claimed that theology was purely practical. Their views, moreover, were echoed in Spinoza's *Tractatus theologico-politicus*, published anonymously in 1670. If theology were practical in the sense claimed by these opponents, it would have as its subject "obedience to precepts and faith in the promises" and nothing more.[28] Theology would lack dogmatic knowledge concerning such issues as Trinity and incarnation and would be reduced to an ethical atheism.[29]

Turretin's solution to the fundamental problem of the nature of theology grows out of three concerns: the soteriological emphasis he inherited from the Reformation; his decided preference for the Augustinian understanding of God as the *summum bonum*, the ultimate object of our enjoyment (*fruitio*); and his need to oppose the Remonstrants and the Socinians with a theological truth that can be known objectively and, at least in some sense, in and for itself.[30] Theology, thus, is defined as a mixed discipline, partly practical and partly speculative or contemplative, with emphasis on the practical. This mixture appears in his consideration of the object of theology: it is both the worship of God as the highest good (*summum bonum*) and the knowledge of God as the ultimate truth (*primum Verum*). Similarly, the *principium* or foundation of theology is both a ground of instruction in piety and a source of knowledge of God, whether that foundation is considered externally as *Verbum* or internally as *Spiritus*. Furthermore, the human subject and the form of theology bear witness to this mixture, the former in a balance of love and faith, the latter in a balance of worship and knowledge. What is more, final blessedness (*hominis beatitudo*) consists both in the enjoyment (*fruitio*) and the vision (*visio*) of God.[31]

This emphasis on the practical aspect of theology also appears in Turretin's discussion of the object of theology (*obiectum theologiae*). Once again he attempts to distance himself from the medieval scholastics, although only for polemical reasons, inasmuch as he has availed himself most fully of their categories of argument. The object of theology, argues Turretin, is indeed God, but not God as he is in himself. Rather, the object of theology is God as he has revealed himself in his Word.[32] "Neither," adds Turretin, "is he to be considered theoretically as deity, as would Thomas and most scholastics after him, for indeed this way of knowing him cannot be saving, but is the destruction of sinners: rather [God is to be considered] even as he is *our God*, that is, covenanted in Christ." Even in the final decades of the seventeenth century, Protestant theology could echo Luther's attack on the *theologia gloriae* in the name of the *theologia crucis*.[33]

The Relationship of Faith and Reason, Theology and Philosophy

The problem of maintaining continuity with the Reformers' theology while at the same time building intellectual bridges to the scholastic past, evident in Turretin's discussion of the genus and object of theology, appears still more prominently in his attempt to describe the rational and philosophical elements in theological system. On the one hand, the institutionalization of Protestant theology in the university context made such rapprochement with philosophy necessary, creating a problem much like that faced by the scholastics of the thirteenth century. On the other hand, the *sola scriptura* of the Reformation demanded a certain reticence in the appropriation of any philosophy in a formative or substantive way. Whereas Aquinas could state the problem of knowing God primarily in terms of the order of being and the difficulty of comprehending something higher in the order than ourselves, Turretin chose to phrase the problem in terms of human sinfulness and the necessity of a redemptive hearing of the Word.[34]

In order to maintain the priority of revelation over reason without descending into the depths of irrationality, Turretin distinguishes between misuse of reason *in excessu* and *in defectu*. Excessive use of philosophy has been, according to Turretin, a problem in all ages of the church. He cites Justin Martyr, Clement of Alexandria, and Origen among the early Fathers as examples of such excess. These writers represent a strain in early Christianity that "came out of Philosophy" but nonetheless retained some of its errors and brought about an unfortunate mixture of Gentile with Christian thought. The scholastics of the Middle Ages, Turretin continues, taught a doctrine "more philosophical than theological, which rested more upon the reasonings of Aristotle and other philosophers than upon the testimonies of the Prophets and the Apostles." Turretin's language itself pinpoints the problem: he has already argued that theology rests essentially on testimony rather than on the evidence of reason. The rationalistic and philosophical perversion of theology continued in the seventeenth century among the Socinians who, writes Turretin, accept as a maxim the thesis that "philosophy interprets scripture." Such profound abuse of philosophy, however, does not justify the other extreme. Turretin argues that those "who are of the opinion that philosophy is the contrary of theology," both useless and "noxious" to the theological enterprise, err on the side of defect. These people, says Turretin, are "Fanatics and Enthusiasts," "Anabaptists and Weiglians," who wage ignorant war against philosophy and the liberal arts.[35]

On this question, the "orthodox" take a mediating (*medium*) position, neither confounding nor opposing theology and philosophy. Philo and those Fathers who used the allegory of Sara and Hagar to describe theology as mistress and philosophy as handmaid (*ancilla*) argued rightly: philosophy may be correctly *used* when its abuses are clearly recognized.[36] The key to the matter for Turretin remains the hierarchy of the "ways of knowing": the senses are *infra rationem* and therefore governed by it; the intellect stands *iuxta rationem*; and faith, which knows things that reason cannot discern, remains *supra rationem*. Echoing Augustine as well as the medieval doctors, Turretin points out that, insofar as all truth issues from God "even as grace does not destroy nature but perfects it, neither does supernatural revelation abrogate nature, but cleanses it."[37] True philosophy (as opposed to the erring disputes of philosophical sects) teaches of divine and human things according to the "light of nature." Therefore, it can confirm theological truth on the basis of natural knowledge. It would be an abuse and a lifting of philosophy beyond its place in the order of knowing, however, to set the light of nature and the conclusions of reason against such revealed truths as creation *ex nihilo* or the virgin birth. Thus, philosophy may be used, but only within its proper bounds. It cannot negate the doctine of the Trinity or the incarnation because it does not teach these things. Geometry, explains Turretin, does not negate medicine nor physics undercut jurisprudence. What is more, truth cannot be contrary to truth: when philosophy speaks the truth, it can only support theology.[38]

This entire argument rests on Turretin's perception that human reason (*ratio humana*) occupies a carefully delimited place in theological discourse. Against the Socinians, he argues that reason can never be the foundation (*principium*) or the norm by which the Christian religion and its theology determine the objects of faith. He has no quarrel with theologians who would use reason to "illustrate" or "collate" theological arguments or scriptural passages, to draw out "inferences," or to produce "arguments" concerning the orthodoxy or heterodoxy of a doctrinal position.[39] Equally, reason may be the "instrument" or "means" by which certain articles of faith are adduced, but it may never be the foundation upon which or principle from which (*principium ex quo*) the articles of faith are derived. For the *principium* of theology must be such that all articles—indeed, all truths—of theology can be drawn from it and ultimately resolved back into it, particularly the principal, saving truths that come from beyond reason. Reason itself is both limited and, following the fall, corrupt.[40] In its corruption, unregenerate reason cannot grasp either law or gospel; the mysteries of the faith transcend its reach. If reason were the *principium* of theology, argues Turretin, then theology would be natural theology and nothing more: "Faith does not ultimately resolve into reason . . . but into the Word which God has spoken surely in scripture."[41]

Reason remains as a standard of "private judgment." It cannot have the power of ultimate judgment in controversy, for that power inheres in the pastors of the church in a derived sense and ultimately "in God alone, speaking in scripture."[42] But reason can help the intellect: subjectively, in discerning the things of faith (*res fidei*); or normatively, in seeking the connections between elements either of natural or of supernatural revelation.[43] By extension, therefore, reason may be permitted to judge in some of the controversies concerning the faith. It cannot pass judgment on the true mysteries of God, such as Trinity and incarnation, nor can it pass judgment on the power of God. All these things transcend the natural order within which reason operates. But reason can adjudge doctrines that are developed as conclusions based on revelation in their logical relation to doctrines that are explicitly revealed. Thus, for example, the doctrine of purgatory may be judged by reason as contradictory to the doctrine that Christ's blood has saved us from all sin. Like Scotus and the nominalists, Turretin distinguishes between doctrines that are "incomprehensible" and therefore beyond the reach of reason, such as Trinity and incarnation, and doctrines that are "incompossible," such as transubstantiation and the ubiquity of Christ's resurrected body. The point concerning incompossibility, the logical irreconcilability of two things in terms of their mutual possibility within the same order, rests on Turretin's denial of double truth: divine truth does not stand in utter defiance, within the natural order, of the principles of the natural order, such as the relation of substance and accidents or the local nature of bodies.[44]

The weight of evidence shows Turretin to be neither a rationalist nor a fideist. In his controversies, he makes no attempt to attack the positive rationalism of his time, Cartesian philosophy, but he does attack the rationalistic theology of the Socinians, in which the Cartesian element was strong. He does not view philosophy itself as the enemy and will not abandon either the gift of reason or the truths that reason is capable of eliciting from perception of the natural order. Yet, he will not ignore the basic insight of Reformed theology that reason has been corrupted by the Fall and now sees with an uncertain, obscure, and frequently erroneous light. The "light of lights," the Word of God, provides the only firm ground—even for a theology that strives for rational expression.[45]

When Turretin addresses directly the question of the foundations of theology (*principia theologiae*), he places himself into a tradition of Protestant argumentation that was almost a century long and that represents one of the first Protestant appropriations of medieval scholastic distinctions. Franciscus Junius, a pupil of Calvin who contributed much to the development of Calvinism in the Netherlands, is generally credited with the formal enunciation of a distinction used by nearly all the later Protestant scholastics, including Turretin, between the *theologia archetypa* or divine self-knowledge and its temporal analogue, the *theologia ectypa*.[46] Since the latter is finite as well as temporal, it is accessible to the human mind. Using this line of thought, Turretin claims that the form of this theology must be suited to our condition: it cannot be a heavenly theology of the blessed, but only a theology of earthly pilgrims (*viatores*) on the way (*in via*) toward eternal life—a *theologia viatorum*. Since he rules out reason as a fundamental principle, Turretin argues that the ectypal *theologia viatorum* also must be a *theologia revelationis*.[47] The idea of a *theologia revelationis* indicates in its very terms both the "Word of God" and the "word concerning God," comments Turretin, "for there could be no speech about God without God."[48] Theology, therefore, recognizes as its *principia* the true God and his self-revelation—the *principium essendi* (God) and the *principium cognoscendi* (the scriptural revelation).

Since it is the purpose of theology to teach savingly of God, the ectypal theology of revelation deemphasizes "natural revelation" as insufficient for salvation and develops primarily the teaching of scripture.[49] God's faithful in the church attend the "school of grace," read the "book of Scripture," and learn supernatural theology illumined by the "light of faith"; the worldly, by contrast, attend the "school of nature," read the "book of creation," and learn natural theology according to the "light of reason."[50] Granting these paradigms, reason and the philosophy based on it can have at best an instrumental or ancillary status in Christian theology. Used principally, reason produces a worldly alternative to the theology of revelation.

Conclusions: Theology for the Reformed Academy and University

Turretin was a codifier and a gatherer of opinion rather than an original thinker. What he produced in his *Institutio theologicae elencticae* was an academic theology for use in the Reformed academies and universities of his time. His "scholasticism" is the result not of a particular philosophical perspective but of an academic intention and method. As he tells his readers in his prefatory letter, his theology, as found in the pages of the *Institutio*, is incomplete—specifically because his theology stands as a academic exercise in elenctics or dispute with adversaries. The genre of the academic exercise excludes other dimensions of the theological enterprise, notably exegesis, positive dogmatic statement, and practical application, all of which were assumed to be necessary elements in the broader theological work of his era.[51]

As a defender of a form of orthodoxy, he strove to weigh options, to refute errors and adversaries, and to present a normative statement of Reformed theology to his students and his peers. What is evident on virtually every page of Turretin's theology is that this normative statement attains its breadth and comprehensive character by a consistent recourse not merely to the thought of the great Reformers but to the whole of the Christian tradition—and specifically to the definitions and paradigms of the medieval doctors. Thus, the movement of Reformed theology from sixteenth-century protest to seventeenth-century orthodoxy, as evidenced in Turretin's *Institutio theologicae*, involved what may well be called a catholicizing tendency. The polemic against Rome remains as bitter as ever, and Turretin makes no effort to enter into dialogue with his Roman Catholic contemporaries. However, he does draw substantively on a part of the tradition that had seemed, at least on a superficial reading of the sources, irrevocably cast aside by his own theological predecessors barely a century and a half before.

Rather than being the result of an incipient rationalism or the product of a systematization of Protestantism around certain central dogmas, then, Turretin's Protestant scholasticism may be seen as the product of an institutionalizing and catholicizing tendency, which was itself a symptom of the desire to forge a theological orthodoxy, a system of "right-doctrine." Turretin's statements concerning reason and theological principles manifest neither a sympathy with rationalist philosophy as developed in the seventeenth century nor a desire to find a theoretical basis for a monistic or deductive system—a desire that would, if present, evidence a certain kinship with the systematizing efforts of the rationalist philosophers.[52] Rather, they manifest a consistent hope that Protestantism might affirm a traditional orthodoxy that rests on the universally recognized essential and cognitive foundations of the theological system, that is, on the God and his biblical revelation.

Turretin's institutionalizing and catholicizing tendency appears in the very process of his system-building. It was certainly not characteristic of seventeenth-century writers to note for their readers issues such as continuity and discontinuity with the past or the underlying problematic of theological formulation, but Turretin's constant balancing of typical Protestant themes like *sola scriptura* and *sola fide* with a substantive use of medieval scholastic theology, together with his occasional disclaimer of any real affinity with the medieval models, demonstrates both a concern to state the theology of the Reformed tradition in a fully systematized and scholastic form and to employ the breadth of the tradition and the techniques of scholasticism in the defense of the orthodox confessional stance without detriment to the original message of Protestantism.

9

The Debate over the Vowel Points and the Crisis in Orthodox Hermeneutics

Although the century-long debate in post-Reformation Protestantism over the origin and antiquity of the vowel points in the Hebrew text of the Old Testament may seem somewhat far removed from the concerns of modern theology, it remains a significant index of the alteration both in doctrine and hermeneutic that took place in Reformed theology as it moved from the period of the Reformation into the age of orthodoxy and rationalism. This debate stands on the divide between exegesis according to the principles of *analogia Scripturae* and *analogia fidei* and the more strictly textual exegesis associated with modern criticism of Scripture.

At the beginning of the Reformation, the system of "jots and tittles" known as vowel points, and used as an aid to the pronunciation of Hebrew in the Massoretic text of the Old Testament, was hardly a source of exegetical difficulty. Whereas rabbinic teaching, following the doctrines of the Kabbala, held the coetaneous revelation of consonants and vowels to Moses on Sinai, medieval Christian interpreters of Scripture had viewed the points as a Jewish attempt to conceal the true meaning of the text and render it useless to Christians. The several patterns of allegorical, spiritual, and typological exegesis practiced in the late Middle Ages and the early sixteenth century, however, made a critical approach to the vowel points unnecessary.[1] Luther argued that the points were merely an imperfect aid to the reader, that they were unknown to Jerome and thus postbiblical in origin, and that they might be altered by the interpreter in order to bring the meaning of the Old Testament into conformity with the revelation of Christ in the New Testament.[2] Zwingli concurred, expressing a low opinion of the vowel points.[3] Neither worried over the possible use of the system of vocalization to corrupt the text. Calvin, more textually oriented in his exegesis than either Zwingli or Luther, had a high regard for the accuracy of the Massoretic editors of the text and, while believing the vowel points to be an invention of these rabbis, approved of alterations in pointing only after critical examination of the meaning of the text.[4]

A crucial juncture in the understanding of the text of the Old Testament occurred in 1538 when Elias Levita published his commentary on the collected scribal annotations, the *Massorah*. Levita was able to show that neither the Talmud nor the Midrash manifested knowledge of the complete Massoretic system of vocalization and inferred that the points were of later origin than these documents. As for variant readings of the vowels, these, he argued, prove theologically that the vowels did not go back to Sinai, since divine origin of the vowels would have precluded any critical variation of vocalizations by the rabbis. Levita also demonstrated that the names of the points were Babylonian and Aramaic, proving them to have originated following the exile of the Jews to Babylon. Throughout his study, Levita asserts the accuracy of the vocalizations and praises the Massoretes for their perspicacity.[5]

Levita's work was at first received enthusiastically by Protestant Hebraists: one year after its publication, Sebastian Munster translated the preface and superintended the reprinting of Levita's entire tome in Basel.[6] There was, moreover, no immediate or intense theological reaction. Neither Calvin's *Institutes* nor Musculus's *Loci communes* nor Ursinus's *Locus de sacra scriptura* nor Zanchi's two works on the doctrine of Scripture take note of Levita. Bishop John Jewell well represented the initial Protestant reception of Levita's theory when he wrote of the disagreements over the origin of the points in the *Defense* (1567–1570) of his *Apologia Ecclesiae Anglicanae*. Jewel's chief opponent, Thomas Harding, had argued against the use of Scripture by laity, using the absence of vowels as evidence that only the learned ought to have access to the holy text. Jewel began his refutation by noting first the varied opinions of the rabbis: some say that the vowel points "were delivered to Moses in the mount; some say that they were invented by Esdras; some by the Tabarites, which were the canonists of the Jews, or doctors of Traditions."[7] Jewel himself seems to have favored the latter opinion, arguing that even as the ancient practice of writing Greek without accents never prevented the common man from reading that language, so the absence of vowels from the Hebrew text of Scripture never hindered the Jews from reading the Bible. "Certainly Mr. Harding knows that even now not only the learned of the Jews, but also the very children of ten years of age, are able to read without pricks or vowels."[8]

Toward the end of the sixteenth century, the debate entered a new phase. Roman polemicists began to suggest that—in view of the probable addition of the vowels to the text by the Massoretes—the text could not be an absolute rule of doctrine. Scripture itself, claimed Gilbertus Genebrardus, Melchior Cano, and Gulielmus Lindanus, could hardly be considered a divine and infallible canon when it contained an element of purely human invention so fundamental as the vowels. The Jews, these three writers claimed, had intentionally altered the vowel points out of malice toward the church:[9] here, the medieval theory is revived as a weapon against Protestantism.

Roman polemic found its most comprehensive formulation in Cardinal Robert Franz Bellarmine's *Disputationes de controversis christianae fidei adversus sui temporis Haereticos*, which appeared between 1581 and 1593 in four enormous volumes containing a total of sixty-four "books." In his treatise *De Verbo Dei*, Bellarmine recognized the Bible, the *verbum Dei scriptum*, to be "the true word of God and the certain and sure rule of faith," but he denied that Scripture could stand alone. It did not contain all necessary doctrine and its meaning was often unclear apart from the tradition of the church, the *verbum Dei non scriptum*.[10] Much of Bellarmine's argument rested on the difficulty of establishing the precise meaning of the original Hebrew and Greek of the Bible. The heretics of his time, he noted, despise the Vulgate while praising excessively the Hebrew and Greek codices. Yet, they contradict their own claims by emending the text.[11]

Bellarmine comments further that Jewish sources such as the Talmud and, presumably, the marginalia of the Massoretic text, demonstrate the need for extensive emendation. The codices are filled with scribal errors. Differences between the Vulgate and the Hebrew, therefore, can be explained as a result of emendations made in the time of Jerome and as the result of errors in the transmission of the Hebrew text since that time. Bellarmine explained the corruption of the available Hebrew codices as the result of "the negligence and ignorance of the scribes," who easily confused the many similarly shaped letters of the Hebrew alphabet, and of "the ignorance of the rabbis who added the points."[12]

Reformed response followed rapidly on the heels of the Roman polemic, reaching a first stage of codification during the three decades following 1590.[13] Amandus Polanus von Polansdorf, the most compendious systematic theologian of the early orthodox period, incorporated the debate into his doctrine of Scripture; and the elder Johannes Buxtorf, the most eminent Protestant philologist of the day, prepared what was thought to be the definitive scholarly conclusion to the controversy over the vowel points. These two formulations coincided with the solidification of the early orthodox doctrine of Holy Scripture as the infallible *principium cognoscendi* of theology.

As an Old Testament scholar as well as a doctrinal theologian, Polanus was probably more conscious of philological debate and its bearing on positive doctrine than many of his contemporaries. Junius and Gomarus—the latter, like Polanus, a professor of Bible—argued the issue, but neither treated it as a systematic locus;[14] the debate is absent also from the systems of Bucanus, Keckermann, Ames, Trelcatius, Festus Hommius, Johannes Scharpius, and Walaeus. None of these thinkers felt the need to corroborate their doctrine of Scripture and their hermeneutic with a statement on the vowel points. It was Polanus who set the stage for subsequent doctrinal formulation by including in his *Syntagma theologiae*, in addition to the usual dogmatic *loci* of the authority, divinity, necessity, perspicuity, and authenticity of the Scriptures, a *locus*, "In quo respondetur adversariis Editionem Hebraeam Veteris Testamenti oppugnantibus." Here he treats both the general question of the authenticity of the Hebrew text and the more restricted issue of the vowel points. In discussing the former question, Polanus takes as his point of departure the treatises of Lindanus, a post-Tridentine Roman polemicist who attempted to buttress the Council's doctrine of the dogmatic superiority of the Vulgate by arguing a textual superiority of the Vulgate over the Hebrew of the Old Testament.[15] In the latter issue, Polanus does not deal with Roman polemic but strikes directly at what he sees to be the source of the problem, Elias Levita's *Massoreth Ha-Massoreth*.[16] Debate had now reached the point at which Levita's philological studies could no longer be viewed as theologically neutral.

Polanus noted that Levita's dating of the work of the Tiberian Massoretes to the middle of the fifth century after Christ implied the origin of the points to be later than the Vulgate. This dating had to be denied not only to establish the purity of the text both in consonants and vowels but also to counter the claim of Lindanus that the Vulgate took priority over extant (i.e., Massoretic) Hebrew codices. Extrabiblical Jewish sources, wrote Polanus, weighed heavily against Levita's argument. Polanus cites the opinion of the Talmud, the Zohar, and the exegete Rabbi David Kimchi to the effect that the points belonged to the original revelation of the Word to Moses and the Prophets and were produced simultaneously with the consonants of the Law, summing up the argument with the rabbinic maxim, "puncta vocalia sunt animae syllabarum et vocum atque adeo vivae pronunciationis."[17] Polanus does not even raise the possibility that the points, whatever their origin, are representations of the sounds necessarily implied by the configuration of the consonants.

The elder Buxtorf buttressed this dogmatic formulation with massive documentation in his *Tiberias sive commentarius Masorethicus* (1620) in which he drew on the Talmud, Midrash, and Zohar and also—in the judgment of Ginzburg—on the more recent statement of conservative rabbinic doctrine against Levita by Azzariah de Rossi.[18] If Buxtorf was ultimately proved incorrect in his arguments, his genuine erudition and vast knowledge of the Hebrew sources made his arguments appear practically invincible to his contemporaries: at last Lindanus, Genebrardus, and Bellarmine had met their match. Buxtorf argues, against Levita, that the Massorah and its basic principles did exist prior to the Talmud, since the Talmud utilizes points and accents. Rather than attribute the Massorah to the school at Tiberias, Buxtorf believed it to have been written by the men of the great synagogue or council called by the prophet Ezra, and he hypothesized a continuity of tradition linking the scholars of the ancient city of Tiberias to the great synagogue. After the destruction of Jerusalem in A.D. 70, there had remained places where the remnants of Israel cast out of Babylon and the Jews remaining in the land gradually restored their schools and synagogues. Tiberias was one of these places.[19]

The Massoretic commentary on the text, argues Buxtorf, by its continual analysis of irregularities in pointing, proves the antiquity of the vowels: the Massoretes would have had no reason to debate and correct the points and accents had they invented them. The Massoretes were editors, not inventors.[20] The men of the great synagogue, in the time of Ezra, produced the basic set of points and accents, or perhaps restored them to their proper use after a period of decline, whereas the Massoretes merely received the various sigla from the tradition and examined them critically.[21] From these arguments, Buxtorf moves toward doctrinal affirmation: if the vowel points and accents were in fact the invention of the Massoretes, then the Holy Scriptures have been augmented, are of an uncertain authority, and are not to be considered as totally divine. Moreover, if the points were of human invention, notes Buxtorf—unwittingly preparing ground both for further polemic and for a new, revolutionary hermeneutical perspective—then the text could be infinitely amended and altered to suit human whim. Nor is it enough to state that the text is incorruptible and immutable in its consonants: the vowels, too, must be immutable, since they are the soul of the words, the vivifying spirit.[22]

An event of seminal importance to the development of Protestant hermeneutics and to the formulation of the high orthodox doctrine of Scripture occurred in 1624: the anonymous publication of Louis Cappel's *Arcanum punctationis revelatum* with a highly laudatory preface by the eminent philologist of the University of Leiden Thomas Erpenius. In this treatise, the erudition of Buxtorf was surpassed and his argument for an early origin of the vowel points soundly refuted—only four years after the publication of his *magnum opus*. The refutation had, moreover, come from a fellow Protestant. It seemed now as if the textual underpinnings of the Reformation's *sola scriptura* were being chipped away from within the ranks of the Reformed.

In response to Buxtorf's strongest argument, Cappel showed that references to the Massorah in the Talmud indicated the tradition of biblical interpretation and not the specific problem of the vowel points.[23] Furthermore, the variety of the pointing of the text, the rabbinic discussion of variants, and the failure of the vocalization to follow a uniform rule indicate not the antiquity of the points but the gradual invention of a system of vocalization by many editors over the course of centuries.[24] As for the comment of Christ (Matthew 5:18) that no jot or tittle of the law can be changed, Cappel could argue, on good rabbinic grounds, that it referred not to the vowel points but to the *figura literae*, the spines and horns (*corniculum*) that distinguish one consonant from another.[25]

After dealing at length with grammatical and historical issues, Cappel finally turns to his theological argument. He recognizes that, in the controversy up to that point, there seemed to be only two options: either insist on the equal antiquity of the vowels and consonants or yield to the "Papist" argument, accept the human origin of the points, and admit that the authority of Scripture depended upon the testimony and the teaching office of the church.[26] Cappel believed that he could contribute a new dimension to the controversy and reinforce the Protestant position on the authority of Scripture. The "Papists" argue thus:

> If the points are from the Massoretes, the authority of the Hebrew text is merely human . . . ;
> But the points are from the Massoretes;
> Therefore, etc.

It is useless to refute the minor of the syllogism, comments Cappel, since the best analysis of the Hebrew text and of rabbinic sources favors it. The issue, then, is to refute the major.[27]

Following Levita, Cappel argued that the vowels, or at least the vocalization, had been passed on as an oral tradition that, although unwritten, was as carefully established as the written text:

> When I say that the points were conceived by the Tiberian Massoretes and added to the consonants. . . . I wish to imply that they expressed by these markings of their invention the reading of the sacred text which had everywhere obtained among the Jews, and which they had been taught by the teachers of their schools.

The Massoretes simply reported the tradition by means of a set of symbols, in the firm faith that their reading represented that of Moses and the Prophets.[28] The tradition itself can in no wise be called arbitrary, since vowels stand in the grammatical series of the words of the text and depend, for their sound, on the order and structure of the sentences. Ultimately, therefore, the vowels depend–even acknowledging the human origin of the system of points–not on human editing but on the divine and inspired canon of Scripture. Because the grammatical structure of the sentence stands, the true and certain text of the Old Testament can be established.[29]

In thus accepting the invention of the vowel points by the Massoretes but insisting on the integrity of the text in its grammatical construction, Cappel stood in somewhat greater continuity with the Reformers on the specific problem of the vowels than did his orthodox contemporaries, but that continuity was established by way of a vastly different hermeneutic. Cappel maintained, even in his later and more radical *Critica Sacra* (1650), that the

> saving doctrine which was stated by Moses, the prophets, the apostles, and the evangelists in their *autographois* . . . is, in the Greek and Hebrew texts and in the translations either old or new, clearly, correctly, and sufficiently conveyed. . . . in respect of their content the Greek and Hebrew texts are authentic, sacred, divine, *theopneustoi*.[30]

Cappel's method, however, more and more assumed that the vowel points had been corrupted in the transmission and that the *textus receptus* needed to be altered on the basis of ancient translations such as the Chaldee, the newly discovered Syriac, and the Septuagint. Differences between these ancient versions and the extant Hebrew codices could be explained by the hypothesization of earlier Hebrew manuscripts substantially different from the *textus receptus*.[31] Without much prompting, Cappel's orthodox contemporaries fulminated against the new hermeneutic as a disastrous repudiation of the *analogia fidei* and as a method suspiciously similar to Roman attempts to correct the Hebrew text from the Vulgate. At the foundation both of the Roman arguments for the priority of the Vulgate and of Cappel's use of ancient versions lay the ascription of postbiblical origin to the vowel points.

Quite in contrast to Cappel, the orthodox stood in continuity with the hermeneutic of the Reformers; even if their exegesis was frequently more dogmatic both in its intention and its result, their norm of interpretation, the *analogia fidei*, also was the norm of Calvin, Bullinger, Vermigli, and other exegetes of the mid-sixteenth century. Ironically, they maintained this hermeneutic by means of a more rigid view of the inspiration of the text than that held by their predecessors, a view that depended (or so it seemed to the early orthodox) on the extension of divine authority beyond the sense of the scripture to the individual words, indeed, to their letters and even to the tiny "jots and tittles" of the system of vocalization.[32] Whereas Luther, Calvin, and their contemporaries viewed the question of the origin of the vowel points as a minor issue to be treated at the level of textual analysis, the early orthodox had, in the process of systematic development of a Reformed dogmatics and under the impact of polemic, raised the question to doctrinal status.

This alteration of the grounds of inquiry is quite evident in Andreas Rivetus's *Isagoge, seu introductio generalis ad Scripturam Sacram*, written shortly after the appearance of Cappel's *Arcanum punctationis revelatum*. Rivetus faced a double problem. In the first place, he recognized that Protestant opinion on the origin of the vowel points had changed since the time of Calvin. In the second place, the philologist Erpenius, who had written such a glowing introduction to Cappel's book, had been Rivetus's colleague on the faculty of the University of Leiden. Rivetus delicately dissociates himself from the opinion of Cappel, bemoans comments of Zwingli and of Calvin on the origin of the points, praises Erpenius's linguistic ability and even Erpenius's gracious judgment of the treatise in question.[33] A final decision in these matters, says Rivetus, must be left to the great philologists: he awaits the response of Buxtorf.[34] Blame for the crisis in hermeneutics Rivetus lays squarely on the shoulders of the long-deceased Elias Levita and the insidious Roman polemicists, such as Genebrardus, "that most petulant persecutor of all good things and bitter enemy of truth." The claim that the Tiberian Massoretes invented the current system of vocalization cannot be allowed to prejudice the authority of the books of Scripture or to impugn the purity of the sources.[35]

"Almost all the Papists agree in this," writes Rivetus, "that the points of the Hebrews are a human invention, which had been used by the Jews, following the advent of Christ, against Christ and to the detriment of Christian piety."[36] But this assertion, even buttressed by the theory of Levita, cannot undermine the normative status of Scripture—for even Genebrardus admits in his study of rabbinic writings that the absence of vowel points does not lead to arbitrary renderings of the text and that the text, without vowels, is neither "crippled" nor "contracted" but is perfectly and fully presented in its essential letters.[37] Without actually advocating Cappel's refinement of Levita and without waiting for a counterargument from Buxtorf, Rivetus could begin to adapt the Reformed orthodox hermeneutic, maintaining the sole authority of Scripture, insisting on the clarity and perspicuity of the text, with or without proof of the Mosaic origin of the vowel points. Perhaps he had seen the handwriting on the wall and noticed that all the letters were consonants. In any case, Rivetus settled on the real issue underlying the debate: the *puritas fontium* and the ability of the exegete to discern the "true sense" of Scripture and the "meaning of the Holy Spirit in things necessary to salvation." He also recognized that not all codices were free from various corruptions, but maintained that by comparison and collation of codices the pure canon of Scripture could be set forth in the "words which the Holy Spirit dictated to his amanuenses."[38]

Reaction to Cappel's arguments and subsequent movement to modify hermeneutics without losing irrevocably the formal doctrine of scriptural authority laid down by the early orthodox is most clearly and definitively seen among the English writers. In 1623, John Weemse had published his hermeneutical and exegetical treatise *The Christian Synagogue*. Both in this and in the second edition of his work (1630), Weemse espoused the theory of Buxtorf, noting that "the points and accents are naturally bred with the Scriptures, delivered by God to Moyses out of Mount Sinai, and so on to posteritie."[39] In the third edition of *The Christian Synagogue*, issued in 1636 as part of his collected works, Weemse reacts to Cappel's theory and develops a statement concerning the vowels more amenable than Cappel's argument to the orthodox doctrine. Weemse, in fact, adumbrates the high orthodox formulation:

> The letters in the Scripture have two sort of points, either in valor or in figure; the points in valor were from the beginning delivered by Moses in mount Sinai, but the figures of them were found out afterwards by the Mazorites, and no consonant can bee pronounced without them. Of the latter points, the Iewes say in the Ierusolymitan Talmud, . . . "Letters without points are like a body without a soule."[40]

Weemse recognized a certain linguistic logic on the part of those who insisted on the simultaneous revelation of vowels and consonants, but admitted that the history of Hebrew and its cognate languages demonstrated otherwise. Creation of vowel signs for Hebrew, Arabic, Syriac, and Chaldee is analogous to the allowing for spaces between words in Greek: these are aids developed for the sake of those "less adept at reading the language."[41]

Perhaps the greatest linguistic scholar of the age, Brian Walton, superintended the printing, between 1653 and 1657, of the great "London Polyglot Bible," which collated all the texts, variants, and versions known in his day. In the *Prolegomena* to this mammoth endeavor, Walton accepted the view of the vowel points developed by Levita and Cappel but strove to avoid the extreme of Cappel's later hermeneutical theory. It was the Massoretes who developed a system of vowel points after Ezra and after the close of the period of the writing of the canonical Old Testament. The present vowel signs in the text are, therefore, of only human authority. Nevertheless, argues Walton, they are in the main an authentic representation of the oral tradition of pronunciation and a valid guide to meaning.[42] By a careful collation of manuscripts and through a conservative use of ancient versions, errors can be excised. Walton limits the use to which ancient versions like the Syriac and Chaldee can be put by affirming the priority of the Hebrew as the original language. He specifically limits the value of the Vulgate, denying the validity of the Roman, post-Tridentine hermeneutic.[43] This being said on the philological level, it remained for the dogmaticians to disengage the problem of the vowel points from the problematic elements of Cappel's late hermeneutic and to arrive at a doctrinal formulation dealing adequately with the interpretation and authority of the scriptures.[44]

The dogmatic solution, which is found in the systems of Turretin and Johann Heidegger and, in a less detailed form, in the *Formula Consensus Helvetica* (1675), embodies three underlying distinctions:[45] the *autographa* or original manuscript copies of the scriptural books as dictated by the Spirit to the biblical authors must be distinguished from the *apographa* or later copies; the authority of scripture considered in terms of the content or meaning of the text ("authoritas . . . in rebus ipsis de quibus id agit") from the authority of the words of the text, the actual *scriptura*; and the vowels considered according to sound, the *valor* or *potestas* of the vowel point from the *figura* or symbol, the vowel point itself.

Against Rome, the orthodox postulated the sole authority of the Hebrew text of the Old Testament, denying the validity of emendations and doctrinal interpretations made on the basis of ancient versions. In contrast to the purely linguistic point made by Walton, Turretin and Heidegger moved toward a theological determination on the question of "authenticity." That writing is authentic which is abundantly sufficient in all things to the building of faith and which conveys accurately the intention of the author.[46] This authenticity, they continue, should be viewed either *primario et originaliter* or *secundario et derivative*. The former authenticity applies to self-authenticating (*autopiston*) or archetypal writings, such as the original copies of royal edicts, parliamentary decrees, and various legal documents, in short, to the original autograph copy from the hand of the author. Secondary authority belongs to all accurate copies—*apographa*—faithfully produced from the archetypes by diligent scribes, such as the copies of edicts made for public distribution. In the former sense, only the autograph copies of biblical books made by Moses, the Prophets, and the Apostles are authentic, but in the latter, all faithful copies can be considered authentic.[47]

In this argument, Turretin allows for an authentic transmission of the text, which must ultimately lead to a priority of the Hebrew codices over the versions: for the value of all apographa is doubly determined—either *materialiter quoad res enunciatas* or *formaliter quoad verba et modum enunciandi*. Even the ancient versions, insofar as they represent a faithful rendition of the original Hebrew, are authentic in a material sense, according to the "things said"; but only Hebrew copies can be formally authentic, according to the mode of speaking.[48] No version can claim to reproduce exactly the words dictated by the Spirit. "If the Hebrew edition of the Old and the Greek of the New Testament are not authentic, no edition is authentic. . . . And no authentic Word of God is in the Church and no end of controversy, since there would be no certain rule of faith and morals in which all might be resolved."[49]

This series of distinctions affirming the priority of the Hebrew text is in no way invalidated by presence of variant readings in the several codices; the correct reading can easily be determined from the coherence of the text itself and from a comparison of codices.[50] This method also frustrates the claim of those adversaries who deny the authenticity of the Hebrew on the ground that the vowels are of recent origin, "as if they were solely of human invention, dreamed up by the Massoretes," and lacking divine authority. Even Bellarmine had been forced to admit that addition of vowel points does not alter the text. As for the professed superiority of the Vulgate, this, Turretin comments, can hardly be concluded unless the Holy Spirit revealed the vowels immediately to Jerome![51] More important, even if it is allowed that the points are a recent addition to the text, it does not follow that they are a merely human invention depending entirely on the human will; the pointing of the text was accomplished according to "the analogy of scripture" with attention to the "genius of Sacred Language, and the sense long received among the Jews." Errors in pointing may be corrected utilizing an identical method. Thus, a distinction must obtain between the *figura* or symbol, which can be erroneously employed and the *sonus* or sound value, the *potestas* of the symbol, which must be coeval with the consonants.[52] In support of this point, Turretin cites the English scholar Prideaux and the "Doctissimus Waltonus." Turretin also takes from Walton the fact that three consonants—aleph, waw, and yod—stood from time immemorial as aids in the conservation of correct pronunciation.[53]

As a parting shot, Turretin cannot resist taunting his adversaries with the continuing disagreement of the philologists. He cites more than a dozen writers, "Protestant and Popish," who attribute the origin of the vowel points either to Moses or to the "great synagogue" in the time of Ezra. If the elder Buxtorf did not live to write a reply to Cappel, there is still his *Tiberias*; and there are the "*solidissimae*" works of the younger Johannes Buxtorf, which refute at length the arguments of Cappel's *Arcanum punctationis revelatum*. No determination of doctrine can be drawn from an unsettled philological battle.[54] The orthodox Reformed doctrine, unlike the argument of its adversaries, no longer depends on the outcome of the debate.

Having thus argued the authenticity of the Hebrew text, Turretin moves to apply his logic to the specific case of the current Massoretic edition of the text. He must now deny the distinction made by his adversaries between the Hebrew text *in se* or the text considered hypothetically and the Massoretic edition, the text as it actually exists: they would drive a methodological wedge between the two and thus render the Massoretic text useless as a norm for interpretation.[55] That method is unsound which would collate the Hebrew text with several ancient versions and, on the basis of the versions, hypothesize a different Hebrew original, for this would constitute the authentic reading of the text according to the human will and the reason of the exegete rather than according to the work of the Spirit.[56] Moreover, by the Hebrew text, the Protestants understand not a single codex but a collation of the variant readings of all extant codices—which, as closest to the *autographa*, has priority over all versions.[57] A distinction must be made between *varia lectio* and *varians interpretatio*: variant readings are indeed present in the Hebrew, but the ancient versions present variant interpretations. There is no reason to assume a variant reading of the Hebrew for each and every varying interpretation found in the ancient versions.[58]

In conclusion: the controversy over the vowel points in the Hebrew text of Scripture was, for the seventeenth-century orthodox, a pivotal debate in which ability to come to terms with the findings of historical analysis was the key to the survival of a hermeneutic based on the sole authority of Scripture. During the period of early orthodoxy (ca. 1565–ca.1640), a rapid development of the formal doctrine of Scripture occurred as a result of polemic with Rome over the question of authority in matters of doctrine. Protestant insistence on the integrity and perfection of Scripture produced a more rigid doctrine and a less flexible hermeneutic than that which had obtained during the Reformation. Indeed, the early orthodox proved incapable of adapting to a theory of the invention of vowel points by the Tiberian Massoretes in the fifth century after Christ, particularly in view of the use to which that theory was put by Roman polemicists.

During the period of high orthodoxy (ca. 1640–ca.1725), exegetes and ultimately theologians refined their hermeneutic so as to affirm the integrity and authenticity of the text of Scripture despite the possible presence of a human element in the vowel points. The orthodox developed a highly refined method of text collation in the attempt to approach ever more closely to the inspired exactitude of the original *autographa*. This method, although frequently condemned for the rigid formulations of the inspiration and authority of the text that accompanied its development, does stand, both in its insistence on the overarching doctrinal harmony of Scripture as a key to interpretation and in its frequently overlooked ability to distinguish between the *Verbum Dei* or underlying essence of the text and the actual *verba* of the text, in hermeneutical continuity with the Reformation.[59]

At this juncture, the orthodox hermeneutic had come full circle: the relatively moderate solution achieved by Turretin, Heidegger, and the *Formula Consensus Helvetica* enabled the orthodox to formulate a doctrine of Scripture as Word of God very much like that of the early orthodox writers—such as Ursinus, Zanchi, Keckermann, and Walaeus—whose systems did not press the issue of verbal inspiration quite as far as Polanus and did not shape doctrine around the problem of the vowels. Leonardus Rijssenius, whose system is based directly on Turretin's *Institutio*, regards the vowel points as a device of the Massoretes intended to preserve the correct reading of the text.[60] Johannes Marckius specifically notes his abandonment of the "Philologis *inquisitio*," while Petrus van Mastricht, despite his usual care for the history of polemic, completely omits consideration of the issue.[61]

Nevertheless, the high orthodox hermeneutic was plagued by an inability or unwillingness to separate the new exegetical method of Cappel from the exegetical method proposed by Roman opponents of *sola scriptura*. Cappel's use of ancient versions in the attempt to reconstruct a Hebrew text prior to the Massoretic text and the similar method proposed by Walton are hardly differentiated in the polemic from the Roman insistence (for entirely different reasons) on the prior authority of the Vulgate and the magisterial position given in matters of interpretation to the exegetical and doctrinal tradition. This association, together with the autonomous position given to the exegete in the determination of the text by Cappel's hermeneutic, barred the way to future cooperation between the critical exegete and the orthodox theologian and to a certain extent ensured the decline of orthodoxy in the eighteenth century. The critical method of Cappel, by contrast, in its emphasis on the minutiae of text and the freedom of the exegete, ultimately lost contact with the orthodox standard of the material integrity of Scripture, the sense of continuity both in text and translation *quoad res*, as witnessed by the orthodox stress on the *analogia Scripturae* and *analogia fidei* in interpretation.

10

Henry Ainsworth and the Development of Protestant Exegesis in the Early Seventeenth Century

Ainsworth's Life and Work

Henry Ainsworth or Aynsworth (1570–1622) was one of the most prominent spokesmen for ecclesiastical separatism or independency and one of the most able and prolific of the Puritan exegetes of the seventeenth century, second only to Andrew Willet in his mastery of the Pentateuch. Daniel Neal identifies Ainsworth both as a leader of the "Brownists or rigid Separatists" and as the author of "a most learned commentary on the five books of Moses, by which he appears to have been a great master of oriental languages and of Jewish antiquities."[1] The details of his biography are somewhat sketchy and there is no major study extant of his life and work.[2] The sad state of study and, indeed, of the intellectually imperialistic way in which seventeenth-century biblical interpretation has been neglected and even dismissed is nowhere more apparent than in Frederick Farrar's single reference to Ainsworth's work as one example among many of the "grotesque" and "melancholy . . . mass of hypotheses" found in the older exegesis about the meaning of the Song of Songs: Ainsworth understood its theme to be the reconciliation of human beings with God.[3] The far more objective Ludwig Diestel lists Ainsworth with Willet and Cartwright as one of the "profitable" seventeenth-century English expositors of the Old Testament.[4]

Only sketchy information is available concerning Ainsworth's early years. He was baptized on January 15, 1569/70, at Swanton Morley, Norfolk, the son of a yeoman farmer, Thomas Ainsworth.[5] He studied at Swanton Morley in a local school for about three years. In late 1586, he arrived at St. John's College, Cambridge. William Whitaker, then master of the college, was one of the most eminent theologians in England at the time and one of the great technical defenders of the Protestant exegesis and doctrine of Scripture against Roman Catholic polemic.[6] Ainsworth's tutor was Ralph Furness, one of the more thoroughgoing of the Puritans at St. John's.

After a year of study—Moody speculates that it was because of the highly charged atmosphere of debate at St. John's—Ainsworth began his advanced studies at Gonville and Caius College, Cambridge.[7] He registered on December 15, 1587, and continued in residence there for four years. It was most certainly during those years that he gained his extensive grounding in Hebrew, was attracted to Puritan theology, and, eventually, adopted a separatistic view of the true church. Ainsworth left Cambridge in 1591 without having received a degree.[8] Probably because of his attachment to the separatist group known polemically as the "Brownists" he found not only residence at Cambridge but also life in England increasingly difficult.[9]

When persecution was directed against the Brownists, Ainsworth fled, first to Ireland and then to Amsterdam. Unable to find employment as a scholar or a clergyman, Ainsworth worked as a porter for an Amsterdam book dealer beginning in 1593. Finally, in 1596, he found a position as a teacher for one of the English separatist congregations in the Netherlands. There, in collaboration with Francis Johnson, he worked to place independency on a firmer theological footing.[10] In the same year, Ainsworth published his first book, *A True Confession of the Faith, which wee falsely called Brownists, doo hold.*

Internal dissensions gradually split the congregation. Some were related to a dispute over the attire of women brought on by the ornate clothing worn by Francis Johnson's wife. Not long before Francis Johnson's release from prison in Southwark, George Johnson, his brother, became the spokesman of a group in the congregation that was dismayed at the "vain apparel" of the pastor's wife, who "wore three, four or five gold rings at once" while "the brethren" were "in great necessity beyond the seas." This dissension gradually healed itself, particularly after George was forced out of the congregation.[11] Other disputes of a nature more dangerous to the long-term health of the church arose from a debate over the interpretation of Matthew 18:17 ("And if he shall neglect to hear them, tell it unto the church: but if he neglect to hear the church, let him be unto thee as a heathen man and a publican") in relation to the power of excommunication. Whereas Francis Johnson held that the power of excommunication belonged solely to pastors and elders, Ainsworth argued from Matthew 18:17 that the power belonged to the entire congregation. In 1610, the congregation split into two groups, mockingly called "Franciscan Brownists" and "Ainsworthian Brownists" by opponents of separatism. Ainsworth believed that Johnson's attempt to place power in the hands of the pastor and the elders alone was a departure from the biblical principles of the foundation of their congregation—and he was deeply disturbed by the conduct of Johnson and his supporters: "daily, in their public doctrines and prayers they inveighed against the truth they formerly professed; wounded the conscience of the brethren; and sought occasions to draw men from the right way and practice of the Gospell."[12]

In December 1610, finding his situation intolerable, Ainsworth and his followers separated themselves from Johnson's party. Whereas Ainsworth attempted to reduce the tensions between parties, Johnson responded to his exit by deposing and excommunicating Ainsworth. Frederick J. Powicke hypothesizes that the larger portion of the congregation left with Ainsworth, even though Johnson remained in possession of the church building.[13] After some months, during which Ainsworth and his followers are reported to have held their services in a synagogue, a lawsuit brought by the owners of the church building was decided in favor of Ainsworth's group, and Ainsworth was left the sole pastor of the congregation. Johnson eventually left Amsterdam with his followers and settled for four years in Emden.[14]

Between 1609 and 1613, Ainsworth also was involved in a theologically significant epistolary debate with an English recusant, John Ainsworth, later published as *The Trying Out of the Truth, Begun and Prosequuted in Certain Letters between John Aynsworth and Henry*

Aynsworth (1618). The debate began when John Ainsworth, imprisoned as a recusant for his abjuration of the Church of England, challenged Henry Ainsworth to debate the issues separating Protestants and Roman Catholics by letter. The letters of the two Ainsworths, gathered and published as *The Trying Out of the Truth*, cover three topics: whether Scripture is a sufficient rule for faith; whether Scripture ought to be interpreted by the church, according to its unwritten traditions; and whether the "Church of Rome" is the true Catholic Church, and therefore capable of making authoritative pronouncements on the "truths of the faith."[15] Whether John and Henry Ainsworth were related—even brothers, as has been suggested on grounds of the even-handed and nonpolemical character of their debate—cannot be ascertained. The sole evidence that remains is Henry Ainsworth's cryptic remark in the published volume, referring to John Ainsworth, "whom for nation and name, (& I know not whither also for neerer alliance,) I regard as is meet."[16] Typically, however, the two writers refer to each with the literary convention "loving friend," which (like Henry Ainsworth's cryptic comment) points away from kinship.[17]

The close of the first decade of the seventeenth century marked a major turning point not only in Ainsworth's career as a minister in Amsterdam but also in his career as a theologian and exegete. During the fifteen years following the publication of his *True Confession of Faith*, his works had been largely doctrinal and polemical: the treatise on *The Communion of Saincts* (1607); the ironically titled *Counterpoyson: Considerations touching the Poynts in Difference between the godly ministers of the Church of England, and the seduced Brethren of the Separation* (1608); *A Defense of the Holy Scriptures, Worship, and Ministrie* (1609); and *An Arrow Against Idolatrie* (1611); and *A Seasonable Discourse; or a Censure upon a dialogue of the Anabaptists, entitled,* A *Description of What God hath Predestinated Concerning Man* (posth. 1623) are noteworthy examples of Ainsworth's skill as a theologian and polemicist.

Once his position in the church was secure, Ainsworth began to exercise his great linguistic abilities in study of the Hebrew text of the Old Testament and to devote far more time to the publication of exegetical works. His first major exegetical effort was *The Book of Psalmes: Englished both in Prose and Metre. With Annotations, opening the Words and Sentences, by Conference with Other Scriptures* (1612). The annotations on Psalms both illustrates well Ainsworth's exegetical method and indicates the pattern of translation and comment that would be followed in his later works—the annotations on Genesis (1616), Exodus (1617), Leviticus (1618), Numbers (1619), Deuteronomy (1619), and the Song of Songs (1623). All seven volumes were printed under the title *Annotations upon the Five Books of Moses, the Book of Psalms, and the Song of Songs* (1626–1627). In each of these volumes, Ainsworth offered his own translation, based on a close reading of the Hebrew text and an examination of ancient versions (most notably the Septuagint and the Chaldee Paraphrase), together with a series of annotations that both explain the meaning of the text and justify the decisions of the translator.

Ainsworth also appears to have written commentaries or annotations on Hosea, the Gospel of Matthew, and the Epistle to the Hebrews. These works were seen in manuscript form some time after his death by John Worthington, who made some inquiries concerning the possibility of having them published. Disputes between Ainsworth's son and Ainsworth's successor in the church in Amsterdam, John Canne, prevented publication and the manuscripts are now lost.[18]

Little is known of the last years of Ainsworth's life. He is reported to have retired from the church after several more internal disputes. He then visited Ireland, where he may have lived before his exile in Amsterdam, perhaps seeking respite from problems of church politics.[19] Other reports have him briefly in London and one highly hostile but potentially reliable source, the antiseparatist polemicist John Paget, who accused Ainsworth of having "turned [his] coate & changed [his] religion *five* severall times," indicated that Ainsworth returned to the Church of England, lapsed once more, and then finally made a reluctant peace with episcopacy while in Ireland, out of fear of punishment.[20] Ainsworth eventually returned to Amsterdam and to the service of his congregation. He died there in 1622 or early 1623. Neal's *History of the Puritans* offers this curious account of his death:[21]

> His death was sudden, and not without suspicion of violence; for it was reported, that having found a diamond of very great value in the streets of Amsterdam, he advertised it in print, and when the owner, who was a Jew, came to demand it, he offered [Ainsworth] any acknowledgement he would desire; but Ainsworth, though poor, would accept nothing but a conference with some of the rabbis upon the prophecies of the Old Testament relating to the Messias, which the other promised; but not having interest enough to obtain it, and Ainsworth being resolute, it is thought he was poisoned.[22]

Neal's editors add that "others say, that he obtained the conference, and so confounded the Jews, that from pique and malice they in this manner [i.e., poison] put an end to his life."[23]

More recent scholarship has dismissed the account as a bit of malicious fiction and has concluded that Ainsworth died of a "fit of gravel . . . brought on or aggravated by sedentary work."[24] The preface to Ainsworth's *Seasonable Discourse* indicates a lingering illness in Ainsworth's last years.[25] More detail is offered in the *Medical Observations* of Nicholas Tulp or Tulpius, the Amsterdam physician who performed an autopsy on Ainsworth and identified his illness as *ischuria lunatica*—a retention of urine brought on, Tulpius believed, by the phases of the moon. Tulpius did find evidence of kidney stones and of obstruction which, as William and Ernest Axon note, most probably caused fatal blood poisoning. The symptoms of Ainsworth's final illness most certainly caused the rumor that he had been poisoned.[26] The rest of the tale, recorded so piously by Neal and Benjamin Brook, was a sorry speculation that drew together Ainsworth's rabbinic and talmudic interests with the antisemitism of the age.

Ainsworth's Approach to the Text and the Work of Translation

Ainsworth's effort, as illustrated both in his prose and his metrical version of the Psalms, was to produce a translation that was both accurate and understandable—and either easily readable or eminently singable. "The Text I set down in such maner," he explains, "as I neither omit the grace of the Hebrue tongue, (wher in the Psalms wer first pened,) minding how the Apostles writing in Greek, doo chuse many Hebraismes as having their weight, neyther yet use I such uncouth phrases, as the common reader understands not."[27] The New Testament's approach to Hebraisms, therefore, provides

Ainsworth with a rule—and, as his use of the New Testament in his annotations shows, an example frequently followed in detail.

Single words are often not easily translated by means of perfectly equivalent words in the translator's language, as evidenced, Ainsworth argued, by the patterns of the New Testament's Hebraisms. The translation and annotations, therefore, strive for clarity and for the careful communication of meaning by using a series of typographical devices and, on occasion, unusual patterns of punctuation. The range of meaning of individual Hebrew words is indicated by amplification of the translation: where single words cannot translate a Hebrew word, Ainsworth does not hesitate to add qualifiers and indicate synonyms: "For this reason," he states, "I add necessary words of explanation, which may be knowen by their different letter": the text of the annotations thus uses both Black Letter and Roman fonts in order to highlight and distinguish the words of the text from the annotation itself.[28] In addition, Ainsworth will often indicate that a Hebrew verb expresses time and mood without the use of auxiliaries by hyphenating the English verb in his translation—for example, "wil-tell" instead of "will tell."

These explanations and typographical changes frequently offer insight into Ainsworth's approach to translation. Thus, in his annotation on Psalm 2:7, "I wil-tel, the decree: Iehovah, sayd unto me, thou *art* my Son . . . ," Ainsworth comments "I wil-tel,] telling, *is often used for* preaching, declaring, shewing."[29] Similarly, in his comment on Psalm 8:8–9, "8. Sheep and oxen al of them: and also, the beasts of the feild. 9. The fowl of the heavens, & the fishes of the sea," Ainsworth offers the qualifier on verse 8, "Sheep and Oxen] *or* Flocks, *and* heards. The *flock* comprehending both *sheep* and *goats*. Levit. 1.10." And of his translation of verse 9, he notes, "The fowl] *that is*, fowles *or* birds: one *is used for* many *or* all."[30] In both of these instances, Ainsworth has striven for a precise verbal equivalency in translation and has found the need to explain even the best English word: in the case of verse 8, the word translated as "sheep" could as easily be rendered "flock"—and Ainsworth is quick to point out that a "flock" might not simply contain sheep, as he infers from Leviticus 1:10, "And if his offering be of the flocks, namely, of the sheep, or of the goats." In the case of verse 9, he translates "fowl" in the singular because the Hebrew is in the singular, but he points out the plural meaning of the word.

Ainsworth's intention as translator, clearly echoing that of a sixteenth-century humanist such as Reuchlin, is thus to come as close to the Hebrew as English will allow and, rather than provide a translation noted for its pleasing English style, to offer a version that directs its readers toward Hebrew words and Hebraic meanings.[31] Ainsworth also strives for verbal equivalency in his punctuation of the text: he not only offers qualifiers, as indicated in the annotations, he also differs "somewhat in phrase from our former Englished Bible" and, indeed, "in pawses, (which are more frequent here,) I follow the Original text: where more are to be seen than our English can wel admit of." These pauses or punctuations, explains Ainsworth, serve "both to shew the sense, and to read with consideration."[32]

Ainsworth's use of the ancient versions also offers insight into his approach and places him with humanistic advocates of what Schwarz identified as the "philological view" of translation, notably Johannes Reuchlin. On the one hand, Ainsworth seldom looks to the patristic and medieval exegetical tradition for answers—while, on the other, he never renounces traditionary readings of the text and, in fact, often obliges the exegetical tradition in his understanding of doctrinal and prophetic issues. His primary interest was in the most ancient sources.[33] Ainsworth was quite aware that the Septuagint often differs from the Hebrew original and he indicates a decided preference to the Hebrew text. Yet, he also evidences considerable respect for the "Seventy" as translators who were able to grasp fine nuances of the original. Similarly, his use of the Chaldee Paraphrase or Targums indicates his respect for the ability of the ancient paraphrase to grasp the meaning of the Hebrew—and very much like Reuchlin, Ainsworth came increasingly to value the Jewish exegesis of the Old Testament, as found not only in the Targums but also in the Talmud and Midrash.[34]

It is worth noting that Ainsworth's versification typically assumes that the titles or subscriptions are integral parts of the text of the Psalms to be included, in his prose version, as part of the first verse or even, in the instances of longer titles, as an entire verse or pair of verses. This procedure is different from that of the King James Version, in which the subscriptions and titles are not included in the versification. Thus, in Psalm 50, his text reads,

> 1. A psalm of Asaph: The God of Gods, Iehovah; speaketh, and caleth the earth: from the rising-up of the Sun, unto the going-in thereof.
> 2. Out of Sion the whole perfection of bewty, God shineth clearly.

By way of contrast, the somewhat longer subscription to Psalm 51 is given two verses:

> 1. To the mayster *of the musick*, a psalm of David. 2. When Nathan the Prophet, came unto him: after he had entered, unto Bathshebangh.
> 3. Be gracious to me O God according to thy kind-mercie: according to the multitude of thy tender-mercies, wipe-away my trespasses.

(Ainsworth, as would be expected, did not set the subscriptions into verse—with the result that his metrical versions frequently begin with verse two or three.)

As Ainsworth himself noted in his preface, much of his translation was finished and partly printed before he was able to examine "our late wel amended Translation," the famous "King James Version" of 1611.[35] Indeed, Ainsworth's renderings, although frequently akin to the King James Version and its predecessors, evidence an independence from it and from the previous translations in the English tradition—the Coverdale, the Geneva, and the Bishop's Bible. The translation of the tetragrammaton as "Jehovah" and the use of transliterations of divine names, like "Jah," typical of Ainsworth's work, is a major mark of distinction between his version and the several translations available to him.

The independence of Ainsworth's efforts from previous versions, particularly in the earlier part of the Psalter, before the appearance of the King James Version, is nowhere more apparent than in his version of Psalm 23. In this Psalm in particular, the ancestors of the King James Version are all quite similar. Thus, Coverdale:

> A psalme of Dauid.
> THE LORDE is my shepherde, I can want nothinge. He fedeth me in a grene pasture, and ledeth me to a fresh water. He quickeneth my soule, and bringeth me forth in the waye of righteousness for his names sake. Though I shulde walke now in the valley of the shadowe of death, yet I feare no euell, for thou art with me: thy staffe and thy shepehoke comforte me. Thou preparest a table before me agaynst mine enemies: thou anoyntest my

> heade with oyle, and fyllest my cuppe full. Oh let thy louinge kyndnes and mercy folowe me all the dayes of my life, that I may dwell in the house of the LORDE for euer.[36]

The Geneva Bible adds versification and makes several changes, some of them approximating more closely the King James Version:

> A Psalme of Dauid.
> 1. The Lorde *is* my shepherd, I shal not want.
> 2. He maketh me to rest in grene pasture, and leadeth me by the stil waters.
> 3. He restoreth my soule, and leadeth me in the paths of righteousnes for his Names sake.
> 4. Yea, thogh I shulde wakle through the valley of the shadow of death, I wil feare no euil: for thou art with me: thy rod and thy staffe, they comfort me.
> 5. Thou doest prepare a table before me, in the sight of mine aduersaries: thou doest anoint mine head with oyle, *and* my cup runneth ouer.
> 6. Douteles kindenes, and mercie shal follow me all the dayes of my life, and I shal remaine a long season in the house of the Lord.[37]

The Bishops' Bible also reflects its predecessors and points toward the King James Version:

> The Lorde is my shepheard: therefore can I lack nothing.
> 2 Hee shall feede mee in a greene pasture: and leade me forth beside the waters of comfort
> 3 He shall convert my soule: and bring me foorth in the paths of righteousnesse, for his names sake.
> 4 Yea, though I walke through the valley of the shadow of death, I will feare no euill: for thou art with me, thy rodde and thy staffe comfort me.
> 5 Thou shalt prepare a table before mee, against them that trouble mee: thou hast anointed my head with oyle, and my cup shall be full.
> 6 But thy loving kindnes an mercy shall follow me all the dayes of my life: and I will dwell in the house of the Lord for euer.[38]

Ainsworth, however, is quite distinctive, in places echoing the tradition of translation but also in each verse offering a unique approach to the words of the text:

> 1. A Psalm of David. Iehovah feedeth me, I shall not lack. [2] In folds of budding grass, he maketh me lie-down: he easily-leadeth me, by the waters of rests. [3] He returneth my soul: he leadeth me in the beaten-paths of justice, for his name sake. [4] Yea, though I should walk, in the vally of the shade of death, I wil not fear, evil; for thou *wilt be* with me: they rod and thy staff, they shal comfort me. [5] Thou furnishest before me, a table; *in* presence of my distressers: thou makest fat my head with oil; my cup *is* abundant. [6] Doubtles, good and mercy shal folow me, al the dayes of my life: and I shal converse in the howse of Iehovah, to length of dayes.

The characteristics of Ainsworth's verbal equivalency method of translation are evident: the use of "Iehovah" rather than "Lord" to translate the tetragrammaton, the hyphenated combinations of English words to indicate the translation of a single Hebrew word ("budding-grass," "lie-down," "easily-leadeth," and "beaten-paths") and the use of punctuation for the sake of indicating speaker's pauses in the Hebrew ("I will not fear, evil" and "before me, a table"). In addition, the many differences between Ainsworth's version and all of the translations in the tradition leading to the King James Version indicate his independence as a translator. The tradition of English translation, for example, consistently offers "green pasture" or "pastures" where Ainsworth translates "folds of budding-grass"; the tradition provides "valley of the shadow of death" while Ainsworth gives "vally of the shade of death." Coverdale, Bishops, and King James translate "I will dwell in the house of the Lord forever," and Ainsworth quite distinctively offers "I shal converse in the howse of Iehovah, to length of dayes."

Even so, Ainsworth's version of the familiar 139th Psalm, probably done with the King James Version in hand, echoes it in places, but also frequently departs from it:

> 1. To the mayster *of the musik*, Davids Psalme: Iehovah thou hast serched me, and known. 2. Thou knowest my sitting and my rising; thou understandest my *familiar*-thought, a farr off. 3. Thou fannest my path and my lying-down: and art accustomed to al my wayes.
>
> 4. When the speech *is* not *yet* in my tongue: loe Iehovah, thou knowest it al. 5. Thou doost besett me behind, and before: and puttest, thy palm upon me. 6. A knowledge too marveilous for me: it is high, I cannot *atteyn* to it.[39]

Perhaps most remarkable from a stylistic perspective is Ainsworth's frequent economy of phrase: where the King James Version gives "Thou knowest my downsitting and my uprising," he offers, following the Geneva Bible, "Thou knowest my sitting and my rising"; where the King James Version, in this verse, identical with Coverdale, renders the text "For there is not a word in my tongue, *but*, lo, O Lord, thou knowest it altogether," and the Geneva, "For there is not a worde in my tongue, but lo, thou knowest it wholly, ó Lord," Ainsworth has "When the speech *is* not *yet* in my tongue: loe Iehovah, thou knowest it al." This latter illustration also exemplifies Ainsworth's desire for precision of meaning: it is not clear from the Geneva or the King James Version whether or not the word has been spoken—Ainsworth makes clear that the sound has not yet been uttered.

Nonetheless, when he feels that a single English word cannot bear the meaning of the Hebrew, economy is set aside. Thus, in Psalm 140, the King James Version (KJV) renders verse one as, "Deliver me, O Lord, from the evil man: preserve me from the violent man."[40] Ainsworth offers, "Release me Ô Iehovah, from the evil earthly-man; from the man of violent wrongs, preserve thou me," qualifying the identity of the "evil man" as tending toward the dust in order more precisely to render the Hebrew *Adam*, and of the "violent man" as a doer of wrong. The following verse evidences a return to strict economy: "Which think evil *things* in hart: every day, they gather warrs" over against the King James Version's "Which imagine mischiefs in *their* hart; continually are they gathered together *for* warr." For the final phrase, Ainsworth will also allow, as offered in his annotations, "they are gathered to warrs"—but the economy remains.[41]

The translation of *Adam* as "earthly-man" belongs to Ainsworth's effort at precise renderings of the meaning of the Hebrew. Thus, in Psalm 4:3, Ainsworth translates the plural of *Ish* simply as "men," but in his annotations adds that this "is the name of *man* in respect of his *power* and *dignity*."[42] When a text calls for a contrast between *Adam* and *Ish*, as in Psalm 49:3, Ainsworth renders the former "base-man" and the latter "nobleman." *Adam*, he notes, "was so called of *Adamah the earth*, whereupon this title is given *to the baser sort of people*," in contrast to the use of *Ish* to refer to the "valor, nobleness, and dignitie" of human beings.[43] Comparison with the King James Version provides a significant index to Ainsworth's originality: "Both sonns of base-man, and sonns of noble-man: togither rich and poor" over against "Both low and high, rich and poor, together" (Psalm 49:2, KJV). Ainsworth understood a strong contrast between *Ish* and *Enosh*: whereas the former refers to human beings according to their dignity, the latter, he argues, is a name "given to al men, to put them in mind of their *miserie and mortality*." *Enosh*, thus, signifies man as "doleful, sory, sorrowful, wretched, and sick incurably."[44] *Geber* also is translated to indicate its distinct meaning—as "perfect man" in Psalm 18:26, where Ainsworth annotates "*man*] or, *mighty-one*" and comments that *Geber* indicates "strength, valor, and superiority." In Psalm 19:6, *Geber* is rendered "mighty-man" and in Psalm 45:4 as "mighty-one": there is no slavish rendition of the Hebrew as one equivalent; rather in each case, Ainsworth attempts to understand the distinctive Hebrew word in its context and to translate it accordingly, typically indicating with a hyphen that his two English words have translated a single Hebrew word.[45]

Ainsworth and the Protestant Exegetical Tradition

Ainsworth's exegesis belongs to the more literal-grammatical side of the Reformed exegetical tradition.[46] He attends closely to the text and, as evidenced throughout his annotations, assumes that exposition begins with grammatical and linguistic analysis and with translation. As is the case with most exegetes of his time, whether Protestant or Roman Catholic, Ainsworth saw a host of christological references in the Psalms and, indeed, throughout the Old Testament. Nevertheless, Ainsworth evidences a clear preference for the more literal patterns of Reformed interpretation—more in the spirit of Calvin, Beza, Perkins, Willet, Rivetus, Diodati, and Poole than of Piscator, the Federal School, Dickson, and Matthew Henry. Where Piscator, the Federalists, Dickson, and Henry consistently sought out the typological and, indeed, allegorical meaning of the Old Testament in order to point the text as much as possible toward its fulfillment in Christ, Ainsworth follows a somewhat more restrained path.[47] Although he notes many of the traditional types, tropes, and doctrinal associations, Ainsworth's emphasis falls on the text and its literal meaning, and on those figures that, arguably, are intrinsic to it.

A clear index of Ainsworth's approach to the Old Testament is his understanding of the relationship of David and Christ in the Psalter. Throughout the history of the Christian exegesis of the Old Testament, David has been understood as a type of Christ and many of the Psalms have been interpreted as direct prophecies of Christ's advent and work. Once this relationship of type and antitype, prophecy and fulfillment had been established, however, the further question of the primary meaning or focus of the text was subject to a variety of answers: it was simple enough, under the terms of the fourfold exegesis of the Middle Ages to identify David as the literal subject and Christ as the allegorical or anagogical subject of a Psalm. Nicholas of Lyra, similarly, could argue a double literal sense, according to which David was the literal subject in an initial historical sense and Christ the literal subject of a Psalm as identified by the New Testament revelation. In the early sixteenth century, Lefèvre d'Étaples could argue single literal reference to Christ in Psalms 1, 2, 17, 18, and 20, on the ground that the Apostle Paul understood Christ as the literal subject of these Psalms: the reference to David virtually disappears and Christ is understood to be the "foundation and goal," "*principium* and *finis*" of the Psalter as a whole.[48]

These interests and interpretive patterns, standing as they did in relation to the historical path of prophecy and revelation given in the canon of Scripture, did not entirely disappear with the Reformation and the beginnings of Protestantism.[49] In particular, Lefèvre's identification of Christ as the sole subject of certain Psalms and the "*principium* and *finis*" of the whole Psalter remained an exegetical option long into the seventeenth century: David Dickson could state that the subject of Psalm 2 was "mainly, if not only . . . Christ," that the primary message of Psalm 8 was the love and grace of God toward human beings as shown forth primarily in Christ, that the basic argument or scope of Psalm 18 was the identification of David "as a type of Christ, and fellow partaker of the sufferings of Christ," and that Psalm 20 was written "to the church in the form of a prayer for the kings of Israel, but with a special eye upon, and relation unto Christ."[50] And if Dickson could find a reference to Christ in Psalm 1 only in the blessed man's delight in the law of the Lord as holding "forth the way of reconciliation with God," he saw no need to mention David at all.[51] Since, moreover, the "scope" of the entire book of Psalms was "not only to teach us the grounds of divinity for our information, but also to direct us how to apply saving doctrines practically to ourselves," once the way of righteousness was identified in Psalm 1, Dickson argued, Christ was announced in Psalm 2 and, given this foundation, the "rest of the Psalms hold forth examples of Christ and his followers . . . in all assaults making use of their covenant with God, and prevailing by his power." Even so, the Psalter closes with praise that looks forward to "that endless and uninterrupted thanksgiving . . . at the great day of our Lord's second coming."[52]

Thus, also in Matthew Henry's commentary, the primary referent of Psalms 2 and 8 is Christ and the David-Christ typology is clearly seen in Psalms 18 and 20,[53] while the christological reference in Psalm 1 is confined to the final pronouncement of blessing on the righteous and doom for the ungodly in Christ's second coming—adumbrating, perhaps, for Henry the eschatological vision of the end of the Psalter where the victory and vindication of Israel ultimately refer "to Christ's victories, by the power of his gospel and grace over spiritual enemies, in which all believers are more than conquerors."[54] For Henry, like Dickson, understood the "scope" of the entire Psalter as an "abstract, or summary, of both Testaments" in which "the exercises of natural religion" and "the excellencies of revealed religion" were advanced, with "Christ, the Crown and Centre of revealed religion . . . clearly spoken of in type and prophecy."[55]

The contrast between this typological or even allegorical emphasis and the more literal approach characteristic of Calvin and his direct heirs in the Reformed exegetical tradition is considerable. Calvin did not deny the christological reference of the Psalms—but, as his commentary on Psalm 18 evidences, he focused his interpretation on David and only discussed Christ insofar as David, in the Psalm "also shows that his reign was an image and type of the kingdom of Christ, to teach and assure the faithful."[56] Thus, the religious life of the historical David provides the setting of the Psalm: "We ought carefully to mark," Calvin writes, "the particular time when this psalm was composed, as it shows us that David, when his affairs were brought to a state of peace and prosperity, was not intoxicated with extravagant joy like irreligious men."[57] Calvin understands Psalm 20 as "a common prayer of the Church on behalf of the King of Israel . . . for in the person of David the safety and well-being of the whole community centered."[58] Here, too, he recognizes the prophetic reference to Christ, but the primary focus of his interpretation remains David. Even in Psalm 2, in which the New Testament use of the text so clearly identified the Psalm as a Messianic prophecy, Calvin still identifies David as the literal subject and Christ as the antitype: after its literal presentation of the perpetuity of the kingdom of David, the Psalm also "contains a prophecy concerning the future kingdom of Christ."[59] What is more, Calvin's sense of the scope or argument of the entire Psalter was directed toward a more strict literal and historical interpretation: rather than a summary of all doctrine and a revelation of Christ, he understood the Psalms as "an anatomy of all parts of the soul" in which the various writers reveal "all their inmost thoughts and affections" as they speak directly in prayer to God.[60] The Psalms are, therefore, "replete with all the precepts which serve to frame our life to every part of holiness, piety, and righteousness" that " principally teach and train us to bear the cross."[61]

Even Calvin, however, was led to argue that certain of the royal Psalms, identified as messianic or christological by the New Testament, were direct references to Christ. Thus, of Psalm 110 he writes "in this psalm David sets forth the perpetuity of Christ's reign." Given Christ's own application of the Psalm to himself (Matt. 22:42–45) and the clear messianic content of the Psalm itself, Calvin comments, "we are able, by the most irresistible arguments, to compel" even the "most obstinate" of Jewish adversaries "to admit that the truths here stated relate neither to David nor to any other person than the Mediator alone."[62] Indeed, comments Calvin, the fourth verse, with its reference to Melchizedek, "is a satisfactory proof that the person here spoken of is none other than Christ."[63] Calvin also offers an extended commentary on the Melchizedek-Christ typology in his commentary on Genesis 14:18–19—a point on which the Reformed exegetical tradition is both unanimous and, in addition, reflective of the larger Christian exegetical tradition.[64]

Ainsworth, although occasionally somewhat less restrained than Calvin, never reaches the christological emphasis of Dickson and Henry. His basic perspective on the Psalter, quite in contrast to the perspectives of all the interpreters just noted, was to view it as hymnody. "Psalms of holy scripture, are perpetually to be sung in the church," Ainsworth writes, "for God hath given his word, partly in prose, to be read; partly in metre to be sung."[65] The Psalter was "by the Prophets, (and specially David), to be left unto the church as a part of the Canonicall word of God" to be sung in worship even as the prose scriptures are read. The Psalms therefore have, according to Ainsworth, hortatory and doxological functions: "the celebrating of God, his name and works . . . the teaching, instructing, comforting, of our selves . . . the alaying of our inordinate passions, anger, greif, and care . . . stirring up good affections in us, joy, comfort, servencie in the spirit . . . facilitie & ease for us to learn the law of God with more delight."[66] At this point, a parallel with Calvin's approach appears and, with it, the motivation to find the primary meaning of the Psalter in the religious life of the historical writers.

Christological interpretations are present in Ainsworth's reading of the Psalter, but do not dominate the exegesis as they tend to do in Dickson's and Henry's commentaries. Unlike most of his contemporaries and many of his predecessors in the Protestant exegetical tradition, Ainsworth saw no reason to identify Christ as the "blessed man" of Psalm 1: the only christological reference he finds is the nurturing effect of the streams or "brooks of water" (v. 3). Ainsworth assumes the Messianic import of Psalm 2 and he cites David as a "type of Christ" in Psalm 18:50, Psalm 40:1, and Psalm 89. In Psalm 2, however, he does not so much replace David with Christ as interpret the text as a prophecy: "David was the writer of this Psalm," Ainsworth comments, "and beginneth with marveling at the rage and folly of the Jewes and Gentiles, in persecuting Christ and his Church; Act. 4.35, &c."[67] In Psalm 8, not the entire Psalm but only verses 2, 3, 6, and 7: the praise of God's name "in all the earth [and] above the heavens" and the reference to strength "out of the mouths of babes and sucklings," are interpreted as prophecies of Christ, by the expected "conference" of the Psalm with New Testament texts. In the first phrase Ainsworth refers to "the spreading of Christ's kingdom and gospel" and in the second to the fulfillment of the prophecy "when children crying *Hosanna* to welcome Christ; the cheif preists and Scribes disdeighned, and sought to destroy him: but he stopped their mouthes, by aledging this scripture."[68] In the sixth and seventh verses, Ainsworth understands a double reference of the words "son of man" to Adam and to Christ. The exposition is similar to Calvin's, which notes the christological referent of the latter two texts only, but then expands on the prophetic character of the middle portion of the Psalm, beginning with verse 4 (KJV), "What is man . . . and the son of man, that thou visitest him. Calvin comments that, in the final prophetic sense, this "passage may properly apply to Christ alone."[69] In his christological reading of Psalm 110, Ainsworth simply concurs with tradition, given the weight of the New Testament evidence.

Ainsworth's caution in drawing out the christological interpretation arises from his close sense of the Hebrew text and, in the case of Psalm 2, out of his interest in the distinctive meanings of the several Hebrew words for "man." His translation runs, "What is sory-man that thou remembrest him: and the son of Adam, that thou-visitest him?" Here, "sory-man" translates *Enosh* while *Adam* is transliterated, rather than rendered as "earthly-man" or "base-man," because of what Ainsworth takes to be the multiple reference—to Adam and to all of Adam's progeny. The focus of Ainsworth's interpretation is the meaning of the words for "man" and, remarkably, in view of the connection drawn by other interpreters between the phrase "son of Man" and Christ,[70] without any initial reference to christological themes. Ainsworth contrasts the two names for human beings:

> *Enosh*, or "sory-man," was the name of Adam's nephew, Gen. 4:26, which signifieth *doleful, sory, sorrowful*. . . . And this name is given to al men, to put them in mind of their *misery and mortality*: as *Psal. 9:21. let the heathens know, that they be Ænosh.*[71]

"Adam," Ainsworth continues, was "the name of both man and woman . . . and is also the name of al their children." And just as human beings are called *Enosh* to remind them of "their doleful estate, by syn," so are they all called *Adam* "to put them in mind of their original, and end; which were made of *Adamah* the *earth*, even of the dust; and to dust shall agayne return. Gen. 2:7. & 3:19."[72] The point of the text is to indicate, granting man's identity, how generous the divine providence is toward him. Reference to Christ appears, in Ainsworth's reading, only in the next verse, based on the citation of the Psalm in Hebrews 2:6–7, but even there the reference of the Psalm to man in general remains and Ainsworth argues that the text may be understood as a reference to human beings before the fall, as they were "first made, in Gods image, and Lord of the world, Gen. 1:26."[73] Similarly, the eighteenth Psalm refers primarily to David, called "servant of Iehovah . . . for his service in administering the kingdom."[74]

We do see a hint of the eschatological reading of the final Psalms in the Psalter in Ainsworth's understanding of the phrase "he hath exalted the horn of his people"

(Ps. 148:14) as a reference to Christ, the "horn of salvation" in Luke 1:69. And in the final verse of the Psalter, which he translated as "Let al breath praise Iah; Halelu-Iah," Ainsworth saw—as had many of his predecessors—the glorious vision "where every creature which is in heaven and on earth and under the earth . . . were heard, saying, Unto him that sitteth upon the Throne unto the Lamb, be blessing, & honour, & glorie, & power for ever & ever."[75] Here, however, as before, the christological readings do not overpower the text and Ainsworth's primary concern remains the significance of Hebrew words and phrases in their biblical and primarily Old Testament context.

Both in the extended title of his annotations on the Psalms and at greater length in the preface to this first major interpretive effort, Ainsworth made an effort to explain and to justify his exegetical method to his readers. The key phrase in the title of the *Psalmes* is "opening the words and sentences, by conference with other scriptures." This method of conferring Scripture with Scripture, which we have observed throughout the preceding examples, is the exegetical analog of the Protestant doctrine of the prior authority of Scripture: inasmuch as no interpretive authority stands above the Scriptures, the text itself must be the key to understanding the text—and when a particular place in the text is unclear, clarity is gained not by going outside the text to the churchly magisterium or to a particular tradition of authoritative exegesis, but by comparing the unclear portion of the text with a clear portion of similar meaning.[76]

The method of "conference" also assumes the underlying unity of individual books of the Bible and of the Bible as a whole.[77] Ainsworth, therefore, does not confine his comparisons of text with text to the other verses in the same Psalm or to the book of Psalms, but frequently searches through the entire Old Testament for similar grammatical usages and often points toward the fulfillment prophecy in the New Testament as the ultimate theological meaning of a text. His cautious approach to the Messianic implications of the Psalms and his primary interest in a literal-grammatical exegesis, moreover, undergird this approach to typology. In most cases, Ainsworth's discoveries of Christ in the Psalter not only reflect traditional patterns of exegesis; they also assume a New Testament use of the passage. Thus, Ainsworth does not always or nearly always identify David as a type of Christ, nor does he view the entire Psalter as primarily christological. Rather, he identifies Christ as a prophetic subject only when another text, typically drawn from the New Testament, offers the identification: the historical subject of the Psalm continues to be David and the primary focus of the exegesis of the whole remains the words of the text, most of which are not references to Christ.

From the perspective of his eminent contemporary, Whitaker, this approach to typology indicated a profound respect for the literal meaning of the text. According to Whitaker, the identification of various figurative meanings in the text, if controlled by Scripture itself, was not a departure from literal exegesis. "We concede," he comments,

> such things as allegory, anagoge, and tropology in scripture; but meanwhile we deny that there are many and various senses. We affirm that there is but one true, proper, and genuine sense of scripture, arising from the words rightly understood, which we call the literal.[78]

"Various collections," "senses," "applications," and "accommodations" of a text remain possible, but only if they arise from the literal, grammatical meaning of the text. Whitaker cites Hosea 11:1, "Out of Egypt have I called my son," and Exodus 12:46, "Thou shalt not break a bone of him," as examples: both texts are clear, so that neither demands an allegorical reading on the ground of the impossibility of the letter:

> It is sufficiently plain that the former is to be understood of the people of Israel, and the latter of the paschal lamb. Who, now, would dare to transfer and accommodate these to Christ, if the Holy Spirit had not done it first, and declared to us his mind and intention?—namely that the *Son* in the former passage denotes not only the people of Israel, but Christ also; and the *bone* in the latter, is to be understood of Christ as well as of the paschal lamb. They who interpret these places merely of the people of Israel or the paschal lamb, bring only part of the meaning, not the whole: because the entire sense is to be understood of the sign and the thing itself together, and consists in the accommodation of the sign to the thing signified. Hereupon emerge not different senses, but one entire sense.[79]

The "letter" or the "literal sense" of a text is not, therefore, restricted to a single historical referent.[80]

Comparison of the work of Ainsworth with that of his contemporary Andrew Willet sheds further light on this interpretive perspective, particularly given their common interest in the Pentateuch, the reputation that both attained in their own day as experts on the language and meaning of the Books of Moses, and the methodological and hermeneutical similarities between the expositions. Willet's method was distinguished by its "sixfold" or, as he called it, "hexapla" approach to a text.[81] The method consisted in an introductory "Analysis" or argument, an examination of the text and translations, a discussion of interpretive difficulties with extensive reference to other commentators past and present, a presentation of theological topics related to the text, a section dealing with theological disputes, and, finally, a homiletical application.[82]

Ainsworth's approach to Genesis, although less elaborate than Willet's, does offer a threefold division in to argument, translation, and annotation. The argument offers a synopsis of the chapter, the translation is Ainsworth's own, and the annotations cover background to the book, textual comments related to Ainsworth's own work of translation, his comparison of the ancient versions, and frequently his use of rabbinic sources.[83] Indeed, if the methods of two exegetes are to be contrasted, the fundamental difference that determines the direction of the comment is not the difference in organization or even the presence of a strong dogmatic thrust in the fourth division of Willet's "hexapla": rather, it is Ainsworth's tendency to gravitate toward rabbinic sources and Willet's tendency to survey the history of Christian comment that create the most significant contrasts between the commentaries.

Ainsworth and Willet on the Identity of Melchizedek

By way of an example related to the christological exegesis of the Psalter, the discussion of the identify of Melchizedek found in the commentaries of Ainsworth and contemporaries like Willet is also instructive. Willet's discussion of the identity of Melchizedek begins with a series of patristic identifications that he examines and, for the most part, rejects at some length. Thus, "*Origen* and *Didymus* thinke that *Melchizedek* was an Angell, but the text is contrary that maketh him King of Salem."[84] More troublesome is the interpretation attributed to Augustine, that identifies Melchizedek as the Holy Ghost.

Willet doubts that the source of this opinion, a treatise of "questions of the Old and new Testament," is actually by Augustine. One of Augustine's genuine works, comments Willet, "numbereth the Melchsedechians among the Heretikes," an "erronious opinion" that at least serves to undermine an attribution of the *Quaestiones Veteris et Novi Testamenti* to Augustine.[85] More important, it makes no sense to identify "a Priest to the most high God" as the Holy Ghost because "every Priest is taken from among men, Heb. 5.1, 2" and because the Holy Ghost, as God, cannot be inferior to God as a Priest must be.

> And whereas the Apostle saith, that *Melckisedeck was without father or mother, and without beginning of dayes, or end of life, Heb.7.3.* whence they would enforce that *Melchisedeck* was not a mortall man, but of an immortall nature; the Apostle hath there relation onely to one story in this place; *Melchisedeck* is not set forth in story by his kindred, his birth and death; he had both father and mother, was borne, and died, but there is no mention made of it, and so *Hierome* expoundeth that word used by the Apostle, *agenealogetos*, genealogie is not expressed or mentioned.[86]

Willet thus refutes a patristic misinterpretation with a careful piece of patristic exegesis. He also, here, quietly disagrees with Calvin, who had viewed the testimony of Hebrews 7:3 to the unknown origin of Melchizedek, "as if he had dropped from the clouds," and the lack of reference to his death as proof positive that God had chosen "a person unknown" who was "a sincere cultivator and guardian of religion" amid "the corruptions of the world."[87]

A third view, which boasted a notable series of theologians and exegetes—"*Irenaeus, Eusebius, Caesarien* [i.e., Basil], *Apollinarius, Eustathius*, as *Hierome* testifieth, and among the new Writers, *Calvin, Iunius, Musculus, Mercerus, Pererius*"—is that Melchizedek "was a King of Canaan, and not of *Abrahams* line."[88] Pererius had argued that Heb. 7:6, "He whose kindred is not counted among them" proved that Melchizedek was not one of Abraham's kindred. Willet counters with the point already taken from Jerome—that the meaning here is identical to that of Heb. 3:2, "not rehearsed in genealogie" and has no significance beyond the form of the story itself. In addition, "seeing Canaan was under Gods curse, and *Sem* had the chief blessing, how is it that one of Canaan should blesse *Abraham* of *Sem*." Even so, none of the Canaanites could be greater than Abraham, as Melchizedek was, granting that God's curse was on Canaan and Abraham is "the father of the faithfull."[89] These considerations appear to Willet to be sufficient to set aside the identification of Melchizedek as an otherwise unknown Canaanite and to rule out the caveat voiced by Calvin and later exegetes that, if Melchizedek were Shem, the text would surely not have given him a new and strange name.[90]

These arguments bring Willet to a fourth opinion, which he believes to be the "most probable": that Melchizedek was "Sem" or "Shem," the son of Noah. As Syracides commented, Willet continues, "Sem and Seth were in great honour among the children of men" and even though, at the time of Abraham, *Arphaxad, Selah*, and *Heber* yet lived, yet *Sem* was most honorable in respect of his yeares" and his receipt of Noah's blessing. What is more, Abraham's immediate ancestors were "idolaters"—leaving Shem the greatest among the living and greater, thus, than Abraham. The Midrash also agrees, granting that Salem or Jerusalem is known to have been the place of residence of Shem. Moreover, as Melanchthon argues, "God brought *Abraham* to *Sem* the father of his ancestors, to joyne together a notable company of the Church."[91] After a series of further arguments concerning the suitability of Shem, Willet offers as final reason the Melckizedek-Christ typology:

> seeing *Melchisedeck* was a type of Christ, *Psal. 110.* that came of *Sem*, and no type or figure of Christ is expressed in Scripture but of *Sems* line, none is more like to be this representer and foreshewer of Christs everlasting Priesthood, than *Sem* himself then living. It is most unlike, that any Priest not of *Sem*, should shadow forth the high Priest Christ . . . and not . . . *Sem*, the father of Christ after the flesh.[92]

Willet notes and answers a series of chronological objections and then approaches the readings of Chytraeus and Cajetan, who had indicated that "Melchizedek" was not a proper name, but "an appellative, signifying that he was a righteous & just king": Cajetan had indicated that such a name, like that of "another King of Jerusalem called *Adoni-zedek*, Lord of justice," might well be a name "not proper to *Sem*, but common to the kings of Salem, as *Caesar* and *Augustus* were to the Emperour of Rome." Willet accepts the derivation, but answers with Selneccer that such a name would indeed be proper to Shem, "in respect of his office, because onely he excelled among the rest, as a just King."[93] Willet's exegesis, thus, is guided by the history of interpretation—patristic, Catholic (Cajetan and Pererius), Lutheran (Chytraeus and Selneccer), and Reformed (Calvin, Junius, Musculus, and Mercerus)—although clearly not bound to any particular trajectory, granting his rejection, on this point, of the Reformed view and his advocacy of the rabbinic position.

Ainsworth, by way of contrast, offers no reference either to the Fathers or to sixteenth- and seventeenth-century exegetes in his comment. He relies almost exclusively on Rabbinic exegesis. This emphasis does not change the result of the exegesis, granting that the identification of Melchizedek and Shem comes from the rabbis—but it does change the tone of the exercise. Ainsworth notes no alternative identifications and moves directly to the rabbinic view and to the question of typology:

> v. 18. *Melchisedek:*] the Ierusalemy Thargum sayth, *he Shem rabba, this* was *Sem the great:* and in *Breshith Rabba* upon this place, it is sayd, *this Melchisedek was Sem the son of Noe.* He was called *Melchisedek*, that is by interpretation, *King of justice, Heb.* 7.2 and therein, was a figure of *Christ*, the *King that reigneth in justice, Esay. 32.1*. . . . Other the best and most ancient Hebrue Doctors, doe also hold *Melchisedek* to be *Sem*: so *Pirke* R. *Eliezer, chapt 8.* and *Thalmod Babyl. in Treatise of vowes, at the end of Chapt.* 3. and *Ben Sirach* sayth, *Sem and Seth, were glorious among men: Ecclus* 49.16.[94]

Ainsworth also makes short work of the identification of "Salem"—it is, as "both the Chaldee paraphrasts say," Jerusalem. This contrasts with the lengthy discussion in Willet, where the identification of Salem as a "town in the region of Sichem," as Jerome and in the sixteenth century Mercerus had argued. For Willet, much of the issue is one of linguistic derivation: Jerome's derivation of Jerusalem from the Greek *hieros* and the Hebrew *salem* is unlikely: he prefers a Jewish interpretation that Shem first called the city Salem and later, after Abraham's visit, the name was altered, following the pattern of Abraham's altar "Jehovah Jireh" (Gen. 22:14), "the Lord will be seene." Thus, the Midrash on Psalm 76 understands Jerusalem as Jireh-salem "which signifieth the vision of peace."[95]

A major point of difference between the two exegetes—traceable to Ainsworth's greater interest in rabbinic exegesis and the resulting difference in his manner of handling doctrinal or dogmatic issues raised by the text–lies in the handling of Melchizedek's offering of bread and wine to Abraham. Willet deals with this issue in the controversial section of his commentary and devotes almost his entire energy to a refutation of Roman Catholic exegesis. The offering of the bread and wine was not a sacrifice nor was Melchizedek's priesthood defined by his offering of the bread and wine. Willet gloats that Cajetan had stated "Nothing is written of the oblation, but of the prolation or producing of bread and wine." This "producing" of bread and wine was in fact a "princely gift" and a priestly act of blessing, given Melchizedek's dual role–as Josephus rightly says, it was a time of refreshment after battle, contrasted with the ill behavior of the Moabites and Ammonites who were "accursed" for not offering refreshment to the Israelites as they "came out of Egypt, Deut. 23.4."[96] Moreover, Willet raises the issue of the Melchizedek-Christ typology primarily in his polemical section, in order to define the nature of Melchizedek's priesthood over against Roman Catholic sacrificial readings of the text: it is the eternity of Melchizedek's priesthood and his spiritual anointing that founds the typology, not his offering of bread and wine. "So that in truth," Willet concludes, "this example of *Melchizedek* . . . maketh altogether against the popish Masse sacrifice, and nothing for it."[97]

Ainsworth, by way of contrast, looks for a rabbinic link and finds it "in *Echah rabbethi* or *Comment on the Lamentations*" in which "the Hebrew Doctors . . . say from Esa. 9.6, *the name of the Messias is called Salom* (*Peace*)." Melchizedek, the type or figure of the Messiah, therefore, "here hath nothing to do with the warrs of the nine kings, but goverened his realm in peace." The story, therefore, parallels that story of David and his followers who were "refreshed in the wildernes, by good men who brought them victuals, 2 Sam.17.27, 28, 29 and as on the contrary, the Ammonites & Moabites might not enter into the congregation of the Lord for ever, *because they mett not Israel with bread and water in the way, when they came out of Egypt, Deut.23.3, 4.*"[98] In this act, Ainsworth adds, Melchizedek may be understood as a type of Christ, "who taketh away the hunger & thirst of al that beleev in him, Iohn.6.35."[99] Significantly, Ainsworth not only fails to mention the polemic with Rome, he also utterly refuses to accept the obvious gambit of a eucharistic connotation for the text. The Melchizedek-Christ typology arises textually, according to the *analogia Scripturae*. Psalm 110:4 intervenes between the story in Genesis and the Apostolic witness in the Epistle to the Hebrews. The typology is grounded on the application of the words of the Psalm, "thow art a preist for ever, according to the order of Melchisedek," to Christ both directly by the Apostle and indirectly by the "Hebrew Doctors" who offer a messianic reading of the Psalm. Christ is also prefigured in the blessing of Abraham, in which "the less is blessed by the better."[100]

Both Ainsworth and Willet evidence a strong appreciation for the tradition of rabbinic interpretation–more indeed, than either the group of earlier Christian exegetes cited by Willet or many later Protestant exegetes, who might have been influenced, if not by Ainsworth and Willet, surely by the rise of Protestant interest in Hebraica in the seventeenth century.[101] To the objection that Jewish opinion was not unanimous, Willet notes that Josephus and Philo, as cited by Pererius, had identified Melchizedek as "a stranger from the kindred of *Abraham*"–but that "for these two, there are alleaged two and twenty Rabbines, and principall writers among the Jewes, as *Aben Ezra, Levi Ben Gerson, David Kimchi*, with others, that make up that number, which all with one consent, hold *Sem* to be *Melchisedek.*"[102] Ainsworth and Willet also share a sense of the priority of the text and its issues over the question of typology—although both also understand the Melchizedek-Christ typology to be resident in the literal meaning of the text and known by the conference of Scripture with Scripture. Like virtually all of the Christian exegetes that they cite, they assume the *analogia Scripturae* and therefore the relevance of the text of Hebrews to the identification of Melchizedek but, significantly, it is not the Melchizedek-Christ typology that is the primary issue addressed, but the way in which Hebrews deals with the story in Genesis and with what might be called the problem of the historical Melchizedek.

Ainsworth's almost overwhelming interest, beginning with his *Annotations upon . . . Genesis*, in rabbinic exegesis not only marks a point of contrast with Willet's more muted interest, it also indicates a change of approach in Ainsworth's own style. In his *Annotations upon . . . the Psalmes*, Ainsworth had used, for the most part, only the Targums or Chaldee Paraphrase and had emphasized its philological and lexical importance. In his work on the Pentateuch, Ainsworth adopted a more positive interpretive approach to the Chaldee Paraphrase and, in addition, drew into discussion a broad spectrum of Mishnaic and Talmudic opinion as a support not only of his basic linguistic work but also of his larger interpretive efforts. This tendency toward rabbinic study and the use of Jewish exegesis for textual and philological assistance places Ainsworth, together with his contemporary, the eminent philologist and rabbinic scholar, Johannes Buxtorf, at the beginning of a seventeenth-century exegetical development that would come to full flower in the next generation of exegetes, in the work of Christopher Cartwright and of the compilers of the *Critici Sacri*.[103]

Ainsworth's exegetical and interpretive efforts, together with those of Willet, Whitaker, and Cartwright, moreover, defy the stereotype of a dogmatizing biblicism that looked away from the context and syntax of a passage toward its use, out of context, in theological system. Instead, the exegesis of the period evidences a variety of methods, some of them not at all dogmatic and some of them—like Willet's—moving from textual study and examination of the exegetical tradition toward a sense of the relationship and application of the results of exegesis to other theological disciplines, not merely to dogmatics but to preaching as well. Ainsworth's work, given its immersion in the theory and techniques of translation, its relative independence over against previous efforts, and its interest in Judaica, was certainly not based primarily on dogmatic concerns and looked toward the doctrines of the church as a remote goal, granting the directions given to interpretation in the exegetical tradition. Ainsworth's central interest was the text and the communication of the literal meaning of the text—as he and his contemporaries understood the "literal" sense—in English. His theory of interpretation indicated the necessity of creating a precise verbal equivalency, even to the point of indicating the root meaning of Hebrew words in compounded English terms. This fundamental interest into Hebrew meanings was, clearly, at the root of Ainsworth's interest in Judaica: his work manifests little or nothing of the traditional Christian polemics against Jewish interpretation of the Old Testament. Rather, it evidences a consistent attempt to engage the rabbis as dialogue partners in eliciting the meaning of words and the interpretation of the text, as witnessed by Ainsworth's nonpolemical Christian adaptation of the Targums and the rabbinic understanding of Wisdom in the interpretation of Genesis 1 and by his full reliance on the rabbis in his interpretation of Melchizedek as Shem.

It is worth commenting here on the potential relationship between Ainsworth's social context and his exegesis: although the doctrinal content belongs to a long tradition of meditation on the various themes and issues noted, there are, additionally, the nuances of interpretation arising out of Ainsworth's rather individualistic theory of translation and out of his use of Judaica. Access to Judaica and contact with practicing rabbis—as oddly and at best partially indicated by the account of Ainsworth's last days—was a concrete possibility in the Amsterdam of Ainsworth's exile (particularly in the book trade, where Ainsworth was employed for a time), but not, given the expulsion of Jews from England in 1290 by order of Edward I, a possibility in Ainsworth's homeland. Ainsworth's profound interest in and easy access to Judaica was certainly furthered, if not generated, by contacts made in Amsterdam, as it is a certainty that the rising Protestant interest in Judaica, pioneered by Ainsworth and continued by Hugh Broughton, Christopher Cartwright, John Weemse, and John Lightfoot, contributed both positively and negatively to the debate, during the time of Cromwell, over the return of the Jews to England.[104]

Such exegesis ought hardly to be called "precritical." Ainsworth and his contemporaries do not, of course, adumbrate later developments in historical-critical method—but they are certainly aware of text-critical issues. And they certainly accept the critical burden of assessing various and diverse readings found in the tradition of interpretation by means of the literal and grammatical exegesis of the text. What separates them from modern exegesis, rather than merely the question of a particular form of critical method, is the way in which they address the text from the vantage point of a long and eminent tradition of textual and theological interpretation, a tradition that has become increasingly *terra incognita* in our century, but that in the seventeenth century still provided a series of interpretive options and hermeneutical models for the exegete. What to twentieth-century eyes might appear curious, overly theologized, somewhat speculative, or even a bit arbitrary, often belongs to highly influential and centuries-old understandings of the text. Among such issues is the problem of the identification of Melchizedek in Genesis 14, generated by the curiosity of the text itself and rendered theologically significant by the references to Melchizedek in the Psalter and in the Epistle to the Hebrews. Because of their immersion in that tradition, exegetes of the seventeenth century, such as Ainsworth and Willet, frequently were able to perceive relationships binding the text and its ancient meanings to the larger scope of Scripture and—borrowing a modern hermeneutical distinction—frequently were able to move from the meaning of the text to its contemporary significance with far more confidence and sensitivity than the modern exegete. As evidenced by the presence of a metrical Psalter in Ainsworth's commentary, seventeenth-century exegetes assumed that the text, as mediated by its tradition of interpretation and construed anew in their present, was capable of speaking directly to the living community of belief.

11

The Covenant of Works and the Stability of Divine Law in Seventeenth-Century Reformed Orthodoxy

A Study in the Theology of Herman Witsius and Wilhelmus à Brakel

The Problem of the Prelapsarian Covenant in Reformed Theology

The doctrine of the covenant of works, which occupied a place of considerable significance in the Reformed theological systems of the seventeenth century, is an example of a doctrinal construct, not explicitly stated in Scripture but drawn as a conclusion from the examination and comparison of a series of biblical *loci* or *sedes doctrinae*. The concept of a covenant of works belongs, therefore, to a secondary or derivative albeit still fundamental category of doctrine—as indicated in the rule of interpretation cited in the Westminster Confession,

> The whole counsel of God, concerning all things necessary for his own glory, man's salvation, faith, and life, is either expressly set down in Scripture, or by good and necessary consequence may be deduced from Scripture.[1]

The identification of the covenant of works as a consequent doctrine surely accounts for the varied terminology (covenant of works, covenant of nature, covenant of creation, covenant of innocency) associated with it and for its absence from some of the major Reformed theological systems of the seventeenth century—just as it accounts for the intimate relationship in which the doctrine of the covenant of works stands with the central soteriological topics in Reformed theology: the Protestant orthodox recognized that a distorted perspective on a logically consequent doctrinal *locus* could, all too easily, become the basis of a retroactive misconception of a primary or logically prior doctrinal *locus*.[2] This intimate relationship of the covenant of works to the right formulation of other topics in the covenantal or federal Reformed systems was stated succinctly by Brakel at the very end of the seventeenth century:

> knowledge of this [covenant] is of the greatest importance, for whoever errs herein or denies this covenant of works, will not understand the covenant of grace, will probably err concerning the suretyship (*borgtocht*) of the Lord Jesus, and will likely deny that Christ by His active obedience has merited a right to eternal life for the elect. . . . Whoever denies the covenant of works, must rightly be suspected to be in error concerning the covenant of grace as well.[3]

Witsius, likewise, connects the denial of the covenant of works with a series of christological and soteriological errors.[4]

Despite these indications of the significance of the doctrine and despite the considerable scrutiny that the Reformed doctrine of the covenant of works has received at the hands of twentieth-century historians and theologians,[5] the doctrine remains little understood and much debated, whether from the perspective of its historical origins or from the perspective of its theological content. By far the larger number of works on Reformed covenant theology have concentrated on aspects of the historical development of the two covenant schema, with emphasis on the covenant of grace.[6] Within this rather extensive literature there is a debate over the implications of the covenant schema for Reformed theology: thus, a series of writers, notably, Trinterud, Moeller, Greaves, and Baker, assume two divergent trends in covenant theology and even, in the case of Baker, two different Reformed traditions defined by differing covenant emphases. According to these writers, the bilateral or two-sided covenant scheme associated with Bullinger and the Rhenish reformers stands as a counter to a unilateral or one-sided covenant scheme grounded in the doctrine of predestination and associated with Calvin and the Genevan Reformation. Other writers, such as Hoekema, Emerson, and Bierma, with strong historical evidence, argue against this bifurcation of the Reformed tradition and do not view covenant theology as representing a point of tension or conflict with Reformed predestinarianism.[7]

Recent studies of the origins of the covenant of works by Letham, Weir, and Lillback point in rather different directions. Letham argues an increasingly clear relationship in early Reformed theology between a covenantal understanding of the Mosaic law and the identification of the natural law known to Adam before the Fall with the Mosaic but, with somewhat less justice, also credits the prevalence of the two-covenant scheme with the rise of interest in Ramist dichotomies. Weir claims, without clear historical warrant, that the notion of a prelapsarian covenant arose in response to questions of theodicy raised by mid-sixteenth-century predestinarian controversy and that the idea of a covenant of works was designed to resolve the "tensions" between Reformed predestinarianism and Reformed covenant theology.[8] Lillback, in contrast to both Letham and Weir, understands the theological and exegetical argumentation leading to the doctrine of a covenant of works as having a much older history, with roots in medieval notions of *pactum* and considerable precedent, including one brief but specific allusion precisely where Weir and others have assumed it could not be found, in the thought of Calvin.[9]

A few essays have addressed the question of the interrelationship of the covenant of works and the covenant of grace, with widely differing results: essays by Kevan, Von Rohr, and Muller indicate a concerted effort to work out a variety of theological tensions between works and grace, human responsibility and divine election.[10] McGiffert develops a variation on the older theme of two diverging tendencies in Reformed theology, but sees late-sixteenth-century covenant theology as representing a legal tendency over against the theology of grace taught by Calvin and his contemporaries.[11] Far less nuanced, the works of Rolston, Torrance, and Poole understand developing covenant theology as a form of legalism and as a declension from the theology of the Reformers. In this view, the covenant of works appears as an illegitimate addition to Reformed theology that disturbs the priority of grace over works by asserting a historical and potentially a theological priority of law over grace or by misunderstanding the biblical concept of *berith* as a legal contract. These writers take great pains to set covenant theology at odds with Calvin, explicitly for the sake of their own Calvinian theological project, and they typically proceed as if Reformed federalism were a monolith with little variety of formulation and with no clear sense of the relationship of the concept of a covenant of works to the doctrines of grace, Christ, and salvation. Poole's work is especially to be criticized for its heavy reliance on secondary sources and for its failure to deal with the breadth of contemporary scholarly reinterpretation of Protestant orthodoxy.[12]

Considering the number of issues and problems raised by the scholarship, the following essay can only hope to address a small number of the questions concerning the covenant of works. The essay's focus on Herman Witsius's and Wilhelmus à Brakel's late-seventeenth-century efforts to define the covenant of works precludes examination of the problems of the origin of the concept of a prelapsarian covenant and of the distinctions in terminology between covenant of works and covenant of nature. It also leaves for another time the question of the relationship between British and continental federalism and between the Reformed orthodox federal theology in general and the work of the federal school of Cocceius, and points only tangentially to the issue of continuity and discontinuity between the teaching of the Reformers and the doctrines of their orthodox and scholastic successors. The issue to be addressed here is the theological content and implication of the fully developed continental Reformed orthodox concept of the covenant of works with emphasis, although not exclusively, on the work of Witsius and Brakel,[13] and with a view to clearing away some of the misapprehensions resident in the work of Torrance, Rolston, and Poole.

The Meaning of "Covenant"

The Reformed orthodox understanding of covenant cannot be reduced to legalism, to extraneous connotations accompanying the translation of a *berith* and *diatheke* by *foedus*, or, indeed, to an attempt to resolve a presumed "tension" between the doctrines of predestination and salvation by grace alone and the problem of human responsibility before God. Rather, it rested on a complex of exegetical, etymological, theological, and legal considerations that evidence concern for the text of Scripture, the culture of the Jews and other ancient Near Eastern peoples, the linguistic and cultural transition from Hebrew into Greek and Latin, the Christian exegetical tradition, and the doctrinal appropriation of ancient covenant language in the light of other fundamental theological questions—notably the relationship of Adam and Christ, the *imago Dei*, the problem of original righteousness and original sin, the history of salvation recorded in Scripture, and the distinction of law and gospel.

As I have argued at length elsewhere, the dogmatic or doctrinal formulations of the seventeenth-century orthodox can only be understood in relation to the exegetical tradition. At virtually no point in the development of the older Protestant dogmatics can one find a case of "proof-texting" in the negative sense of the term: the older dogmatics consistently folded the best exegesis of its day into its pattern and method of formulation. That exegesis, moreover, was not only linguistically and textually sophisticated, it also was rooted in—and frequently explicitly cognizant of—the older Christian exegetical tradition and its theological results.[14] The Reformed doctrine of covenant offers a primary example of this close relation between exegesis and seventeenth-century dogmatics. Most of the accusations of "proof-texting" and "eisegesis" arise out of an encounter of modern writers, schooled in or influenced by the results of modern critical exegesis, with the doctrinal results of precritical exegesis: in other words, it would be impossible to build a seventeenth-century theological system on the basis of a collection of twentieth-century biblical commentaries—but not nearly so difficult to build such a system on the basis of sixteenth- and seventeenth-century biblical commentaries.[15]

Witsius begins his massive *De oeconomia foederis* with an extensive etymological and exegetical discussion in which he recognizes the complexity of biblical covenant language and the diversity of issues, both linguistic and cultural, impinging on the interpretation of the biblical words for covenant, *berith* and *diatheke*.[16] The etymology of *berith*, Witsius indicates, points in three exegetically and theologically relevant directions. First, he notes that the root, in its *piel* form, "signifies *to cut down*"—a meaning that relates to the biblical concept of covenant inasmuch as "covenants used to be solemnly ratified by cutting animals asunder." Second, the root is also related to the verb *bara*, "to *create* (*creare*), thus metaphorically to *ordain* (*ordinare*) or to *dispose* (*diatithesthai*)." And, third, to *barah*, the verb to choose or elect—insofar as "in covenants, especially of friendship, there is a choice of persons, between whom, of things about which, and of conditions on which, a covenant is entered into."[17] Brakel singles out the third of these derivations as correct, inasmuch as "one chooses persons and makes stipulations" in covenant.[18]

These several possible implications of the term in turn point to a variety of biblical usages, which Witsius distinguishes into a "proper" or strict usage of *berith* and an extended or "improper" usage. In its proper sense, covenant "signifies a mutual agreement between parties with respect to something." Specifically, such covenants were made "between Abraham and Mamre, with Eschol and Aner, who are called *confederates* [*foederati*] *with Abraham*" (Gen. 14:13) between Isaac and Abimelech (Gen. 26:28–29), and between Jonathan and David (1 Sam. 18:2). In this sense also, Scripture teaches of a covenant "between God and man."[19] The extended or improper senses of covenant derive from other aspects of the etymology: thus covenant can refer to "an immutable ordinance" in the sense of a "declared or definite statute [*delineatum vel definitum statutum*]" such as God's "covenant of the day and of the night" (Jer. 33:20). In this sense of a clearly delineated statute, a covenant can also indicate "a *testament*, or . . . a last and irrevocable will," as illustrated by Numbers 18:19, "I have given thee, and thy sons and thy daughters with thee, by a statute for ever; it is a covenant of salt for ever." This usage, Witsius notes, is particularly applicable to the covenant of grace "which the apostle proposes under the similitude of a testament, the execution of which depends upon the death of the testator." A second usage of covenant is as "a sure and stable promise" even in the sense of a promise that is one-sided and lacks mutual agreement: thus, "Behold, I make a covenant; before all thy people I will do marvels" (Exod. 34:10). Third, a covenant can indicate a "precept." The biblical usage "to cut" or "make" a covenant can mean "to give a precept," as in Jeremiah 34:13–14, "I made a covenant with your fathers . . . saying, At the end of seven years let ye go every man his brother."[20]

The Greek term, *diatheke*, is also "equivocal." Witsius notes several meanings: very often, both in classical and biblical Greek, the term indicates a "testament [*testamentum*]."[21] *Diatheke* can, however, also denote a "law that functions as a rule of life [*legem quae* vivendi *regula sit*]"—as Grotius indicates, "the Orphics and Pythagoreans styled the rules of living prescribed to their pupils, *diathekai*"—and it can also signify "an engagement [*sponsio*] or agreement [*pactio*]" or even be used in the sense of *synomosia* or confederacy, as in Hesychius.[22] "There is none of these significations," Witsius concludes, "that will not be of use in the progress of this work": all, in short, illuminate the interpretation of Scripture.[23]

This initial analysis of the meaning of *berith* and *diatheke* is both more exegetically sophisticated and more linguistically refined than indicated by the studies of Torrance and Poole, which attempt to argue that the translation of *berith* and *diatheke* as *foedus* (or, in German, as *Bund*) misunderstand and misrepresent the biblical concept as a legal contract rather than as a promise, an oath, a pledge, or a command.[24] Quite to the contrary, Witsius and Brakel (like the covenant tradition as a whole) find implications of promise, oath, pledge, and command imbedded in the etymology and biblical usage of *berith* and *diatheke*—but they also find, contrary to the exegetical and theological assumptions of Torrance and Poole, the concept of a mutual pact and agreement in which elements of promise and of law are combined.

Witsius goes on to note that the Hebrew idiom for the initiation of a covenant relationship refers to "cutting" or "striking" a covenant—a phrase found also in ancient Greek practice and in the Latin idioms "*ferire, icere,* and *percutere foedus.*" Such language clearly originated, Witsius comments, in "the ancient ceremony of slaying animals, by which covenants are ratified." Even so, "ancient traces" of this rite can be found in Genesis 15:9–10 and also in Jeremiah 34:18, where the ceremonial ratification consisted in the passage of the parties in covenant between "the divided parts of the victim cut asunder." As Witsius notes, this issue received considerable elaboration at the hands of Grotius, Bochart, and Owen.[25] Such rites were to be found among ancient pagan nations, but the form of the rites in ancient Israel points to a still more solemn and weighty act, inasmuch as God himself was one of the covenant partners. As Jeremiah 34:18–20 indicates, in the case of Israel's covenant with God, the "cutting of animals asunder" pointed toward the penalty inflicted on those who broke covenant—that they "should be cut asunder by the vengeance of God."[26] Even here, however, Witsius notes, the instability of human covenanting with God points toward the "stability [*firmitatem*] of the covenant of grace . . . founded [*fundatam esse*] on the sacrifice of Christ" inasmuch as in that sacrifice, "the body and soul of Christ were . . . pulled asunder."[27]

Witsius's general definition of covenant, which follows on and grows out of these linguistic and exegetical arguments, even more than that of Perkins and the earlier covenant theologians looks to the broader theological context of covenant and to the identification of theology as practical wisdom characteristic of Ramist, English Puritan, and continental covenant theology.[28]

> A covenant of God with man is an agreement [*conventio*] between God and man, about the method of obtaining ultimate blessedness [*beatitudinis*], with the addition of a threat of eternal destruction, against anyone contemptuous of this blessedness.[29]

With this basic definition in view, Witsius indicates that a covenant between God and human beings is, fundamentally and primarily, a covenant "of one party [*unius lateris*]" grounded in "the utmost majesty of the most high God" and incapable of being initiated by any but God.[30]

As instituted by God, covenant has three aspects—a promise, a condition, and a sanction. The promise offers "ultimate blessedness in life eternal"; the condition indicates what must be performed for human beings to inherit the promise; and the sanction is to be leveled against those who do not fulfill the condition. Such a covenant addresses the whole person, "soul and body":

> to each part [soul and body] God promises blessedness [*beatitudinem*], of each he requires holiness [*sanctitatem*], and to each he threatens destruction [*exitium*]. And he makes this covenant, to the end that God may appear glorious in the whole man.[31]

In a manner reminiscent of Anselm's argument concerning the necessity or fittingness of Christ's satisfaction and indicative of the shape of his own views on the work of the Mediator in the covenant of grace, Witsius argues that it was "entirely becoming God and worthy of him" to enter covenant with "a rational creature formed after his own image." Indeed, it was "impossible" for God not to present himself to such a creature "as a pattern of holiness [*exemplar sanctitatis*]." Given the nature of God, "God cannot but bind man to love, worship, and seek him, as the chief good" and, moreover, will himself to be found by those who love, worship, and seek him. Not only the express statements of Scripture, therefore, but also a rational "consideration of the divine perfections" lead to the doctrine of covenant and to recognition of the covenant requirement of holiness. Covenant, thus, implies the law as "the condition of enjoying happiness [*conditionem potiundae felicitatis*]" or more precisely, as the condition for the ultimate enjoyment or "fruition" of God. Even so, covenant also implies the threat of punishment for disobedience.[32] Similar arguments are found in Brakel's *Redelijke Godsdienst*.[33] Only secondarily does such a covenant become "a covenant of two parties": the ground of the covenant is the divine initiative.

In order for the covenant to become "a covenant of two parties [*utriusque lateris*]," the rational creature must "consent" to the covenant by "embracing the good promised by God, engaging to an exact observance of the condition required," and acknowledging the propriety of punishment in the case of violation. Thus, Moses enjoins Israel to "enter into covenant with the Lord thy God, and into his oath" or, as the text of Nehemiah somewhat more sharply states, "into a curse, and into an oath, to walk in God's law."[34] Human response to God's covenant is by nature a "voluntary adstipulation of the faithful soul" but it is also in some sense a necessary response. Given the dependence of all creatures on God and the universally binding character of God's law, there can be no ground for refusal of the covenant: "not to desire the promises, is to refuse the goodness of God; to reject the precepts, is to deny the eminence and holiness of God [*Dei eminentiam & sanctitatem*]." Even so, "to disallow the sanction is to deny the righteousness or justice of God [*Dei iustitiam*]"—in this sense, the Apostle indicates that covenants "are rendered into the form of law [*in legis formulam redactum sit*], Heb. 8:6, cf. 7:2." The covenants of God are, therefore, "*injunctions* or *covenants from commands*"—as indicated by Hebrews 9:20, ". . . the blood of the testament, which God hath enjoined unto you."[35] In short, divine covenants cannot be refused because they rest on "God's power and right over creature [*potestas et jus Dei in creaturas*]." Yet, once accepted in faith, they in turn bind God to fulfill his promises and to be "a source of ultimate blessedness" to his creatures.[36]

According to Witsius and Brakel, both of the divine covenants, the covenant of works or nature and the covenant of grace conform to these definitions, inasmuch as it is to these covenants that the Apostle refers in his distinction between "the law of works" and "the law of faith." According to the former, "the man which doeth these things, shall live by them"; while according to the latter, "whoever believeth in him, shall not be ashamed."[37] Even so,

> In the covenant of works, man is considered as *working*, and the reward as to be given *of debt* (*ex debito*); and consequently man's *glorying* is not excluded, by which as a faithful servant he may glory upon the right discharge of his duty. . . . In the covenant of grace, the man in covenant [*homo foederatus*], ungodly in himself [*in se impius*], is considered as *believing* [*ut credens*]; eternal life being given to man, as the merit of the Mediator, *out of grace*, which excludes boasting, except that by which the believing sinner glories in God, as a merciful Savior.[38]

In their understanding of both covenants, moreover, both Witsius and Brakel bear witness to a resolution of the seeming problem of unilateral and bilateral definitions of covenant—and, in so doing, evidence yet another aspect of continuity with the intentions of the Reformers. Over against the view that has tended to set unilateral against bilateral definitions,[39] as if the former indicated a reliance on the doctrine of election and the latter an almost synergistic emphasis on human responsibility, the lengthy etymological and exegetical discussion offered by Witsius indicates that all covenants between God and human beings are founded on divine initiative and are, in that sense, unilateral. At the same time, these covenants, once made, bespeak a mutuality: the human partner must in some way consent to the covenant and exercise responsibility within it. (Of course, in the covenant of grace, the voluntary consent to the covenant and its terms rests on the gracious election of God and is the regenerate will's response in grace.) It is easily argued that the unilateral emphasis with bilateral overtones found in Calvin's covenant language, the opposite usage in Bullinger's, and the recourse to two definitions in Perkins's writings point toward precisely the same issue,[40] and that the finely tooled arguments of later federalists such as Witsius and Brakel are merely the result of more than a century of refinement of definition. It is not the case, as some have argued, that covenant language cuts against election and grace and that covenant doctrine either relaxes the strict doctrine of the decrees or is itself rigidified by contact with the doctrine of predestination during the scholastic era of Reformed theology.[41]

The Prelapsarian Covenant, Law, and the Natural Order

The concept of a covenant of works—or, as it also was called by Reformed writers of the sixteenth and seventeenth centuries, the covenant of nature or covenant of creation—most probably entered Reformed theology in the mid-sixteenth century in works such as Musculus's *Loci communes*, Hyperius' *Methodus theologiae*, and Ursinus's *Summa theologiae* or, as it is often called, *Catechesis maior*.[42] Musculus understood the order of creation as a *foedus generale*; Hyperius had proposed to construct his theological system around the distinction between humanity *ante* and *post lapsum*, including discussions of the law and the gospel *ante* and *post lapsum*; and Ursinus identified the law as a *foedus naturale in creatione*.[43] Particularly in the case of Musculus, there is an arguable antecedent in Bullinger's theology,[44] and—granting the training of both Musculus and

Hyperius in the older theology—there is also considerable medieval precedent. Ursinus presumably drew on Melanchthon, but also on Calvin: Calvin, without connecting the concept explicitly to covenant language, had evidenced considerable interest in the relationship between the natural order and the divine law as grounded in the goodness and sovereignty of God.[45] As Bierma has pointed out, Calvin used the concept of a *ius creationis* or "right of creation" in a manner that adumbrates Olevianus's later explicitly covenantal use of the term,[46] and, as Lillback has shown, there are a series of other concepts as well in Calvin's thought—an emphasis on the legal relationship between God and Adam, an identification of the tree of life as sacramental, the assumption (noted elsewhere) that sacraments are covenantal signs, and an identification of the Mosaic law as a *pactio legalis*, and an insistence on the relationship between Adam and Christ as the basis for understanding Christ's redemptive satisfaction of the law—that stand in a positive relation to the later langauge of a covenant of works or nature.[47]

The notion of a prelapsarian covenant, whatever its precise origins, did take on a dual focus, indicated in the variety of terms used—such as *foedus naturalis* or *foedus naturale*, *foedus legalis* and *foedus operum*. As Letham has quite correctly noted,[48] the virtually identical content of the natural and the Mosaic law also makes its contribution here: the covenantal understanding of the Mosaic law was, certainly, developed prior to the identification of the prelapsarian covenant of works, as was the identity of the Mosaic law with the law of nature. Both of these conclusions appear in the thought of Calvin without the corresponding doctrine of a *foedus naturale* in creation or a *foedus operum* in Eden: if Calvin did not typically speak of the prelapsarian state as bounded by covenant, he certainly assumed that it was governed by law.[49]

In the work of Ursinus in particular, as in the writings of subsequent generations of Reformed theologians, the idea of an initial, fundamental, prelapsarian covenant was rooted in the concept of creation as an order instituted by God and it was also connected with the basic exposition of the doctrine of law and grace in its relation to the problem of the creation of man according to the *imago Dei*.[50] The concept of the prelapsarian covenant functions, on the one hand, therefore, as a pattern of interpretation for the obedient life of man before the Fall and as an explanation of the problem of the holy law of God as it confronts and condemns man after the Fall; and, on the other, as illustrated by Musculus and, without the use of covenantal language, by Calvin, it functions as broad category of divine order and natural law, resembling and probably drawing on the late medieval emphasis on the divine *potentia ordinata* as *pactum*, capable of explaining the human predicament in a larger theological context. This relationship of the doctrine to the understanding of sin and of sinful human nature, moreover, placed the covenant of works in an explanatory role over against the doctrine of salvation, specifically, of the covenant of grace and its Mediator. In addition, and equally importantly, the concept of a covenant of creation, nature, or works provided nascent Reformed theological system with an alternative to the traditional Augustinian view of the transmission of sin as resting on an inherent concupiscence: the Pauline statement that all people sinned "in Adam" could now be interpreted federally, with profound ramifications for Christology and soteriology.[51]

This theological setting of the doctrine is made clear by the exegetical emphasis of the various expositions of the mature federal theology on the problem of law and grace in its relation to the first and second Adam—Adam and Christ—in the epistle of Paul to the Romans, with collateral citation of the Pauline covenant language in the epistle to the Galatians. In other words, the Reformed theologians of the sixteenth and seventeenth centuries who raised and developed the issue of the covenants did not understand their sole exegetical starting point to be the text of Genesis chapters two and three or such texts as Hosea 6:7 ("like Adam [or man] they have transgressed the covenant") and Job 31:33 ("If I covered my transgressions as Adam").[52] In the case of the text from Hosea, there was debate in the sixteenth and seventeenth centuries over the translation, with the Swiss and English Reformed, following Calvin and the Geneva Bible (1560), tending toward the generic reading, "man," and the Dutch and German Reformed almost uniformly reading "Adam."[53] As noted earlier, the doctrine was a conclusion drawn from a large complex of texts, among them, Genesis 1:26–27; Leviticus 18:4–5; Matthew 19:16–17; 22:37–39; Romans 1:17; 2:14–15; 5:12–21; 7:10; 8:3–4; 10:5; Galatians 3:11–12; 4:4–5, with Hosea 6:7 and Job 31:33 offered only as collateral arguments.[54] It was, moreover, a conclusion largely in accord with the exegetical tradition: Witsius can, for example, cite Chrysostom on Romans 7:10 to the effect that the natural law was given to Adam at the Creation.[55]

In the theology of Witsius and Brakel, the intrinsic relationship between law and covenant and the identification of the law revealed under the covenant of works with both the law of nature and the Mosaic law are assumed, given that "a knowledge of conformity to the law was implanted in [man's] nature" and given, moreover, the very "nature of God" as Lord and sovereign over his creation: "as soon as a creature exists, is [God] above the creature and that creature is subordinate to Him . . . not only because [God] has created him, or because he has entered into a covenant with man, or because man has become sinful, but especially because of God's nature, for He is Jehovah."[56] Thus, the law stands prior both to the fact of sin and to the fact of any covenant.[57] When considered as the prescribed condition of the covenant of works, the law is "twofold," consisting in "the law of nature, implanted in Adam at his creation [*Lex Naturae Adamo increata*]" and "the symbolical law [*Lex Symbolica*], concerning the tree of the knowledge of good and evil."[58] The former law, the *ius naturalis*, is "binding" on human beings "by divine authority" inasmuch as it is "inscribed by God on man's conscience [*hominis conscientiae . . . a Deo inscripta*]" in the act of creation and therefore an aspect of the fundamental nature of humanity. Since, moreover, even pagan nations understand the difference between right and wrong and, in their laws, evidence much of the substance of the divine commands revealed in the decalogue, we can assume a full knowledge of the law in Adam, "newly formed after the image of God."[59]

Stability of Promise and Law and the Order of Redemption

As Kevan has shown, there was not only considerable agreement among Reformed theologians in the seventeenth century concerning the identity of the prelapsarian relationship between God and Adam as a covenant, virtually all of the Reformed theologians of the era recognized, albeit in varying degrees, that there could be no relationship between God and the finite, mutable creature apart from grace.[60] This was also the burden of the medieval doctrine of the *donum superadditum*, particularly in its fully Augustinian form, a doctrine most probably at the root of the idea of the covenant of works.[61] Here, too, there is more continuity between the thought of Reformers such as Calvin and Bullinger (neither of whom made reference to a prelapsarian covenant) and the later federal thinkers than is typically indicated.

Indeed, major discontinuity in substance at this point can only be argued, as witnessed in Rolston's and Torrance's work, by exaggerating Calvin's views on the prelapsarian graciousness of God and by minimizing his comments on Adam's duties before God and God's law—and then by arguing precisely the opposite distortion of the thought of Witsius and other federal thinkers. Calvin, thereby, is seen to emphasize grace far beyond law and the federalists, law to the virtual exclusion of grace.[62] Witsius, however, indicates that Adam's original condition could not have been "so merely natural" that Adam's understanding was based purely on "the consideration of nature."[63] Even so, the Protestant form of the *donum superadditum* enters here: in no condition, not even in the state of original righteousness, can any "creature be, or conceived to be capable of doing anything independent of the Creator." Thus, God not only "furnished" the first pair "with sufficient powers" to stand "pure and inviolate," he also acted to "preserve those powers by the continual influence of his providence."[64] If the medieval parallel is invoked, this formulation arguably echoes the teaching of Aquinas and of the more Augustinian doctors who insisted that the *donum* was part of the original constitution of the human being and not a gift given on the basis of an initial probation—any more than grace, as provided to sinners after the Fall, is given on the basis of a human act. Aquinas had, moreover, specifically opposed the understanding of the *donum* as superadded following probation, inasmuch as this would indicate the possibility of a similar Pelagianizing understanding of the work of grace as a divine response to merit.[65] From the perspective of these historical foundations and the debate that surrounded them, the Reformed view of the covenant of works, therefore, was constructed for the sake of undergirding the Reformation principle of salvation by grace alone.

Thus, contrary to the allegations of Rolston and Torrance, Witsius's and Brakel's perspective on the conditions of the prelapsarian covenant, rooted in a sense of the congruity of the divine goodness with God's righteousness and of righteousness with a requirement that the creature conform to divine law, is hardly a legalism—certainly not in the usual negative sense. Witsius cites an unnamed opponent who had argued that there could have been no law before the Fall, inasmuch as "then the love of God prevailed, which requires no law." Only when "love is violated" must this natural state be altered and "a precept [be] superadded."[66] Witsius responds with a series of points: first, "it is not the rigor of coercion that properly constitutes a law, but the obligatory virtue of what is enjoined, proceeding both from the power of the lawgiver, and from the equity of the thing commanded; which is here founded in the most holy nature of God, insofar as it is imitable by man." Apart from and prior to the problem of coercion, there is what the apostle James has called "the perfect law of liberty."[67]

Second and third—from somewhat different perspectives—Witsius and Brakel note that there is no contradiction between nature and law, whether in general or with reference to the natural loving relationship between parent and child, which itself is regulated by law. Fourth, it is contrary to the basic understanding of law to argue that it arises only after the entrance of sin, inasmuch as sin is itself "the transgression of the law."[68] And, fifth, love is not "rendered less voluntary by the precept" granting that the law itself "enjoins a love in every way perfect, and therefore as voluntary as possible, not extorted by servile fear of [divine] threatening."[69] The fundamental, natural law of God, identical in substance with the decalogue,[70] is therefore inseparable from the goodness and love of God and, indeed, from the eventual promise of grace following sin. (The claim of the opponent, that the love of God "requires no law" ultimately opposes law to love and opens the way for an assault on the necessity of Christ's satisfaction for sin and for an alternative atonement theory: Brakel's argument that misunderstanding of the covenant of works will lead to error concerning Christ's work has struck home.)

Given these relationships between law and grace, the two covenants, and the problems of sin and salvation, it should not be surprising that a central issue addressed in the Reformed doctrine of the covenant of works was the issue of federal headship and, therefore, the parallels between the first and the second Adam, the federal heads of the covenants of works and of grace. It is at this point that the soteriological ground of the doctrine of the covenant of works is most clearly presented, particularly in terms of its relationship to the doctrine of Christ's mediatorial headship and work of satisfaction.

Adam, in the covenant of works, "stood as the head of mankind [*caput totius generis humani*]," in his person "representing" the entire human race.[71] By the same token, as indicated by the Apostle in Romans 5:11–15, Christ as the antitype of Adam stands as the representative of humanity in the covenant of grace and the "surety" of fulfillment or substitute for mankind before the law of God, in effect, in fulfillment of the demands of the violated covenant of works.[72] After all, the violation of the covenant of works abrogated the law as a covenant, not as the ultimate "rule of life."[73] It is both the permanence of the divine promise of fellowship and the stability of the divine law as the standard of holiness and righteousness and, therefore, as the basis for fellowship with the holy and righteous God, that relates the covenants to one another: "the law declares, that there is no admission for any to eternal life, but on the account of a perfect and absolutely complete righteousness; [and] also, that every sinner shall undergo the penalty of death, the dominion of which is eternal" unless the penalty of sin is paid and "the dominion of death . . . abolished."[74]

Drawing on the epistles to the Romans and the Galatians, Witsius argues the equivalency of the promises of the two covenants. Paul, he notes, "distinguishes the righteousness of the law from the evangelical" while at the same time indicating that "life" is promised under both covenants. Concerning legal righteousness, Paul writes "that the man which doth these things shall live by them" (Rom. 10:5) and concerning evangelical righteousness, "the just shall live by faith" (Rom 1:17).[75] Even so,

> On both sides, the promise of life is the same, proposed in the very same words. For the apostle does not hint by the least expression, that one kind of life is promised by the gospel, another by the law. . . . But the apostle places the whole difference, not in the thing promised, but in the condition of obtaining the promise. . . . That very life therefore was promised by the law to the man that worketh, which he now receives by faith in Christ. But to what man thus working was it promised? to the sinner only? Was it not to man in his innocency? Was it not then when it might truly be said, If you continue to do well, you shall be the heir of that life upon that condition. Which could be said to none

> but to upright Adam. Was it not then, when the promise was actually made? For after the entrance of sin, there is not so much a promise, as a denunciation of wrath, and an intimation of a curse, proposing that as the condition for obtaining life, which is now impossible. I therefore conclude, that to Adam, in the covenant of works, was promised the same eternal life, to be obtained by the righteousness which is the law, of which believers are made partakers through Christ.[76]

The identical point is made by Brakel with reference to the same texts.[77]

Arguably, both theologians here manifest the central reason for the doctrine of a covenant of works and its fundamental relationship to the doctrines of justification by grace through faith and Christ's satisfaction for sin: the issue is not to hammer home a legalistic view of life and salvation but precisely the opposite, while at the same time upholding the stability of divine law. There can be no salvation by works, but only by a means that excludes works–in short, through faith in Christ. Nonetheless, the law is not void. Indeed, the law remains the representation of divine goodness, holiness, and righteousness placed in the heart and mind of Adam even as he was created in the image of God. Given the fact of sin, such a law can no longer hold forth its original promise of fellowship with God, but it remains the condition of fellowship just as it remains the temporal indication of the goodness, holiness, and righteousness of God. The covenant of works takes on for the fallen Adam the function of the second or pedagogical use of the law–precisely the function of the Mosaic law understood as the legal covenant or covenant of works: "The Lord willed," Brakel writes, that Adam "would now turn away from the broken covenant of works, and, being lost in himself, would put all hope in the seed of the woman, which was promised to him immediately thereafter."[78]

The covenant of works, then, was violated and made void from the human side by the sin of Adam and Eve, rendering the promises of the covenant inaccessible to their posterity–but it was also, Witsius argues, abrogated from the divine side in the sense that God has clearly willed not to renew or recast the covenant of works for the sake of offering to fallen humanity a promise of life grounded in its own personal righteousness. In other words, God will not now, in the context of human sinfulness "prescribe a condition of obedience less perfect than that which he stipulated" in the original covenant of works.[79] Nonetheless, so far as the promise of eternal life is concerned, all of mankind remains bound to "a perfect performance of duty" and, so far as the law is concerned, all mankind remains subject to its "penal sanction": thus, sin does not render void nor the divine abrogation of the covenant of works remove "the unchangeable truth" of God's "immutable and indispensable justice."[80] Even so, Calvin had argued the "perpetual validity" of the law and had insisted that "the law has been divinely handed down to us to teach us perfect righteousness; there no other righteouness is taught than that which conforms to the requirements of God's will."[81]

The divine abrogation of the covenant of works, then, does not abolish the promise of God or the condition of holiness and righteousness required for the fulfillment of the promise. And it is precisely because of this coordinate stability of promise and law that the covenant of grace becomes effective in Christ alone. When the Apostle Paul writes, "Do we then make void the law through faith? God forbid: yea, we establish the law," he indicates both that "the covenant of grace does not abrogate, but supposes the abrogation of the covenant of works" and that

> the covenant of grace is not [itself] the abolition, but rather the confirmation of the covenant of works, inasmuch as the Mediator has fulfilled all the conditions of that covenant, so that all believers may be justified and saved according to the covenant of works, to which satisfaction was made by the Mediator. . . . The very law of the covenant, which formerly gave up the human sinner to sin, when his condition is once changed by union with Christ the surety, does now, without any abolition, abrogation, or any other change whatever, absolve the man from the guilt and dominion of sin, and bestow on him that sanctification and glorification, which are gradually brought to perfection, which he shall obtain at the resurrection of the dead.[82]

The stability of the law, guaranteed in the divine maintenance of the terms of the covenant of works, points not to a legalistic view of salvation but to the fullness of Christ's work of satisfaction and to the totally unmerited character of the salvation provided by grace through faith to believers. "Recognize," writes Brakel, that "the Lord Jesus placed Himself under" the "same law Adam had . . . and thereby He merited redemption and adoption as children for the elect."[83]

The ultimate relationship of the covenant of works to the covenant of grace and, equally so, of Adam to Christ as the old and new federal heads of the humanity, is established and outlined by Witsius, Brakel, and virtually all of the major Reformed covenant theologians of the seventeenth century in their discussion of the "covenant of redemption" or *pactum salutis* between God the Father and God the Son.[84] Here, also, as in the case of the covenant of works, we encounter a doctrinal construct, elicited according to the terms of the older Reformed hermeneutic, from the collation and exegetical analysis of a series of biblical passages. The doctrine itself probably originated with Cocceius, but its roots are most probably to be found in the earlier Reformed meditation on the trinitarian nature of the divine decrees.[85] While not attempting to offer a discussion of the entire doctrine of the covenant of redemption, we can note here its function with respect to the two other covenants. In the first place, it is the eternal foundation of the covenant of grace, according to which Christ is established, in the depths of the Trinity, as the Redeemer, the new federal head of humanity, and the surety and sponsor of humanity in covenant: in short, the covenant of redemption is an "agreement between God and the Mediator" that makes possible the covenant of grace as an agreement between God and his elect. The covenant of grace thus also "presupposes" the covenant of redemption and "is founded upon it."[86]

In the second place, the covenant of redemption established the eternal remedy for the problem of sin and ensured the full manifestation and exercise of the divine righteousness and justice both in the covenant of works and beyond its abrogation. As Brakel comments, "The fact that God from eternity foreknew the fall, decreeing that He would permit it to occur, is not only confirmed by the doctrines of His omniscience and decrees, but also from the fact that God from eternity ordained a Redeemer for man, to deliver him from sin: the Lord Jesus Christ whom Peter calls the Lamb, "who was foreknown [*voorgekend*] before the foundation of the world."[87] By the covenant of redemption, the Son binds himself to the work of salvation and, therefore, to the fulfillment of the condition of fellowship with God for the sake of God's covenant people. Thus the promises, the conditions, and the penalties for failure to fulfill the conditions remain—but the conditions are met and the penalties satisfied in Christ. As eternally guaranteed by the covenant of redemption, "conditions are offered, to which eternal salvation is annexed; conditions not to be performed again by us, which might throw the mind into despondency; but by him, who would not part with his life, before he had truly said, 'It is finished.'"[88]

Conclusions

The concept of the covenant of works that I have outlined in the thought of Herman Witsius and Wilhelmus à Brakel bears little resemblance to the caricature of Reformed federalism presented by writers such as Rolston, Torrance, and Poole. The doctrine is so clearly based on a careful consideration of the etymology of *berith* and *diatheke* and on the exegesis of numerous passages in Scripture that the rather simplistic claim that the mistranslation of *berith* produced an unbiblical legalism cannot be maintained: as in the case of the biblical terms themselves, the implications of *foedus*, when used as the Latin equivalent of *berith* or *diatheke*, rested on its context–on the specific meaning given to the term by its usage–rather than on a set of preconceived theological priorities, such as the radical priority of grace over law in the Barthian theology of Torrance and Rolston.[89]

What is more, the older Reformed language of covenant of works did not indicate a radical priority of law over grace as these writers have argued. The clear implication of the doctrine is the ultimate parity of the divine attributes of righteousness and mercy or graciousness and the resultant balance of righteousness or justice (*iustitia*) with mercy and grace in the plan and work of God. The formulation of an eternal covenant of redemption, moreover, together with the consistent priority of promise over condition in all of Witsius's and Brakel's definitions of covenant, point toward the priority of the gracious divine will over law, of the divine intention of fellowship with the creature over the stipulation of conditions. Beyond this, the conditions themselves–the natural law and its revealed form, the decalogue–are not arbitrary: they represent both the divine nature itself in its attributes of goodness, holiness, and righteousness, and the image of God in Adam and Eve. The sole condition for fellowship, therefore, is the divinely given reflection of God himself in his creature, understood as the fundamental law or order for creaturely existence.

The purported legalism of the continuing covenant of works as presented in the demands of the law is nothing less than permanence of the original divine intention to ground fellowship in the nature of God and in the *imago Dei*. Witsius and Brakel recognized in their debate with seventeenth-century Arminian and Socinian adversaries that as long as covenant refers to a relationship between God and human beings, law must belong to covenant as much as promise. They also understood–as we should perhaps recognize in the theological presuppositions of the contemporary critics of the doctrine–that the denial of the covenant of works, the attempt to deny the legal element of covenant in general (and, today, the attempt to pit the Reformers against their successors), represent not only an alternative view of the original relationship between God and human beings but also an alternative theory of Christ's atonement and a theology that, at best, is less than traditionally Reformed.

The elements of the Reformed doctrine of the covenant of works that I have described here indicate the result of a process of doctrinal development in the Reformed tradition. As such, the language of the doctrine is certainly different from the language of the Reformers and even from that of earlier successors to the original Reformers such as Ursinus and Olevian or, indeed, in a slightly later time, William Perkins. Yet, the fundamental points of the doctrine, that the work of redemption must be understood both in terms of law and of grace, that human beings were created in and for fellowship with God under terms both of promise and of law, that Adam's fall was a transgression of God's law, that human inability after the Fall in no way removes the standard or the demands of the law, and that the gift of salvation through Christ's satisfaction for sin both sets believers free from the law's condemnation and upholds the law's demands, remain virtually identical. The free gift of grace in the one covenant respects the stability of law in the other, while the presence of law under different uses in both covenants echoes both the immutability of the divine nature and the constancy of the divine promises.

Afterword

A legitimate and productive intellectual history of post-Reformation Protestantism must step past the self-indulgent theologism of the older historiography and cease to read the materials of the sixteenth and seventeenth centuries through the lenses of macrotheological questions arising out of nineteenth, twentieth, and (now) twenty-first century dogmatic concerns. The essays in this volume have been written with such a history in mind. All are intentionally definitional and programmatic: the definitions and the program for research are detailed in part I, with an emphasis on approach and method—examples of the program, illustrative of the definitions, are offered in part II. The central convictions embodied in all of the essays carry both negative and positive implications. On the negative side, stands the conviction that the older scholarship on Reformed orthodoxy, with its language of central dogmas, doctrinal tensions, antinomies, and problems, its strict bifurcation of scholasticism and humanism, and its consistently dogmatic reading of the entire development of Reformed thought toward its seventeenth-century institutionalization not only was incorrect in its presentation of particulars but also was fundamentally flawed in its method and approach to the sixteenth- and seventeenth-century materials. Indeed, it has been the underlying approach, applied as a restrictive grid over the materials of the history, that has caused the distorted presentation of the particulars. The scholarship has been so profoundly rooted in its own dogmatic projects—all of them originating in the nineteenth and twentieth centuries—that it consistently failed to read and interpret the documentation of the Reformation and subsequent Protestant orthodoxy in its historical context and on its own terms.

On the positive side, there is a vast reservoir of important material to be investigated—much of it for the first time—and to be integrated interpretively into a new understanding of late-sixteenth- and seventeenth-century Protestant thought. Concentration on what I have denominated macrotheological issues, together with fundamental biases against even examining the documents of the seventeenth-century theological development, left the bulk of Protestant literature of the late sixteenth and seventeenth centuries largely unexamined in the scholarly literature of the nineteenth and twentieth centuries. Given the assumption that Beza had created a "predestinarian system" that was duplicated and reduplicated by the Reformed orthodox, the theological systems of thinkers such as Keckermann, Bucanus, Polanus, Trelcatius, Walaeus, Maccovius, Maresius, Heidanus, Mastricht, and Heidegger needed little or no discussion. Given the assumption that "rigid orthodoxy" prevailed over exegesis and, as far as some of the older literature was concerned, little in the way of careful philology or cogent interpretation occurred in the seventeenth century, the exegetical opera of Gomarus, Rivetus, Amama, Diodati, Piscator, Walaeus, Davenant, Broughton, Willet, Weemse, and others too numerous to mention, consistently have been ignored.

The literature surveys found in various of the preceding essays indicate genuine progress, both in the broad strokes of reappraisal and in the narrow task of the reasonably objective examination of individual writers, documents, and ideas. The work of basic reappraisal of these materials has certainly moved forward in the last twenty years and has received considerable impetus for future in the work of a larger group of scholars in the last decade. These advances have, in turn, provided a foundation for the twenty-first century examination of a rare storehouse of interrelated and still largely untouched materials. Once the dogmatizing grids have been set aside, therefore, there remains an enormous amount of work to be done to uncover the actual developments of the era. In many cases, the extant secondary literature has neglected major thinkers and significant trajectories of argument. In fact, one of the issues confronting scholarly examination of the late sixteenth and the seventeenth century is simply identifying who were the major figures and what were the major issues in debate—and then sufficiently raising the profile of the figures or issues in order to bring about an alteration of the broader surveys of the era.

This point is particularly relevant in the areas of biblical interpretation and philosophy, not to mention the interfaces between these areas and the development of Protestant theology. By way of example: one might ask the question of the philosophers most influential on the method and logic of Reformed theology in the seventeenth century. It is unlikely at present that thinkers such as Thomas Spencer, Franco Burgersdijk, or Adrian Heereboord would be brought forward. Similarly, one might raise the question of major Hebraists who contributed to the development of Reformed exegesis and theology in the same era. Given the relative fame of the debate over the vowel points, Johannes Buxtorf Sr. and Louis Cappel might come to mind, but British scholars such as Henry Ainsworth, Hugh Broughton, and John Weemse would probably escape notice. What is more, a perusal of the works of these less-known thinkers immediately demonstrates the relevance of their work to the doctrinal theology of the era, and, in addition, demonstrates the sensitivity of the theological or dogmatic formulators to a host of issues not typically discussed in older analyses of Reformed orthodoxy. The three philosophers just noted reveal, among other things, that a strict dichotomy between Ramists and Aristotelians cannot be maintained—while the exegetes reveal the impact of Judaica on the Reformed orthodox and the consistent interplay of theology and exegesis that occurred in the era of orthodoxy.

Scholarship on the era of orthodoxy needs not only to move away from the tendency to identify emblematic documents but also to study the documents of the era of orthodoxy at a level of detail suitable to an understanding of the detail in the materials themselves—not only the writings of the individual thinker under examination but also the collateral literature of the era, particularly the bibliography of the thinker in question. One ought not to be content, for example, to read the piety of Richard Baxter or John

Owen apart from the larger corpus of their writings. That larger corpus, in turn, leads the student of Baxter and Owen to a significant doctrinal, exegetical, polemical, and historical bibliography with works both in English and in Latin. Baxter and Owen, like Edward Leigh, Joseph Caryl, Samuel Rutherford, and other British theologians of the era, read heavily in the works of continental theologians, whether Reformed, Lutheran, or Roman, and studied a series of medieval scholastics and Renaissance-era theologians and philosophers as well. As indicated in several places in the preceding essays, examination of this broader field of literature often reveals motivations for theological statements that do not oblige what might be called macrotheological patterns. The theologies of the late sixteenth and seventeenth century were not constructed with a view to the "tensions" and "problems" that arise for modern dogmaticians who peruse the older orthodoxy largely in order to find foils for their own formulations. Rather, they were constructed in view of contemporary problems, issues, and debates that may not be altogether obvious to the modern reader of a seventeenth-century theological system. Such problems, issues, and debates only appear on close examination of the context of a document or the context of the debate in which the document is situated—and it is these exegetical, philosophical, ecclesial, institutional, and cultural contexts that promise the most fruitful grounds for future research.

I close with a challenge both to my colleagues in the reappraisal and to those who remain entrenched in the older models and continue to pose "Calvin against the Calvinists." For the reappraisal to move forward, there is much to be done in the way of cross-disciplinary study and examination of writers whose work has been neglected, in some cases for centuries. The challenge is to return to the documents with renewed vigor and an ever-clearer sense of the historical context. For the proponents of the older paradigms, the challenge is to shed their twentieth-century dogmatic criteria, to recognize the failure of an emblematic, decontextualized use of documents such as Beza's *Tabula*, to avoid the excessive levels of generalization belonging to their standard claims about "Aristotelianism," "rationalism," "scholasticism," and the like, and to argue their thesis from actual documents, using the actual terms found in the documents, respecting the limits of meaning determined by historical context, and expanding their bibliography to include and respond to the collateral literature cited by exponents of the reappraisal. Of course, my own assumption is that the older paradigm cannot stand exposure to such methodological rigor. I can only hope that this book will contribute to the revival of interest in the late-sixteenth- and seventeenth-century materials and will stimulate the efforts at reappraisal begun in the last two decades toward further insight into the era of Protestant scholasticism and confessional orthodoxy.

Notes

1. Approaches to Post-Reformation Protestantism

1. Thus, e.g., Basil Hall, "Calvin and Biblical Humanism," in *Huguenot Society Proceedings*, 20 (1959–1964), pp. 195–209; idem, "Calvin Against the Calvinists," in *John Calvin: A Collection of Distinguished Essays*, ed. Gervase Duffield (Grand Rapids, MI: Eerdmans, 1966), pp. 19–37; Charles S. McCoy, "Johannes Cocceius: Federal Theologian," in *Scottish Journal of Theology*, 16 (1963), pp. 352–370; and Brian G. Armstrong, *Calvinism and the Amyraut Heresy: Protestant Scholasticism and Humanism in Seventeenth Century France* (Madison: University of Wisconsin Press, 1969).

2. See the emergent consensus of recent scholarship in Willem J. van Asselt, "Protestantse scholastiek: Methodologische kwesties bij de bestudering van haar ontwikkeling," in *Tijdschrift voor Nederlandse Kerkgeschiedenis*, 4/3 (Sept. 2001), pp. 64–69; Willem J. van Asselt, P. L. Rouwendal, et al., *Inleiding in de Gereformeerde Scholastiek* (Zoetermeer: Boekencentrum, 1998); Carl R. Trueman and R. Scott Clark, eds., *Protestant Scholasticism: Essays in Reappraisal* (Carlisle: Paternoster Press, 1999), and Willem J. Van Asselt and Eef Dekker, *Reformation and Scholasticism: An Ecumenical Enterprise* (Grand Rapids, MI: Baker Book House, 2001).

3. Paul Oskar Kristeller, *Renaissance Thought: The Classic, Scholastic, and Humanist Strains* (New York: Harper & Row, 1961).

4. Lewis Spitz, "Humanism and the Protestant Reformation," in *Renaissance Humanism*, ed. Albert Rabil, 3 vols. (Philadelphia: University of Pennsylvania Press, 1988), vol. 3, p. 393; J. D'Amico, "Humanism and Pre-Reformation Theology," in ibid., vol. 3, pp. 367–368; also, James H. Overfield, *Humanism and Scholasticism in Late Medieval Germany* (Princeton, NJ: Princeton University Press, 1984), pp. 59–60, 94–100, 329–330 and idem, "Scholastic Opposition to Humanism in Pre-Reformation Germany," in *Viator*, 7 (1976), pp. 391–420.

5. See Heiko A. Oberman, *Forerunners of the Reformation* (New York: Holt, Rinehart and Winston, 1966), pp. 1–65; idem, "The Shape of Late Medieval Thought: The Birthpangs of the Modern Era," in *The Dawn of the Reformation: Essays in Late Medieval and Early Reformation Thought* (Edinburgh: T. & T. Clark, 1986), pp. 18–38.

6. Richard A. Muller, "The Use and Abuse of a Document: Beza's *Tabula praedestinationis*, the Bolsec Controversy, and the Origins of Reformed Orthodoxy," in *Protestant Scholasticism: Essays in Reappraisal*, ed. Carl Trueman and Scott Clark (Carlisle: Paternoster Press, 1999), pp. 33–61.

7. For a historical survey of these confessions, see Richard A. Muller, "Reformed Confessions and Catechisms," s.v. in *Dictionary of Historical Theology*, ed. Trevor Hart (Carlisle: Paternoster Press /Grand Rapids, MI: Eerdmans, 2000).

8. See Thomas C. Pfizenmaier, *The Trinitarian Theology of Dr. Samuel Clarke (1675–1729): Context, Sources, and Controversy* (Leiden: E. J. Brill, 1997).

9. See, e.g., J. H. Kurtz, *Church History*, trans. John Macpherson, 3 vols. (New York: Funk & Wagnalls, 1890), pp. 146–147; Bengt Hägglund, *History of Theology*, trans. Gene Lund (St. Louis: Concordia, 1968), pp. 343–344.

10. Thus, J. Wayne Baker, *Heinrich Bullinger and the Covenant: The Other Reformed Tradition* (Athens: Ohio University Press, 1980) and idem, "Heinrich Bullinger, the Covenant, and the Reformed Tradition in Retrospect," in John H. Leith (ed.), *Calvin Studies VIII: The Westminster Confession in Current Thought*, papers presented at the Colloquium on Calvin Studies (Davidson College, January 26–27, 1996), pp. 58–75; also published in *Sixteenth Century Journal*, 29/2 (1998), pp. 359–376. Cf. the critiques of Baker in Lyle D. Bierma, "Federal Theology in the Sixteenth Century: Two Traditions?" in *Westminster Theological Journal*, 45 (1983), pp. 3043–21; idem, *German Calvinism in the Confessional Age: The Covenant Theology of Caspar Olevian* (Grand Rapids, MI: Baker Book House, 1996), pp. 31–62; and in Richard A. Muller, *The Unaccommodated Calvin* (New York: Oxford University Press, 2000), pp. 155, 183, 253n89–90, 254n93.

11. See Paul Rorem, "Calvin and Bullinger on the Lord's Supper: Part I. The Impasse," in *Lutheran Quarterly*, NS 2 (1988), pp. 155–184; and idem, "Calvin and Bullinger on the Lord's Supper: Part II. The Agreement," in *Lutheran Quarterly*, NS 2 (1988), pp. 357–389.

12. Jan Rohls, *Reformed Confessions: Theology from Zurich to Barmen*, trans. John Hoffmeyer, intro. by Jack Stotts (Louisville, KY: Westminster John Knox Press, 1998), pp. 9–28.

13. Armstrong, *Calvinism and the Amyraut Heresy*, pp. xvii–xix, 158–226, 263–269, et passim.

14. Leonard Trinterud, "The Origins of Puritanism," in *Church History*, 20 (1951), pp. 37–57; Jens Moeller, "The Beginnings of Puritan Covenant Theology," in *Journal of Ecclesiastical History*, 14 (1963), pp. 46–67; Richard Greaves, "The Origins and Early Development of English Covenant Thought," in *The Historian*, 21 (1968), pp. 21–35; J. Wayne Baker, *Heinrich Bullinger and the Covenant*, pp. 165–177, 193–198.

15. CF. William Perkins, *A Golden Chaine*, in *The Workes of . . . Mr. William Perkins*, 3 vols. (Cambridge: John Legate, 1612–1619), vol. 1, pp. 32, col. 1; p. 71, col. 1; idem, *An Exposition of the Creede*, in *Workes*, vol. 1, p. 167, col. 2; with Johannes Cocceius, *Summa doctrina de foedere et testamento Dei*, I.5–7, in *Opera omnia theologica, exegetica, didactica, polemica, philologica*, 12 vols. (Amsterdam, 1701–1706), vol. 7, pp. 45–46.

16. See Muller, *Unaccommodated Calvin*, pp. 102–111.

17. See the discussion in, chapter 6.

18. See Richard A. Muller, *Post-Reformation Reformed Dogmatics*, 4 vols. (Grand Rapids, MI: Baker Book House, 2003), vol. 2, pp. 149–159, 338–368.

19. See Muller, *Post-Reformation Reformed Dogmatics*, vol. 2, pp. 93–118, 180–193, 228–253.

20. On this subject, see, e.g., Susan E. Schreiner, *Where Shall Wisdom be Found? Calvin's Exegesis of Job from Medieval and Modern Perspectives* (Chicago: University of Chicago Press, 1994); Richard A. Muller and John L. Thompson, *Biblical Interpretation in the Era of the Reformation: Essays Presented to David C. Steinmetz in Honor of His Sixtieth Birthday* (Grand Rapids, MI: Eerdmans, 1996); Craig S. Farmer, *The Gospel of John in the Sixteenth Century: The Johannine Exegesis of Wolfgang Musculus* (New York: Oxford University Press, 1997); Irena Backus, *Reformation Readings of the Apocalypse: Geneva, Zurich, and Wittenberg* (New York: Oxford University Press, 2000).

21. Note that the terms "infralapsarian" and "supralapsarian" derive from debates of the late sixteenth and early seventeenth century and relate, specifically, to the way in which the human object of God's eternal electing and reprobating is defined – viz., as a possibility for creation and fall (supralapsarian) or as actually created and fallen (infralpsarian). Inasmuch as Calvin and his contemporaries did not pose the issue in precisely this way, the terms are not applied to their teachings with any precision.

22. As is characteristic of J. Wayne Baker, *Heinrich Bullinger and the Covenant: The Other Reformed Tradition* (Athens: Ohio University Press, 1980), pp. 27–54, 213–214. See the careful comparison of Bullinger with Calvin in Cornelis P. Venema, "Heinrich Bullinger's Correspondence on Calvin's Doctrine of Predestination, 1551–1553," in *Sixteenth Century Journal*, 17/4 (1986), pp. 435–450.

23. Muller, "The Use and Abuse of a Document," pp. 58–59; cf. Lynne Courter Boughton, "Supralapsarianism and the Role of Metaphysics in sixteenth Century Reformed Theology," in *Westminster Theological Journal*, 48/1 (1986), pp. 63–96.

24. See Lyle D. Bierma, "Federal Theology in the Sixteenth Century: Two Traditions?" in *Westminster Theological Journal*, 45 (1983), pp. 304–321; and idem, "The Role of Covenant Theology in Early Reformed Orthodoxy," in *Sixteenth Century Journal*, 21/3 (1990), pp. 453–462; contra Baker, *Heinrich Bullinger and the Covenant*, pp. 53–54, 193–215.

25. See Willem van Asselt, *The Federal Theology of Johannes Cocceius (1603–1669)* (Leiden: E. J. Brill, 2001); also on the British development, see Andrew Alexander Woolsey, "Unity and Continuity in Covenantal Thought: A Study in the Reformed Tradition to the Westminster Assembly," 2 vols. (Ph. D. Dissertation: University of Glasgow, 1988).

26. Contra Baker, *Heinrich Bullinger and the Covenant*, p. 215 and McCoy, "The Covenant Theology of Johannes Cocceius," pp. 276–319.

27. Willem J. Van Asselt, "Johannes Cocceius Anti-Scholasticus?" in van Asselt and Dekker (eds.), *Protestant Scholasticism*, pp. 227–251.

28. See Robert A. Peterson, *Calvin's Doctrine of the Atonement* (Phillipsburg, NJ: Presbyterian and Reformed Publishing Co., 1983); and Jonathan H. Rainbow, *The Will of God and the Cross: An Historical and Theological Study of John Calvin's Doctrine of Limited Redemption* (Allison Park, PA: Pickwick Publications, 1990).

29. Thus, William R. Godfrey, *Tensions within International Calvinism the Debate on the Atonement at the Synod of Dort, 1618–1619* (Ph.D. dissertation, Stanford University, 1974); idem, "Reformed Thought on the Extent of the Atonement to 1618," in *Westminster Theological Journal*, 37/2 (Winter, 1975), pp. 133–171; also note Stephen Strehle, "The Extent of the Atonement and the Synod of Dort," in *Westminster Theological Journal*, 51 (1989), pp. 1–23 and idem, "Universal Grace and Amyraldianism," in *Westminster Theological Journal*, 51 (1989), pp. 345–357.

30. See Brian G. Armstrong, *Calvinism and the Amyraut Heresy Protestant Scholasticism and Humanism in Seventeenth Century France* (Madison: University of Wisconsin Press, 1969).

31. The two main sections of this chapter were previously published as *Scholasticism and Orthodoxy in the Reformed Tradition: An Attempt at Definition*, P. J. Zondervan Professor of Historical Theology Inaugural Address, delivered in the Calvin Seminary Chapel, September 7, 1995, (Grand Rapids, MI: Calvin Theological Seminary, 1995) and as "Protestant Scholasticism: Methodological Issues and Problems in the Study of Its Development" in *Areopagus [Uitgegeven door de Faculteit Godgeleerdheid van de Universiteit Utrecht]*, Nieuwe Jaargang 3/3 (1999), pp. 14–19.

32. Previously published as *Ad fontes argumentorum: The Sources of Reformed Theology in the seventeenth Century* [Belle van Zuylenleerstoel Inaugural Address, delivered May 11, 1999, Universiteit Utrecht. *Utrechtse Theologische Reeks*, deel 40] (Utrecht: Faculteit der Godgeleerdheid, 1999).

33. Previously published, "Part I," in *Calvin Theological Journal*, 30/2 (November, 1995), pp. 345–75; "Part II," in *Calvin Theological Journal*, 31/1 (April, 1996), pp. 125–160.

34. Previously published as "The Era of Protestant Orthodoxy," in *Theological Education in the Evangelical Tradition*, ed. Daryl G. Hart and R. Albert Mohler (Grand Rapids, MI: Baker Book House, 1997), pp. 101–128.

35. Cf. Carl R. Trueman, "A Small Step Toward Rationalism: The Impact of the Metaphysics of Tommaso Campanella on the Theology of Richard Baxter," in Trueman and Clark (eds.), *Protestant Scholasticism*, pp. 147–164.

36. Previously published in *The Sixteenth Century Journal,* 15/3 (Fall 1984), pp. 341–365.
37. Previously published in *Church History,* 55/2 (June 1986), pp. 193–205.
38. Previously published in *The Journal of Medieval and Renaissance Studies,* 10/1 (Spring 1980), pp. 53–72.
39. Not previously published.
40. Previously published in *Calvin Theological Journal,* 29/1 (1994), pp. 75–101.
41. Jack B. Rogers and Donald K. McKim, *The Authority and Interpretation of the Bible: An Historical Approach* (San Francisco: Harper and Row, 1979), pp. 180–181, 183–184.

2. Scholasticism and Orthodoxy in the Reformed Tradition

1. This essay presupposes an extensive bibliography, found, e.g., in Willem J. van Asselt, P. L. Rouwendal, et al., *Inleiding in de Gereformeerde Scholastiek* (Zoetermeer: Boekencentrum, 1998); and in the next three chapters in this volume, namely, *Ad fontes argumentorum: The Sources of Reformed Theology in the seventeenth Century,* and "Calvin and the Calvinists: Assessing Continuities and Discontinuities Between the Reformation and Orthodoxy," Parts One and Two.
2. Cf. David Bagchi, "Sic et Non: Luther and Scholasticism," in Trueman and Clark, *Protestant Scholasticism: Essays in Reappraisal,* pp. 3–15, with Richard A. Muller, "Scholasticism in Calvin: a Question of Relation and Disjunction," in *The Unaccommodated Calvin: Studies in the Formation of a Theological Tradition* (New York: Oxford University Press, 2000), pp. 39–61.
3. A most egregious example of the latter problem is Karl Barth, *The Theology of John Calvin,* trans. G. W. Bromiley (Grand Rapids, MI: Eerdmans, 1995). See the discussion in Muller, *Unaccommodated Calvin,* pp. 4–8 on the application of dogmatic grids to Calvin.
4. See the discussions of the problematic apparatus of modern editions of the *Institutes* in Muller, *Unaccommodated Calvin,* pp. 72–78, 140–142, 187–188.
5. Jack Bartlett Rogers, *Scripture in the Westminster Confession: A Problem of Historical Interpretation for American Presbyterianism* (Grand Rapids, MI: Eerdmans, 1967); also note Jack B. Rogers and Donald K. McKim, *The Authority and Interpretation of the Bible: An Historical Approach* (San Francisco: Harper & Row, 1979). Cf. the alternative perspective in Paul R. Schaefer, "Protestant 'Scholasticism' at Elizabethan Cambridge: William Perkins and a Reformed Theology of the Heart," in Trueman and Clark, eds., *Protestant Scholasticism,* pp. 147–164.
6. E.g., John Arrowsmith, *Armilla Catechetica; A Chain of Principles: Or, an Orderly Concatenation of Theological Aphorisms and Exercitations* (Cambridge, 1659); Thomas Ridgley, *A Body of Divinity: Wherein the Doctrines of the Christian Religion are Explained and Defended, being the Substance of Several Lectures on the Assembly's Larger Catechism,* 2 vols. (London, 1731–1733).
7. Cf. M. Fabius Quintilianus, *Institutiones oratoriae libri XII,* ed. Ludwig Rademacher, 2 vols. (Leipzig: Teubner, 1907–1911), III.vi.44 (I, p. 148) with Rudolph Agricola, *De inventione dialectica lucubrationes* (Cologne, 1539), II.2 (pp. 227–228) and Philip Melanchthon, *Elementa rhetorices,* in *Philippi Melanchthonis opera quae supersunt omnia,* ed. C. G. Bretschneider and H. E. Bindseil (28 vols. Halle/Braunschweig, 1834–1860), 13, col. 424, 574.
8. Richard A. Muller, "Grace, Election, and Contingent Choice: Arminius' Gambit and the Reformed Response," in *The Grace of God and the Bondage of the Will,* ed. Thomas Schreiner and Bruce Ware, 2 vols. (Grand Rapids, MI: Baker Book House, 1995), vol. 2, pp. 251–278, offers discussion of contingency and freedom in Reformed scholastic thought.
9. Cf. Richard A. Muller, *Christ and the Decree: Christology and Predestination in Reformed Theology from Calvin to Perkins* (Durham, NC: Labyrinth Press, 1986; Grand Rapids, MI: Baker Book House, 1988) and idem, "Found (No Thanks to Theodore Beza): One 'Decretal' Theology," in *Calvin Theological Journal,* 32/1 (April 1997), pp. 145–51.

10. Peter Lombard, *Sententiae in IV libris distinctae*, editio tertia, 2 vols. (Grottaferrata: Collegium S. Bonaventurae ad Claras Aquas, 1971–1981), Lib. I, dist. xlv, cap. 5.

11. See the discussion in Heinrich Heppe, *Reformed Dogmatics Set Out and Illustrated from the Sources*, revised and edited by Ernst Bizer, trans. G. T. Thomson (London, 1950; repr. Grand Rapids, MI: Baker Book House, 1978), pp. 85–92.

12. The text of Beza's address is found in *Leges Academiae Genevensis* (Geneva: Stephanus, 1559; facsimile repr. Geneva: J. G. Fick, 1859), fol. a.iii, recto–b.ii, recto and also in *Le Livre du recteur de l'Académie de Genève*, ed. S. Stelling-Michaud (6 vols. Geneva: Droz, 1959–80), I, pp. 64–65. Cf. Gillian Lewis, ""The Geneva Academy," in *Calvinism in Europe, 1540–1620* (Cambridge: Cambridge University Press, 1994), p. 39.

13. Cf. Donald W. Sinnema, "The Distinction Between Scholastic and Popular: Andreas Hyperius and Reformed Scholasticism," in Trueman and Clark (eds.), *Protestant Scholasticism: Essays in Reassessment*, pp. 125–143.

14. *Leges Academiae Genevensis*, fol. c.i, verso; also *L'Ordre du College de Geneve* (Geneva: Stephanus, 1559; facsimile repr. Geneva: J. G. Fick, 1859), fol. c.i, verso.

15. Cf. *Leges Academiae Genevensis*, fol. c.ii, recto–c.iii, recto; with *L'Ordre du College de Geneve*, fol. b.ii, recto–verso; b.iii, verso with the discussion in Irena Backus, "L'enseignement de la logique à l'Académie de Genève entre 1559 et 1565," in *Revue de Théologie et de Philosophie*, 111 (1979), pp. 153–163.

16. See *Renaissance Student Life: The Paedologia of Petrus Mosellanus*, trans., with an intro. by Robert Francis Seyboldt (Chicago: University of Illinois Press, 1927).

17. Cf. A. Bömer, *Die lateinischen Schülergespräche der Humanisten*, 2 vols. (Berlin, 1897–1899) with L. Massebieau, *Les colloques scolaires de seizième siècle, et les auteurs, 1480–1570* (Paris, 1878) and idem, *Répertoire des ouvrages pédagogiques du XVIe siècle* (Paris, 1886).

18. Stephanus Szegedinus, *Theologiae sincerae loci communes de Deo et Homine perpetuis Tabulis explicati et scholasticorum dogmatis illustrati* [The standard topics of sound theology concerning God and Humanity explained in running tables and illustrated with scholastic or academic doctrinal formulae] (Basel, 1588).

19. Leigh, *A Systeme or Body of Divinity* (London, 1664), I.i.

20. Franz Burman, *Synopsis theologiae et speciatim oeconomiae foederum Dei* (Geneva, 1678), I.ii.42; cf., in the eighteenth century, the similar view of method in Salomon van Til, *Theologiae utriusque compendium cum naturalis tum revelatae* (Leiden, 1704; second edition, 1719), II.i.

21. See Armand Maurer, *Medieval Philosophy* (New York: Random House, 1962), p. 90; David Knowles, *The Evolution of Medieval Thought* (New York: Vintage Books, 1962), p. 87; J. A. Weisheipl, "Scholastic Method," in NCE, 12, p. 1145; G. Fritz and A. Michel, "Scholastique," in DTC, 14/2, col. 1691; cf. the similar comments concerning Protestant scholasticism in David C. Steinmetz, "The Theology of Calvin and Calvinism," in *Reformation Europe: A Guide to Research*, ed. Steven Ozment (St. Louis: Center for Reformation Research, 1982), p. 225, and William T. Costello, *The Scholastic Curriculum at Early Seventeenth-Century Cambridge* (Cambridge, MA: Harvard University Press, 1958), pp. 11, 35.

22. See, e.g. Antoine Chandieu, *De verbo Dei scripto . . . Praefatio de vera methodo theologice simul et scholastice disputandi*, in *Opera theologica* (Geneva, 1593) with Johann Heinrich Alsted, *Theologia scholastica didactica exhibens locos communos theologicos methodo scholastica* (Hanover, 1618) and cf. Donald W. Sinnema, "Antoine De Chandieu's Call for a Scholastic Reformed Theology (1580)," in *Later Calvinism: International Perspectives*, ed. W. Fred Graham (Kirksville, MO: Sixteenth Century Journal Publishers, 1994), pp. 159–190 with Muller, *Post-Reformation Reformed Dogmatics*, vol. 1, pp. 110–116, 193–208, 428–435.

23. Burman, *Synopsis theologiae*, I.ii.47; cf. the similar objections, at length, in Voetius, *De theologia scholastica*, in *Selectarum disputationum theologicarum* (Utrecht, 1648–1669), I: 12–29.

24. Leigh, *Body of Divinity*, I.i.

25. On Ramus, see Walter J. Ong, *Ramus: Method and the Decay of Dialogue* (Cambridge, MA.: Harvard University Press, 1958) and Neal W. Gilbert, *Renaissance Concepts of Method* (New York: Columbia University Press, 1960), pp. 129–163.

26. Cf. Backus, "L'enseignement de la logique," pp. 154–155 with and Joan Lechler, *Renaissance Concepts of the Commonplaces* (New York: Pageant Press, 1962).

27. Cf. the conclusions of Willem van Asselt, *The Federal Theology of Johannes Cocceius (1603–1669)* (Leiden: E. J. Brill, 2001), pp. 101–105 and idem, "Johannes Cocceius Anti-Scholasticus?" in van Asselt and Dekker (eds.), *Protestant Scholasticism*, pp. 227–251.

28. Cf. Lyle D. Bierma, "Federal Theology in the Sixteenth Century: Two Traditions?" in *Westminster Theological Journal*, 45 (1983), pp. 304–321; idem, *German Calvinism in the Confessional Age: The Covenant Theology of Caspar Olevian* (Grand Rapids, MI: Baker Book House, 1996), pp. 31–62.

29. Note the examples in Muller, *Post-Reformation Reformed Dogmatics*, vol. 1, pp. 108–117, 176–188, 339–353.

30. See Donald W. Sinnema, *The Issue of Reprobation at the Synod of Dort (1618–19) in the Light of the History of this Doctrine* (Ph.D. dissertation, University of St. Michael's College, 1985).

31. I have commented further on this issue in "Reformation, Orthodoxy, 'Christian Aristotelianism,' and the Eclecticism of Early Modern Philosophy," in *Nederkands Archief voor Kerkgeschiedenis*, 81/3 (2001), pp. 306–325.

32. Cf. Van Asselt, *Federal Theology of Johannes Cocceius*, pp. 81–94, with Martin I. Klauber, "Reason, Revelation, and Cartesianism: Louis Tronchin and Enlightened Orthodoxy in Late Seventeenth-Century Geneva," in *Church History*, 59 (1990), pp. 326–339, and with Michael Heyd, *Between Orthodoxy and the Enlightenment: Jean-Robert Chouet and the Introduction of Cartesian Science in the Academy of Geneva* (The Hague: De Graff, 1982); and idem, "From a Rationalist Theology to a Cartesian Voluntarism: David Derodon and Jean-Robert Chouet," in *Journal of the History of Ideas*, 40 (1979), pp. 527–542.

33. I.e., the declared hermeneutic of the Reformed orthodox, as stated e.g., in the *Westminster Confession*, i.6; cf. Muller, *Post-Reformation Reformed Dogmatics*, vol. 2, pp. 495–498.

34. This point may seem methodologically self-evident, but the number of essays in the history of Christian doctrine that assume doctrine is its own explanation, not to mention the number of studies of Calvin that cite only Calvin's *Institutes* and a few of his commentaries or treatises, render the point worthy of frequent reiteration. Cf. the arguments in Quentin Skinner, "Meaning and Understanding in the History of Ideas," in *History and Theory*, 8 (1969), pp. 3–53.

35. E.g., Heiko A. Oberman, *Forerunners of the Reformation* (New York: Holt, Rinehart and Winston, 1966); idem, *The Harvest of Medieval Theology: Gabriel Biel and Late Medieval Nominalism*, rev. ed. (Grand Rapids, MI: Eerdmans, 1967); and idem, *Masters of the Reformation: Emergence of a New Intellectual Climate in Europe*, trans. Dennis Martin (Cambridge: Cambridge University Press, 1981).

36. Cf. the similar methodological point made in Quentin Skinner, *Reason and Rhetoric in the Philosophy of Hobbes* (Cambridge: Cambridge University Press, 1996), p. 7.

37. Paul Oskar Kristeller, *Renaissance Thought: The Classic, Scholastic, and Humanist Strains* (New York: Harper & Row, 1961); *Medieval Aspects of Renaissance Learning*, ed. E. P. Mahoney (Durham, NC: Duke University Press, 1974).

38. John Patrick Donnelly, *Calvinism and Scholasticism in Vermigli's Doctrine of Man and Grace* (Leiden: E. J. Brill, 1975) and idem, "Calvinist Thomism," in *Viator*, 7 (1976), pp. 441–455.

39. E.g., David C. Steinmetz (ed.), *The Bible in the Sixteenth Century* (Durham, NC: Duke University Press, 1990); idem, *Calvin in Context* (Oxford: Oxford University Press, 1995); idem, *Luther and Staupitz: An Essay in the Intellectual Origins of the Protestant Reformation* (Durham,

NC: Duke University Press, 1980); Susan E. Schreiner, *Where Shall Wisdom be Found? Calvin's Exegesis of Job from Medieval and Modern Perspectives* (Chicago: University of Chicago Press, 1994); Irena Backus, *Reformation Readings of the Apocalypse: Geneva, Zurich, and Wittenberg* (New York: Oxford University Press, 2000); Peter T. van Rooden, *Theology, Biblical Scholarship and Rabbinical Studies in the Seventeenth Century: Constantijn L'Empereur* (1591–1648), *Professor of Hebrew and Theology at Leiden*, trans. J. C. Grayson (Leiden: Brill, 1989); Stephen George Burnett, *From Christian Hebraism to Jewish Studies: Johannes Buxtorf* (1564–1629) *and Hebrew Learning in the Seventeenth Century* (Leiden: E. J. Brill, 1996).

40. See, e.g., Jerrold E. Siegel, *Rhetoric and Philosophy in Renaissance Humanism* (Princeton, NJ: Princeton University Press, 1968); Debora K. Shuger, *Sacred Rhetoric: The Christian Grand Style in the English Renaissance* (Princeton, NJ: Princeton University Press, 1988); Peter Mack, *Renaissance Argument: Valla and Agricola in the Traditions of Rhetoric and Dialectic* (Leiden: Brill, 1993); Manfred Hoffmann, *Rhetoric and Theology: The Hermeneutic of Erasmus* (Toronto: University of Toronto Press, 1994).

41. E.g., Serene Jones, *Calvin and the Rhetoric of Piety* (Louisville, KY: Westminster John Knox, 1995); Don H. Compier, *John Calvin's Rhetorical Doctrine of Sin* (Lewiston, NY: Mellen Press, 2001).

42. E.g., Heinz Schilling, ed., *Die reformierte Konfessionalisierung in Deutschland: das Problem der "Zweiten Reformation": Wissenschaftliches Symposion des Vereins für Reformationsgeschichte 1985* (Gutersloh: Gutersloher Verlagshaus G. Mohn, 1986); and idem, *Civic Calvinism in Northwestern Germany and the Netherlands: Sixteenth to Nineteenth Centuries*, Sixteenth Century Essays and Studies, vol. 17 (Kirksville, MO.: Sixteenth Century Journal Publishers, 1991).

43. Cf. Muller, *Unaccommodated Calvin*, pp. 4–8 with Skinner, "Meaning and Understanding," pp. 7–22.

44. E.g., the programmatic essay of Robert M. Kingdon, "A New View of Calvin in the Light of the Registers of the Geneva Consistory," in Wilhelm Neuser and Brian G. Armstrong (eds.), *Calvinus Sincerioris Religionis Vindex: Calvin as Protector of the Purer Religion*. Die Referate des Internationalen Kongresses für Calvinforschung, vom 13. bis 16. September in Edinburgh (Kirksville, MO: Sixteenth Century Journal Publishers, 1997), pp. 21–33; also note William G. Naphy, "Calvin's Letters: Reflections on their Usefulness in Studying Genevan History," in *Archiv für Reformationsgeschichte* 86 (1995), pp. 67–90.

45. See Richard A. Muller, "The Use and Abuse of a Document: Beza's *Tabula praedestinationis*, the Bolsec Controversy, and the Origins of Reformed Orthodoxy," in Trueman and Clark, eds., *Protestant Scholasticism*, pp. 33–61.

3. *Ad fontes argumentorum*

1. Cf., e.g., Alister McGrath, *Reformation Thought: An Introduction*, second edition (Grand Rapids, MI: Baker Book House, 1993), pp. 129–130; James B. Torrance, "Strengths and Weaknesses of the Westminster Theology," in *The Westminster Confession*, ed. Alisdair Heron (Edinburgh: Saint Andrews Press, 1982), pp. 40–53; idem, "Calvin and Puritanism in England and Scotland—Some Basic Concepts in the Development of 'Federal Theology,'" in *Calvinus Reformator* (Potchefstroom: Potchefstroom University for Christian Higher Education, 1982), pp. 264–277; Frederic W. Farrar, *History of Interpretation* (New York: Dutton, 1886; repr. Grand Rapids, MI: Baker Book House, 1961); *The Cambridge History of the Bible*, 3 vols., ed. P. R. Ackroyd, C. F. Evans, G. W. H. Lampe, and S. L. Greenslade (Cambridge: Cambridge University Press, 1963–1970).

2. Notable exceptions here are the essays of Michael McGiffert on the covenant of works: e.g., "Grace and Works: The Rise and Division of Covenant Divinity in Elizabethan Puritanism," in *Harvard Theological Review*, 75/4 (1982), pp. 463–502; "From Moses to Adam: The

Making of the Covenant of Works," in *Sixteenth Century Journal*, 19/2 (1988), pp. 131–155; "The Perkinsian Moment of Federal Theology," in *Calvin Theological Journal*, 29/1 (April 1994), pp. 134–136.

3. For a summary of arguments and literature, see "Calvin and the Calvinists: Assessing Continuities and Discontinuities Between the Reformation and Orthodoxy," Parts One and Two.

4. These are the conclusions of Carl Beck, "Das Princip des Protestantismus. Anfrage in einem Schreiben an *D.* Ullmann," in *Theologische Studien und Kritiken*, 24 (1851), pp. 408–411; and Albrecht Ritschl, "Über die beiden Principien des Protestantismus," in *Zeitschrift für Kirchengeschichte*, 1 (1876), pp. 397–413.

5. See Willem J. van Asselt, P. L. Rouwendal, et. al. *Inleiding in de Gereformeerde Scholastiek* (Zoetermeer: Boekencentrum, 1998) and note the discussion in Muller, *Post-Reformation Reformed Dogmatics*, vol. 1, pp. 96–123, 220–237, et passim.

6. Note that Paul Althaus, *Die Prinzipien der deutschen reformierten Dogmatik im Zeitalter der aristotelischen Scholastik* (Leipzig: Deichert, 1914) never inquired of the sixteenth- and seventeenth-century theologians what their *principia* were, but instead examined doctrines like predestination and providence as if they were the *principia* of the older theology.

7. Thus, Frederic W. Farrar, *History of Interpretation* (New York: Dutton, 1886; repr. Grand Rapids, MI: Baker Book House, 1961; Basil Hall, "Biblical Scholarship: Editions and Commentaries," in *Cambridge History of the Bible*, vol. 3, pp. 38–93; and Norman Sykes, "The Religion of Protestants," in ibid. vol. 3, pp. 175–198. One has the distinct impression when reading these essays that none of the authors troubled himself to look at any commentaries of the era.

8. See, e.g., Stephen G. Burnett, *From Christian Hebraism to Jewish Studies: Johannes Buxtorf (1564–1629) and Hebrew Learning in the Seventeenth Century* (Leiden: E. J. Brill, 1996); Peter T. van Rooden, *Theology, Biblical Scholarship and Rabbinical Studies in the Seventeenth Century: Constantijn L'Empereur (1591–1648), Professor of Hebrew and Theology at Leiden*, trans. J. C. Grayson (Leiden: E. J. Brill, 1989); Jai Sung Shim, *Biblical Hermeneutics and Hebraism in the Early Seventeenth-Century as Reflected in the Work of John Weemse (1579–1636)* (Ph. D. dissertation, Calvin Theological Seminary, 1998).

9. Thus, Theodore Beza, *Novum D.N. Iesu Christi Testamentum Latine iam olim a veteri interprete, nunc denuo a Theodoro Beza versum; cum eiusdem annotationibus, in quibus ratio interpretationis redditur* (Geneva: Robertus Stephanus, 1556); idem, *Iesu Christi D.N. Novum testamentum, sive Novum foedus: cuius Graeco textui respondent interpretationes duae: una, vetus, altera, noua, Theodori Bezae, diligenter ab eo recognita / eiusdem Th. Bezae annotationes, quas itidem hac secunda editione recognouit, & accessione non parua locupletauit ; indices etiam duo, theologis (praesertim Hebraicae, Graecae & Latinae linguae studiosis) multum profuturi, adiecti sunt* (Geneva: Henricus Stephanus, 1565); and idem, *Testamentum Novum, sive Nouum foedus Iesu Christi, D.N.: cuius Graeco contextui respondent interpretationes duae: vna, vetus, altera Theodori Bezae / nunc quartò diligenter ab eo recognita* (Geneva: Henricus Stephanus, 1589).

10. See Irene Backus, *The Reformed Roots of the English New Testament: The Influence of Theodore Beza on the English New Testament* (Pittsburgh, PA: Pickwick Press, 1980); Marvin Anderson, "The Geneva (Tomson/Junius) New Testament Among Other English Bibles of the Period," in *The Geneva Bible: The Annotated New Testament, 1602 Edition*, edited by Gerald T. Sheppard, (New York: The Pilgrim Press, 1989), pp. 5–17.

11. See Peter William van Kleek, *Hermeneutics and Theology in the Seventeenth Century: the Contribution of Andrew Willet* (Th.M. thesis, Calvin Theological Seminary, 1998).

12. E.g., Andrew Willet, *Hexapla in Genesin* (Cambridge, 1605; second ed., enlarged, 1608); *Hexapla in Exodum* (London, 1608); *Hexapla in Leviticum* (London, 1631); *Hexapla in Danielem* (Cambridge, 1610); and *Hexapla: That is, a Six Fold Commentarie upon the Epistle to the Romans* (Cambridge, 1620).

13. See the discussion in Muller, *Post-Reformation Reformed Dogmatics*, vol. 2, pp. 507–508.

14. Cf. John Calvin, *Letter to Sadoleto*, in *Selected Works of John Calvin: Tracts and Letters*, ed. Henry Beveridge and Jules Bonnet, 7 vols. (Grand Rapids, MI: Baker Book House, 1983), vol. 1, pp. 37–38, in which Calvin identifies the Reformation with the unperverted truth of the ancient tradition of the church and appeals to a formula of universality reminiscent of the Vincentian canon, with Calvin, *Institutes*, IV.ix.1-14, in which Calvin subordinates the authority of councils to the Word of God, and with *Institutes*, II.ii.6; III.xiv.11 (references to *saniores scholastici*).

15. Turetin, *Institutio theologiae elencticae*, I.xiv.22.

16. Cf. Theodore Beza, *Ad Acta Colloqui Montisbelgardensis Tubingae edita Theodori Bezae responsionis* (Geneva, 1588) with Jill Raitt, *The Colloquy of Montbéliard: Religion and Politics in the Sixteenth Century* (New York: Oxford University Press, 1993); and note the tenor of the Leipzig Colloquy (1631) in H. A. Niemeyer, *Collectio confessionium in ecclesiis reformatis publicatarum* (Leipzig, 1840), pp. 653–668; also J. K. Seidemann, *Die Leipziger Disputation* (Dresden, 1843).

17. Cf. Franciscus Turretinus, *Institutio theologiae elencticae*, 3 vols. (Geneva, 1679–1685; a new edition, Edinburgh, 1847); now available as *Institutes of Elenctic Theology*, 3 vols., trans. George Musgrave Giger, ed. James T. Dennison, Jr. (Phillipsburg, NJ: Presbyterian and Reformed Publishing, 1992–1997), III.xxiv.12–14.

18. Second Helvetic Confession, xx.5; xi.14, in Philip Schaff, *The Creeds of Christendom: with a History and Critical Notes*, 6th ed., 3 vols. (1931; repr., Grand Rapids, MI: Baker Book House, 1983), vol. 3, pp. 290–291, 257.

19. Heidelberg Catechism, q. 80, in Schaff, *Creeds*, vol. 3, pp. 335–336.

20. Belgic Confession, xxxvi, in Schaff, *Creeds*, vol. 3, pp. 432–433.

21. Gallican Confession, xxviii, in Schaff, *Creeds*, vol. 3, pp. 375–376.

22. E. g., Johannes Hoornbeeck, *Socinianismus confutatus*, 3 vols. (Utrecht, 1650–1664) and idem, *Summa controversiarum religionis, cum infidelibus, haereticis, schismaticis* (Utrecht, 1653).

23. See, e.g., Peter Fraenkel, *Testimonia Patrum: The Function of Patristic Argument in the Theology of Philip Melanchthon* (Geneva: Droz, 1961); E. P. Meijering, *Melanchthon and Patristic Thought: The Doctrines of Christ, Grace, the Trinity, and Creation* (Leiden: E. J. Brill, 1983); Luchesius Smits, *Saint-Augustine dans l'oeuvre de Jean Calvin*, 2 vols. (Assen: Van Gorcum, 1957–1958); Johannes van Oort (ed.), *De kerkvaders in Reformatie en Nadere Reformatie* (Zoetermeer: Boekencentrum, 1997); Anthony N. S. Lane, *John Calvin: Student of the Church Fathers* (Grand Rapids: Baker Books, 1999); further, Manfred Schultze, "Martin Luther and the Church Fathers," in Irena Backus (ed.), *The Reception of the Church Fathers in the West: From the Carolingians to the Maurists*, 2 vols. (Leiden: E. J. Brill, 1997), vol. 2, pp. 573–626; Irena Backus, "Ulrich Zwingli, Martin Bucer, and the Church Fathers," in ibid., vol. 2, pp. 627–660; Johannes van Oort, "John Calvin and the Church Fathers," in ibid., vol. 2, pp. 661–700; Irena Backus, "The Fathers in Calvinist Orthodoxy: Patristic Scholarship," in ibid., vol. 2, pp. 839–866; E. P. Meijering, "The Fathers in Calvinist Orthodoxy: Systematic Theology," in ibid., vol. 2, pp. 867–888. Also see G. L. C. Frank, "A Lutheran Turned Eastward: The Use of the Greek Fathers in the Eucharistic Theology of Martin Chemnitz," in *St. Vladimir's Theological Quarterly*, 26 (1982), pp. 155–171; and Robert A. Kelly, "Tradition and Innovation: The Use of Theodoret's *Eranistes* in Martin Chemnitz's *De Duabus Naturis in Christo*," in Marguerite Shuster and Richard A. Muller (eds.), *Perspectives on Christology: Essays in Honor of Paul K. Jewett* (Grand Rapids, MI: Zondervan, 1991), pp. 105–125.

24. Thus, Johann Gerhard, *Patrologia, sive de primitivae ecclesiae christianae doctores vita ac lucubrationibus* (Jena, 1653); cf. Johannes Quasten, *Patrology*, 4 vols. (Utrecht: Spectrum; Westminster, MD: Christian Classics, 1950–1986), vol. 1, p. 1.

25. Abraham Scultetus, *Medulla theologiae patrum in quo theologia priscorum primitivae ecclesiae doctorum qvi ante et post Concilium Nicaenum floruerunt, methodo analyticâ & syntheticâ expressa, atque à Roberti Bellarmini, Caesaris Baronii, Gregorii de Valentia, aliorumque pontificiorum corruptelis ita vindicatur: ut liquido appareat, penes solas Reformatas Ecclesias esse doctrinae & veritatis evangelicae antiquitatem* (Amberg, 1598).

26. Thus, Turretin, *Institutio theologiae elencticae*, II.xxi.5–6, 9; Jean Daillé, *A Treatise concerning the Right use of the Fathers, in the Decision of the Controversies that are this Day in Religion* (London: John Martin, 1675); cf. Friedrich Kropatscheck, *Das Schriftprinzip der lutherischen Kirche. Geschichte und dogmatische Untersuchungen. I. Die vorgeschichte. Das Erbe des Mittelalters* (Leipzig: Deichert, 1904) with Paul de Vooght, *Les Sources de la doctrine chrétienne d'après les théologiens du XIVe siècle et du début du XVe* (Paris: Desclée, 1954), idem, "Le rapport écriture-tradition d'après saint Thomas d'Aquin et les théologiens du XIII siècle," in *Istina*, 8 (1962), pp. 499–510 and Muller, *Post-Reformation Reformed Dogmatics*, vol. 2, pp. 23–61.

27. Thus, John Forbes of Corse, *Instructiones historico-theologicae de doctrina christiana* (Amsterdam, 1645); and the detailed but arguably ahistorical George Bull, *Defensio fidei nicaenae: Defence of the Nicene Creed, out of the Extant Writings of the Catholick Doctors, who Flourished during the First Three Centuries of the Christian Church* [1685], 2 vols. (Oxford: Parker, 1851).

28. See D. W. Dockrill, "Authority of the Fathers in the Great Trinitarian Debates of the Sixteen Nineties," in *Studia Patristica*, 18/4 (1983), pp. 335–347, and Johan van den Berg, "The Idea of the Pre-existence of the Soul of Christ: an Argument in the Controversy between Arian and Orthodox in the Eighteenth Century," in *Tradition and Re-interpretation*, ed. J. Henten, H. Jonge, et al. (1986), pp. 284–295; and see the introduction in Thomas C. Pfizenmaier, *The Trinitarian Theology of Dr. Samuel Clarke (1675–1729): Context, Sources, and Controversy* (Leiden: E. J. Brill, 1997), pp. 102–128.

29. Cf. Pfizenmaier, *Trinitarian Theology*, pp. 128–141.

30. E.g., Turretin, *Institutio theologiae elencticae*, III.xxiii.6, 10; xxvii.17.

31. E.g., James Ussher, *Gotteschalci et praedestinatianae controversiae ab eo motae, historia: Unà cum duplice ejusdem Confessione* (Dublin: Ex Typographià Societatis Bibliopolarum, 1631); Cornelius Jansen, *Augustinus, in quo haereses et mores Pelagii . . . ex Augustino recensentur et refutantur . I. In quo haereses & mores Pelagii contra naturae humanae sanitatem, aegritudinem & medicinam ex S. Augustino recensentur ac refutantur. II. In quo genuina sententia S. Augustini de humanae naturae stantis, lapsae, purae statu & viribus eruitur & explicatur. III. In quo genuina sententia profundissimi doctoris de auxilio gratiae medicinalis Christi salvatoris, & de praedestinatione hominum & angelorum proponitur, ac dilucide ostenditur* (Louvain: Jacobus Zeger, 1640); Gerardus Vossius, *Historiæ de controversiis, quas Pelagius eiusque reliquiæ moverunt, libri septem* (Leiden: Joannes Patius, 1618); Melchior Leydecker, *De historia Jansenismi libri VI, quibus de Cornelii Jansennii vita et morte, nec non de ipsius et sequacium dogmatibus disseritur* (Utrecht: Halma, 1695).

32. See, for example, the consistent referencing of Calvin's commentaries in Edward Leigh, *A Treatise of Divinity* (London, 1646), I.iii–iv (pp. 42–83).

33. On Arminius's Molinism, see: Eef Dekker, "Was Arminius a Molinist?" in *Sixteenth Century Journal*, 27/2 (1996), pp. 337–352; idem, *Rijker dan Midas: Vrijheid, genade en predestinatie in de theologie van Jacobus Arminius, 1559–1609* (Zoetermeer: Boekencentrum, 1993); and Richard A. Muller, *God, Creation and Providence in the Thought of Jacob Arminius: Sources and Directions of Scholastic Protestantism in the Era of Early Orthodoxy* (Grand Rapids, MI: Baker Book House, 1991), pp. 154–166.

34. See Armand Aime LaVallee, *Calvin's Criticism of Scholastic Theology* (Ph.D. dissertation: Harvard University, 1967) and Karl Reuter, *Das Grundverständnis der Theologie Calvins* (Neukirchen: Neukirchner Verlag, 1963).

35. On Daneau's work, see Olivier Fatio, *Méthode et théologie: Lambert Daneau et les débuts de la scholastique reformée* (Geneva: Droz, 1976).

36. Franciscus Junius, *De vera theologia*, in *Opuscula theologica selecta*, ed. Abraham Kuyper (Amsterdam: F. Muller, 1882) and see the discussion in Muller, *Post-Reformation Reformed Dogmatics*, vol. 1, pp. 113-117, 224-237, 254-268, et passim.

37. Thus, e.g., Johannes Altenstaig, *Vocabularius theologicae* (Gratz, 1517); republished as *Lexicon theologicum* (Köln, 1619); Gregory of Rimini, *Super Primum et secundum sententiarum* (Venice, 1521); Henry of Ghent, *Summa quaestionum ordinariarum theologi* (Paris, 1520); Thomas Aquinas, *Summa totius theologiae . . . in tres partes ab auctore suo distributa* (Antwerp, 1575, 1585); Pierre D'Ailly, *Quaestiones super libros sententiarum cum quibusdam in fine adjunctis* (Strasbourg, 1490); Thomas of Strasbourg, *Commentaria in IIII libros Sententiarum* (Venice, 1564); Durandus of Sancto Porciano, *In Petri Lombardi sententias theologicas commentariorum libri IV* (Venice, 1571); Marsilius of Inghen, *Quaestiones Marsilii super quattuor libros sententiarum* (Strasbourg, 1501); Nicolaus of Lyra, *Biblia sacra cum Glossa interlineari, ordinaria, et Nicolai Lyrani Postilla*, 7 vols. (Venice, 1588); Richard of Middleton, *In IV libros sententiarum* (Venice, 1507-1509).

38. See, e.g., Turretin, *Institutio theologiae elencticae*, III.i–ii and Stephen Charnock, *Discourses upon the Existence and Attributes of God*, 2 vols. (New York: Robert Carter, 1853), vol. 1, pp. 89-175.

39. Cf. Jean Calvin, *Institutio christianae religionis*, I.iii.1–2.

40. See John Platt, *Reformed Thought and Scholasticism: The Arguments for the Existence of God in Dutch Theology, 1575–1650* (Leiden: E. J. Brill, 1982).

41. Cf. Eef Dekker, *Rijker dan Midas: vrijheid, genade en predestinatie in de theologie van Jacobus Arminius (1559–1609)* (Zoetermeer: Boekencentrum, 1993); with Willem van Asselt and Evert Dekker (eds.), *De scholastieke Voetius, een luisteroefening aan de hand van Voetius' Disputationes Selectae* (Zoetermeer: Boekencentrum, 1995).

42. Cf. Alsted, *Praecognita theologiae* (Hanau, 1614), II.x; Turretin, *Institutio theologiae elencticae*, I.xii-xiii; and see the discussion in Muller, *Post-Reformation Reformed Dogmatics*, vol. 1, pp. 359-403.

43. Turretin, *Institutio theologiae elencticae*, I.ix.1–5; xi.3–5

44. Cf. Martin I. Klauber, "The Use of Philosophy in the Theology of Johannes Maccovius (1578-1644)," in *Calvin Theological Journal*, 30/2 (1995), pp. 376–391 with Lynne Courter Boughton, "Supralapsarianism and the Role of Metaphysics in Sixteenth-Century Reformed Theology," in *Westminster Theological Journal*, 48 (1986), pp. 63–96.

45. See, at greater length, Richard A. Muller, "Scholasticism, Reformation, Orthodoxy and the Persistence of Christian Aristotelianism," in *Trinity Journal*, NS 19/1 (1998), pp. 91–96; in response to Ronald N. Frost, "Aristotle's *Ethics*: The *Real* Reason for Luther's Reformation," in *Trinity Journal*, NS 18/2 (1997), pp. 223–241.

46. Eef Dekker, "Was Arminius a Molinist?" in *Sixteenth Century Journal*, 27/2 (1996), pp. 337–352.

47. See Stanislav Sousedík, "Arriagas Universalienlehre," in Tereza Saxolvá and Stanislav Sousedík (eds.), *Rodrigo de Arriaga (†1667): Philosoph und Theolog* (Prague: Univerzity Karlovy, 1998), pp. 41–49.

48. Cf. Thomas Barlow, *Exercitationes aliquot metaphysicale, de Deo: quod sit objectum metaphysicae* (London, 1637).

49. Voetius, *Testimonium Academiae Ultrajectinae, et Narratio Historica qua defensae, qua exterminatae novae Philosophiae* (Utrecht, 1643); also see M. Schoock, *La Querelle d'Utrecht* (Paris: Impressions Nouvelles, 1988), and the discussion by J. A. van Ruler, "New Philosophy to Old Standards: Voetius' Vindication of Divine Concurrence and Secondary Causality," in *NAKG* 71 (1991), pp. 58–91. For Protestant response to Spinoza, see, e.g., John Howe, *The Living Temple, or, A Designed Improvement of that Notion, that a Good Man is the Temple of God: Part I. Concerning God's Existence and His Conversableness with Man against Atheism, or the Epicurean Deism*

(1676). *Part II. Containing Animadversions on Spinoza, and a French Writer Pretending to Refute Him* (1702), in *The Works of the Rev. John Howe, M.A.*, 3 vols. (London: William Tegg, 1848; repr. Ligonier, PA: Soli Deo Gloria Publications, 1990), vol. 1, pp. 1–344.

50. Cf. Michael Heyd, "From a Rationalist Theology to a Cartesian Voluntarism: David Derodon and Jean-Robert Chouet, in *Journal of the History of Ideas*, 40 (1979), pp. 527–542, with Maria-Cristina Pitassi, "Un manuscrit genevois du XVIIIe siécle: la 'Refutation du système de Spinosa par Mr. Turrettini,'" in *Nederlands Archief voor Kerkgeschiedenis*, 68 (1988), pp. 180–212. Also see Ernst Bizer, "Die reformierte Orthodoxie und der Cartesianismus," in *Zeitschrift für Theologie und Kirche* (1958), pp. 306–372, and Josef Bohatec, *Die cartesianische Scholastik in der Philosophie und reformierten Dogmatik des 17. Jahrhunderts* (Leipzig: Deichert, 1912).

51. Cf. Mastricht, *Theoretico-practica theologia*, II.vi.8.

52. See, further, the studies of Theo Verbeek, *Descartes and the Dutch: Early Reactions to Cartesianism (1637–1650)* (Carbondale: Southern Illinois University Press, 1992); "Descartes and the Problem of Atheism: the Utrecht Crisis," in *Nederlands Archief voor Kerkgeschiedenis*, 71/2 (1991), pp. 211–223; and "From 'Learned Ignorance' to Scepticism: Descartes and Calvinist Orthodoxy," in Richarc H. Popkin and Arjo Vanderjagt, eds., *Scepticism and Irreligion in the Seventeenth and Eighteenth Centuries* (Leiden: E. J. Brill, 1993), pp. 31–45.

53. Muller, *Post-Reformation Reformed Dogmatics*, vol. 1, pp. 339–353.

54. Wilhelmus à Brakel, *Logiké Latreia, dat is Redelijke Godsdienst in welken de goddelijke Waarheded van het Genade-Verbond worden verklaard* (Dordrecht, 1700); in translation, *The Christian's Reasonable Service in which Divine Truths concerning the Covenant of Grace are Expounded, Defended against Opposing Parties, and their Practice Advocated*, 4 vols., trans. Bartel Elshout (Ligonier, PA: Soli Deo Gloria Publications, 1992–1996); Petrus van Mastricht, *Theoretico-practica theologia* (Utrecht, 1714; editio nova, 1724).

55. Thus, e.g., Turretin, *Institutio theologiae elencticae*, III.ii., on the unity of God: §1–4, on the state of the question; §5, on proof from Scripture; §6–7, on proof from reason; §8–13, sources of explanation; III.xiii, on "middle knowledge": §1, definition of the term; §2–4, origins of the concept; §5–8, on the state of the question; §9–14, argument against the concept; §15–23, sources of explanation—with §15–17 being drawn from scripture, §18–23 being discursive.

56. Cf. Leigh, *A System or Body of Divinity*, I.i; Burman, *Synopsis theologiae*, I.ii.42.

57. See the discussion in Muller, *Post-Reformation Reformed Dogmatics*, vol. 1, pp. 188–219.

58. Hans Emil Weber, *Reformation, Orthodoxie und Rationalismus*, 2 vols. (Gütersloh, 1937–1951; repr. Darmstadt: Wissenschaftliche Buchgesellschaft, 1966); Johannes Henricus Scholten, *De leer der Hervormde Kerk in hare grondbeginselen, uit de bronnen voorgesteld en beoordeeld* (Leiden: Engels, 1870).

4. *Calvin and the "Calvinists": Part 1*

1. E.g., Alexander Schweizer, "Die Entwickelung des Moralsystems in der reformirten Kirche," in *Theologische Studien und Kritiken*, 23 (1850), pp. 5–78, 288–327, 554–580; idem, *Die Glaubenslehre der evangelisch-reformirten Kirche dargestellt und aus den Quellen belegt*, 2 vols. (Zürich: Orell, Füssli, 1844–1847); idem, "Moses Amyraldus: Versuch einer Synthese des Universalismus und des Partikularismus," in *Theologische Jahrbücher*, 11 (1852), pp. 41–101, 155–207; idem, *Die protestantischen Centraldogmen in ihrer Entwicklung innerhalb der reformierten Kirche*, 2 vols. (Zürich: Orell, Füssli, 1854–1856).

2. Heinrich Heppe, *Die Bekenntnisschriften der reformirten Kirche Deutschlands, Schriften zur reformirten Theologie*, Band I (Elberfeld: Friederichs, 1860), idem, "Der Charakter der deutsch-reformirten Kirche und das Verhältniss derselben zum Luthertum und zum Calvinismus," in

Theologische Studien und Kritiken, 1850 (Heft 3), pp. 669–706; idem, *Die confessionelle Entwicklung der altprotestantischen Kirche Deutschlands, die altprotestantische Union und die gegenwärtige confessionelle Lage und Aufgabe des deutschen Protestantismus* (Marburg: Elwert, 1854); idem, *Die Dogmatik der evangelisch-reformierten Kirche*, Neu durchgesehen und herausgegeben von Ernst Bizer (Neukirchen: Moers, 1935) [Originally published in 1861 as *Schriften zur reformirten Theologie*, Band II]: in translation, *Reformed Dogmatics Set Out and Illustrated from the Sources*, revised and edited by Ernst Bizer; trans. G. T. Thomson (London, 1950; repr. Grand Rapids, MI: Baker Book House, 1978); idem, *Die Dogmatik des deutschen Protestantismus im sechzehnten Jahrhundert*, 3 vols. (Gotha: Perthes, 1857); idem, *Theodor Beza: Leben und ausgewählte Schriften* (Elberfeld: Friederichs, 1861).

3. Paul Althaus, *Die Prinzipien der deutschen reformierten Dogmatik im Zeitalter der aristotelischen Scholastik* (Leipzig: Deichert, 1914).

4. Hans Emil Weber, *Der Einfluss der protestantischen Schulphilosphie auf die orthodox-lutherische Dogmatik* (Leipzig: Deichert, 1908), idem, *Die philosophische Scholastik des deutschen Protestantismus in Zeitalter der Orthodoxie* (Leipzig: Quelle und Meyer, 1907); idem, *Reformation, Orthodoxie und Rationalismus*, 2 vols. in 3 parts (Gütersloh: Bertelsmann, 1937–1951; repr. Darmstadt: Wissenschaftliche Buchgesellschaft, 1966).

5 Carl R. Trueman and R. Scott Clark, eds., *Protestant Scholasticism: Essays in Reappraisal* (Carlisle: Paternoster Press, 1999); Willem J. Van Asselt and Eef Dekker, *Reformation and Scholasticism: An Ecumenical Enterprise* (Grand Rapids, MI: Baker Book House, 2001). W. Fred Graham, ed., *Later Calvinism: International Perspectives*, ed. (Kirksville, MO: Sixteenth Century Journal Publishers, 1994) evidences the continuing disagreement among scholars, with essays by Brian Armstrong, David Foxgrover, and David Willis-Watkins, together with commentary by the editor, representing the older approach—and essays by Stephen Spencer, Martin Klauber, Donald Sinnema, Lyle Bierma, John Farthing, Robert Letham, and Richard Muller representing various aspects of the reappraisal.

6. Cf. the similar results in a somewhat differently organized paradigm of the history of scholarship in Willem van Asselt and Eef Dekker, "Introduction," in Van Asselt and Dekker, eds., *Reformation and Scholasticism*, pp. 14–39; also note, Carl Trueman and Scott Clark, "Introduction," in *Protestant Scholasticism*, pp. xv–xix.

7. Cf. the history of scholarship in Van Asselt and Dekker, *Reformation and Scholasticism*, pp. 18–30.

8. Alexander Schweizer, "Die Synthese des Determinismus und der Freiheit in der reformirten Dogmatik. Zur Vertheidigung gegen Ebrard,' in *Theologische Jahrbücher*, 8 (1849), pp. 153–209, especially pp. 163–166, 185–187; cf. idem, "Die Prädestinationslehre aus der Literargeschichte der reformirten Dogmatik nachgewiesen und wider Ebrard vertheidigt," in *Theologische Jahrbücher*, 10 (1851), pp. 391, 393–394.

9. Heppe, "Der Charakter der deutsch-reformirten Kirche," pp. 671–672, 677–678.

10. Matthias Schneckenburger, "Die neueren Verhandlungen, betreffend das Prinzip des reformirten Lehrbegriffs," in *Theologische Jahrbücher*, 7 (1848), pp. 71–144; cf. idem, "Recension von Alexander Schweizer, *Die Glaubenslehre der evangelisch-reformirten Kirche . . .* ," in *Theologische Studien und Kritiken*, 20 (1847), pp. 947–983; idem, "Die reformirte Dogmatik mit Rückblick auf: Al. Schweizer's *Glaubenslehre der evang.-reformirten Kirche*," in *Theologische Studien und Kritiken*, 21 (1848), pp. 68–110, 600–631; and idem, *Vergleichende Darstellung des lutherischen und reformirten Lehrbegriffs*, ed. Edward Guder, 2 vols. (Stuttgart, 1855).

11. Weber, *Reformation, Orthodoxie und Rationalismus*, 1/2, pp. 290–312.

12. Weber, *Reformation, Orthodoxie und Rationalismus*, 1/2, pp. 240–256; II, pp. 98–108.

13. Cf. Bizer, *Frühorthodoxie und Rationalismus*, pp. 6–15 on Beza's concept of predestination, pp. 16–32 on Ursinus's language of "necessity," pp. 32–50 on Daneau's doctrine of creation; cf. Muller, *Christ and the Decree*, pp. 6–7.

14. Thus, Basil Hall, "Calvin Against the Calvinists," in *John Calvin: A Collection of Distinguished Essays*, ed. Gervase Duffield (Grand Rapids, MI: Eerdmans, 1966), pp. 23-27; Brian Armstrong, *Calvinism and the Amyraut Heresy: Protestant Scholasticism and Humanism in Seventeenth Century France* (Madison: University of Wisconsin Press, 1969), pp. 31-40; Ernst Bizer, *Frühorthodoxie und Rationalismus* (Zurich: EVZ Verlag, 1963), pp. 7-9; Otto Gründler, *Die Gotteslehre Girolami Zanchis und ihre Bedeutung für seine Lehre von der Prädestination* (Neukirchen: Neukirchner Verlag, 1965); Johannes Dantine, "Das christologische Problem in Rahmen der Prädestinationslehre von Theodor Beza," in *Zeitschrift für Kirchengeschichte*, 77 (1966), pp. 81-96; idem, "Les Tabelles sur la doctrine de la prédestination par Théodore de Bèze," in *Revue de théologie et de philosophie*, 16 (1966), pp. 365-377; Walter Kickel, *Vernunft und Offenbarung bei Theodor Beza* (Neukirchen: Neukirchner Verlag, 1967), pp. 136-146.

15. Holmes Rolston III, *John Calvin versus the Westminster Confession* (Richmond, VA: John Knox, 1972); James B. Torrance, "Strengths and Weaknesses of the Westminster Theology," in *The Westminster Confession*, ed. Alisdair Heron (Edinburgh: Saint Andrews Press, 1982), pp. 40-53; idem, "Covenant or Contract? A Study of the Theological Background or Worship in Seventeenth-Century Scotland," in *Scottish Journal of Theology*, 23 (1970), pp. 51-76; idem, "Calvin and Puritanism in England and Scotland—Some Basic Concepts in the Development of 'Federal Theology,'" in *Calvinus Reformator* (Potchefstroom: Potchefstroom University for Christian Higher Education, 1982), pp. 264-277.

16. E.g., Wilhelm Niesel, *Theology of Calvin*, trans. Harold Knight (London, 1956; repr. Grand Rapids, MI: Baker, 1980), pp. 26-30, 35-37; John T. McNeill, "The Significance of the Word for Calvin," *Church History*, 28/2 (June 1959), pp. 140-145; J. K. S. Reid, *The Authority of Scripture: a Study of Reformation and Post-Reformation Understanding of the Bible* (London: Methuen, 1962), pp. 36-45. Much of the extensive literature on both sides of this debate is surveyed in Richard A. Muller, *Post-Reformation Reformed Dogmatics*, 4 vols (Grand Rapids, MI: Baker Book House, 2003), vol. 2, pp. 27-28, 64-66, 95-97, 228-253.

17. Paul Jacobs, *Prädestination und Verantwortlichkeit bei Calvin* (Neukirchen: Moers, 1937); Ronald S. Wallace, *Calvin's Doctrine of the Word and Sacrament* (Grand Rapids, MI: Eerdmans, 1957); idem, *Calvin, Geneva and the Reformation: A Study of Calvin as Social Reformer, Churchman, Pastor and Theologian* (Grand Rapids, MI: Baker Book House, 1988); and the works of Niesel and Reid cited in, note 14.

18. Richard A. Muller, *Christ and the Decree: Christology and Predestination in Reformed Theology from Calvin to Perkins* [*Studies in Historical Theology*, vol. 2] (Durham, NC: Labyrinth Press, 1986; paperback edition, Grand Rapids, MI: Baker Book House, 1988), pp. 1-9.

19. See the discussion of this problem with reference to Calvin and the Reformation in Muller, *Unaccommodated Calvin*, pp. 4-7, 12; also note Richard A. Muller, "Directions in Current Calvin Research," in *Calvin Studies IX*, papers presented at the Colloquium on Calvin Studies (Davidson College, January 30-31, 1998), pp. 71-72, 78-79.

20. Leonard Trinterud, "The Origins of Puritanism," in *Church History*, 20 (1951), pp. 37-57; Jens Moeller, "The Beginnings of Puritan Covenant Theology," in *Journal of Ecclesiastical History*, 14 (1963), pp. 46-67; Charles S. McCoy, "The Covenant Theology of Johannes Cocceius" (Ph.D. Dissertation, Yale University, 1956); idem, "Johannes Cocceius: Federal Theologian," in *Scottish Journal of Theology*, 16 (1963), pp. 352-370; and J. Wayne Baker, *Heinrich Bullinger and the Covenant: The Other Reformed Tradition* (Athens, OH: Ohio University Press, 1980).

21. Cf. Baker, *Heinrich Bullinger and the Covenant*, pp. 204-215; and Charles S. McCoy and J. Wayne Baker, *Fountainhead of Federalism: Heinrich Bullinger and the Covenantal Tradition*, with a translation of *De testamento seu foedere Dei unico et aeterno* (1534) by Heinrich Bullinger (Louisville, KY: Westminster / John Knox, 1991) with Michael McGiffert, "Grace and Works:

the Rise and Division of Covenant Divinity in Elizabethan Puritanism," in *Harvard Theological Review*, 75/4 (1982), pp. 463–502 and idem, "From Moses to Adam: the Making of the Covenant of Works," in *Sixteenth Century Journal*, 19/2 (1988), pp. 131–155; and with the devastating critique of the claim of "legalism" in idem, "The Perkinsian Moment of Federal Theology," in *Calvin Theological Journal*, 29/1 (April 1994), pp. 134–36. Further survey and analysis of this bibliography can be found, in chapter 11.

22. Note James B. Torrance, "Interpreting the Word by the Light of Christ or the Light of Nature? Calvin, Calvinism, and Barth," in *Calviniana*, pp. 255–267, where the central issue is not historical analysis but the theologically loaded rhetorical query, "Is Barth or Federal Calvinism the More Faithful Interpreter of Calvin?" (p. 261); cf. the essays by Rolston and Torrance, cited in, note 13, and Kickel, *Vernunft und Offenbarung*, pp. 136–146, 167–169, with John L. Farthing, "*Foedus Evangelicum*: Jerome Zanchi on the Covenant," in *Calvin Theological Journal*, 29/1 (1994), pp. 149–167; also see Muller, *Post-Reformation Reformed Dogmatics*, vol. 2, pp. 62–64, 182–197, 239–270, et passim on the analysis of the doctrine of Scripture; and note Hall, "Calvin Against the Calvinists," pp. 22–23, for strictures against the Barthianization of Calvin studies.

23. Hall, "Calvin Against the Calvinists," pp. 24–27.

24. Peter Toon, *The Emergence of Hyper-calvinism in English Nonconformity 1689-1765* (London: Olive Tree Press, 1967), pp. 12–13.

25. Otto Gründler, *Die Gotteslehre Girolami Zanchis und ihre Bedeutung für seine Lehre von der Prädestination* (Neukirchen: Neukirchner Verlag, 1965); also note idem, *Thomism and Calvinism in the Theology of Girolamo Zanchi (1516–1590)* (Th.D. dissertation, Princeton Theological Seminary, 1961); Cornelis van Sliedregt, *Calvijns opvolger Theodorus Beza, zijn verkiezingsleer en zijn belijdenis van de drieënige God* (Leiden: Groen, 1996).

26. Philip C. Holtrop, *The Bolsec Controversy on Predestination, From 1551 to 1555*, 2 vols. in 4 parts (Lewiston: Edwin Mellen, 1993), 1/1, pp. 3-9, 14–15; 1/2, pp. 822–878; and cf. my review of Holtrop in *Calvin Theological Journal*, 29/2 (1994), pp. 581–589.

27. Armstrong, *Calvinism and the Amyraut Heresy*, p. 32; cf. the citations of the definition in Bray, *Theodore Beza's Doctrine of Predestination*, pp. 12–15; Donnelly, "Italian Influences in the Development of Calvinist Scholasticism," pp. 82–83; idem, *Calvinism and Scholasticism*, pp. 199–202; S. van der Linde, "Het 'Griekse' Denken in Kerk, Theologie en Geloofspraktijk," p. 260; David N. J. Poole, *The History of the Covenant Concept from the Bible to Johannes Cloppenburg "De Foedere Dei"* (San Francisco: Mellen Research University Press, 1992), p. 173; and Holtrop, *The Bolsec Controversy*, 1/1, pp. 27–28.

28. Armstrong, *Calvinism and the Amyraut Heresy*, p. 31, note 84; cf. Paul Oskar Kristeller, *Renaissance Thought: The Classic, Scholastic, and Humanist Strains* (New York: Harper & Row, 1961), p. 116.

29. Holtrop, *The Bolsec Controversy*, 1/2, pp. 822ff.

30. Cf. Armstrong, *Calvinism and the Amyraut Heresy*, p. 32, with Emil Brunner, *The Christian Doctrine of God*, trans. Olive Wyon (Philadelphia: Westminster, 1950), pp. 131, 203, 293, 297, 299, et passim.

31. Charles S. McCoy, "Johannes Cocceius: Federal Theologian," in *Scottish Journal of Theology*, 16 (1963), p. 366; Hall, "Calvin Against the Calvinists," p. 27; cf. Armstrong, *Calvinism and the Amyraut Heresy*, pp. 39–40.

32. R. T. Kendall, *Calvin and English Calvinism to 1649* (New York: Oxford University Press, 1978), pp. 6-7, 29–30; idem, "The Puritan Modification of Calvin's Theology," in *John Calvin: His Influence in the Western World*, ed. W. Stanford Reid (Grand Rapids, MI: Zondervan, 1982), pp. 197-214; cf. Althaus, *Die Prinzipien*, p. 193.

33. This issue will be discussed at length in the second part of this essay.

34. Kickel, *Vernunft und Offenbarung*, pp. 167-169.

35. Armstrong, *Calvinism and the Amyraut Heresy*, p. 42.

36. Holtrop, *The Bolsec Controversy*, 1/2, pp. 822–878, especially 843–844; cf. idem, "Decree(s) of God," s.v. in *Encyclopedia of the Reformed Faith*, ed. Donald K. McKim (Louisville, KY: Westminster / John Knox, 1992), p. 98, col. 2.

37. S. van der Linde, "Het 'Griekse' Denken in Kerk, Theologie en Geloofspraktijk: Een eerste Inleiding," in *Theologia Reformata*, 28 (1985), pp. 248–268; W. van 't Spijker, "Gereformeerde Scholastiek II: Scholastiek, Erasmus, Luther, Melanchthon," *Theologia Reformata*, 29 (1986), pp. 7–27; idem, "Gereformeerde Scholastiek III: Zwingli en Bucer," *Theologia Reformata*, 29 (1986), pp. 136–160; S. van der Linde, "Gereformeerde Scholastiek IV: Calvijn," in *Theologia Reformata*, 29 (1986), pp. 244–266; C. Graafland, "Gereformeerde Scholastiek V: De Invloed van de Scholastiek op de Gereformeerde Orthodoxie," in *Theologia Reformata*, 30 (1987), pp. 4–25; idem, "Gereformeerde Scholastiek VI: De Invloed van de Scholastiek op de Nadere Reformatie," in *Theologia Reformata*, 30 (1987), pp. 109–131; 313–340; also note, C. Graafland, "De Gereformeerde Orthodoxie en het Piëtisme in Nederland," in *Nederlands Theologisch Tijdschrift*, 19 (1964-65), pp. 466–479.

38. Notably, Olevianus and Voetius, as is apparent in Graafland's *De zekerheid van het geloof: Een onderzoek naar de geloofsbeschouwing van enige vertegenwoordigers van reformatie en nadere reformatie* (Wageningen: Veenman, 1961); *Van Calvijn tot Barth: Oorsprong en ontwikkeling van de leer der verkiezing in het Gereformeerd Protestantisme* ('s-Gravenhage: Boekencentrum, 1987); and *Van Calvijn tot Comrie: Oorsprong en ontwikkeling van de leer van het verbond in het Gereformeerd Protestantisme*, 3 vols. (Zoetermeer: Boekencentrum, 1992–1994).

39. John S. Bray, *Theodore Beza's Doctrine of Predestination* (Nieuwkoop: DeGraaf, 1975), pp. 12–15, 141–142; John Patrick Donnelly, "Italian Influences in the Development of Calvinist Scholasticism," in *The Sixteenth Century Journal*, 7/1 (1976), pp. 81–101; and idem, "Calvinist Thomism," in *Viator*, 7 (1976), pp. 441–445.

40. Cf. Donnelly, *Calvinism and Scholasticism*, pp. 199–202; Bray, *Theodore Beza's Doctrine of Predestination*, pp. 245–226.

41. J. C. McClelland, "The Reformed Doctrine of Predestination according to Peter Martyr," in *Scottish Journal of Theology*, 8 (1955). pp. 255–271; Marvin W. Anderson, "Theodore Beza: Savant or Scholastic?" in *Theologische Zeitschrift*, 43/4 (1987), pp. 320–332; "Peter Martyr, Reformed Theologian (1542–1562)," in *The Sixteenth Century Journal*, 4 (1973), pp. 41–64; *Peter Martyr: A Reformer in Exile* (Nieuwkoop: De Graaf, 1975).

42. Ian McPhee, *Conserver or Transformer of Calvin's Theology? A Study of the Origins and Development of Theodore Beza's Thought, 1550–1570* (Ph.D. dissertation: Cambridge University, 1979).

43. See, in particular, Willem van 't Spijker, *Principe, methode en functie van de theologie bij Andreas Hyperius*, Apeldoornse Studies, 26 (Kampen: J. H. Kok, 1990) and "Reformation and Scholasticism," in Van Asselt and Dekker, *Reformationand Scholasticism*, pp. 84–85.

44. I will introduce major essays in reappraisal in the following paragraphs, but reserve fuller discussion of the secondary literature belonging to the reappraisal of orthodoxy to the specific elaboration of the eleven premises of reappraisal.

45. Cf. Muller, *Post-Reformation Reformed Dogmatics*, vol. 1, pp. 125–132 with idem, *Christ and the Decree*, pp. 1–5 and with Brian A. Gerrish, *Tradition and the Modern World: Reformed Theology in the Nineteenth Century* (Chicago: University of Chicago Press, 1978), pp. 119–136.

46. Cf. Weber, *Reformation, Orthodoxie und Rationalismus*, 1/1, pp. 179–82, 188–92; vol. 2, pp. 213–215 with idem, "Zur Reformiert-Lutherischen Auseinandersetzung," in *Gesammelte Aufsätze*, ed. Ulrich Seeger (Munich: Chr. Kaiser, 1965), pp. 154–64.

47. E.g., Paul de Vooght, *Les Sources de la doctrine Chrétienne d'après les théologiens du XIVe siècle* (Paris, 1954); Heiko A. Oberman, *Forerunners of the Reformation* (New York: Holt, Rinehart,

and Winston, 1966); idem, *The Harvest of Medieval Theology: Gabriel Biel and Late Medieval Nominalism* (rev. ed., Grand Rapids, MI: Eerdmans, 1967); idem, *Masters of the Reformation: Emergence of a New Intellectual Climate in Europe*, trans. Dennis Martin (Cambridge: Cambridge University Press, 1981); and idem, "The Shape of Late Medieval Thought: the Birthpangs of the Modern Era," in Trinkaus and Oberman (eds.), *The Pursuit of Holiness*, pp. 3–25; Karl Reuter, *Das Grundverständnis der Theologie Calvins* (Neukirchen, 1963); David C. Steinmetz, *Misericordia Dei: The Theology of Johannes von Staupitz in its Late Medieval Setting* (Leiden: Brill, 1968); idem, "Calvin and the Absolute Power of God," in *Journal of Medieval and Renaissance Studies*, 18/1 (Spring, 1988), pp. 65–79; Susan E. Schreiner, "Exegesis and Double Justice in Calvin's Sermons on Job," in *Church History*, 58 (1989), pp. 322–338; idem, *The Theater of His Glory: Nature and the Natural Order in the Thought of John Calvin* (Durham, NC: Labyrinth Press, 1991).

48. Cf. W. van 't Spijker, "Gereformeerde Scholastiek III: Zwingli en Bucer," pp. 139–140, 156–159; S. van der Linde, "Gereformeerde Scholastiek IV: Calvijn," pp. 247–253; John Patrick Donnelly, *Calvinism and Scholasticism in Vermigli's Doctrine of Man and Grace* (Leiden, 1975); idem, "Calvinist Thomism," in *Viator*, 7 (1976), pp. 441–455; idem, "Italian Influences on the Development of Calvinist Scholasticism," in *The Sixteenth Century Journal*, 7/1 (1976), pp. 81–101; Paul Helm, "Calvin (and Zwingli) on Divine Providence," in *Calvin Theological Journal*, 29/2 (1994), pp. 388–405, and Muller, *Christ and the Decree*, pp. 47–67, passim.

49. Cf. Helm, "Calvin (and Zwingli) on Divine Providence," p. 401, with François Wendel, *Calvin: The Origins and Development of His Religious Thought*, trans. Philip Mairét (New York: Harper & Row, 1963), p. 122.

50. James H. Overfield, *Humanism and Scholasticism in Late Medieval Germany* (Princeton, NJ: Princeton University Press, 1984), pp. 59–60, 94–100, 329–330, and idem, "Scholastic Opposition to Humanism in Pre-Reformation Germany," in *Viator*, 7 (1976), pp. 391–420; cf. Donnelly, *Calvinism and Scholasticism*, p. 201–202.

51. Lewis Spitz, "Humanism and the Protestant Reformation," in *Renaissance Humanism*, ed. Albert Rabil (Philadelphia: University of Pennsylvania Press, 1988), vol. 3, p. 393, and note the similar opinion expressed by J. D'Amico, "Humanism and Pre-Reformation Theology," in ibid., vol. 3, pp. 367–368.

52. Cf. Kristeller, *Renaissance Thought*, pp. 92–119 with idem, "Humanism," in *The Cambridge History of Renaissance Philosophy*, pp. 113–114, and with Charles B. Schmitt, *Aristotle and the Renaissance* (Cambridge, MA: Harvard University Press, 1983), pp. 24–25.

53. Cf. Richard A. Muller, *The Unaccommodated Calvin: Studies in the Foundation of a Theological Tradition* (New York: Oxford University Press, 2000), pp. 39–58, 101–117.

54. Cf. John Schneider, *Philip Melanchthon's Rhetorical Construal of Biblical Authority: Oratio Sacra* (Lewiston, NY: Edwin Mellen, 1990), pp. 67–78, with Ian McPhee, *Conserver or Transformer of Calvin's Theology? A Study of the Origins and Development of Theodore Beza's Thought, 1550–1570* (Ph.D. dissertation: Cambridge University, 1979), pp. xviii–xxi, xxv. Also note the reappraisal of Beza in Marvin W. Anderson, "Theodore Beza: Savant or Scholastic?" in *Theologische Zeitschrift*, 43/4 (1987), pp. 320–332; Robert Letham, "Theodore Beza: A Reassessment," in *Scottish Journal of Theology*, 40 (1987), pp. 25–40.

55. Cf. Schneider, *Philip Melanchthon's Rhetorical Construal of Biblical Authority*, pp. 73–75, with W. van 't Spijker, *Principe, methode en functie van de theologie bij Andreas Hyperius*, Apeldoornse Studies, 26 (Kampen: J. H. Kok, 1990); Ian McPhee, "Conserver or Transformer," pp. xv–xviii; Donnelly, *Calvinism and Scholasticism*, p. 193; Peter Fraenkel, *De l'écriture à la dispute: Le cas de l'Académie de Genève sous Théodore de Bèze* (Lausanne: Revue de Théologie et de Philosophie, 1977), pp. 5–7, 36–39; Irena Backus, "L'enseignement de la logique à l'Academie de Genève entre 1559 et 1565," in *Revue de Théologie et de Philosophie*, 111 (1979), pp. 153–163; William T. Costello, *The Scholastic Curriculum at Early Seventeenth-Century Cambridge* (Cambridge, MA: Harvard University Press, 1958), pp. 15–35; Mark H. Curtis, *Oxford and*

Cambridge in Transition, 1558-1642: An Essay on Changing Relations between the English University and English Society (Oxford: Clarendon Press, 1959), p. 96; and with Stephen Spencer, *Reformed Scholasticism in Medieval Perspective: Thomas Aquinas and François Turrettini on Incarnation* (Ph.D. Dissertation, Michigan State University, 1988), pp. 88–95.

56. Cf. Donald W. Sinnema, *The Issue of Reprobation at the Synod of Dort (1618–19) in the Light of the History of this Doctrine* (Ph.D. Dissertation, University of St. Michael's College, Toronto, 1985), pp. 21–40.

57. Cf. Richard A. Muller, *God, Creation and Providence in the Thought of Jacob Arminius: Sources and Directions of Scholastic Protestantism in the Era of Early Orthodoxy* (Grand Rapids, MI: Baker Book House, 1991), pp. 153–166, 253–261, with Eef Dekker, *Rijker dan Midas: Vrijheid, genade en predestinatie in de theologie van Jacobus Arminius, 1559–1609* (Zoetermeer: Boekencentrum, 1993) and idem, "Was Arminius a Molinist?" in *Sixteenth Century Journal*, 27/2 (1996), pp. 337-352.

58. See especially here the magisterial work of Olivier Fatio, *Méthode et théologie: Lambert Daneau et les débuts de la scholastique reformée* (Geneva, 1976); cf. Jill Raitt, *The Eucharistic Theology of Theodore Beza: Development of the Reformed Doctrine* (Chambersburg, PA.: American Academy of Religion, 1972), pp. 70–73; Donnelly, *Calvinism and Scholasticism*, pp. 9–10, 19, 42–43, 197–207; similar issues are addressed in chapters 7 and 8, "*Vera Philosophia cum sacra Theologia nusquam pugnat*: Keckermann on Philosophy, Theology, and the Problem of Double Truth" and "Scholasticism Protestant and Catholic: Francis Turretin on the Object and Principles of Theology."

59. See Anthony N. S. Lane, *Calvin and Bernard of Clairvaux, Studies in Reformed Theology and History*, N.S. 1 (Princeton, NJ: Princeton Theological Seminary, 1996); idem, *John Calvin: Student of the Church Fathers* (Grand Rapids, MI: Baker Books, 1999); Luchesius Smits *Saint-Augustine dans l'oeuvre de Jean Calvin*, 2 vols. (Assen, 1957–1958); John Walchenbach, *John Calvin as Biblical Commentator: An Investigation into Calvin's Use of John Chrysostom as an Exegetical Tutor* (Ph.D. dissertation: University of Pittsburgh, 1974); J. Marius Lange van Ravenswaay, *Augustinus totus noster: das Augustinverstandnis bei Johannes Calvin* (Göttingen: Vandenhoeck & Ruprecht, 1990); W. Stanford Reid, "Bernard of Clairvaux in the Thought of John Calvin," in *Westminster Theological Journal*, 41/1 (1978), pp. 127–145; Peter Fraenkel, *Testimonia Patrum: the Function of the Patristic Argument in the Theology of Philip Melanchthon* (Geneva, 1961).

60. E.g., Abraham Scultetus, *Medulla theologiae patrum syntagma* (Frankfurt, 1609-1615); Johann Gerhard, *Patrologia sive de primitivae ecclesiae christianae doctor. vitae ac lucubrationibus* (Jena, 1653); and cf. E. P. Meijering, *Reformierte Scholastik und Patristische Theologie: die Bedeutung des Väterbeweises in der* Institutio Theologiae elencticae *F. Turretins unter besonderer Berücksichtung der Gotteslehre und Christologie* (Nieuwkoop: De Graaf, 1991).

61. Armstrong, *Calvinism and the Amyraut Heresy*, p. 32 (point 1); and see my essay, "Reformation, Orthodoxy, 'Christian Aristotelianism,' and the Eclecticism of Early Modern Philosophy," in *Nederkands Archief voor Kerkgeschiedenis*, 81/3 (2001), pp. 306–325.

62. Cf. Kristeller, *Renaissance Thought*, pp. 24–47; John Dillenberger, *Protestant Thought and Natural Science: A Historical Interpretation* (Nashville: Abingdon, 1960), pp. 51–54; Max Wundt, *Die Deutsche Schulmetaphysik des 17. Jahrhunderts* (Tübingen, 1939); Ernst Lewalter, *Spanisch-jesuitisch und deutsch-lutherische Metaphysik des 17. Jahrhunderts* (Hamburg, 1935; repr. Darmstadt, 1968); Paul Dibon, *L'Enseignement philosophique dans les Universités néerlandaises à l'époque précartesienne* (Amsterdam, 1954); Schmitt, *Aristotle and the Renaissance*, pp. 10–33; and Joseph S. Freedman, *European Academic Philosophy in the Late Sixteenth and Early Seventeenth Centuries: the Life, Significance, and Philosophy of Clemens Timpler (1563/4–1624)* (Hildesheim: Olms, 1988).

63. See Walter J. Ong, *Ramus: Method and Decay of Dialogue* (Cambridge, MA: Harvard University Press, 1958); Keith L. Sprunger, "Ames, Ramus, and the Method of Puritan Theol-

ogy," in *Harvard Theological Review*, 59 (1966), pp. 133–151; Donald K. McKim, *Ramism in William Perkins' Theology* (New York: Peter Lang, 1987).

64. Cf. Jürgen Moltmann, "Zur Bedeutung des Petrus Ramus für Philosophie und Theologie im Calvinismus," *Zeitschrift für Kirchengeschichte*, LXVII (1956–1957), pp. 295–318, and Graafland, "Gereformeerde Scholastick VI: De Invloed van de Scholastiek op de Nadere Reformatie," pp. 313–325, with the critique of this perspective in Lyle D. Bierma, *German Calvinism in the Confessional Age: The Covenant Theology of Caspar Olevianus* (Grand Rapids, MI: Baker Book House, 1996), pp. 24–25, 162–168.

65. Heinrich Heppe, *Geschichte des Pietismus und der Mystik in der reformirten Kirche, namentlich der Niederlande* (Leiden: Brill, 1879), pp. 24–26.

66. Contra C. Graafland, "Gereformeerde Scholastiek V," pp. 13–17, and idem, *Van Calvijn tot Comrie: oorsprong en ontwikkeling van de leer van het verbond in het Gereformeerd Protestantisme*, 3 vols. (Zoetermeer: Boekencentrum, 1992–1994), in which an artificial contrast is made between a "Bezan," predestinarian line of thought and the development of covenant theology. Cf. the reappraisal in Andreas J. Beck, "Gisbertus Voetius (1589–1676): Basic Features of his Doctrine of God," in Van Asselt and Dekker, eds., *Reformation and Scholasticism*, pp. 205–226; Joel R. Beeke, "Gisbertus Voetius: Toward A Reformed Marriage of Knowledge and Piety," in Trueman and Clark, eds., *Protestant Scholasticism*, pp. 227–243 and Paul R. Schaefer, "Protestant 'Scholasticism' at Elizabethan Cambridge: William Perkins and a Reformed Theology of the Heart," in ibid., pp. 147–164.

67. See Muller, *Post-Reformation Reformed Dogmatics*, vol. 1, pp. 188–208.

68. See Olivier Fatio, "Présence de Calvin à l'époque de l'orthodoxie réformée: Les abrégées de Calvin à la fin du 16e et au 17e siècle," in *Calvinus Ecclesiae Doctor*, ed. W. H. Neuser (Kampen: J. H. Kok, 1978), pp. 171–207.

69. Armand Maurer, *Medieval Philosophy* (New York: Random House, 1962), p. 90.

70. J. A. Weisheipl, "Scholastic Method," in NCE, 12, p. 1145; cf. the similar remarks of G. Fritz and A. Michel, "Scholastique," in DTC, 14/2, col. 1691.

71. David Knowles, *The Evolution of Medieval Thought* (New York: Vintage Books, 1962), p. 87; cf. the similar definitions relative to Protestant scholasticism in David C. Steinmetz, "The Theology of Calvin and Calvinism," in *Reformation Europe: A Guide to Research*, ed. Steven Ozment (St. Louis: Center for Reformation Research, 1982), p. 225 and Costello, *The Scholastic Curriculum*, pp. 11, 35.

72. Armstrong, *Calvinism and the Amyraut Heresy*, p. 32 (point 1).

73. See Meijering, *Reformierte Scholastik und Patristische Theologie*, pp. 21–41; cf. Spencer, "Reformed Scholasticism in Medieval Perspective," pp. 195–198, 249.

74. Cf. the distinction between scholastic method and doctrinal content in Beza in Raitt, *The Eucharistic Theology of Theodore Beza*, pp. viii, 69–73, and the rather misplaced critique of the point in Holtrop's review (*Calvin Theological Journal*, 11/1 [1976], pp. 92–94), in which he contrasts Calvin's "integrated psychology" with the "Aristotelian faculty psychology" of Beza, as if Calvin somehow escaped the sixteenth-century worldview.

75. See the discussion of *dicta probantia* Muller, *Post-Reformation Reformed Dogmatics*, vol. 2, pp. 507–518.

76. On the problem of central dogmas, see the discussion in part two of this essay.

77. *Westminster Confession*, i.6, in Philip Schaff, *Creeds of Christendom*, 3 vols. (1931; repr. Grand Rapids, MI: Baker Book House, 1983), vol. 3, p. 603; cf. Sinnema, "Antoine De Chandieu's Call for a Scholastic Reformed Theology," in Graham, ed., *Later Calvinism*, pp. 176–79, and idem, "The Distinction Between Scholastic and Popular: Andreas Hyperius and Reformed Scholasticism," in Trueman and Clark, eds., *Protestant Scholasticism: Essays in Reassessment*, pp. 125–143.

78. Armstrong, *Calvinism and the Amyraut Heresy*, p. 32 (point 1); cf. Graham, in *Later Calvinism*, pp. 3–4.

79. Donnelly, "Italian Influences on Calvinist Scholasticism," pp. 90–91; but cf. John L. Farthing, "Christ and the Eschaton: The Reformed Eschatology of Jerome Zanchi," in *Later Calvinism*, pp. 333–354, and idem, "*De coniugio spirituali*: Jerome Zanchi on Ephesians 5:23–33," in *Sixteenth Century Journal* 24 (1993), pp. 621–652 on the christological piety in Zanchi's work.

80. Cf. chapter 11, "The Covenant of Works and the Stability of Divine Law."

81. Cf. Muller, *Post-Reformation Reformed Dogmatics*, vol. 1, pp. 188–208, with Sinnema, "Reformed Scholasticism and the Synod of Dort," pp. 467–506; idem, "Antoine De Chandieu's Call," pp. 159–190.

82. Cf. Armand Duckert, *Théodore de Bèze: Prédicateur* (Geneva, 1891); Jill Raitt, "Beza, Guide for the Faithful Life," in *Scottish Journal of Theology*, 39/1 (1986), pp. 83–107; and Scott Manetsch, "Psalms before Sonnets: Theodore Beza and the *Studia humanitatis*," in Andrew C. Gow and Robert J. Bast (eds.), *Continuity and Change: The Harvest of Late Medieval and Reformation History. Essays Presented to Heiko A. Oberman on his Seventieth Birthday*. Leiden: E. J. Brill, 2000), pp. 400–416.

83. Cf. Donald Sinnema, "Antoine De Chandieu's Call for a Scholastic Reformed Theology," in Graham (ed.), *Later Calvinism*, pp. 159–189 and idem, "Reformed Scholasticism and the synod of Dort (1618–1619), in B. J. Van er Walt (ed.), *John Calvin's Institutes: His Opus Magnum* (Potchefstroom: Potcheftstroom University for Christian Higher Education, 1986), pp. 467–506.

84. Cf., e.g., John Calvin, *Institutio christianae religionis* (Geneva: Robert Stephanus, 1559), III.ii.33—a critique of the scholastic definition of faith that actually obliges the definition—and III.ii.1–2, in which Calvin criticizes the scholastics for identifying God *simpliciter* as the object of faith, a criticism applicable to very few of the medieval doctors.

85. Cf. Gisbertus Voetius, *De theologia scholastica* in *Selectae disputationes theologicae*, 5 vols. (Utrecht, 1648–1669), vol. 1, pp. 12–29, with the discussion in Muller, *Post-Reformation Reformed Dogmatics*, vol. 1, pp. 188–219.

86. Cf. Anton Dumitriu, *History of Logic*, 4 vols. (Tunbridge Wells, Kent: Abacus Press, 1977), vol. 2, pp. 224–225, 230–233, with Arno Seifert, *Logik zwischen Scholastik und Humanismus: Das Kommentarwerk Johann Ecks* (Munich: Wilhelm Fink, 1978), pp. 26–28, 39–42.

87. Cf. A. Gardeil, "La notion du lieu théologique,' in *Revue des Sciences Philosophiques et Théologiques* (1908), pp. 51–73, 246–276, 484–505, with Robert Kolb, "Teaching the Text: The Commonplace Method in Sixteenth Century Lutheran Biblical Commentary," in *Bibliothèque d'Humanisme et Renaissance*, 49 (1987), pp. 571–585.

88. C. Constantin, "Rationalisme," in *Dictionnaire de théologie catholique*, ed. A. Vacant et al., 15 vols. (Paris: Librairie Letouzey et Ané, 1923–1950), 13/2, col. 1689, also, cols. 1725–1730; cf. Bernard Williams, "Rationalism," s.v. in *The Encyclopedia of Philosophy*, 7 vols. (New York: Collier-Macmillan, 1967).

89. Contra Bizer, *Frühorthodoxie und Rationalismus*, pp. 5–6, 9, 11–12; see the discussion in F. A. Tholuck, "Rationalism and Supranaturalism," s.v. in *A Religious Encyclopedia or Dictionary of Biblical, Historical, Doctrinal and Practical Theology*, ed. Philip Schaff, revised edition, 3 vols. (New York: Christian Literature Company, 1888); H. Hohlwein, "Rationalismus: I. Philosophisch; II. Rationalismus und Supranaturalismus, kirchengeschichtlich," s.v. in *Die Religion in Geschichte und Gegenwart: Handwörterbuch für Theologie und Religionswissenschaft*, 3rd edition, ed. H. Campenhausen, et al., 7 vols. (Tübingen: Mohr, 1957–1965); and Muller, *Post-Reformation Reformed Ddogmatics*, 1, pp. 80–84, 132–146.

90. See R. Scott Clark, "The Authority of Reason in the Later Reformation: Scholasticism in Caspar Olevian and Antoine de la Faye," in Trueman and Clark, eds., *Protestant Scholasti-*

cism, pp. 111–126. Cf. chapters 7 and 8 in this volume, with Sinnema, "Antoine De Chandieu's Call for a Scholastic Reformed Theology (1580)," pp. 159–190; and Spencer, "Reformed Scholasticism in Medieval Perspective," p. 249.

91. Armstrong, *Calvinism and the Amyraut Heresy*, p. 32 (point 2); cf. the careful rebuttal the "stereotyped criticism" of scholasticism inherent in Armstrong's definition in McPhee, "Conserver or Transformer," pp. xxi–xxiv.

92. Cf. Etienne Gilson, *Reason and Revelation in the Middle Ages* (New York: Scribner, 1938) with De Vooght, *Les Sources de la doctrine Chrétienne*, pp. 40–42, 80–89, et passim. And note the discussions in Muller, *Post-Reformation Reformed Dogmatics*, vol. 1, pp. 269–309, 386–394, 438–444; vol. 2, pp. 30–45, 149–221.

93. Thus, e.g., Samuel Maresius, *De abusu philosophiae Cartesianae, surrepente & vitando in rebus theologicis & fidei, dissertaio theologica* (Groningen, 1670); Suetonius Tranquillus [Gisbertus Voetius], *Nader openinge van eenighe stucken in de Cartesiaensche Philosophie raeckende de H. Theologie* (Leiden, 1656); Petrus van Mastricht, *Novitatum Cartesianarum Gangraena . . . seu theologia Cartesiana detecta* (Amsterdam, 1677); John Howe, *The Living Temple, or, A Designed Improvement of that Notion, that a Good Man is the Temple of God: Part I. Concerning God's Existence and His Conversableness with Man against Atheism, or the Epicurean Deism* (London, 1676); *Part II. Containing Animadversions on Spinoza, and a French Writer Pretending to Refute Him* (London, 1702); cf. Ernst Bizer, "Die reformierte Orthodoxie und der Cartesianismus," in *Zeitschrift für Theologie und Kirche* (1958), pp. 306–372, and Thomas A. McGahagan, *Cartesianism in the Netherlands, 1639–1676: the New Science and the Calvinist Counter-Reformation* (Ph.D. dissertation, University of Pennsylvania, 1976).

94. Cf. Theo Verbeek, "Descartes and the Problem of Atheism: the Utrecht Crisis," in *Nederlands Archief voor Kerkgeschiedenis*, 71/2 (1991), pp. 222–223; idem, *Descartes and the Dutch, Descartes and the Dutch: Early Reactions to Cartesianism (1637–1650)* (Carbondale: Southern Illinois University Press, 1992); Aza Goudriaan, *Philosophische Gotteserkenntnis dei Suarez und Descartes in Zusammenhang mit die niederländischen reformierten Theologie und Philosophie des 17. Jahrhunderts* (Leiden, 1999).

95. C. Louise Thijssen-Schoute, "Le cartésianisme aux Pays-bas," in E. J. Dijksterhius et al., *Descartes eet le cartésianisme hollandais* (Paris: Editions Françaises d'Amsterdam, 1950), pp. 239–259, and Ernestine G. E. van der Wall, "Cartesianism and Cocceianism: a natural alliance?" in M. Magdelaine et al (ed.), *De l'humanisme aux lumières, Bayle et le protestantisme*, pp. 445–455.

96. See Michael Heyd, "From a Rationalist Theology to a Cartesian Voluntarism: David Derodon and Jean-Robert Chouet, in *Journal of the History of Ideas*, 40 (1979): 527–542; also see Martin I. Klauber, "Reason, Revelation, and Cartesianism: Louis Tronchin and Enlightened Orthodoxy in Late Seventeenth-Century Geneva," in *Church History*, 59 (1990), pp. 326–339; and idem, *Between Reformed Scholasticism and Pan-Protestantism: Jean-Alphonse Turretin (1671–1737) and Enlightened Orthodoxy at the Academy of Geneva* (Selinsgrove, PA: Susquehanna University Press, 1994).

97. E.g., Daniel Wyttenbach, *Tentamen theologiae dogmaticae* (Frankfurt, 1747–1749), prol. 7–9; see the discussion in Muller, *Post-Reformation Reformed Dogmatics*, vol. 1, pp. 386–397.

5. *Calvin and the "Calvinists": Part 2*

1. Cf. G. Fritz and A. Michel, "Scolastique," DTC 14/2, cols. 1691–1728; J. A. Weisheipl, "Scholastic Method," in NCE, 12, pp. 1145–1146; I. C. Brady, J. E. Gurr and J. A. Weisheipl, "Scholasticism," in NCE, 12, pp. 1153–1170.

2. Maurer, *Medieval Philosophy*, p. 90.

3. On the Neo-Platonism of Aquinas, see W. J. Hankey, *God in Himself: Aquinas' Doctrine of God as Expounded in the Summa theologiae* (New York: Oxford University Press, 1987).

4. William T. Costello, *The Scholastic Curriculum at Early Seventeenth-Century Cambridge* (Cambridge, MA: Harvard University Press, 1958), pp. 7–11.

5. See Timothy Wengert, *Philip Melanchthon's Annotationes in Johannem in Relation to its Predecessors and Contemporaries* (Geneva: Librairie Droz, 1987), pp. 167–177; and Schneider, *Philip Melanchthon's Rhetorical Construal of Biblical Authority*, pp. 67–80; G. P. Hartvelt, "Over de methode der dogmatiek in de eeuw der Reformatie. Bijdrage tot de geschiedenis van de gereformeerde dogmatiek," in *Gereformeerde Theologisch Tijdschrift*, 62 (1962), pp. 97–149; and note Steinmetz, "The Theology of Calvin and Calvinism," pp. 225–226.

6. Cf. Leroy E. Loemker, "Leibniz and the Herborn Encyclopedists," in *Struggle for Synthesis: The Seventeenth Century Background of Leibniz's Synthesis of Order and Freedom* (Cambridge, MA: Harvard University Press, 1972), pp. 276–277, with Donald W. Sinnema, "Aristotle and Early Reformed Orthodoxy: Moments of Accommodation and Antithesis," in *Christianity and the Classics: The Acceptance of a Heritage*, ed. Wendy Helleman (Lanham, MD: University Press of America, 1990), pp. 119–148; and Martin I. Klauber, "Reason, Revelation, and Cartesianism: Louis Tronchin and Enlightened Orthodoxy in Late Seventeenth-Century Geneva," in *Church History*, 59 (1990), pp. 326–339.

7. Cf. Muller, *Post-Reformation Reformed Dogmatics*, vol. 1, pp. 329, 331–337; Martin I. Klauber, "Reason, Revelation, and Cartesianism," pp. 326–339; idem, "Francis Turretin on Biblical Accommodation: Loyal Calvinist or Reformed Scholastic?" in *Westminster Theological Journal*, 55 (1993), pp. 73–86; idem, "Reformed Orthodoxy in Transition: Bénédict Pictet (1655–1724) and Enlightened Orthodoxy in Post-Reformation Geneva," in *Later Calvinism*, pp. 93–113; Michael Heyd, "From a Rationalist Theology to a Cartesian Voluntarism: David Derodon and Jean-Robert Chouet," in *Journal of the History of Ideas*, 40 (1979), pp. 527–542, and idem, *Between Orthodoxy and the Enlightenment: Jean- Robert Chouet and the Introduction of Cartesian Science in the Academy of Geneva* (The Hague, 1982).

8. Cf. David C. Steinmetz, "The Theology of Calvin and Calvinism,"*Reformation Europe: A Guide to Research*, ed. Steven Ozment (St. Louis: Center for Reformation Research, 1982), p. 225.

9. Cf. Richard A. Muller, "Arminius and the Scholastic Tradition," in *Calvin Theological Journal*, 24/2 (1989), pp. 263–277, with Donald W. Sinnema, *The Issue of Reprobation at the Synod of Dort (1618–1619) in the Light of the History of this Doctrine* (Ph.D. Dissertation, University of St. Michael's College, Toronto, 1985).

10. Cf. Muller, *God, Creation, and Providence*, pp. 269–278, with Sinnema, "The Issue of Reprobation," pp. 383–384, 447–450.

11. E.g., the Lutheran usage in Johann Wilhelm Baier, *Compendium theologiae positivae, adjectis notis amplioribus* . . . denuo edendum curavit C. F. G. Walther, 3 vols. in 4. (St. Louis: Concordia, 1879), vol. 1, pp. 93–118; cf. Robert D. Preus, *The Theology of Post-Reformation Lutheranism*, 2 vols. (St. Louis: Concordia, 1970–1972) and Muller, *Post-Reformation Reformed Dogmatics*, vol. 2, pp. 222–228.

12. Cf. Robert Kolb, "Teaching the Text: The Commonplace Method in Sixteenth Century Lutheran Biblical Commentary," in *Bibliothèque d'Humanisme et Renaissance*, 49 (1987), pp. 571–585, with A. Gardeil, "Lieux théologiques," in *Dictionnaire de théologie catholique*, 9/1, cols. 712-747.

13. Calvin, Commentary on Exodus 3:14 (*CTS Harmony*, I, pp. 73–74).

14. Armstrong, *Calvinism and the Amyraut Heresy*, p. 32 (point 4).

15. Peter Lombard, *Sententiae in IV libris distinctae*, 2 vols. (Grottaferrata: Collegium S. Bonaventurae ad Claras Aquas, 1971–1981), I, d. 45, c. 5–7.

16. Cf. Lynne Courter Boughton, "Supralapsarianism and the Role of Metaphysics in Sixteenth-Century Reformed Theology," in *Westminster Theological Journal*, 48 (1986), pp. 68–69,

82, 84–96, with the similar conclusions in Richard A. Muller, "Perkins' A *Golden Chaine*: Predestinarian System or Schematized Ordo Salutis?" in *The Sixteenth Century Journal*, 9/1 (April 1978), pp. 69–81 and see the discussion of distinctions in the divine will in idem, "Grace, Election, and Contingent Choice: Arminius' Gambit and the Reformed Response," in *The Grace of God, the Bondage of the Will*, ed. Thomas Schreiner and Bruce Ware, 2 vols. (Grand Rapids, MI: Baker Book House, 1995), vol. 2, pp. 251–278.

17. See Elsie Anne McKee, "Exegesis, Theology, and Development in Calvin's *Institutio*: A Methodological Suggestion, in *Probing the Reformed Tradition: Historical Studies in Honor of Edward A. Dowey, Jr.*, ed. Brian G. Armstrong and Elsie A. McKee (Louisville, KY: Westminster/John Knox, 1989), pp. 154–172; cf. Muller, *Unaccommodated Calvin*, pp. 101–117, 140–158.

18. C. Graafland, "Gereformeerde Scholastiek V," pp. 20–22.

19. Cf. the discussion in Muller, *Unaccommodated Calvin*, pp. 104–117.

20. Armstrong, *Calvinism and the Amyraut Heresy*, p. 32 (point 3).

21. Cf. Muller, *Post-Reformation Reformed Dogmatics*, vol. 2, pp. 204–221, 490–491.

22. Note the stereotype offered in Frederick W. Farrar, *History of Interpretation* (New York: Dutton, 1886; repr. Grand Rapids, MI: Baker Book House, 1961), pp. 357–378, and echoed in *The Cambridge History of the Bible*, ed. P. R. Ackroyd, C. F. Evans, G. W. H. Lampe, and S. L. Greenslade, 3 vols. (Cambridge: Cambridge University Press, 1963-70), vol. 3, pp. 175–178.

23. See, e.g., L. Fuks, "Hebreeuws en Hebraisten in Franecker in de 17e en 18e Eeuw," in *Travels in the World of the Old Testament: Studies Presented to Professor M. A. Beek on the Occasion of his 65th Birthday*, ed. M. S. H. G. Heerma Van Goss, et al. (Assen: Van Gorcum, 1974), pp. 50-70; Peter T. van Rooden, *Theology, Biblical Scholarship and Rabbinical Studies in the Seventeenth Century: Constantijn L'Empereur (1591–1648), Professor of Hebrew and Theology at Leiden*, trans. J. C. Grayson (Leiden: E. J. Brill, 1989); Jean-Robert Armogathe (ed.), *Le Grand Siècle de la Bible: Bible de tous les temps*, vol. 6 (Paris: Beauchesne, 1989); Stephen George Burnett, *The Christian Hebraism of Johann Buxtorf (1564–1629)* (Ph.D. dissertation, University of Wisconsin, Madison, 1990).

24. See the descriptions of these efforts, with citation of numerous examples in Muller, *Post-Reformation Reformed Dogmatics*, vol. 2, pp. 440–449.

25. E.g., David C. Steinmetz, "Calvin and the Absolute Power of God," in *Journal of Medieval and Renaissance Studies*, 18/1 (Spring 1988), pp. 65–79; idem, "Calvin Among the Thomists," in *Biblical Hermeneutics in Historical Perspective* (Grand Rapids, MI: Eerdmans, 1991), pp. 198–214; Susan E. Schreiner, "Through a Mirror Dimly: Calvin's Sermons on Job," in *Calvin Theological Journal*, 21 (1986), pp. 175–193; idem, "Exegesis and Double Justice in Calvin's Sermons on Job," in *Church History*, 58 (1989), pp. 322–338, and idem, *Where Shall Wisdom Be Found? Calvin's Exegesis of Job from Medieval and Modern Perspectives* (Chicago: University of Chicago Press, 1994); John L. Thompson, *John Calvin and the Daughters of Sarah: Women in Regular and Exceptional Roles in the Exegesis of Calvin, His Predecessors and His Contemporaries* (Geneva: Droz, 1992); idem, "The Immoralities of the Patriarchs in the History of Exegesis: A Reappraisal of Calvin's Position," in *Calvin Theological Journal* 26 (1991), pp. 9-46; and idem, "Patriarchs, Polygamy and Private Resistance: John Calvin and Others on Breaking God's Rules," in *Sixteenth Century Journal*, 25/1 (1994), pp. 3–28; cf. Muller, *Post-Reformation Reformed Dogmatics*, vol. 2, pp. 93–146, 440–522.

26. Cf. Hall, "Calvin Against the Calvinists," pp. 19–37; with Torrance, "Calvin and Puritanism in England and Scotland—Some Basic Concepts in the Development of 'Federal Theology,'" pp. 264–277; Kendall, "The Puritan Modification of Calvin's Theology," pp. 197–214; David Willis-Watkins, "The Third Part of Christian Freedom Misplaced," in *Later Calvinism*," pp. 471–488.

27. I adduce the example as part of an ongoing discussion between Brian Armstrong and me, evidenced by the essays cited in subsequent notes and the as-yet-unpublished paper, "Jean

Calvin and Pierre du Moulin on the Knowledge of God," delivered by Armstrong at the Sixteenth Century Studies Conference in St Louis, MO, December 11, 1993.

28. John Calvin, *Institutio christianae religionis* (Geneva: Robert Stephanus, 1559), I.xv.7; II.i.8-9; ii.2; cf. Muller, *Unaccommodated Calvin*, pp. 164–170, for a discussion of faculty psychology in Calvin's *Institutes* and commentaries.

29. Cf. Richard A. Muller "*Duplex cognitio dei* in the Theology of Early Reformed Orthodoxy," in *The Sixteenth Century Journal*, 10 (1979), pp. 58–59 with David C. Steinmetz, "Calvin and the Natural Knowledge of God," in *Via Augustini: Augustine in the later Middle Ages, Renaissance, and Reformation: essays in honor of Damasus Trapp*, O.S.A., ed. Heiko A. Oberman and Frank A. James, in cooperation with Eric Leland Saak (Leiden: E.J. Brill, 1991), pp. 142–156; and Muller, *Post-Reformation Reformed Dogmatics*, vol. 1, pp. 269–309.

30. Armstrong, "The Changing Face of French Protestantism," pp. 145-149.

31. Cf. Lyle D. Bierma, *German Calvinism in the Confessional Age: The Covenant Theology of Caspar Olevian* (Grand Rapids: Baker Book House, 1994); idem, "Covenant or Covenants in the Theology of Olevianus," in *Calvin Theological Journal*, 22 (1987), pp. 228–250; and idem, "Federal Theology in the Sixteenth Century: Two Traditions?" in *Westminster Theological Journal*, 45 (1983), pp. 304–321; contra J. Wayne Baker, *Heinrich Bullinger and the Covenant: The Other Reformed Tradition* (Athens: Ohio University Press, 1980).

32. Cf. the rather extravagant and highly tendentious theological claims made in James B. Torrance, "Strengths and Weaknesses of the Westminster Theology," in *The Westminster Confession*, ed. Alisdair Heron (Edinburgh: Saint Andrews Press, 1982), pp. 40–53; idem, "Covenant or Contract? A Study of the Theological Background or Worship in Seventeenth-Century Scotland," in *Scottish Journal of Theology*, 23 (1970), pp. 51–76; idem, "Calvin and Puritanism in England and Scotland–Some Basic Concepts in the Development of 'Federal Theology,'" in *Calvinus Reformator* (Potchefstroom: Potchefstroom University for Christian Higher Education, 1982), pp. 264–277; and David N. J. Poole, *The History of the Covenant Concept from the Bible to Johannes Cloppenburg "De Foedere Dei"* (San Francisco: Mellen Research University Press, 1992); with Anthony Hoekema, "Calvin's Doctrine of the Covenant of Grace," in *Reformed Review*, 15 (1962), pp. 1–12; idem, "The Covenant of Grace in Calvin's Teaching," in *Calvin Theological Journal*, 2 (1967), pp. 133–161; Peter Alan Lillback, "Ursinus Development of the Covenant of Creation: A Debt to Melanchthon or Calvin," in *Westminster Theological Journal*, 43 (1981), pp. 247–288; idem, "The Binding of God: Calvin's Role in the Development of Covenant Theology" (Ph.D. dissertation: Westminster Theological Seminary, 1985); and my review of Poole in *Calvin Theological Journal*, 28/1 (1993), pp. 217–218.

33. W. Robert Godfrey, *Tensions within International Calvinism: the Debate on the Atonement at the Synod of Dort, 1618–1619* (Ph.D. dissertation, Stanford University, 1974); idem, "Reformed Thought on the Extent of the Atonement to 1618," in *Westminster Theological Journal*, 37/2 (Winter 1975), pp. 133–171; Donald W. Sinnema, *The Issue of Reprobation at the Synod of Dort (1618–1619) in the Light of the History of this Doctrine* (Ph.D. Dissertation, University of St. Michael's College, Toronto, 1985); idem, "Aristotle and Early Reformed Orthodoxy: Moments of Accommodation and Antithesis," pp. 119–148; and idem, "Reformed Scholasticism and the Synod of Dort," pp. 467–506; and cf. the similar results in Robert Letham, "Faith and Assurance in Early Calvinism: A Model of Continuity and Diversity," in *Later Calvinism*, pp. 355–384 and idem, *Saving Faith and Assurance in Reformed Theology: Zwingli to the Synod of Dort*, 2 vols. (Ph.D. dissertation: University of Aberdeen, 1979).

34. Cf. Keith L. Sprunger, "Ames, Ramus, and the Method of Puritan Theology," in *Harvard Theological Review*, 59 (1966), pp. 133–151; idem, "Technometria: A Prologue to Puritan Theology," in *Journal of the History of Ideas*, 29 (1968), pp. 115–122; with Jürgen Moltmann, "Zur Bedeutung des Petrus Ramus für Philosophie und Theologie im Calvinismus," *Zeitschrift für Kirchengeschichte*, 67 (1956–1957), pp. 295–318; and with Lyle D. Bierma, "The Role of

Covenant Theology in Early Reformed Orthodoxy," in *Sixteenth Century Journal*, 21/3 (1990), pp. 453-462.

35. Cf. Armstrong, *Calvinism and the Amyraut Heresy*, p. 38 with Willis-Watkins, "The Third Part of Christian Freedom Misplaced," pp. 482–488.

36. Jacob Burckhardt, *The Civilization of the Renaissance in Italy*, trans. S. C. G. Middlemore, edited by Ludwig Goldscheider, with an intro. by Hajo Holborn (New York: Modern Library, 1954), pp. 100, 148, 153–156, etc.

37. For the tone and scope of the reappraisal, see in particular Wallace K. Ferguson, *The Renaissance in Historical Thought: Five Centuries of Interpretation* (Boston: Heath, 1948), William H. Werkmeister (ed.) *Facets of the Renaissance: Essays by Wallace K. Ferguson, Garrett Mattingly, E. Harris Harbison, Myron P. Gilmore, and Paul Oskar Kristeller* (New York: Harper & Row, 1963); and Albert Rabil Jr. (ed.), *Renaissance Humanism: Foundations, Forms, and Legacy*, 3 vols. (Philadelphia: University of Pennsylvania Press, 1988); still not to be ignored is the trenchant critique of the entire concept of "Renaissance" in Lynn Thorndike, "Renaissance or Prenaissance?" in *Journal of the History of Ideas*, 4 (1943), pp. 65–74.

38. Cf. Charles Homer Haskins, *The Renaissance of the Twelfth Century* (1927; repr. New York: Meridian, 1957); idem, *The Rise of the Universities* (1923; repr. Ithaca, NY: Cornell University Press, 1957); Robert L. Benson and Giles Constable (eds.), *Renaissance and Renewal in the Twelfth Century* (Cambridge, MA: Harvard University Press, 1982); R. R. Bolgar, *The Classical Heritage and its Beneficiaries* (Cambridge: Cambridge University Press, 1954), esp. pp. 183ff.; and Etienne Gilson, "Humanisme médiévale et Renaissance," in *Les idées et les lettres*, second edition (Paris: Vrin, 1955).

39. On the roots and sources of Calvin's humanism, Ford Lewis Battles, "The Sources of Calvin's Seneca Commentary," in *John Calvin: A Collection of Distinguished Essays*, ed. G. E. Duffield (Appleford, England: Sutton Courtney Press, 1966), pp. 38–66; the introductory essays in *Calvin's Commentary on Seneca's De Clementia* with intro., trans., and notes by Ford Lewis Battles and André Malan Hugo (Leiden: E. J. Brill, 1969); Quirinus Breen, *Jonh Calvin: A Study in French Humanism* (Grand Rapids, MI: Eerdmans, 1931); idem, "John Calvin and the Rhetorical Tradition," in *Christianity and Humanism: Studies in the History of Ideas* (Grand Rapids, MI: Eerdmans, 1968), pp. 107–129; Benoit Girardin, *Rhétorique et théologique: Calvin, le Commentaire de l'Epître aux Romains* (Paris: Beauchesne, 1979); and Olivier Miller, *Calvin et la dynamique de la parole: Etude de rhétorique réformée* (Paris: Librairie Honoré Champoin, 1992).

40. See the lucid discussion of the complexity of humanism in Jean-Claude Margolin, *Humanism in Europe at the Time of the Renaissance*, trans. John L. Farthing (Durham, NC: Labyrinth Press, 1989), pp. 2–6, 21–39, 41–52; cf. Charles Trinkaus, "Italian Humanism and Scholastic Theology," in *Renaissance Humanism*, ed. Rabil, vol. 3, pp. 327–348 and John F. D'Amico, "Humanism and Pre- Reformation Theology," in ibid, pp. 349–379; also note Charles Trinkaus, *In Our Image and Likeness: Humanity and Divinity in Italian humanist Thought*, 2 vols. (Chicago: University of Chicago Press, 1970), pp. 60–61, 332–333.

41. See Hanna H. Gray, "Renaissance Humanism: The Pursiut of Eloquence," in *Renaissance Essays: From the Journal of the History of Ideas*, ed. Paul Oskar Kristeller and Philip P. Wiener (New York: Harper & Row, 1968), pp. 199–216.

42. See *Renaissance Student Life: The Paedologia of Petrus Mosellanus*, trans. with an intro. by Robert Francis Seyboldt (Chicago: University of Illinois Press, 1927); cf. A. Bömer, *Die lateinischen Schülergespräche der Humanisten*, 2 vols. (Berlin, 1897–1899) with L. Massebieau, *Les colloques scolaires de seizième siècle, et les auteurs, 1480–1570* (Paris, 1878) and idem, *Répertoire des ouvrages pédagogiques du XVIe siècle* (Paris, 1886).

43. Cf. Kristeller, *Renaissance Humanism*, pp. 4–23; cf. D'Amico, "Humanism and Pre-Reformation Theology," pp. 350–352, and John Herman Randall Jr., "The Development of

Scientific Method in the School of Padua," in Kristeller and Wiener (eds.) *Renaissance Essays*, pp. 217–251.

44. E. David Willis, "Persuasion in Calvin's Theology," in *Calvin and Christian Ethics*: Papers and Responses presented at the Fifth Colloquium on Calvin and Calvin Studies, sponsored by the Calvin Studies Society, May 8–9, 1985, ed. Peter De Klerk (Grand Rapids, MI: Calvin Studies Society, 1987), p. 83; cf. William J. Bouwsma, *John Calvin: A Sixteenth-Century Portrait* (New York: Oxford University Press, 1988), pp. 2–5, 113–127.

45. Cf. John B. Payne, *Erasmus: His Theology of the Sacraments* (Richmond, VA: John Knox Press, 1970), pp. 12–14, 19–23, 238–239; E.-W. Kohls, *Die Theologie des Erasmus*, 2 vols. (Basel: F. Reinhardt, 1966), I, pp. 193–196, 223 and Christian Dolfen, *Die Stellung des Erasmus von Rotterdam zur scholastischen Methode* (Osnabrück: Meinders & Elstermann, 1936), pp. 64–82; also see Cornelis Augustijn, *Erasmus: His Life, Works, and Influence* (Toronto: University of Toronto Press, 1991), p. 103; cf. Margolin, *Humanism in Europe*, pp. 4, 24, 30–2, 41–50 with Kristeller, *Renaissance Thought*, pp. 8, 10, 32–43, 98–119.

46. See Eugene F. Rice, "Erasmus and the Religious Tradition, 1495–1499," in Kristeller and Wiener (eds.), *Renaissance Essays*, pp. 162–186; cf. Payne, *Erasmus*, p. 22.

47. Cf. Erika Rummel, *The Humanist-Scholastic Debate in the Renaissance and Reformation* (Cambridge, MA: Harvard University Press, 1995), pp. 1–40, 140–147 with idem, "The Conflict between Humanism and Scholasticism Revisited," in *Sixteenth Century Journal*, 23 (1992), pp. 713–726; Charles Nauert, "The Clash of Humanists and Scholastics: An Approach to Pre-Reformation Controversies," in *Sixteenth Century Journal*, 4 (1973), pp. 1–18, and with A. Perreiah, "Humanist Critiques of Scholastic Dialectic," in *Sixteenth Century Journal*, 13 (1982), pp. 3–22.

48. Cf. David Bagchi, "Sic et Non: Luther and Scholasticism," in *Protestant Scholasticism: Essays in Reappraisal*, ed. Trueman and Clark, pp. 3–15 with Muller, *Unaccommodated Calvin*, pp. 39-61.

49. Rummel, *Humanist-Scholastic Debate*, pp. 153–154.

50. On Beza's humanist leanings and biblical scholarship, see Scott Manetsch, "Psalms before Sonnets: Theodore Beza and the *Studia humanitatis*," in Andrew C. Gow and Robert J. Bast (eds.), *Continuity and Change: The Harvest of Late Medieval and Reformation History: Essays Presented to Heiko A. Oberman on his Seventieth Birthday* (Leiden: E. J. Brill, 2000), pp. 400-416; cf. Irena Backus, *The Reformed Roots of the English New Testament: the Influence of Theodore Beza on the English New Testament* (Pittsburgh, PA: Pickwick Press, 1980) and Robert D. Linder, "Calvinism and Humanism: The First Generation," in *Church History*, 44/2 (1975), pp. 167–181. Also note the discussions of the continuity of humanism with the nominally "scholastic" Protestantism of the seventeenth century in Sebastian Rehnman, "John Owen: A Reformed Scholastic at Oxford," in Van Asselt and Dekker, eds., *Reformation and Scholasticism*, pp. 181–203.

51. Pierre Fraenkel, *De l'Écriture à la dispute: Le cas de l'Académie de Genève sous Théodore de Bèze* (Lausanne: Revue de théologie de de Philosophie, 1977), pp. 4–7, 24–28, 33–39.

52. See Paul Dibon, *L'Enseignement philosophique dans les Universités néerlandaises à l'époque précartesienne (1575–1650)* (Amsterdam: Elsevir, 1954); idem, "L'influence de Ramus aux universités néerlandaises du 17e siècle," in *Actes du XIème congrès Internationale de Philosophie*, 14 (1953), pp. 307–311; Walter J. Ong, *Ramus: Method and the Decay of Dialogue* (Cambridge, MA: Harvard University Press, 1958); Keith L. Sprunger, "Ames, Ramus, and the Method of Puritan Theology," in *Harvard Theological Review*, 59 (1966), pp. 133–151; Donald K. McKim, *Ramism in William Perkins' Theology* (New York: Peter Lang, 1987); Randall, "The Development of Scientific Method," pp. 238–250.

53. Cf. Bray, *Theodore Beza's Doctrine of Predestination*, p. 15; Poole, *History of the Covenant*, p. 173; Holtrop, *The Bolsec Controversy*, 1/1, p. 28, with Muller, *Unaccommodated Calvin*, 159–173; idem, "The Priority of the Intellect in the Soteriology of Jacob Arminius," in *The*

Westminster Theological Journal, 55 (1993), pp. 55–72; Joel R. Beeke, *Assurance of Faith: Calvin, English Puritanism, and the Dutch Second Reformation* (New York and Bern: Peter Lang, 1991), pp. 47–56, 78–82, 174–82, 292–302; idem, "Faith and Assurance in the Heidelberg Catechism and its Primary Composers: A Fresh Look at the Kendall Thesis," in *Calvin Theological Journal*, 27/1 (1992), pp. 45–51, 59, 61; idem, "Personal Assurance of Faith: The Puritans and Chapter 18.2 of the *Westminster Confession*," in *Westminster Theological Journal*, 55 (1993), pp. 73–86; Norman Shepherd, "Zanchius on Saving Faith," in *Westminster Theological Journal*, 36 (1973), pp. 31–47; and Otto Gründler, "From Seed to Fruition: Calvin's Notion of the *semen fidei* and Its Aftermath in Reformed Orthodoxy," in *Probing the Reformed Tradition: Historical Essays in Honor of Edward A. Dowey, Jr.*, ed. Elsie Anne McKee and Brian G. Armstrong (Louisville, KY: Westminster/John Knox, 1989), pp. 108–115, in which Gründler argues the continuity in doctrinal intention between Calvin and his early orthodox successors.

54. Cf. Armstrong, *Calvinism and the Amyraut Heresy*, p. 139; Bray, *Theodore Beza's Doctrine of Predestination*, p. 15; Gründler, *Die Gotteslehre Girolamo Zanchis*, p. 49; Poole, *History of the Covenant*, p. 173; Holtrop, *The Bolsec Controversy*, 1/1, p. 28. Note the alternative reading of Zanchi in Harm Goris, "Thomism in Zanchi's Doctrine of God," in Van Asselt and Dekker, eds., *Reformation and Scholasticism*, pp. 121–139.

55. J. H. Alting, *Methodus theologiae didacticae*, cited in Heppe, *Reformed Dogmatics*, p. 531; and note that Alting's language of *cognitio certa* is a nearly perfect mirror of Calvin's "*firmam certamque cognitionem*" (*Institutio*, III.ii.7) while *fiducialis apprehensio*, understood as a volitional act, reflects Calvin's *firmam illam stabilemque cordis constantiam* (*Institutio*, III.iii.33).

56. Cf. Robert D. Preus, *The Theology of Post-Reformation Lutheranism*, 2 vols. (St. Louis: Concordia, 1970-72), vol. 1, pp. 219–222, 232, 405, 412; with Friedrich Kalb, *Theology of Worship in Seventeenth Century Lutheranism*, trans. Harry Hamann (St. Louis: Concordia, 1965), pp. x–xi, 157–171; Hans Leuba, *Orthodoxie und Pietismus: Gesammelte Studien* (Bielefeld: Luther-Verlag, 1975), pp. 50–59; and Richard A. Muller, "J. J. Rambach and the Dogmatics of Scholastic Pietism," in *Consensus: A Canadian Lutheran Journal of Theology*, 16/2 (1990), pp. 7–27.

57. See Willem van 't Spijker, "Orthodoxie en Nadere Reformatie," in *Theologische Aspecten van de Nadere Reformatie*, ed. T. Brienen et al. (Zoetermeer: Uitgeverij Boekencentrum, 1993), pp. 11–27; also, Beeke, *Assurance of Faith*, pp. 389–392 and idem, "The Dutch Second Reformation (*Nadere Reformatie*)," in *Calvin Theological Journal*, 28/2 (1993), pp. 298–327.

58. Petrus van Mastricht, *Theoretico-practica theologia, qua, per capita theologica, pars dogmatica, elenchtica et practica, perpetua sumbibasei conjugantur, praecedunt in usum operis, paraleipomena, seu sceleton de optima concionandi methodo*, 2 vols. (Amsterdam: Henricus & Theodorus Boom, 1682-1687; later editions, Utrecht: van de Water, Poolsum, Wagens & Paddenburg, 1714, 1724).

59. Contra the bifurcations in Cornelis Graafland, *De zekerheid van het geloof: een onderzoek naar de geloofsbeschouwing van enige vertegenwoordigers van reformatie en nadere reformatie* (Wageningen: Veenman, 1961); idem, "Gereformeerde Scholastiek VI: De Invloed van de Scholastiek op de Nadere Reformatie," pp. 109-131; 313-340 and idem, "De Gereformeerde Orthodoxie en het Piëtisme in Nederland," pp. 478--479.

60. On this history, see Peter Petersen, *Geschichte der aristotelischen Philosophie im protestantischen Deutschland* (Leipzig, 1921; repr. Stuttgart, 1964); Max Wundt, *Die deutsche Schulmetaphysik des 17. Jahrhunderts* (Tübingen, 1939); Josef Bohatec, *Die cartesianische Scholastik in der Philosophie und reformierten Dogmatik des 17. Jahrhunderts* (Leipzig, 1912); Ernst Bizer, "Die reformierte Orthodoxie und der Cartesianismus," in *Zeitschrift für Theologie und Kirche* (1958), pp. 306–372; E. P. Bos and H. A. Krop (eds.) *Franco Burgersdijk (1540–1635): Neo-Aristotelianism in Leiden* (Amsterdam: Rodopi, 1993); Siegfried Wollgast *Philosophie in Deutechland zwischen Reformation und Aufklärung, 1550–1650* (Berlin: Akademie Verlag, 1988); and Jean-Pierre Schobinger, *Die Philosophie des 17. Jahrhunderts*, 3 vols. in 4 parts (Basel: Schwabe, 1988–1993).

61. Cf. Charles S. McCoy, *The Covenant Theology of Johannes Cocceius* (Ph.D. Dissertation, Yale University, 1956); with idem, "Johannes Cocceius: Federal Theologian," in *Scottish Journal of Theology*, 16 (1963), pp. 352–370; Charles S. McCoy, and J. Wayne Baker, *Fountainhead of Federalism: Heinrich Bullinger and the Covenantal Tradition* (Louisville, KY: Westminster / John Knox, 1991), pp. 69-75; and Holtrop, *The Bolsec Controversy*, 1/1, p. 19.

62. Cf. Bizer, "Die reformierte Orthodoxie und der Cartesianismus," pp. 308–329, 347–372, with Thomas A. McGahagan, *Cartesianism in the Netherlands, 1639–1676: The New Science and the Calvinist Counter-Reformation* (Ph.D. dissertation, University of Pennsylvania, 1976).

63. Michael Heyd, *Between Orthodoxy and the Enlightenment: Jean-Robert Chouet and the Introduction of Cartesian Science in the Academy of Geneva* (The Hague: De Graff, 1982); and idem, "From a Rationalist Theology to a Cartesian Voluntarism: David Derodon and Jean-Robert Chouet," in *Journal of the History of Ideas*, 40 (1979), pp. 527–542; cf. Martin I. Klauber, "Reason, Revelation, and Cartesianism: Louis Tronchin and Enlightened Orthodoxy in Late Seventeenth-Century Geneva," in *Church History*, 59 (1990), pp. 326–339.

64. Martin I. Klauber, "The Drive Toward Protestant Union in Early Eighteenth-Century Geneva," in *Church History*, 61 (1992), pp. 334, 347–349; and idem, "Reason, Revelation, and Cartesianism," pp. 328–329, 339; idem, *The Context and Development of the Views of Jean-Alphonse Turrettini (1671–1737) on Religious Authority* (Ph.D. Dissertation, University of Wisconsin-Madison, 1987); also note Maria C. Pitassi, *Entre croire et savoir: le problème de la méthode critique chez Jean LeClerc* (Leiden: Brill, 1987), p. 2; and cf. Martin I. Klauber and Glenn S. Sunshine, "Jean-Alphonse Turrettini on Biblical Accommodation: Calvinist or Socinian?" in *Calvin Theological Journal*, 25 (1990), pp. 7–27.

65. Thus, e.g., Edward A. Dowey, *The Knowledge of God in Calvin's Theology* (New York: Columbia University Press, 1952); Thomas F. Torrance, *Calvin's Doctrine of Man* (Grand Rapids, MI: Eerdmans, 1957); Paul Van Buren, *Christ in our Place: the Substitutionary Character of Calvin's Doctrine of Reconciliation* (Edinburgh: T. & T. Clark, 1957); Ronald S. Wallace, *Calvin, Geneva and the Reformation: A Study of Calvin as Social Reformer, Churchman, Pastor and Theologian* (Grand Rapids, MI: Baker Book House, 1988); idem, *Calvin's Doctrine of the Word and Sacrament* (Grand Rapids, MI: Eerdmans, 1957).

66. Thus, Brian A. Gerrish, *Grace & Gratitude: The Eucharistic Theology of John Calvin* (Minneapolis: Fortress Press, 1993) and Randall C. Zachman, *The Assurance of Faith: Conscience in the Theology of Martin Luther and John Calvin* (Minneapolis: Fortress Press, 1993).

67. James Daane, *The Freedom of God: A Study of Election and Pulpit* (Grand Rapids, MI: Eerdmans, 1973), pp. 7–8, 36, 38–42, 55–64, etc; cf. Holtrop, *The Bolsec Controversy*, 1/1, pp. 3, 5.

68. Kristeller, *Renaissance Thought*, p. 100.

69. Holtrop, *The Bolsec Controversy*, I/1, pp. 3-5.

70. Cf., e.g., Jack B. Rogers, "The Authority and Interpretation of the Bible in the Reformed Tradition," in *Major Themes in the Reformed Tradition*, ed. Donald K. McKim (Grand Rapids, MI: Eerdmans, 1992), pp. 58–61, with Jack B. Rogers and Donald K. McKim, *The Authority and Interpretation of the Bible: An Historical Approach* (San Francisco: Harper & Row, 1979), pp. 172–188, 270–271, 273, 279–282, 295–296 and with Holtrop, *The Bolsec Controversy*, 1/1, pp. 25–27, p. 39, notes 70–73 and idem, "Decree(s) of God," pp. 98–99.

71. Thus Holtrop, *The Bolsec Controversy*, 1/1, pp. 23–25, 62, with David Foxgrover, "Self-Examination in Calvin and Ames," in *Later Calvinism*, p. 466; Van der Linde, "Het 'Griekse' Denken in Kerk, Theologie en Geloofpratik," pp. 248–268.

72. See in particular, James Barr, *The Semantics of Biblical Language* (Oxford: Oxford University Press, 1961), pp. 10–12, 46-88, in which Barr presents the case against standard Greek-Hebrew dichotomies against Thomas F. Torrance, "The Doctrine of Grace in the Old Testa-

ment," in *Scottish Journal of Theology*, 1 (1948), pp. 55-65. Barr's strictures apply equally to Holtrop's view of a "biblical" notion of "truth as troth" over against propositional understandings of truth: see Holtrop, *The Bolsec Controversy*, 1/2, pp. 893-916.

73. Muller, *Post-Reformation Reformed Dogmatics*, vol. 1, pp. 306–309, 440–443.

74. Hermann Bauke, *Die Probleme der Theologie Calvins* (Leipzig, 1922), pp. 22, 30–31.

75. Cf. J. Bohatec, "Die Methode der reformierten Dogmatik," in *Theologische Studien und Kritiken*, 81 (1908), pp. 277–281, 286–287, 292–298, with G. P. Hartvelt, "Over de methode der dogmatiek in de eeuw der Reformatie. Bijdrage tot de geschiedenis van de gereformeerde dogmatiek," in *Gereformeerde Theologisch Tijdschrift*, 62 (1962), pp. 121–132.

76. Cf. Hartvelt, "Over de methode der dogmatiek in de eeuw der Reformatie," pp. 124–125.

77. Schneckenburger, "Die neuren Verhandlungen," pp. 74–75.

78. Cf. Raitt, *The Eucharistic Theology of Theodore Beza*, pp. 10–30, 73; idem, "The Person of the Mediator: Calvin's Christology and Beza's Fidelity," *Occasional Papers of the Society for Reformation Research*, 1 (Dec. 1977), pp. 53–80; Tadataka Maruyama, *The Ecclesiology of Theodore Beza: The Reform of the True Church* (Geneva: Droz, 1978), pp. 139–148, 198–199; McPhee, "Conserver or Transformer," pp. 81–84; Muller, *Christ and the Decree*, 79–96; Farthing, "*De coniugio spirituali*: Jerome Zanchi on Ephesians 5:23–33," pp. 621–652; Letham, "Theodore Beza: A Reassessment," pp. 25–40.

79. Bray, *Theodore Beza's Doctrine of Predestination*, p. 140, and cf. Richard A. Muller, "The Myth of 'Decretal Theology,'" in *Calvin Theological Journal*, 30/1 (April 1995), pp. 159–167.

80. Muller, *Post-Reformation Reformed Dogmatics*, vol. 1, pp. 123–131, 428–444; cf. vol. 2, pp. 220–221.

81. Helm, "Calvin (and Zwingli) on Divine Providence," p. 391.

82. Cf. Van 't Spijker, *Principe, methode en functie van de theologie bij Andreas Hyperius*, pp. 32–33, 35–36 with Preus, *Theology of Post-Reformation Lutheranism*, vol. 1, pp. 86-88.

83. Muller, *Christ and the Decree*, pp. 113–115, 143–144, 164–168, 171–173, 181.

84. Thus, Raitt, "The Person of the Mediator: Calvin's Christology and Beza's Fidelity," pp. 53-80; Maruyama, *The Ecclesiology of Theodore Beza*, pp. 139–148, 198–199; Muller, *Christ and the Decree*, pp. 79–96.

85. Cf. Bray, *Theodore Beza's Doctrine of Predestination*, p. 140, with McPhee, "Conserver or Transformer of Calvin's Theology," pp. 287, 350–351, 356–357; Muller, *Christ and the Decree*, pp. 79–83, 87–88, 132, 160–162 and idem, "Perkins' *A Golden Chaine*," pp. 69–81; and note the conclusions of Farthing, "*De coniugio spirituali*," pp. 650–652.

86. Cf. Sinnema, "The Issue of Reprobation," pp. 449–450 with Muller, *Christ and the Decree*, pp. 106–107, 112, 154–155, 162, 181.

87. Armstrong, *Calvinism and the Amyraut Heresy*, p. 32 (point 4).

88. Cf. Muller, *Christ and the Decree*, pp. 69–75, 83, 121–125, 175–182, with idem, *Post-Reformation Reformed Orthodoxy*, vol. 1, pp. 108–131, 428–443; vol. 2, pp. 127, 164–180, 204–221.

89. Karl Barth, *Church Dogmatics*, 4 vols., ed. G. W. Bromiley and T. F. Torrance (Edinburgh: T. & T. Clark, 1936-69), 2/2, pp. 127–130.

90. See Barth, *CD*, 2/2, pp. 333–340, and G. C. Berkouwer, *Divine Election* (Grand Rapids, MI: Eerdmans, 1960), pp. 279–306, in which there is a detailed analysis of the Barth-Niesel debate over the *syllogismus practicus*. Cf. Wilhelm Niesel *The Theology of Calvin*, trans. Harold Knight (London: Lutterworth, 1956), pp. 178–179; M. Charles Bell, *Calvin and Scottish Theology: The Doctrine of Assurance* (Edinburgh: Scottish Academic Press, 1985), p. 31; David N. J. Poole, *The History of the Covenant Concept from the Bible to Johannes Cloppenburg "De Foedere Dei"* (San Francisco: Mellen Research University Press, 1992), p. 125.

91. Muller, *Christ and the Decree*, pp. 180–182.

92. See also the discussion in Muller, *Unaccommodated Calvin*, pp. 101–117; also idem, *Post- Reformation Reformed Dogmatics*, vol. 1, pp. 176–219.

93. Cf. Muller, *Unaccommodated Calvin*, pp. 135–136; contra the theologized explanations in, e.g., Edward A. Dowey, *The Knowledge of God in Calvin's Theology* (New York, 1952; third edition, Grand Rapids, MI: Eerdmans, 1994), p. 186.

94. Contra Basil Hall, "Calvin Against the Calvinists," in *John Calvin*, edited by Gervase Duffield (Appleford, England: Sutton Courtnay Press, 1966), p. 27, citing as his proof of the point, Beza's *Summa sive descriptio et distributio causarum salutis electorum, et exitu reproborum* from Theodore Beza, *Tractationes theologicae*, 3 vols. (Geneva, 1570–1582), vol. 1, pp. 170ff. Cf. Peter Toon, *The Emergence of Hyper-Calvinism in English Nonconformity 1689–1765* (London, The Olive Tree Press, 1967), pp. 12–13; Charles S. McCoy, "Johannes Cocceius: Federal Theologian," in *Scottish Journal of Theology*, 16 (1963), p. 366; Alister McGrath, *Reformation Thought: An Introduction*, second edition (Grand Rapids, MI: Baker Book House, 1993), pp. 129–130.

95. Weber, *Foundations of Dogmatics*, vol 1, pp. 350, 397; I address this issue in *Post-Reformation Reformed Dogmatics*, vol. 3 (forthcoming).

96. Discussed in Muller, *Post-Reformation Reformed Dogmatics*, vol. 2, pp. 97–100.

97. Cf. Skinner, "Meaning and Understanding in the History of Ideas," pp. 7–10, 27–28.

98. McCoy, "The Covenant Theology of Johannes Cocceius," pp. 136–137.

99. McCoy, "The Covenant Theology of Johannes Cocceius," pp. 136–137; cf. Dorner, *History of Protestant Theology*, II, pp. 41-42; Baker, *Heinrich Bullinger and the Covenant*, pp. 199–207.

100. See Van Asselt, *Federal Theology of Johannes Cocceius*, pp. 212–218.

101. William Perkins, *A Golden Chaine*, in *The Workes of . . . Mr. William Perkins*, 3 vols. (Cambridge: John Legate, 1612–1619), vol. 1, pp. 32, col. 1; p. 71, col. 1; idem, *An Exposition of the Creede*, in *Workes*, vol. 1, p. 167, col. 2.

102. Karl Barth, *Church Dogmatics*, ed. G. W. Bromiley and T. F. Torrance, 4 vols. (Edinburgh: T. & T. Clark, 1936–1975), 2/2, pp. 60–88, 106–115, 127–145.

103. Barth, *Church Dogmatics*, 2/2, p. 111.

104. Cf. Barth, *Church Dogmatics*, 2/2, pp. 103–115, with J. K. S. Reid, "The Office of Christ in Predestination," in *Scottish Journal of Theology*, 1 (1948), 5–19, 166–183; idem, "Introduction" in Calvin, *Concerning the Eternal Predestination of God* (London: James Clarke, 1961), pp. 41–44; Philip C. Holtrop, "Decree(s) of God," s.v. in *Encyclopedia of the Reformed Faith*, ed. Donald K. McKim (Louisville, KY: Westminster / John Knox, 1992), pp. 97–99.

105. Muller, *Christ and the Decree*, pp. 154–159.

106. Cf. Burckhardt, *The Civilization of the Renaissance in Italy*, p. 100.

107. Cf. the attempts at definition in Richard A. Muller, "Arminius and the Scholastic Tradition," in *Calvin Theological Journal*, 24/2 (November 1989), pp. 275–277, and idem, *Post-Reformation Reformed Dogmatics*, vol. 1, pp. 34–37, 188–203.

6. *Calling, Character, Piety, and Learning*

1. Cf. E. G. Schwiebert, *Luther and His Times: The Reformation From a New Perspective* (St. Louis: Concordia, 1950), pp. 293–302, with Heinrich Boehmer, *Martin Luther: Road to Reformation*, trans. J. W. Doberstein and T. G. Tappert (Philadelphia: Muhlenberg, 1946), pp. 157–163.

2. Gordon Rupp, *Luther's Progress to the Diet of Worms* (New York: Harper & Row, 1964), pp. 24–25.

3. Discussion of the Lutheran development can be found in Robert D. Preus, *The Theology of Post-Reformation Lutheranism*, 2 vols. (St. Louis: Concordia, 1970–1972).

4. On Erasmus, see, e.g., Carl S. Meyer, "Erasmus on the Study of the Scriptures," in *Concordia Theological Monthly*, 40 (1969), pp. 734–746; Albert Rabil Jr., *Erasmus and the New Testament:*

The Mind of a Christian Humanist (San Antonio: Trinity University Press, 1972); Heinz Holeczek, *Humanistische Bibelphilologie als Reformproblem bei Erasmus von Rotterdam, Thomas More, und William Tyndale* (Leiden: E. J. Brill, 1975); Marjorie O'Rourke Boyle, *Erasmus on Language and Method in Theology* (Toronto: Univ. of Toronto Press, 1977); W. van 't Spijker, "Gereformeerde Scholastiek II: Scholastiek, Erasmus, Luther, Melanchthon," *Theologia Reformata*, 29 (1986), pp. 7-27.

5. Melanchthon, *Brevis discendae theologiae ratio*, in *Philippi Melanchthonis Opera quae supersunt omnia*, ed. C. G. Bretschneider and H. E. Bindseil, 28 vols. (Halle/Braunschweig, 1844-), vol. 2, cols. 455–462.

6. Philip Melanchthon, *De Rhetorica libri tres* [later, *Elementa rhetorices*], in *Opera quae supersunt omnia*, vol. 13, cols. 413–506; *De officiis concionatoris*, in *Suppelmenta Melanchthonia*, V. Abteilung, Teil II, *Homiletische Schriften*, ed. P. Drews and F. Cohrs (Leipzig, 1929), pp. 5-14; and *De modo et arte concionandi*, in ibid., pp. 33–55; also see Uwe Schnell, *Die homiletische Theorie Philipp Melanchthons* (Hamburg: Lutherisches Verlagshaus, 1968), pp. 54–57, for a discussion of these treatises plus Melanchthon's two unpublished works on the subject, *Quomodo concionator novitus concionem suam informare debet* (ca. 1532–1536) and *De ratione concionandi* (1552); both treatises are edited in *Homiletische Schriften* (pp. 17–19 and 59–79, respectively).

7. Philip Melanchthon, *Loci communes* (1533) in *Opera quae supersunt omnia*, vol. 21, col. 253–254. The definitive study of Melanchthon's concept of historical or scriptural *series* is Peter Fraenkel, *Testimonia Patrum: The Function of Patristic Argument in the Theology of Philip Melanchthon* (Geneva, 1961), pp. 52–109; also see the discussions of Melanchthon's contribution to theological method in Robert D. Preus, *The Theology of Post-Reformation Lutheranism*, 2 vols. (St. Louis: Concordia, 1970–1972), vol. 1, pp. 77–82; and Richard A. Muller, *Post-Reformation Reformed Dogmatics* 4 vols. (Grand Rapids, MI: Baker Book House, 2003), vol. 1, pp. 101-102; and also see Robert Kolb, "Teaching the Text: The Commonplace Method in Sixteenth Century Lutheran Biblical Commentary," in *Bibliothèque d'Humanisme et Renaissance*, 49 (1987), pp. 571-585.

8. Heinrich Bullinger, *Ratio studiorum, sive de institutione eorum, qui studia literarum sequuntur, libellus aureus. Accessit eodem dispositio locorum communium, tam philosophicorum, quam theologicorum. Item, Christianae fidei perspicue & breviter proposita quaedam axiomata* (Zürich, 1594).

9. Bullinger, *Ratio studiorum*, pp. 2v–3r.

10. Bullinger, *Ratio studiorum*, pp. 7v–9v. Bullinger devotes several successive chapters to the various types of profane letters that ought to be studied and mastered: pp. 10r–22r.

11. Bullinger, *Ratio studiorum*, p. 22v, citing Wisdom 1:4.

12. Bullinger, *Ratio studiorum*, pp. 22v–23r.

13. Bullinger, *Ratio studiorum*, pp. 27v–28v.

14. Bullinger, *Ratio studiorum*, p. 26v.

15. Bullinger, *Ratio studiorum*, pp. 30r–32r. On the "scope" of Scripture, see Boyle, *Erasmus on Language and Method*, pp. 75–79, and Muller, *Post-Reformation Reformed Dogmatics*, vol. 2, pp. 204–221.

16. On Bullinger's life, career, and basic thought, see David C. Steinmetz, *Reformers in the Wings* (Philadelphia: Fortress, 1971), pp. 133–142; and note the major study by Fritz Blanke, *Der junge Bullinger, 1504–1531* (Zürich, 1942).

17. David Chytraeus, *De Studio theologiae* (Wittenberg, 1562); cf. the discussion in Preus, *Theology of Post-Reformation Lutheranism*, vol. 1, pp. 104–107.

18. Cf. the survey of propaedeutic works in Hagenbach, pp. 121–123, with Muller, *Post-Reformation Reformed Dogmatics*, vol. 1, pp. 67–72; and Preus, *The Theology of Post-Reformation Lutheranism*, vol. 1, pp. 100–110.

19. Preus, *Theology of Post-Reformation Lutheranism*, vol. 1, pp. 105–106.

20. Andreas Hyperius, *De Theologo, seu de ratione studii theologici, libri IIII* Basel, 1559); cf. W. van 't Spijker, *Principe, methode en functie van de theologie bij Andreas Hyperius*, Apeldoornse Studies, 26 (Kampen: J. H. Kok, 1990).

21. Andreas Gerardus Hyperius, *De formandis concoinibus sacris seu de interpretatione scripturarum populari libri II* (Marburg, 1553); also printed at Dortmund (1555), Marburg (1562), Basel (1563, 1579) and Halle (1781); the treatise is available in a modern German translation with an introduction by Ernst Christian Achelis and Eugen Sachsse in *Die Homiletik und die Katechetik des Andreas Hyperius* (Berlin: Reuther & Reichard, 1901).

22. Andreas Hyperius, *De sacrae scripturae lectione ac meditatione quotidiana, omnibus omnium ordinum hominibus Christianis perquam necessaria, libri II* (Basel, 1561); translated as *The Course of Christianitie: or, As touching the Dayly Reading and Meditation of the Holy Scriptures*, trans. Iohn Ludham (London, 1579).

23. Hyperius, *De theologo*, p. 40, citing 1 Cor. 1 (cf. 1 Cor. 1:28–31, 2:7).

24. Hyperius, *De theologo*, p. 34.

25. Hyperius, *De theologo*, p. 36, citing Prov. 13:20.

26. Hyperius, *De theologo*, pp. 45–52 (lib. I, cap. 4).

27. Hyperius, *De theologo*, pp. 52–55 (lib. I, cap. 5).

28. Hyperius, *De theologo*, pp. 55–57 (lib. I, cap. 6).

29. Hyperius, *De theologo*, p. 57–64 (lib. I, cap. 7).

30. Hyperius, *De theologo*, pp. 64–65 (lib. I, cap. 8).

31. Hyperius, *De theologo*, pp. 65–80 (lib. I, cap. 9).

32. Hyperius, *De theologo*, p. 47; and cf. the discussion in Van 't Spijker, *Principe, methode en functie*, pp. 25–29.

33. Hyperius, *De theologo*, pp. 80–425 (lib. II, cap. 1–38).

34. Hyperius, *De theologo*, pp. 425–562 (lib. III, cap. 1–8).

35. Hyperius, *De theologo*, pp. 562–756 (lib. IV, cap. 1–10).

36. Modifying the arguments of Edward Farley, *Theologia: The Fragmentation and Unity of Theological Education* (Philadelphia: Fortress, 1983), pp. 78–79.

37. Van 't Spijker, *Principe, methode en functie*, p. 29.

38. For further discussion and definition of Protestant scholasticism, see Van Asselt (ed), *Inleiding*, pp. 9–17; also note Muller, *Post-Reformation Reformed Dogmatics*, vol. 1, pp. 33–37, 193–196, 221–224, and chapter 1 here. The best histories of the theology of the period remain Wilhelm Gass, *Geschichte der protestantischen Dogmatik in ihrem Zusammenhange mit der Theologie*, 4 vols. (Berlin, 1854–1867); Isaac A. Dorner, *History of Protestant Theology Particularly in Germany*, trans. Robson and Taylor, 2 vols. (Edinburgh: T. & T. Clark, 1871); and Otto Ritschl, *Dogmengeschichte des Protestantismus: Grundlagen und Grundzüge der theologischen Gedanken–und Lehrbildung in den protestantischen Kirchen*, 4 vols. (Leipzig: J.C. Hinrichs, 1908–1912; Göttingen: Vandenhoeck & Ruprecht, 1926–1927).

39. For further discussion of the impact of the scholastic revival on Protestant thought, see Hans Emil Weber, *Die philosophische Scholastik des deutschen Protestantismus in Zeitalter der Orthodoxie* (Leipzig, 1907); idem., *Der Einfluss der protestantischen Schulphilosophie auf die orthodox-lutherische Dogmatik* (Leipzig, 1908); Ernst Lewalter, *Spanisch-jesuitisch und deutsch-lutherische Metaphysik des 17. Jahrhunderts* (Hamburg, 1935; repr. Darmstadt, 1968); Paul Dibon, *L'Enseignement philosophique dans les Universités neerlandaises à l'epoque précartesienne* (Amsterdam, 1954); and Richard A. Muller, *God, Creation and Providence in the Thought of Jacob Arminius: Sources and Directions of Scholastic Protestantism in the Era of Early Orthodoxy* (Grand Rapids, MI: Baker Book House, 1991).

40. See further in chapters 7 and 8.

41. I have traced some of these issues of continuity and discontinuity in *Christ and the Decree: Christology and Predestination in Reformed Theology from Calvin to Perkins* (Durham,

NC: Labyrinth Press, 1986; Grand Rapids, MI: Baker Book House, 1988); and *Post-Reformation Reformed Dogmatics*, vol. 1, pp. 164–175, 269–309; vol. 2, pp. 93–102, 159–193, 228–253, et passim.

42. Cf. Hagenbach, pp. 123–125 with Muller, *Post-Reformation Reformed Dogmatics*, vol. 1, pp. 208–219; and Preus, *Theology of Post-Reformation Lutheranism*, vol. 1, pp. 120–128.

43. Johann Gerhard, *Methodus studii theologiae* (Jena, 1620); note also the prolegomena to his *Loci Theologici*, 9 vols., ed. Preuss (Berlin, 1863–1875); cf. Preus, *Theology of Post-Reformation Lutheranism*, vol. 1, pp. 120–121.

44. Gisbertus Voetius, *Exercitia et bibliotheca studiosi theologiae* (Utrecht, 1651).

45. Cf. Farley, *Theologia*, pp. 62–80. Farley quite correctly argues that much of the unity of pre-Enlightenment theological study arose out of the stress on theology as a *praxis* or *scientia practica* and on the cultivation of a theological disposition or *habitus* combining in students learning and piety. Farley does, however, overemphasize the modern, post-Schleiermacherian character of the fourfold encyclopedia and, in his interpretation of the older theology, he overestimates the weight of the subjective disposition in relation to the objective content of theology. For an appreciation and critique of Farley, see Richard A. Muller, *The Study of Theology* (Grand Rapids, MI: Zondervan, 1991), pp. 28–37, 45–50.

46. Gisbertus Voetius, *Selectae disputationes theologicae*, 5 vols. (Utrecht, 1648–1669). The standard biography of Voetius remains Arnoldus Cornelis Duker, *Gisbertus Voetius*, 3 vols. (Leiden: Brill, 1897–1914); also see Jan Anthony Cramer, *De theologische faculteit de Utrecht ten tijde van Voetius* (Utrecht: Kemink, 1932) and C. Graafland, "Gereformeerde scholastiek VI: De invloed van de scholastiek op de Nadere Reformatie" in *Theologia Reformata*, 30 (1987), pp. 109–131, 313–340 (pp. 118–128 deal specifically with Voetius).

47. Cf. Johannes Hoornbeeck, *Socinianismus confutatus*, 3 vols. (Utrecht, 1650–1664) and idem, *Summa controversiarum religionis, cum infidelibus, haereticis, schismaticis* (Utrecht, 1653).

48. See W. J. van Asselt and E. Dekker, *De scholastieke Voetius: Een luisteroefening aan de hand van Voetius' Disputationes Selectae* (Zoetermeer: Boekencentrum, 1995).

49. Cf. Charles S. McCoy, *The Covenant Theology of Johannes Cocceius* (Ph.D. Dissertation, Yale University, 1956) and idem, "Johannes Cocceius: Federal Theologian," in *Scottish Journal of Theology*, 16 (1963), pp. 352–370 with the alternative view in Muller, *Post-Reformation Reformed Dogmatics*, vol. 2, pp. 118–122; similarly, J. Van Oort, et al. *De onbekende Voetius* (Kampen: J. H. Kok, 1990); and F. G. M. Broeyer and E. G. E. van der Wall, *Een richtingenstrijd in de Gereformeerde Kerk: Voetianen en Coccejianen, 1650–1750* (Zoetermeer: Boekencentrum, 1994).

50. On Voetius's balance of piety and academic theology, see Willem van 't Spijker, *Vroomheid en wetenschap bij Voetius* (Apeldoorn: Theologische Universiteri, 1998). Also note van 't Spijker's essay on Voetius in T. Brienen, et al., *De Nadere Reformatie: Beschriving van haar voornamste vertegenwoordigers* (The Hague: Uitgeverij Boekencentrum, 1986), pp. 49–84.

51. Gisbertus Voetius, *Ta asketica sive Exercitia pietatis in usum juventutis academicae nunc edita. Addita est, ob materiam affinitatem, Oratio de pietate cum scientia conjungenda habita anno 1634* (Gorinchem, 1664); also Gisbertus Voetius, *Inaugurele rede over Godzaligheid te verbinden met de wetenschap*: Latijnse tekst opnieuw uitgegeven met Nederlandse vertaling, inleiding en toelichtingen door Dr. Aart De Groot (Kampen: J. H. Kok, 1978).

52. Voetius, *Exercitia et bibliotheca*, pp. 1–2.

53. Voetius, *Exercitia et bibliotheca*, pp. 3–4.

54. Voetius, *Exercitia et bibliotheca*, p. 5.

55. Following the order of Voetius, *Exercitia et bibliotheca*, pp. 37–41, 48–56, 60–66, in which the series is given, in direct relation to the theological curriculum, as *lectio, meditatio, auditio, scriptio, collatio, collegia, enotatio, institutio*, and *apparatus*; but cf. ibid., pp. 22–28, where Voetius offers his general definitions in terms of preparatory study and arranges the series as *lectio, meditatio, enotatio, scriptio, collatio, collegia, auditio, institutio*, and *apparatus*.

56. Voetius, *Exercitia et bibliotheca*, pp. 22–23, cf. p. 39.
57. Voetius, *Exercitia et bibliotheca*, p. 40.
58. Voetius, *Exercitia et bibliotheca*, pp. 23–25, 40.
59. Voetius, *Exercitia et bibliotheca*, pp. 22–23, cf. pp. 40–42.
60. Voetius, *Exercitia et bibliotheca*, pp. 27–28.
61. Voetius, *Exercitia et bibliotheca*, pp. 31–33.
62. Voetius, *Exercitia et bibliotheca*, pp. 33–34.
63. Voetius, *Exercitia et bibliotheca*, pp. 35, 43.
64. Voetius, *Exercitia et bibliotheca*, pp. 35–36.
65. Voetius, *Exercitia et bibliotheca*, p. 36.
66. Voetius, *Exercitia et bibliotheca*, pp. 36–37.
67. Voetius, *Exercitia et bibliotheca*, pp. 37–38.
68. Voetius, *Exercitia et bibliotheca*, pp. 39–41.
69. Voetius, *Exercitia et bibliotheca*, pp. 43–44.
70. Voetius, *Exercitia et bibliotheca*, pp. 44–45.
71. Voetius, *Exercitia et bibliotheca*, pp. 47–48, cf. 49–50, for clearer indication of historical emphases.
72. Voetius, *Exercitia et bibliotheca*, p. 48.
73. Voetius, *Exercitia et bibliotheca*, pp. 49–50.
74. Voetius, *Exercitia et bibliotheca*, p. 50.
75. Voetius, *Exercitia et bibliotheca*, pp. 50–58.
76. Voetius, *Exercitia et bibliotheca*, pp. 69–100.
77. Voetius, *Exercitia et bibliotheca*, p. 69.
78. Voetius, *Exercitia et bibliotheca*, pp. 60–61.
79. Voetius, *Exercitia et bibliotheca*, p. 62.
80. Voetius, *Exercitia et bibliotheca*, p. 62–67.
81. Voetius, *Ta Asketika sive de exercitiis pietatis*, pp. 1–2. Note the translation, with notes and introduction, *De praktijk der godzaligheid*, 2 vols., ed. C. A. de Niet (Utrecht: De Bannier, 1995). The term *militia spiritualis* or spiritual warfare reflects Voetius's strong ties to the Puritan tradition of conscience with its militant language of inward conflict against temptation: cf. John Downham, *The Christian Warfare wherein is first generally shewed the malice, power, and politike strategems of the spiritual enemies of our salvation, Satan and his assistants the world and our flesh* (London, 1604; second edition, 1608). A second part was published in 1611 and the third edition, enlarged to four parts, in 1612. The language of warfare is also found in Thomas Brooks, *Precious Remedies Against Satan's Devices* (London, 1652), idem, *Heaven on Earth: A Treatise of Christian Assurance* (London, 1654) and in John Bunyan, *The Pilgrim's Progress from this World to That Which is to Come* (London, 1687) and idem, *The Holy War made by Shaddai upon Diabolus for the Regaining of the Metropolis of the World; or, the Losing and Taking Again of the Town of Mansoul* (London, 1682).
82. Voetius, *Ta Asketika sive de exercitiis pietatis*, pp. 3–6.
83. Voetius, *Ta Asketika sive de exercitiis pietatis*, p. 12.
84. Herman Witsius, *On the Character of the True Divine: An Inaugural Oration, Delivered at Franecker, April 16, 1675*, trans. John Donaldson, preface by William Cunningham (Edinburgh: James Wood, 1855). Some two decades later, on his inauguration as professor of theology at Leiden, Witsius's views had changed but little: at that time, he offered as an address his *Theologus modestus, delineatus. Oratione inaugurali, qua publicam theologiae professionem in Academia Lugduno-Batava auspicatus est, die sexto decimo Octobris 1698* (Leiden, 1698). On Witsius' life and thought, see J. van Genderen, *Herman Witsius: bijdrage tot de kennis der gereformeerde theologie* (s'Gravenhage: Guido de Bres, 1953).
85. Witsius, *Character*, p. 8.

86. Witsius, *Character*, pp. 9–10.
87. Witsius, *Character*, pp. 13–14.
88. Witsius, *Character*, pp. 14, 16.
89. Witsius, *Character*, p. 16.
90. Witsius, *Character*, pp. 17–18.
91. Witsius, *Character*, pp. 18–19.
92. Witsius, *Theologus modestus*, p. 29.
93. Witsius, *Character*, pp. 24–25.
94. Witsius, *Character*, pp. 28, 30.
95. Witsius, *Character*, pp. 31–33.
96. Witsius, *Character*, p. 40.
97. Wilhelmus à Brakel, *Logike Latreia, dat is Redelijke Godsdienst in welken de goddelijke Waarheded van het Genade-Verbond worden verklaard* (Dordrecht, 1700), trans. as *The Christian's Reasonable Service in which Divine Truths concerning the Covenant of Grace are Expounded, Defended against Opposing Parties, and their Practice Advocated*, 4 vols., translated by Bartel Elshout, with a biographical sketch by W. Fieret and an essay on the "Dutch Second Reformation" by Joel Beeke (Ligonier, PA: Soli Deo Gloria Publications, 1992–1995).
98. Petrus van Mastricht, *Theoretico-practica theologia*, 2 parts (Utrecht, 1682–1687).
99. For an appreciation of Mastricht's method, see Richard A. Muller, "Giving Direction to Theology: the Scholastic Dimension," in *Journal of the Evangelical Theological Society*, 28/2 (June, 1985), pp. 183–193.
100. Witsius, *Theologus modestus*, p. 35, citing Chrysostom, *Homily XXX on Acts*.
101. On pietism and its relation to orthodoxy, see F. Ernest Stoeffler, *The Rise of Evangelical Pietism* (Leiden: E. J. Brill, 1965); idem., *German Pietism During the Eighteenth Century* (Leiden: E. J. Brill, 1973); I. A. Dorner, *History of Protestant Theology*, trans. George Robson and Sophia Taylor, 2 vols. (Edinburgh, 1871); Hans Leuba, *Orthodoxie und Pietismus: Gesammelte Studien* (Bielefeld: Luther-Verlag, 1975).
102. Cf. Richard A. Muller, "J. J. Rambach and the Dogmatics of Scholastic Pietism," in *Consensus: A Canadian Lutheran Journal of Theology*, 16/2 (1990), pp. 7–27, with Preus, *Theology of Post-Reformation Lutheranism*, vol. 1, pp. 219–222, 232, 405, 412; Friedrich Kalb, *Theology of Worship in Seventeenth Century Lutheranism*, trans. Harry Hamann (St. Louis: Concordia, 1965), pp. x–xi, 157–171; and Leuba, *Orthodoxie und Pietismus*, pp. 50–59.
103. Farley, *Theologia*, pp. 80–81.

7. *Vera Philosophia cum sacra Theologia nusquam pugnat*

1. Thesis 44: "Immo theologus non sit nisi id fiat sine Aristotele" in *D. Martin Luthers Werke* (*WA*) (Weimar, 1883ff), 1, p. 226, line 15.
2. Cf. Paul Vignaux, *Luther Commentateur des Sentences* (Paris: J. Vrin, 1935), pp. 24–30; also Paul Althaus, *The Theology of Martin Luther*, trans. R.C. Schultz (Philadelphia: Fortress Press, 1966), pp. 9–11, 18–19. Whether or not Luther's position and, in addition, that of late medieval nominalism imply a theory of double truth has been debated. See Bengt Hägglund, *Theologie und Philosophie bei Luther und in der occamistischen Tradition: Luthers Stellung zur Theorie von der doppelten Wahrheit* (Lund: Gleerup, 1955); Heiko Oberman, *The Harvest of Medieval Theology: Gabriel Biel and Late Medieval Nominalism*, rev. ed. (Grand Rapids, MI: Eerdmans, 1967), pp. 32–42. Oberman argues, against Hägglund, that Biel presses a radical *diastasis* between theology and philosophy but does not claim double truth. I tend to agree with Oberman and find *diastasis* between theology and philosophy and not double truth in Luther's locus *classicus, Disputatio theologica . . . an haec propositio sit vera in philosophim Verbum caro factum est*, in *WA*, 39/2, pp. 3–33.

3. John Calvin, *Institutio christianae religionis*, II.ii.18: "... sparsim quaedam apud philosophos de Deo legi scite et apposite dicta ... sed its viderunt quae videbant, ut tali intuitu minime ad veritatem dirigerentur, nedum pertingerent," in *Joannis Calvini Opera Selecta*, ed. Barth and Niesel, 3rd ed. (Munich: Kaiser, 1967–1974), 3, pp. 260–261. For further analysis of Calvin's view of philosophy, see Charles Partee, *Calvin and Classical Philosophy* (Leiden: E. J. Brill, 1977) and Armand La Vallee, *Calvin's Criticism of Scholastic Theology*, (Ph.D. diss., Harvard University, 1967).

4. See David Bagchi, "Sic et Non: Luther and Scholasticism" and David C. Steinmetz, "The Scholastic Calvin" in Carl R. Trueman and Scott Clark, *Protestant Scholasticism: Essays in Reappraisal* (Carlisle: Paternoster Press, 1999), pp. 3–15; and Richard A. Muller, "Scholasticism in Calvin: A Question of Relation and Disjunction," in *The Unaccommodated Calvin: Studies in the Foundation of a Theological Tradition* (New York: Oxford University Press, 2000), pp. 39–61.

5. On the relation of philosophy to theology in Melanchthon's thought, see Franz Hildebrandt, *Melanchthon: Alien or Ally?* (Cambridge: Cambridge University Press, 1946), pp. 1–33, who finds Melanchthon to be "suspiciously near to Thomas Aquinas" (p. 25); also Wilhelm Neuser, *Der Ansatz der Theologie Philipp Melanchthons* (Neukirchen: Verlag der Buchhandlung des Erziehungsvereins, 1957), pp. 30–40, 43–45, 132–133. Neuser points to the connection between the development of Melanchthon's *Loci communes*, the humanism of Melanchthon's educational program, and the reintroduction of Aristotelian thought in Lutheran theology: "Die Rehabilitierung der Philosophie muss notwendig in der erneunten Thronerhebung des Aristoteles in ihren Abschluss finden" (p. 40). A very careful analysis of Melanchthon in relation to the rising philosophy of the Renaissance and humanism appears in Wilhelm Maurer, *Melanchthon-Studien* (Gütersloh: Gerd Mohn, 1964), pp. 28–38. Also see Maurer's magisterial treatment of Melanchthon's early intellectual pilgrimage, *Der junge Melanchthon*, 2 vols. (Gottingen: Vandenhoeck & Ruprecht, 1967–69), 1: 86–98; 2: 19, 488–489. Hans Engelland's important essay on Melanchthon's theology appears in *Melanchthon on Christian Doctrine: Loci Communes 1555*, trans. and ed. C. Manschreck, intro. by Hans Engelland (New York: Oxford, 1965); in particular, see pp. xxx–xxii. On the thought of Peter Martyr Vermigli, see Joseph C. McLelland, *The Visible Words of God: An Exposition of the Sacramental Theology of Peter Martyr Vermigli, A.D. 1500–1562* (London: Oliver and Boyd, 1957). On the issue of Vermigli's relation to Thomism, see John Patrick Donnelly, "Italian Influences on the Development of Calvinist Scholasticism," *The Sixteenth Century Journal*, 7/1 (1976), pp. 81–101, and "Calvinist Thomism," *Viator*, 7 (1976), pp. 441–445; also by Donnelly, *Calvinism and Scholasticism in Vermigli's Doctrine of Man and Grace* (Leiden: E. J. Brill, 1976), especially chapters 2 and 3, in which Donnelly presents the sources of Vermigli's thought and Vermigli's views on reason and revelation. Also note Marvin W. Anderson, *Peter Martyr, a Reformer in Exile (1542–1562): A Chronology of Biblical Writings in England and Europe* (Nieuwkoop: De Graaf, 1975).

6. Cf. Melanchthon's *Loci communes* (1521): "Et in hoc quidem loco, cum prorsus christiana doctrina a philosophia et humana ratione dissentiat, tamen sensim irrepsit philosophia in christianismum. . . . Additum est e Platonis philosophia vocabulum rationis aeque perniciosum. Nam perinde atque his posterioribus ecclesiae temporibus Aristotelem pro Christo sumus amplexi, ita statim post ecclesiae auspicia per Platonicam philosophiam christiana doctrina labefactata est," in *Melanchthons Werke in Auswahl*, ed. R. Stupperich, 7 vols. (Gütersloh: C. Bertelsmann, 1951–1975), 2/1, pp. 8–9 with the corresponding section of the *Loci praecipui theologici* (1559), in ibid., pp. 236–237. On the law of nature, see *Loci praecipui theologici* (1559), *De Lege divina: Divisio Legum*, in ibid., p. 280, 11.25–30: "Lex naturae, ut infra dicam, est notitia naturalis de Deo et de morum gubernatione seu discrimine honestorum et turpium, divinitus humanis mentibus insita est. Ideo congruit cum ea parte Legis Dei, quae dicitur moralis." Cf. *De Deo*, ibid., pp. 172–173: "Vult enim Deus agnosci et celebrari, et fulsisset illustris et firma notitia Dei in mentibus hominum, si natura hominum mansisset integra. . . . Sed humanae mentes in

hac corruptione naturae in magna et tristi caligine vagantur quaerentes, an sit Deus . . . et quae sit Dei voluntas. . . . Et quamquam utcunque mens humana agnoscit Deum punire sontes, tamen de reconciliatione nihil novit sine revelatione divinae promissionis."

7. Cf. Engelland's introduction in *Melanchthon on Christian Doctrine*, p. xxx. The reader should be aware that, contrary to Manschreck's argument in the preface to this translation of the 1555 (German) *Loci*, the 1559 (Latin) *Loci* do in fact contain large portions of material, not present in the German, concerning the relation of philosophy and theology, e.g., the entire introductory section of *De Lege Dei* (Melanchthon, *Werke*, 2/1, pp. 278–280). It is also the case that the Latin conveys, more clearly than the German, the technical implications of Melanchthon's argumentation.

8. *Loci praecipui theologici* (1559), in Melanchthon, *Werke*, 2/1, pp. 219–223. But note that the proofs occur not in a prolegomenon seeking to justify rationally the theological enterprise or as part of the doctrine of God, rather they occur in the locus on creation, beginning with the 1535 edition (cf. ibid., note, pp. 219–221). Engelland summarizes the proofs in *Melanchthon on Christian Doctrine*, pp. xxix–xxx, but they do not, ironically, appear in the text of Manschreck's translation (cf. pp. 39–44) of the German *Loci*.

9. See Ernest Schwiebert, *Luther and His Times: The Reformation from a New Perspective* (Saint Louis: Concordia, 1950), pp. 298–299.

10. Joseph Freedman, "Philosophy Instruction within the Institutional Framework of Central European Schools and Universities during the Reformation Era," in *History of Universities*, 5 (1985), pp. 124–125.

11. *Loci communes D. Petri Martyri Vermigli* (London, 1576) is the *editio princeps*; citations follow the augmented edition of 1583. The locus concerned with natural knowledge of God in book I, chapter ii. Also note the extended discussion of the knowledge of God in Peter Martyr Vermigli, *In librum Iudicum . . . commentarii doctissimi, cum tractatione, pertuli rerum & locorum* (Zurich: Froschauer, 1561), 6:22, in loc. (fol. 84 verso–88 verso); translated in *The Peter Martyr Reader*, ed. John Patrick Donnelly, Frank A. James III, and Joseph C. McLelland (Kirksville, MO: Truman State University Press, 1999), pp. 107–123.

12. Vermigli, *Loci communes* (1583), II.iii.

13. Vermigli, *Loci Communes* [1583], I.ii.1 [from Vermigli's commentary on Romans 1:19]: "Ut est, Deum velle nos gratis iustificare: per Christum crucifixum condonare peccata: atque in aeterna foelicitate haec nostra corpora eadem restituere. Haec & alia id genus, rerum natura non docet. Ideo Paulus inquit, Quod potuit cognosci de Deo, illis est manifestatum. Declarat illo loco, quaenam sit ea veritas, quam illi detiunerunt in iniustitia. Fuit cognitio divinarum rerum, quam naturali lumine adepti sunt. Redigit autem Paulus ea omnia quae cognoverunt, ad duo capita: nimirum sempiternam Dei potentiam, & divinitatem." Also ibid., I.ii.3: "alii vero, quibus magis assentior, quod Deus inseruit animas nostris *prolepsois*, hoc est anticipationes & informationes, per quas impellimur ad opinandum praeclara atque eximia de natura Dei. Atque hoc notitiae de Deo nobis naturaliter insitae observatione rerum creatarum indies magis ac magis confirmantur & expoliuntur. Inepte, nec minus impie aliqui dicunt, has veritates ab Aristotle, aut Platone se didicisse."

14. Vermigli, *Loci Communes* [1583], II.iii. 5, 7, 8 [from Vermigli's commentary on Aristotle's *Ethics*]: "5. Omnis nostra notitia vel est revelata vel acquisita: in primo membro Theologia, in altero Philosophia. Nomen Philosophiae compositum est. Sapientia dicitur a nonullis omnium rerum quae sunt notitia. . . . Aiunt alii eam esse divinarum & humanarum rerum scientiam . . . Sed videtur definienda, ut sit, Habitus mentis humanis a Deo concessus, industria & exercito auctus, quo comprehenditur omnia quae sunt. . . . 7. . . . Philosophia ipsum animum alit & instruit. . . . 8. . . . Vera philosophia cum ex notitia creaturarum colligitur, & multa concludat ex his praepositionibus de iustitia & rectitudine quae Deus naturaliter mentibus hominum inseriut, iure accusare non potest: est enim Dei opus & absque illius munere singulari ab

hominibus haberi non potuit. Sed Paulus eam Philosophiam reprehendit, quae hominum inventis & ambitiosa certaminibus Philosophorum est vitiata." Cf. Donnelly, *Calvinism and Scholasticism*, pp. 42–67.

15. See chapter 2 for a discussion of the term "scholastic" in its sixteenth- and seventeenth-century context, and cf. Muller, *Unaccommodated Calvin*, pp. 39–61, for an examination of Calvin's use of the term and his relation to "scholasticism."

16. E.g., Hans Emil Weber, *Reformation, Orthodoxie und Rationalismus*, 2 vols. (Gütersloh: Gerd Mohn 1937–1940); Paul Althaus, *Die Prinzipien der deutschen reformierten Dogmatik im Zeitalter der aristotelischen Scholastik* (Leipzig: Deichert, 1914); and Brian G. Armstrong, *Calvinism and the Amyraut Heresy: Protestant Scholasticism and Humanism in Seventeenth Century France* (Madison: University of Wisconsin Press, 1969).

17. E.g., Olivier Fatio, *Méthode et théologie: Lambert Daneau et les débuts de la scholastique réformée* (Geneva: Droz, 1976); Jill Raitt, *The Eucharistic Theology of Theodore Beza: Development of the Reformed Doctrine* (Chambersburg, PA: Amrerican Academy of Religion, 1972); idem, "The Person of the Mediator: Calvin's Christology and Beza's Fidelity," *Occasional Papers of the Society for Reformation Research*, I (Dec. 1977), pp. 53–80; Richard A. Muller, *Christ and the Decree: Christology and Predestination in Reformed Theology from Calvin to Perkins* (Durham, NC: Labyrinth Press, 1986; repr. with corrections, Grand Rapids, MI: Baker Book House, 1988); idem, *God, Creation and Providence in the Thought of Jacob Arminius: Sources and Directions of Scholastic Protestantism in the Era of Early Orthodoxy* (Grand Rapids, MI: Baker Book House, 1991); the essays in Carl R. Trueman and R. Scott Clark, *Protestant Scholasticism: Essays in Reassessment* (Carlisle: Paternoster Press, 1999); Willem J. van Asselt, P. L. Rouwendal, et. al. *Inleiding in de Gereformeerde Scholastiek* (Zoetermeer: Boekencentrum, 1998); and the essays in Willem J. van Asselt and Eef Dekker, eds., *Reformation and Scholasticism: an Ecumenical Enterprise* (Grand Rapids, MI: Baker Book House, 2001).

18. Related arguments for continuity can be found in Richard A. Muller, "*Duplex cognitio dei* in the Theology of Early Reformed Orthodoxy," in *The Sixteenth Century Journal*, 10/2 (1979), pp. 51–61; "Perkins' *A Golden Chaine*: Predestinarian System or Schematized Ordo Salutis?" in *The Sixteenth Century* Journal, 9/1(1978), pp. 69–81; and "Christ in the Eschaton: Calvin and Moltmann on the Duration of the *Munus Regium*, " in *Harvard Theological Review*, 74/1 (1981), pp. 51–59. Continuity as well as development is seen in the studies by Donnelly, cited earlier.

19. The problem of Aristotelianism as a manifestation of doctrinal discontinuity is emphasized by Ernst Bizer, *Friihorthodoxie und Rationalismus* (Zurich: EVZ Verlag, 1963) and Walter Kickel, *Vernunft und Offenbarung bei Theodor Beza* (Neukirchen: Neukirchner Verlag, 1967); these works, together with Basil Hall, "Calvin Against the Calvinists," in *John Calvin*, ed. G. Duffield (Appleford: Sutton Courtnay Press, 1966), emphasize the discontinuity between the Reformation and orthodoxy, particularly in terms of the doctrine of predestination. Aristotelian philosophy and scholastic method in Protestant theology are discussed at length in Hans Emil Weber, *Die philosophische Scholastik des deutschen Protestantismus in Zeitalter der Orthodoxie* (Leipzig: Quelle & Meyer, 1907); Peter Petersen, *Geschichte der aristotelischen Philosophie in protestantischen Deutschland* (Leipzig: F. Meiner 1921); and Max Wundt, *Die deutsche Schulmetaphysik des 17 Jahrhunderts* (Tiibingen: J.C.B. Mohr, 1939). All of these works fall under the strictures noted earlier in chapters 4 and 5.

20. On the basic problem of double truth in the history of thought, see Etienne Gilson, *Reason and revelation in the* Middle *Ages* (New York: Scribners, 1938), pp. 53–63; idem, "La doctrine de la double vérité," in *Etudes de philosophie médiévale* (Strasbourg: Commission des publications de la Facultb des lettres, 1921), pp. 50–69; and idem, "Boéce de Dacie et la double vérité," in *Archives d'histoire doctrinale et littéraire du moyen age*, 30 (1955), pp. 81–99; also, Armand Maurer, "Boetius of Dacia and the Double Truth," *Medieval Studies*, 17 (1955), pp. 233–239;

on the problem as it resurfaces in early sixteenth-century thought, see Martin Pine, "Pomponazzi and the Problem of 'Double Truth,'" in *Journal of the History of Ideas*, 29 (1968), pp. 163–176. Whereas the Latin Averroists—Siger of Brabant, John of Jandun, and Boetius of Dacia—asserted the separation of philosophy from theology and insisted on the truth of revelation, Pomponazzi argued in the opposite direction and equated truth with philosophy as superior to theology. Cf. Pine, "Pomponazzi," pp. 174–175. In neither case do we see a real denial of the principle of non-contradiction, and in the case of the Latin Averroists, there was probably no thought of impugning theological truth, merely a freeing of philosophical investigation from theological system. See, further, Stuart MacClintock, *Perversity and Error, Studies on the "Averroist" John of Jandun* (Bloomington: University of Indiana Press, 1956).

21. See Joseph S. Freedman, "Aristotle and the Content of Philosophy Instruction at Central European Schools and Universities during the Reformation Era (1500–1650)," in *Proceedings of the American Philosophical Society* 137/2 (1993), pp. 213–253; and cf. William T. Costello, *The Scholastic Curriculum at Early Seventeenth-Century Cambridge* (Cambridge, MA: Harvard University Press, 1958), pp. 71–102, 108–128.

22. Arthur Cushman McGiffert, *Protestant Thought Before Kant* (London: Duckworth, 1911), p. 145.

23. See Bartholomaus Keckermann, *Operum omnium quae extant*, 2 vols. (Geneva, 1614). Volume 1 contains lectures on the presuppositions of philosophy, logic, physics, astronomy, geography, metaphysics; volume 2, on ethics, economics, politics, rhetoric (secular), Christian rhetoric, and systematic theology. Keckermann's contemporary J. H. Alsted wrote on all the philosophical topics as well as on theology; see the essays by E. F. Karl Muller in *Realencyklopädie für protestantische Theologie und Kirche*, 3d ed., s.v. "Alsted, Joh. Heinrich" and "Keckermann, Bartholomaus."

24. See Howard Hotson, *Johann Heinrich Alsted, 1588–1638: Between Renaissance, Reformation, and Universal Reform* (Oxford: Clarendon Press, 2000).

25. Thus, Johannes Donner, *Themata X contra systema logicum Keckermanni directa* (Wittenberg, 1610); Cornelius Martinius, *Praelectiones in systema logicum Keckermanni* (Wittenberg, 1612).

26. W. H. Zuylen, *Bartholomaus Keckermann: Sein Leben und Wirken* (Borna-Leipzig: R. Noske, 1934), pp. 15, 20–21. Zuylen's perspective is largely determined by the works of Weber and Althaus with the exception, of course, of *Reformation, Orthodoxie und Rationalismus* which appeared in 1937. Althaus also, in particular, stresses the importance of Keckermann in the development of Protestant scholasticism: see Althaus, *Die Prinzipien*, pp. 11–13, 73–85, 241–249.

27. Zuylen, *Keckermann*, p. 21.

28. Zuylen, *Keckermann*, p. 21.

29. Economics, "oeconomica," is the one term employed by Keckermann unfamiliar in its meaning to the modern reader; it indicates the *prudentia* according to which the family is governed and it contrasts, as a subset of ethics with politics, the *prudentia* concerned with the public good and the ordering of the state.

30. See Hotson, *Johann Heinrich Alsted*, pp. 29–39; also see Leroy E. Loemker, "Leibniz and the Herborn Encyclopedists," in *Journal of the History of Ideas*, 22 (1961), pp. 323–338, and idem, *Struggle for Synthesis: The Seventeenth Century Background of Leibniz's Synthesis of Order and Freedom* (Cambridge, MA.: Harvard University Press, 1972).

31. Andreas Hyperius, *De theologo, seu de ratione studii theologici, libri III* (Basel, 1556), I.iv–ix (pp. 45–80).

32. For a survey of the controversy, see Isaak August Dorner, *History of Protestant Theology*, trans. Robson and Taylor, 2 vols. (Edinburgh, 1871), vol. 2, pp. 110–113; also Paul Tschackert's article in *Realencyklopädie für Protestantische Theologie und Kirche*, 3d ed., s.v. "Hoffmann, Daniel." Cf. Althaus, *Die Prinzipien*, pp. 103–104.

33. Dorner, *History of Protestant Theology*, vol. 2, pp. 112–113.

34. Bartholomaus Keckermann, *Systema ss. theologiae*, I.i, in *Opera*, vol. 2, at end, second pagination, cols. 67–68.

35. Keckermann, *Systema ss. theologiae*, col. 68–69: "Finis Theologiae est ipsa salus, de qua in sequentibus agetur. Salus sive felicitas, est fruitio Dei tanquam summi boni."

36. Keckermann, *Systema ss. theologiae*, col. 67: "Quin & magis ille Ursinus in Catechesi sua diserte Theologiam dicit esse operatricem disciplinam, & idcirco methodo analytica tradendam."

37. Cf. Erdmann K. Sturm, *Der junge Zacharias Ursin: Sein Weg vom Philippismus zum Calvinismus* (Neukirchen: Neukirchner Verlag, 1972), pp. 33–48, 78, 169–170, 173, 177–178, 211–212; also see Bard Thompson, "Historical Background of the Catechism," in *Essays on the Heidelberg Catechism* (Philadelphia: United Church Press, 1963), p. 24; and Julius Ney, in *Realencyklopädie für protestantische Theologie und Kirche*, 3d ed., s.v. "Ursinus, Zacharias."

38. See *D. Zachariae Ursini theologi celeberrimi . . . opera theologica quibus orthodoxae religionis capita perspicue & breviter explicantur*, ed. Q. Reuter, 3 vols. (Heidelberg, 1612), the *Loci theologici, locus primus, de scriptura sacra*, col. 426–458, especially, col. 429–431. This locus, which may not have been part of the original catechetical lectures of Ursinus but, rather, the initial discussion of a fragment system, was included in several of the early versions of the catechetical lectures—all posthumous): e.g., *Doctrinae christianae compendium* (Oxford, 1585), pp. 1–50.

39. The Protestant scholastics were profoundly aware of the medieval debate over theology as contemplative or practical and, indeed, of the works of individual medieval scholastics who debated the issue; in this sense, the use of convenient labels such as "Thomist" or "Scotist" does injustice by way of oversimplification to the early Protestant scholastics. Johannes Gerhard, for example, cites both Scotus and Gregory of Rimini as viewing theology as purely practical; Marsilius of Inghien as denominating it speculative; Bonaventure and Albert viewing theology as neither practical nor speculative but affective; Godfrey of Fontaines calling it both speculative and practical; Thomas Aquinas as concurring with Godfrey but emphasizing the speculative; Richard of Middleton accepting the speculative-practical definition but pressing the priority of the practical, in agreement with Thomas of Strasbourg. Gerhard—who is often classified as a Thomist—favors the view of Scotus, Rimini, Bonaventure, and Albert, adding, by way of confirmation, the statement of Alexander of Hales, "Theologia magis est virtutis, quam artis, sapientia magis quam scientia, magisque consistit in virtute et efficacia, quam in contemplatione et notitia." See Johannes Gerhard, *Loci theologici* (1610–1621), ed. Preuss (Berlin, 1863–1875), 1, *Prooemium de natura theologiae*, sections 11-12. Keckermann, even more radically than Gerhard, sets aside the Thomistic view for a view approximating the Scotist position or the position of a late medieval Augustinian like Gregory of Rimini.

40. Keckermann, *Praecognitorum philosophicorum libri duo*, in *Opera*, vol. 1, col. 7B, F: "habitus mentis, per quem divina, naturalia & humana scimus. Qua latissime significatione philosophae nomen apud Graecos & Latinos veteres communi usu usur patur, & Aristoteles quoque hac significatione utitur I. Metaph. 8. ubi philosophum esse ait eum, qui omnia scit. . . . Propria denique Philosophia significatio est, quae comprehendit eas disciplinas, quas proprie vel Scientiam vel Prudentiam vocamus."

41. Keckermann, *Praecognitorum philosophicorum*, col. 9E: "Philosophiam ait esse habitum animi qui scientia & prudentia constat." He differs with Crellius in calling philosophy a collection of disciplines rather than one unified discipline. Cf. ibid., col. 9G, H.

42. Keckermann, *Praecognitorum philosophicorum*, cols. 11E, 7F, 9E. Cf. Althaus, *Die Prinzipien*, pp. 241–244. Althaus comments that, under the impact of an Aristotelian and generally rationalist perspective, Keckermann tended to reduce sacred history to exemplar status, while at the same time refusing history, as a discipline, any place in the (Aristotelian) construction of the curriculum. Indeed, for Keckermann, history is not a discipline.

43. Cf. Keckermann, *Praecognitorum philosophicorum*, cols. 7–11.

44. Keckermann, *Opera*, vol. 1, col. 68F–G: ". . . atque adeo unica tantum & simplex veritas est Theologiae & Philosophiae, ut non statuenda sit veritas alia Philosophica, alia Theologia."

45. Keckermann, *Opera*, vol. 1, col. 68G: ". . . aliquid verum in Philosophia, quod sit falsum in Theologia."

46. Keckermann, *Opera*, col. 68H, 69A–C.

47. Keckermann, *Opera*, col. 69D.

48. Keckermann, *Opera*, vol. 1, col. 69H: "Dona dei inter se non pugnant: / At Philosophia est donum Dei; Exod 31 vers 3. Psalm 94 vers 10. Syrac 1 vers 1. 2 Chronic 1 vers 12. Danielis 2 *dat sapientibus sapientiam*, Rom 1 vers 19. Iac 1 vers 17. / Ergo non pugnat cum dono Dei, nimirum cum sacra Theologia." Note the citation of Sirach in the minor of the syllogism: Protestants were not averse to citing Apocrypha as collateral proofs!

49. Keckermann, *Opera*, vol. 1, col. 69E–70A.

50. Keckermann, *Opera*, vol. 1, col. B–C: "VII. Unicum & simplex sibiipsi non contrariatur. / Veritas est unica & simplex, sive tradatur in Theologia, sive in Philosophia, & verum vero constans ubicunque tractetur (distinctio enim disciplinarum non multiplicat veritatem). / Ergo veritas sibi non contrarietur, sive tradatur in Theologia sive in Philosophia. VIII. Unicum & simplex non multiplicatur: / Veritas est unica & simplex: / Ergo veritas non multiplicatur, & per consequens, nec dividitur, ut alia sit Theologica alia Philosophica. IX. Bonum bono non repugnat, sed perpetua concordat: / Philosophia ipsa bona est & tractat de duplici bono, naturali & moralis: / Ergo non pugnat cum S. Theologia, qua & ipsa bona est, & tractat de bono spirituali"

51. Keckermann, *Opera*, vol. 1, col. 70D–E.

52. Keckermann, *Opera*, vol. 1, col. 70F: "In summa, cognitio Dei naturalis non contrariatur supernaturali, cognitio per naturam non repugnat cognitioni per gratiam, liber naturae non evertit librum scripturae: Ergo nec Philosophia pugnat cum Theologia."

53. Keckermann, *Opera*, vol. 1, col. 70G–71A.

54. Keckermann, *Opera*, vol. 1, col. 24H.

55. Keckermann, *Opera*, vol. 1, col. 71F.

56. Keckermann, *Opera*, vol. 1, col. 71G: "Humana divinis & naturalia supernaturalibus non repugnat sed subordinantur. . . . pendent creaturae a creatore tanquam effectus a causa; inter causam autem & effectum non est pugna, sed summa concordia."

57. Keckermann, *Opera*, vol. 1, col. 71G–H: ". . . ea et si philosophia non tractat, tamen propterea non refutat, sed concedit & amplectitur tanquam alibi confirmata."

58. Keckermann, *Opera*, vol. 1, col. 72D–E; cf. Althaus, *Die Prinzipien*, pp. 103–104; 106–107.

59. Keckermann, *Opera*, vol. 1, col. 72H–I.

60. Keckermann, *Opera*, vol. 1, col. 73B–C. I hesitate to call this balance of the disciplines and absence of contradiction "Thomist." Althaus, (pp. 77, 84–85) places Keckermann between Thomism and nominalism, ontologism and "terminism." Keckermann is at best eclectic. His restriction of metaphysics to the discussion of *ens* or *essentia* coupled with the declaration that metaphysics does not, as such, deal with God (the subject of theology) but only points to a ground of being, has a Scotist sound. In addition, Scotus clearly stood against a theory of double truth, even though he did not establish as close a relation in his theology between philosophy and theology as did Thomas. On Scotus, see P. Parthenius Minges, *Ioannis Duns Scoti Doctrina Philosophica et Theologica quoad res praecipuas proposita et exposita*, 2 vols. (Ad Claras Aquas: ex Typographia Conegii S. Bonaventurae, 1930), pp. 509, 514–518, 562–568; for Keckermann's views on metaphysics, see *Opera*, vol. 1: 16–17 and the lectures on metaphysics in ibid., especially col. 2015 on the subject of metaphysics as *ens* viewed in a primary and general sense. There is, moreover, a strong Scotist component in Reformed theology, see François Wendel, *Calvin: the Origins and Development of his Religious Thought*, trans. Philip Mairet (New York:

Harper & Row, 1963), pp. 127–129, 231. We note also the impact of Scotus on the discussion of *principia theologiae* in the *Syntagma theologiae christianae* (Geneva, 1617) of Keckermann's contemporary, Amandus Polanus; see *Syntagma, I.iii* (p. 3, col. 1). On Keckermann's metaphysics, see Zuylen, *Keckermann*, pp. 44–47; Polanus's thought has been discussed as primarily Thomistic by Heiner Faulenbach, *Die Struktur der Theologie des Amandus Polanus von Polansdorf* (Zurich: EVZ-Verlag, 1967), which also misses entirely the non-Thomist accents found throughout the Reformed theology of the era.

61. Keckermann, *Opera*, vol. 1, col.73D, G.

62. Keckermann, *Opera*, vol. 1, col. 73H–74A: "Deum qui est infinitae potentiae, ad productionem rerum non agere aliqua praexistente materia."

63. Keckermann, *Opera*, vol. 1, col. 74C: "Unum non est trinum, ex ipso respectu quo unum est. . . . Deum esse unum respectu essentia, trinum vero respectu non essentiae, sed personarum."

64. Recent analyses of late medieval theology have manifested a certain degree of continuity between the theology of the reformers and the thought of the age immediately preceding the Reformation; in particular, see Heiko Oberman, *Forerunners of the Reformation: the Shape of Late Medieval Thought* (New York: Holt, Rinehart and Winston, 1966) and idem, *Masters of the Reformation: the Emergence of a New Intellectual Climate in Europe* (Cambridge: Cambridge University Press, 1981); also see *The Reformation in Medieval Perspective*, ed. Steven Ozment (Chicago: Quadrangle Books, 1971). The continuity of nominalism as a negative cause of the Reformation was announced by Joseph Lortz, *The Reformation in Germany*, 2 vols. (New York; Herder and Herder, 1968), but here, again, several modifications have occurred. On the one hand, Oberman has done much to place nominalism in a positive light; see his *The Harvest of Medieval Theology*. On the other, Donnelly, in his *Calvinist Thomism* (pp. 453–454), has shown, in explicit contrast to Lortz, the continuity of Thomism in Vermigli and Zanchi. On the medieval roots of Calvin's thought, see Karl Reuter, *Das Grundverständnis der Theologie Calvins* (Neukirchen: Neukirchner Verlag, 1963).

65. On Luther's relationship to scholasticism, see Dennis Janz, *Luther and Late Medieval Thomism: A Study in Theological Anthropology* (Waterloo: Wilfrid Laurier University Press, 1983) and David Bagchi, "Sic et Non: Luther and Scholasticism," in Trueman and Clark, *Protestant Scholasticism: Essays in Reappraisal*, pp. 3–15. On Calvin, see Muller, *Unaccommodated Calvin*, pp. 39–61 and David C. Steinmetz, "The Scholastic Calvin," in Trueman and Clark, *Protestant Scholasticism: Essays in Reappraisal*, pp. 16–30.

66. Cf. Donnelly, "Calvinist Thomism," p. 452 and idem, *Calvinism and Scholasticism*, pp. 51–64,196–207.

67. Keckermann, *Praecognitorum philosophicorum*, col. 35C: "Ad studium Theologiae summa est Philosophiae tum utilitas, tum Necessitas: primo quoad ipsam *didaskalian*, sive praecepta Theologiae: 2. quoad *elenchon*, sive disputationes & controversias Theologicas."

68. Keckermann, *Praecognitorum philosophicorum*, col. 36A. Note the comment of Weber, "Den humanistischen Preis der Dialektic nimmt für die weiterdrängende Orthodoxie ein Keckermann auf, indem er die besondere Notwendigkeit der Logik für die Theologie, und zwar gerade auch wegen ihrer Gebundenheit an das Offenbarungszeugnis betont" (Weber, *Reformation, Orthodoxie und Rationalismus*, 1/2, p. 296).

69. Keckermann, *Praecognitorum philosophicorum*, col. 37A: "Principium rei in Theologia Deus est. At vero quid sit eius essentia, quid existentiae modi sive persona, nemo unquam accurate explicabit sine Metaphysics."

70. Keckermann, *Praecognitorum philosophicorum*, col. 37D–H; cf. Althaus, *Die Prinzipien*, pp. 73–75, 96–99.

71. Cf. Althaus, *Die Prinzipien*, p. 81.

72. Althaus, *Die Prinzipien*, p. 77; see Keckermann, *Systema ss. theologiae*, col. 69–70, 83; cf. Zuylen, *Keckermann*, p. 45.

73. Althaus, *Die Prinzipien*, pp. 80–81, cf. pp. 138–139.

74. Zuylen, *Keckermann*, pp. 118–120, 122–123.

75. Keckermann, *Systema ss. theologiae*, I.ii, col. 69H–70I.

76. Keckermann, *Praecognitorum philosophicorum*, col. 37I–38B.

77. Keckermann, *Praecognitorum philosophicorum*, col. 38H, citing Melchior Cano, *Locorum theologicorum*, Lib. 9, cap. 3.

78. Keckermann, *Praecognitorum philosophicorum*, col. 38E–H.

79. Cf. Preus, *Theology of Post-Reformation Lutheranism*, vol. 1, p. 36; in a more formative theological pattern, Gomarus could develop a catena of citations on the Trinity reaching from the Fathers to Thomas Aquinas, Bonaventure, Occam, Biel, Alexander of Hales, and Duns Scotus. See *Disputationes theologicae*, VI. xl–xliii, in *Opera theologica omnia, maximam partem posthuma*, 2 vols. (Amsterdam, 1644). See also note 25 (above) on Gerhard's positive citation of medieval scholastics.

80. Cf. Petersen, *Geschichte der aristotelischen Philosophie*; Paul Dibon, *La philosophie néerlandaise au siècle d'or* (Paris: Elsevier, 1954); Frederick Copleston, *A History of Philosophy*, vol. 3, *Late Medieval and Renaissance Philosophy* (Westminster, MD: Newman Press, 1953); and William Costello, *The Scholastic Curriculum at Early Seventeenth Century Cambridge* (Cambridge, MA: Harvard University Press, 1958).

81. Paul Oskar Kristeller, *Renaissance Thought: The Classic, Scholastic, and Humanist Strains* (New York: Harper & Row, 1961), pp. 34–35.

82. Lambert Daneau, *Physica Christiana, sive de rerum creaturarum cognitione et usu* (Geneva, 1576); see the highly negative evaluation of this piece in Ernst Bizer, *Frühorthodoxie und Rationalismus*, pp. 32–50; an echo of this reading of Daneau is found in John Dillenberger, *Protestant Thought and Natural Science: a Historical Study* (Nashville: Abingdon, 1960), pp. 60–61. Fatio's *Méthode et théologie* presents a reappraisal and a far more positive analysis of Daneau's contribution to Protestant orthodoxy.

83. Cf. the summation of Althaus's argument in *Die Prinzipien*, pp. 271–274, and note, p. 274, "Das gewaltige Pathos, das durch Calvins scharfgeschliffene Sätze oft genug hindurchzittert, darf man bei Keckermann und Alsted, Maccovius und Polanus nicht suchen." Also see Zuylen, *Keckermann*, pp. 110–132.

84. For a specific declaration of Protestant catholicity at the wellsprings of the reform (1539), see Calvin's debate with Sadoletto, in *Ioannis Calvini Opera quae supersunt omnia* in *Corpus Reformatorum* ed. Baum, Cunitz, Reuss (Brunswick, 1863-1900), vol. 5, cols. 385-416; note especially Calvin's declaration, based on the Vincentian Canon, of the Reformation as representing the beliefs of the saints throughout the whole world and in all ages, the unity of the one faith of the church (col. 392).

85. See Musculus, *Loci communes theologiae sacrae* (Basel, 1560), pp. 233, 234, 409.

86. This, at least, was Keckermann's assessment of Pomponazzi: "Petrus Pomponatius, qui publice defendit animum hominis mortalem esse, & cuius etiam adhuc extant impiae de Dei providentia deque Christi miraculis in scriptis assertiones. Sed vitia artificum nemo prudens ascribit artibus: nemo cordatus eorum qui Philosophorum titulo gaudent, ipsius philosophiae vitia esse iudicabit," Keckermann, *Praecognitorum philosophicorum*, col. 33H. Cf. the comments on Protestant scholasticism and double truth in Dillenberger, *Protestant Thought and Natural Science*, pp. 57–58.

87. Cf. *Systema ss. theologiae*, I.ii–vi, including (iii–iv) Keckermann's analysis of the Trinity with Calvin's Institutio, I.x.2; xiii.1, 6, 21; xiv.2; xvi.2; III.xx.40–41. Note the antispeculative manner of Calvin's treatment.

88. Musculus, *Loci communes*, cap. 41–54: chapters beginning with the name, nature, sufficiency, omnipotence, will, and truth of God and moving on to the communicable attributes like mercy and justice.

89. Keckermann, *Systema ss. theologiae*: cf. I.ii–vi with the locus de verbi divini materia, I.viii.

90. Zuylen, *Keckermann*, pp. 123–125.

91. Cf. Keckermann, *Systema ss. theologiae*, col. 117D

92. Cf. Calvin, *Institutes*, I.i–v; cf. David C. Steinmetz, *Calvin in Context*, chapter 12, and note the discussion in Muller, *Post-Reformation Reformed Dogmatics*, vol. 1, pp. 269–309, particularly with reference to Vermigli's views.

93. Calvin, *Institutio*, I.ii.2; iii.1–3. In I.x.1. Calvin states that clear and valid knowledge of the creator comes most surely through Scripture, but even here he does not rule out "Dei notitiam, quae in mundi machina universisque creaturis non obscuri alioqui proponitur."

94. Vermigli, *Loci communes*, I.ii.5.

95. Zuylen, *Keckermann*, p. 123.

96. Thus, Calvin, *Institutes*, I.ii.1; vi.1–2; II.vi.1; cf. Muller, "*Duplex cognitio dei*," pp. 54–56.

97. See Ursinus, *Explicationes catecheseos*, in *Opera*, vol. 1, col. 123–126; the text of the catechism, Q. 26, appears in col. 122.

98. Zuylen, *Keckermann*, p. 123.

99. E.g., *Systema ss. theologiae*, III.iv, *De officio Christi Sacerdotali*, a doctrine of the strict limitation of effective satisfaction to the elect, or III.vi, *De Ecclesia*, in which the church is defined as the object of Christ's work in the threefold office. Here dogmatic concerns predominate rather than philosophical, and we see the working out of the implications and the development of the internal logic of doctrinal patterns.

100. Cf. Donnelly's conclusions concerning Zanchi's balance of Thomist philosophy with Calvinist theology in "Calvinist Thomism," pp. 451–453, especially p. 452, note 66, in which the views of Bizer and Kickel are singled out for criticism. Also see my "*Duplex cognitio Dei* in the Theology of Early Reformed Orthodoxy," p. 61.

8. *Scholasticism Protestant and Catholic*

1. Joseph Lortz, *The Reformation in Germany*, trans. R. Walls, 2 vols. (New York: Herder and Herder, 1968), 1: 194–201; Lortz has continued to maintain his basic thesis but has developed a greater appreciation of Luther as a theologian; see Joseph Lortz, "The Basic Elements of Luther's Intellectual Style," in *Catholic Scholars Dialogue with Luther*, ed. Jared Wicks (Chicago: Loyola University Press, 1970), pp. 3–33; and Louis Bouyer, *The Spirit and the Forms of Protestantism*, trans. A.V. Littledale (Westminster, MD: Newman Press, 1958), pp. 7–11.

2. Heiko A. Oberman, *The Harvest of Medieval Theology: Gabriel Biel and Late Medieval Nominalism*, rev. ed. (Grand Rapids, MI: Eerdmans, 1967), and *Masters of the Reformation: the Emergence of a New Intellectual Climate in Europe*, trans. Dennis Martin (Cambridge: Cambridge University Press, 1981); Bengt Hägglund, *Theologie und Philosophie bei Luther und in der occamistischen Tradition: Luthers Stellung zur Theorie von der doppetten Wahrheit* (Lund: C. W. K. Gleerup, 1955), and *The Background of Luther's Doctrine of Justification in Late Medieval Theology* (Philadelphia: Fortress Press, 1971); David C. Steinmetz, *Misericordia Dei: The Theology of Johannes von Staupitz in its Late Medieval Setting* (Leiden: E. J. Brill, 1968).

3. For example, Gabriel Buescher, *The Eucharistic Teaching of William of Ockham* (Saint Bonaventure, NY: Franciscan Institute, 1950); Philotheus Boehner, *Collected Articles on Ockham*, ed. Eligius M. Buytaert (Saint Bonaventure, NY: Franciscan Institute, 1958).

4. John Patrick Donnelly, *Calvin and Scholasticism in Vermigli's Doctrine of Man and Grace* (Leiden: E. J. Brill, 1976), and "Calvinist Thomism," in *Viator*, 7 (1976), pp. 441–445.

5. For example, Olivier Fatio, *Méthode et théologie: Lambert Daneau et les débuts de la scholastique réformée* (Geneva: Droz, 1976); Robert P. Scharlemann, *Thomas Aquinas and John Gerhard* (New Haven, CT: Yale University Press, 1964). Typical of the older scholarship, which

viewed Protestant scholasticism in term of central dogmas and the rise of rationalism, are Hans Emil Weber, *Reformation, Orthodoxie und Rationalismus*, 2 vols. (Gütersloh: Gerd Mohn, 1937–1940), and Ernst Bizer, *Frühorthodoxie und Rationalismus* (Zürich: EVZ Verlag, 1963). For further bibliography and discussion, see Richard A. Muller, "*Duplex cognitio Dei* in the Theology of Early Reformed Orthodoxy," in *The Sixteenth Century Journal*, 10 (1979), pp. 51–61, and "*Vera Philosophia cum sacra Theologia nusquam pugnat:* Keckerman on Philosophy, Theology and the Problem of Double Truth," chapter 7 of this book.

6. Scharlemann, *Thomas Aquinas and John Gerhard*, pp. 15–17. Note, among the Reformed, Lucas Trelcatius, *Scholastica et methodia locorum communium institutio* (London, 1604), and Johannes Scharpius, *Cursus theologicus in quo controversiae omnes de fidei dogmatibus hoc seculo exagitatae* (Geneva, 1620), both of whom develop polemical loci following their positive statement of doctrine, chiefly against Bellarmine; also see William Ames, *Bellarminus enervatus, sive disputationes anti-Bellarminianae*, 3rd ed. (London, 1629).

7. See Paul Althaus, *Die Prinzipien der deutschen reformierten Dogmatik im Zeitalter der aristotelischen Orthodoxie* (Leizig: Deichert, 1914), pp. 230–233; also note the direct citation of medieval theologians on these issues in Johannes Gerhard, *Loci theologici* (1610–1621), ed. Preuss, 9 vols. (Berlin, 1863-1875), vol. 1, pp. 11–12.

8. For example, Amandus Polanus, *Syntagma theologiae christianae* (Geneva, 1617), 1:3–4; Scharpius, *Cursus theologicus*, cols. 2–3; Franciscus Gomarus, *Disputationes theologicae*, in *Opera theologica omnia* (Amsterdam, 1644), *Disp.* I.45–49. A Scotist or at least *via moderna* accent appears in these works in the basic distinction between archetypal and ectypal theology: see Muller, *Post-Reformation Reformed Dogmatics*, vol. 1, pp. 224–236.

9. Franciscus Turrettinus, *Institutio theologiae elencticae* (Geneva, 1679–1685; new ed., Edinburgh, 1847). Note also the translation: *Institutes of Elenctic Theology*, 3 vols. trans. George Musgrave Giger, ed. James T. Dennison, Jr. (Phillipsburg, NJ: Presbyterian and Reformed Publishing, 1992–1997). To my knowledge, Eugène de Budé, *Vie de François Turrettini, théologien Genevois (1623–1687)* (Lausanne: Bridel, 1871), and Gerrit Keizer, *Francois Turrettini, sa vie, ses oeuvres et le Consensus* (Kampen: J. A. Bus, 1900), remain the only major biographies. Among the studies of Turretin's theology should be mentioned John W. Beardslee, *Theological Development at Geneva under Francis and Jean-Alphonse Turretin* (Ph.D. diss., Yale University, 1956); Stephen R. Spencer, *Reformed Scholasticism in Medieval Perspective: Aquinas and François Turrettini on the Incarnation* (Ph.D. diss., Michigan State University, 1988); Paul T. Jensen, *Calvin and Turrettini: A Comparison of Their Soteriologies* (Ph.D. diss., University of Virginia, 1988); and E. P. Meijering, *Reformierte Scholastik und patristische Theologie: Die Bedeutung des Vaterbeweises in der Institutio theologiae elencticae F. Turretins: unter besonderer Berucksichtigung der Gotteslehre und Christologie* (Nieuwkoop: De Graaf, 1991).

10. On the rise of scholastic philosophy within Protestantism and the influence of Zabarella and Suarez, see Emil Weber, *Die philosophische Scholastik des deutschen Protestantismus im Zeitalter der Orthodoxie* (Leipzig: Quelle & Meyer, 1907); Max Wundt, *Die deutsche Schulphilosophie des 17. Jahrhunderts* (Tübingen: J. C. B. Mohr, 1939); and Peter Petersen, *Geschichte der aristotelischen Philoosphie im protestantischen Deutschland* (1921; repr. Stuttgart: F. Frommann, 1964).

11. Compare the previously cited works by Weber and Bizer with Basil Hall, "Calvin Against the Calvinists," in *John Calvin*, ed. Gervase Duffield (Grand Rapids, MI: Eerdmans, 1966); Brian Armstrong, *Calvinism and the Amyraut Heresy: Protestant Scholasticism and Humanism in Seventeenth Century France* (Madison: University of Wisconsin Press, 1969), and, on a more popular level, Jack B. Rogers and Donald K. McKim, *The Authority and Interpretation of the Bible: An Historical Approach* (San Francisco: Harper & Row, 1979), pp. 172–188 on Turretin.

12. Francis Burgersdijck, *Institutionum logicarum libri duo* (Cambridge, 1637), II.xx.99.

13. Turretin, *Institutio theol. elencticae*, I.vi.1; "Systematice et Objective per modum disciplinae" or "habitualiter et subjective, per modum habitus in intellectu residentis."

14. Compare Turretin, *Institutio theol. elencticae*, I.vi.3 with Thomas Aquinas, *Summa theologiae*, 1-2ae, q.50, a.4; and Parthenius Minges, *Ioannis Duns Scoti Doctrina Philosophica et Theologica*, 2 vols. (Quaracchi: Collegium S. Bonaventurae1930), I, pp. 465–467.

15. On faculty psychology, see Frederick C. Copleston, *Thomas Aquinas* (Baltimore: Penguin Books, 1955), pp. 163–164, 179–180, 194.

16. Turretin, *Institutio theol. elencticae*, I.vi.3.

17. Turretin, *Institutio theol. elencticae*, I.vi.4; compare Beardslee, "Theological Development," pp. 86–91.

18. The use and status of logical conclusions in theological argument was discussed and debated by the Protestant scholastics, typically with the assertion that the middle term of a syllogism (which forces the particular conclusion from a universal premise) must be taken from scripture; see the discussion in Bernhard Punjer, *History of the Christian Philosophy of Religion from the Reformation to Kant*, trans. W. Hastie (Edinburgh: T. & T. Clark, 1887), pp. 164–166. The importance of the issue for doctrine is evident in the *Westminster Confession of Faith*, I.vi, in Philip Schaff, *Creeds of Christendom*, 3 vols. (New York: Scribner, 1919), vol. 3, p. 603.

19. Turretin, *Institutio theol. elencticae*, I.vi.5.

20. Turretin, *Institutio theol. elencticae*, I.vi.5.

21. Compare Thomas Aquinas, *Summa theologiae*, I, q.1, a.2, with Johann Wilhelm Baier, *Compendium theologiae positivae* (Jena, 1685), prolegomena, I.iii.15 (Lutheran); and Gisbertus Voetius, *Disputationum theologicarum pars prima* (Utrecht, 1648), disp. 1 and 2 (Reformed).

22. Minges, *Ioannes Duns Scoti Doctrina*, vol. I, pp. 510–517, on the difficulty of identifying theology as *scientia* insofar as we do not have immediate evidence of the object of theology, God; and see ibid., vol. I, p. 508, on the distinction between *theologia in se* and *theologia nostra*.

23. Turretin, *Institutio theol. elencticae*, I.vi.5.

24. Turretin, *Institutio theol. elencticae*, I.vi.7. Turretin's citations of classical authors, like his use of the scholastics, do not represent "research" into earlier sources of philosophy or theology but rather the use of a received tradition of references. The use of ancient anthologies like Stobaeus or Suidas is typical.

25. Turretin, *Institutio theol. elencticae*, I.vii.1.

26. Turretin, *Institutio theol. elencticae*, I.vii.1. Again the paradigm belongs to a received tradition: see Gerhard, *Loci theologici*, I.11–12; Gomarus, *Disputationes*, I.45–49.

27. Turretin, *Institutio theol. elencticae*, I.vii.3.

28. Compare Turretin, *Institutio theol. elencticae*, I.vii.2, with Philipp van Limborch, *Theologia christiana adpraxin pietatis ac promotionem pacis Christianae unice directa* (Amsterdam, 1734), I.i.5, for the Remonstrant view, and Benedict de Spinoza, A *Theologico-Political Treatise*, in *Works of Spinoza*, trans. R. H.M. Elwes, 2 vols. (New York: Dover, 1951), vol. I, pp. 9–10, 182–199. (N.B., in its first edition, 1686, Limborch's work was entitled *Institutiones theologiae christianae*.)

29. Turretin, *Institutio theol. elencticae*, I.vii.2.

30. Turretin, *Institutio theol. elencticae*, I.vii.6,10,14.

31. Turretin, *Institutio theol. elencticae*, I.vii.6.

32. Turretin, *Institutio theol. elencticae*, I.v.4.

33. Turretin's polemic against excessively metaphysical theology, like Luther's assault on *theologia gloriae*, does of course find echoes in the very medieval perspective it attacks: Turretin's *Deus noster* looks very much like Scotus's *theologia nostra*, inasmuch as it distinguishes between God as he is *in se* and God as he is known to us. In addition, late medieval discussion of the *obiectum theologiae* took note that God is known to us as *redemptor* and *glorificator*: see Gregory of Rimini, *Lectura super primum et secundum sententiarum*, ed. Damasus Trapp and Venicio Marcolino (Berlin: De Gruyter, 1981), bk. 1, prol., q.4, art.2, and Aegidius Romanus, *Primus*

sententiarum (Venice, 1521), bk. 1, prol., q.3. Note also Yves Congar, A *History of Theology*, trans. Hunter Guthrie (Garden City: Doubleday, 1968), pp. 124–125.

34. Turretin, *Institutio theo. elencticae*, I.iv.5.

35. Turretin, *Institutio theo. elencticae*, I.xiii.1.

36. Turretin, *Institutio theo. elencticae*, I.xiii.2.

37. Turretin, *Institutio theo. elencticae*, I.xiii.3.

38. Turretin, *Institutio theo. elencticae*, I.xiii.4–6, 7, 13. Here again we are dealing with a standardized set of arguments: see above, "*Vera Philosophia*," for their use by Keckerman, and compare Beardslee, "Theological Development," pp. 78–80, 177–182.

39. Turretin, *Institutio theo. elencticae*, I.viii.3.

40. Turretin, *Institutio theo. elencticae*, I.viii.1.

41. Turretin, *Institutio theo. elencticae*, I.viii.4.

42. Turretin, *Institutio theo. elencticae*, I.ix.2.

43. Turretin, *Institutio theo. elencticae*, I.xi.3.

44. Turretin, *Institutio theo. elencticae*, I.x.9; cf. I.ix.9.

45. Turretin, *Institutio theo. elencticae*, I.viii.21.

46. Franciscus Junius, *De theologia vera* (Leiden, 1594) and *Theses theologicae* (ca. 1592), in *Opera theologica* (Geneva, 1608), vol. 1, cols. 1592–1785; compare Althaus, *Die Prinzipien*, pp. 230–231, who identifies the development as Thomist, not recognizing the parallels with Scotus; cf. Muller, *Post-Reformation Reformed Dogmatics*, vol. 1, pp. 220–224.

47. Turretin, *Institutio theo. elencticae*, I.ii.6.

48. Turretin, *Institutio theo. elencticae*, I.i.7.

49. Turretin, *Institutio theo. elencticae*, I.ii.6–7.

50. Turretin, *Institutio theo. elencticae*, I.ii.9. These paradigms again are drawn from medieval scholastic models. See, for example, Johannes Altenstaig, *Vocabularius theologiae* (Hagenau, 1517), s.v. "Lumen," "Lux," and "Speculum," citing Pierre d'Ailly, Jacobus de Valencia, Alexander of Hales, Thomas Aquinas, Bonaventure, and Jean Gerson.

51. N.B., the full spectrum of the exercise is found in Petrus van Mastricht, *Theoretico-practica theologia, qua, per capita theologica, pars dogmatica, elenchtica et practica, perpetua successione conjugantur, praecedunt in usum operis, paraleipomena, seu sceleton de optima concionandi methodo*, 2 vols. (Amsterdam: Henricus & Theodorus Boom, 1682–1687). The balance of dogmatic and practical seen in Wilhelmus à Brakel, *ΛΟΓΙΚΗ ΛΑΤΡΕΙΑ, dat is Redelijke Godsdienst in welken de goddelijke Waarheden van het Genade-Verbond worden verklaard . . . alsmede de Bedeeling des Verbonds in het O. en N.T. en de Ontmoeting der Kerk in het N. T. vertoond in eene Verklaring van de Openbaringen aan Johannes*, 3 parts (Dordrecht, 1700; second printing, Leiden: D. Donner, 1893–1894)

52. See the comments of Hermann Bauke, *Die Probleme der Theologie Calvins* (Leipzig: J. C. Hinrichs, 1922), pp. 22, 30–31, concerning the origin of the idea of central dogmas in the "deductive" and "Systematic monism" of Enlightenment philosophy, rather than in the theology of the sixteenth and seventeenth centuries. Note that Turretin does not attack Cartesianism directly but instead notes that "theological certainty" is not a "mathematical certainty"; compare Turretin, *Institutio theol. elencticae*, II.iv.22, with the argument noted above that theology cannot be a science, since it does not rest on rational evidence (Turretin, *Institutio theol. elencticae*, I.vi.5).

9. *The Debate over the Vowel Points*

1. A survey of medieval exegesis with emphasis on the late medieval developments leading to the Reformation can be found in *Forerunners of the Reformation*, ed. Heiko A. Oberman (New York: Holt, Rinehart, Winston, 1966), pp. 281–296; also useful are Beryl Smalley, *The Study of the Bible in the Middle Ages* (Notre Dame, IN: Notre Dame University Press, 1964), and James

S. Preus, *From Shadow to Promise: Old Testament Interpretation from Augustine to the Young Luther* (Cambridge, MA: Harvard University Press 1969): and the various essays on the text and interpretation of Scripture in *The Cambridge History of the Bible* (Cambridge: Cambridge University Press, 1969), hereinafter cited as *CHB*. On the problem of the vowel points in medieval exegesis both Jewish and Christian, see Christian D. Ginzburg, *The Massoreth Ha-Massoreth of Elias Levita* (1867; repr., New York: Ktav, 1968), pp. 45–48. On the method of Jacobus Perez de Valencia (d. 1480), who taught of the rabbinic falsification of vowels, see Wilfrid Werbeck, *Jacobus Perez von Valencia: Untersuchung zu seinem Psalmenkommentar* (Tübingen: Mohr, 1959).

2. Martin Luther, *Enarratio in Genesin* (at 47:31) in *D. Martin Luthers Werke: Kritische Gesamtausgabe* (Weimar: Hermann Böhlaus Nachfolger, 1883 ff.), XLIV, 683: "Tempore Hieronymi nondum sane videtur fuisse usus punctorum, sed absque illis tota Biblia lecta sunt. Recentiores vero Hebraeos, qui iudicium de vero sensu et intellectu linguae sibi sumunt, qui tamen non amici, sed hostes scripturae sunt, non recipio. Ideo saepe contra puncta pronuncio, nisi congruat prior sententia cum novo testamento. Hic locus vero manet ambiguus propter varietatem punctorum."

3. *Huldreich Zwinglis sämmtliche Werke*, ed. Emil Egli, et al. (Berlin: Schwetschke, 1905 ff): Corpus Reformatorum, 101, col. 98–101.

4. *Ioannis Calvini Opera quae supersunt omnia*, ed. Baum, Cunitz, and Reuss (Brunswick: Schwetschke, 1863–1900), vol. 44, cols. 305–306; also in John Calvin, *Commentaries on the Twelve Minor Prophets*, tr. John Owen, vol. 5, *Zechariah and Malachi* (Grand Rapids, MI: Baker, 1950), 313–314.

5. Ginzburg, *Massoreth*, pp. 126–127, 129, 131–132, 137; for a survey of the work of the Massoretes and the problem of vocalization as seen by recent scholarship, cf. *CHB*, vol. 2, pp. 1–13. Also see, John Bowman, "A Forgotten Controversy," in *The Evangelical Quarterly*, 20 (1948), pp. 46–68.

6. Ginzburg, *Massoreth*, p. 48.

7. John Jewel, *The Works of John Jewel, Bishop of Salisbury*, 4 vols. (Cambridge: Parker Society, 1848), vol. 2, p. 678.

8. Jewel, *Works*, vol. 2, p. 679.

9. Cf. the arguments with the several Roman polemicists, in William Whitaker, *A Disputation on Holy Scripture* (Cambridge: Parker Society, 1849), pp. 110–111; a fairly compendious list of writers, both Protestant and Roman, who dealt with this issue is found in John Owen's *A Vindication of the Purity and Integrity of the Hebrew and Greek Texts of the Old and New Testament* (1659) in *The Works of John Owen*, ed. William Goold (London: Johnstone & Hunter, 1850–1853), 16, in particular pp. 371–373. A more recent survey of the debate, from a philological point of view, is Georg Schnedermann, *Die Controverse des Ludovicus Cappellus mit den Buxtorfen über das Alter der hebäschen Punctation: ein Beitrag zu der Geschichte des Studiums der hebräischen Sprache* (Leipzig: J. C. Hinrichs, 1879). Because of the extraordinary breadth of the controversy and the number of writers involved, this chapter traces only the Reformed orthodox side of debate and omits consideration of such Lutheran writers as Flaccius and Gerhard who also argued the Mosaic origin of the points. This allows for a more detailed description of the internecine conflict that plagued Reformed orthodoxy on this issue and for an analysis of the direct line of doctrinal dispute running from Polanus through Buxtorf and Cappel to the dogmatic solution presented by Turretin, Heidegger, and the *Formula Consensus Helvetica*. The following list, although not exhaustive, gives some idea of the number of writers involved just among the Reformed: (a) upholding Mosaic origin: Gerardus, Junius, Gomarus, Polanus, Whitaker, Buxtorf Sr. and Jr., Ussher, Rainolds, Voetius, Deodatus, Lightfoot, Turretin, Heidegger; (b) favoring Massoretic origin: Zwingli, Calvin, Jud, Fagius—who was a student of Levita—Martinius, Jewel, Prideaux, Piscator, Casaubon, Erpenius, Walton, Cappel; (c) mediating or undecided: Scaliger, Drusius, Rivet, Daillé, Leigh.

10. Robert Franz Romulus (Cardinal) Bellarmine, *Disputationes de controversis christianae fidei adversus sui temporis Haereticos*, 4 vols, (Rome, 1581–1593). I have used the *Opera omnia*, 6 vols. (Naples, 1856–1862). *De Verbo Dei* is in Volume I of both editions: Lib. 1, cap. i, "verum esse Verbum Dei, et certum ac stabilem regulam fidei"; cf. IV.iii on the *verbum Dei non scriptum*.

11. Bellarmine, *Disputationes*, II.ii: "Ac primum haeretici hujus temporis odio editionis vulgatae nimium tribuunt editioni hebraicae. Calvinus enim in Antid. conc. trid., necnon Kemnitus in exam. eiusdem conc., et Georgius maior praefat. in psal. omnia examinari, et emendari volunt ad hebraeum textum, quem purissimum fontem non semel appellant."

12. Bellarmine, *Disputationes*, II.ii: "Scripturas Hebraicas non esse in universum depravatas, opera et malitia judaeorurn, nec tamen omnino esse integras et puras, sed habere suos quosdam errores, qui partim irrepserint negligentia et ignorantia librariorum, praesertim cum in hebraeo facile sit errare ob literas quasdam simillimas, partim ignorantia Rabbinorum qui addiderunt puncta."

13. Both in controversial works like William Whitaker's *Disputatio de sacra scriptura* (Cambridge, 1588; tr. 1599) and William Ames's most elaborate work, *Bellarminzu enervatus: sive disputationes Anti-Bellarmini*, 4 vols. (Oxford, 1629) and in theological systems like Festus Hommius, LXX *disputationes theologicae*, second ed. (Oxford, 1630); Robert Rollock, *Tractatus de vocatione efficaci* (Edinburgh, 1597); Johannes Scharpius, *Cursus theologicus* (Geneva, 1620); and Lucas Trelcatius, *Scholastica et methodica locorum communium institutio* (London, 1604), the *locus de scriptura sacra* took its form from the issues faced in the polemic.

14. Schnedermann, p. 31; cf. Francis Junius, *Theses tbeologicae de variis doctrinae Christianae capitibus*, in *Opera theologica* (Geneva? 1608), vol. 1, cols. 1592 et seq. and Franciscus Gomarus, *Disputationes et Tractatus theologicus*, in *Opera theologica omnia* (Amsterdam, 1644), pars III.

15. Amandus Polanus von Polansdorf, *Syntagma theologiae Christianae* (Geneva, 1617), II.xxxvii (p. 74, cols. 2 ff.).

16. Polanus, *Syntagma*, I.xxxvii (p. 75, col. 2).

17. Polanus, *Syntagma*, "Illa Eliae Levitae narratio, historiae verae fidem non meretur. Nam evidentibus argumentis constat, puncta vocalis et puncta distinguentia quae accentus vocantur, in libris Veteris Testamenti non esse demum a Judaeis Tyberiadis excogitata, sed ab ipso Mose et Prophetis adscripta . . . puncta vocalia sunt animae syllabarum et vocum atque adeo vivae pronunciationis."

18. Johannes Buxtorf Sr., *Tiberias sive commentarius Masorethicus triplex: historicus, didacticus, criticus, Ad illustrationem operis biblici Basiliensis conscriptus, quo primum historia Masoretharum Tiberiensium, sive a quibus Masora conscripta sit, excutitur. . . .* Recognitus . . . a Johanne Buxtorfio Fil. (Basel, 1665); cf. Ginzburg, p. 52.

19. Buxtorf, *Tiberias*, cap. viii on the Talmud, cap. iii on the great synagogue, and cap. v on the Massoretic tradition.

20. Buxtorf, *Tiberias*, cap. ix.

21. Buxtorf, *Tiberias*, cap. xi: "An autem ipsimet viri synagogae magnae, Vocalium et Accentum notas primo his invenerint, aut ab aliis inventas, sed in usu neglectas, restauraverint et perfecerint, ac Masoram de iis quoque conscribi curarint, facile nec dici, nec probari facile potest. Supra per complura exempla declarare conati sumus, Masorethas istos, qui voces Vocalibus et accentibus vestitas, recensuerunt, non videri simul et punctorum vocalium inventores, et istarum Notarum censoriarum authores fuisse."

22. Buxtorf, *Tiberias*, cap. ix.

23. Louis Cappel, *Arcanum punctationis revelatum, sive de punctorum vocalium et accentum apud Hebraeos vera et germanae Antiquitate*. Libri duo. in *Ludovici Capelli Commentarii et notae criticae in Vetus Testamentum* (Amsterdam, 1689), pp. 697–790. On this point, see *Arcanum punctationis revelatum*, II.ix.

24. Cappel, *Arcanum punctationis*, II.x.5.

25. Cappel, *Arcanum punctationis*, II.xvi.1–3.

26. Cappel, *Arcanum punctationis*, II.xxii.i.

27. Cappel, *Arcanum punctationis*, II.xxii.2: "Atque sic imprudentes Pontificiis rem longe gratissimam faciunt, eorumque causam agunt strenue. Nam ad majorem quem illis ultro dant isti Theologi, nempe si *puncta sunt a Masorethis, textus Hebraici auctoritas est mere humana*, Pontificii subsumunt, *atqui puncta sunt a Masorethis*, Ergo etc. Hanc minorem longe evidentibus demonstrare possunt Pontificii adversus Theologos illos (ut manifestum esse potest ex iis quae in priore hujus Diatribes parte dicta sunt) quam possunt Theologi isti eius contradictoriam adversus Pontificos probare, uti ex iis quae hac posteriore huius Diatribes parte diximus. liquere cuilibet potest. Satius est ergo concedendo minorem, Majoris consequentiam negare, quam consequentiam illam concedendo, minorem negare, cum minore ista facile demonstrare potest." The italics are Cappel's. The irony of Cappel's position is that he sought to strengthen the Reformed position rather than undermine it, while his brethren in the faith saw his entire work as damaging to doctrine.

28. Cappel, *Arcanum punctationis*, II.xvii.5: "Cum dico a Masorethis Tiberiensibus excogitata esse puncta et consonis addita . . . hoc duntaxat volo, expressam esse ab iis notulis a se excogitatis. lectionem sacri textus, quae tum ubique inter judaeos obtinebat, quem ipsi edocti fuerant a suis magistris scholastica institutione, atqui orali, et πατροπαραδότω traditione ab iis acceperant, quem lectionem credebant Judaci antiquae Mosaicae et Propheticae authenticae conformam esse."

29. Cappel, *Arcanum punctationis*, II.xxii.13 and II.xxvii.2.

30. Cappel, *Critica sacra, sive De variis quae in sacris Veteris Testamenti libris occurrunt lectionibus libri sex* (Paris, 1650), VI.v.11: "Satis ergo est quod eadem salutaris doctrina quae fuit a Mose, prophetis, apostolis, et evangelistis in suis αὐτογράφοι" primum literis consignata, eadem omnino pariter in textibus Graeco et Hebraco, et in translationibus cum veteribus, tum recentibus, clare, certo et sufficienter inveniatur. Pariter illae omnes una cum textibus Graeco et Hebraeo—sunt et dici possunt authenticae, sacrae, divinae, θεόπνευστοι—respectu materiae." Note that Cappel does not hold the authenticity of the Hebrew and Greek *respectu verborum* and can thus equate the Hebrew and Greek with the ancient versions in terms of relative textual integrity.

31. Cappel, *Critica sacra*, VI.x.

32. Cf. Gijsbertus Voetius, *Selectarum disputationum tbeologicarum*, pars. I–V (Utrecht, 1648–1699), vol. 1, 33: cited in Heinrich Heppe, *Reformed Dogmatics Set Out and Illustrated from the Sources*, foreword by Karl Barth; rev. ed. Ernst Bizer; trans. G. T. Thomson (London: George Allen & Unwin, 1950), p. 27.

33. Andreas Rivetus, *Isagoge, seu introductio generalis ad Scripturam Sacram Veteris et Novi Testamenti. In qua, eius natura, existentia, necessitas, puritas, versionem et interpretationem rationes et modi indagantur*, in *Operum theologicorum*, 3 vols. (Rotterdam, 1651–1660), vol. 2, p. 889, col. 1 to 890, col. i (*Isagoge*, VIII.11–14).

34. Rivetus, *Isagoge*, VIII.14 (p. 890, col. i). The elder Buxtorf, who survived the publication of Cappel's treatise by five years (d. 1629), never published a reply. Defense of the *Tiberias* devolved to his son, Johannes Buxtorf the Younger, who in 1648 published his *Tractatus de punctorum vocalium, et accentum, in libris Veteris Testamenti hebraicis, origine, antiquitate, et authoritate: oppositus arcano pwnctationis revelato Ludovici Cappelli*. Together, despite their ultimate failure to prove the antiquity of the vowel points, the Buxtorfs contributed greatly to the Protestant use and appreciation of the Hebrew language and to defense of the Massoretic text of the Old Testament against its various detractors.

35. Rivetus, *Isagoge*, VII.15 (p. 890, col. 2): "Ipse Genebrardus, petulantissimus bonorum omnium insectator, et veritatis hostis acerrimus." Citing Cappel, Rivetus focuses an the central issue: ". . . principium est, quod autor anonymus probat, cap. 27. *Haberi posse certo verum et germanum textus Ebraici sensum, sine punctorum*, quae masorethica vocat, *subsidio*" (italics in Rivetus text).

36. Rivetus, *Isagoge*, VIII.12 (p. 889, col. 2): "omnes fere Pontificos in eo consentiunt, puncta Ebracorum esse inventum humanum, et quidem Judaeorum post Christum adventum, adversus Christum, et pietatem Christianam male affectorum."

37. Rivetus, *Isagoge*, VIII.15 (p. 890, col. 2).

38. Rivetus, *Isagoge*, VIII.18 (p. 891, col. i): "verus Scripturae sensus, vel sententia Sp. Sancti, in rebus ad salutem necessariis. . . . Sed status controversiae is est; an nulla hoc tempore reperiantur exemplaria Ebraica eo usque pura, ut ex collatione, in omnibus ad salutem necessariis veritas deprehendi possit, lectiones quam Sp. Sanctus suis amanuensibus dictavit."

39. John Weemse, *The Christian Synagogue, wherein is contained the diverse reading, the right poynting, translation, and collation of scripture with scripture*, 2 pts. (London, 1623), p. 38; in the edition of 1630, p. 37. On Weemse's thought, see Jai Sung Shim, *Biblical Hermeneutics and Hebraism in the Early Seventeenth-Century as Reflected in the Work of John Weemse (1579–1636)* (Ph. D. dissertation, Calvin Theological Seminary, 1998).

40. John Weemse, *The Christian Synagogue*, in *The Workes of Mr. J. Weemse*, 3 vols. (London, 1636), vol. 1, p. 48.

41. Weemse, *Christian Synagogue*, pp. 49–50.

42. Brian Walton, *Prolegomena*, in *Biblia sacra polyglotta, complectentia textus originales Hebraicum, cum Pentateucho Samaritano, Chaldaicum, Graecum*, 6 vols. (London, 1653–1657), vol. 1: see, in particular, iii.8 and iii.42.

43. Walton, *Prolegomena*, vii.1; cf. vi.8–10, 12.

44. Opposition even to Walton's very scholarly and highly constructive adaptation of Levita's and Cappel's theories was intense. Even the great philologist John Lightfoot—who had participated in the editing of the Samaritan Pentateuch for the London Polyglot—differed violently with Walton over the origin of the vowel points: see his *Horae hebraicae et talmudicae: impensae, I. in chorographiam aliquam terrae israeliticae. II. in evangelium S. Matthei* (Cambridge, 1658), pars 1, cap. lxxxi. Among the theologians, John Owen was particularly dismayed by Walton's advocacy of Levita and Cappel. He responded to the new hermeneutic in his *Of the Divine Original, Authority, Selfevidencing Light, and Power of the Scriptures: with an answer to that inquiry, how we know the scriptures to be the Word of God. Also,* A *Vindication of the Purity and Integrity of the Hebrew and Greek Texts of the Old and New Testament; in some considerations on the Prolegomena and Appendix to the late Biblia Polyglotta* (Oxford, 1659).

45. Francis Turretin, *Institutio theologiae elencticae* (Geneva, 1679–1685; a new edition, Edinburgh: John Lowe, 1848); Johann Heinrich Heidegger, *Corpus theologiae christianae* (Zürich, 1700); and *Formula Consensus Helvetica, in Collectio Confessionum in Ecclesiis Reformatis Publicatarum*, ed. H. A. Niemeyer (Leipzig: Julius Klinkhardt, 1840), pp. 729–739. For an excellent discussion of the *Formula*, with further bibliography, see Philip Schaff, *The Creeds of Christendom, with a History and Critical Notes*, 3 vols. 6th ed. (New York, 1919), vol. 1, pp. 477–489.

46. Turretin, *Institutio*, II.xi.3.

47. Turretin, *Institutio*, II.xi.3; cf. Heidegger, *Corpus theologiae*, II.xcvii: "Est autem authentia Scripturae dignitas illa eximia, secundum et propter quam illa pro verbo Dei infallibili et αὐτοπίστῳ pro potente nos obligate ad omne illud credendum et praestandum, quod credi praestarique jubet, habetur. Quae quidem . . . primo, immediate, irrefragabiliter et plenissime tum quoad res, tum quoad verba singula et idioma textui originali."

48. Turretin, *Institutio*, II.xi.5: "Denique *Authentia* bifariam spectatur, vel *materialiter* quoad *res enunciatas*, vel *formaliter* quoad verba et *modum enunciandi*. Non quaeritur hic de authentia priori sensu, hanc enim Versionibus non denegamus, quando cum fontibus consentiunt, sed tantum posteriori quae solis fontibus competit." Cf. Heidegger, II.xcix: "Tametsi vero authentia versionibus inest *quoad res*, non *absolute*, sed *relate*, eo quo diximus sensu, tamen quoad *idioma*, quo res caetera Divinae exprimuntur, nulla versio, quantumvis exquisita, et fontibus proxima

absolute authentica est, ut praedicationis, expositionis, et aliarum versionum norma, a qua nullo praetextu discedere liceat."

49. Turretin, *Institutio*, II.xi.7: "si Editio Hebraea V. et Graeca N.T. non est authentica nulla erit editio authentica. . . . Sic nullum esset Dei Verbum authenticum in Ecclesia, nullus esset contentionum finis, quia nulla esset certa regula fidei et morum in qua omnino sit acquiescendum."

50. Heidegger, *Corpus theologiae*, II.xlvii: "Nam quoad *varias lectiones. . . . Keri* et *Cethibh* nomine distinctas, nullus falsationis conatus fuit, cum semper Masorethae optima fide variam a Scriptura lectionem, ex Codicibus variis collatis, vel ex Anagnostarum recepta in Synagogis lectione, observatam, relicto Ecclesiae secundum analogiam fidei et contextus ac locorum parallelorum judicio, repraesentaverint." Cf. Turretin, II.xi.8: "*Variae Lectiones* quae occurrunt in Scriptura, authentiam eius non evertunt, quia facile deprehenduntur et dijudicantur, partim ex cohaerentia Textus, partim ex collatione meliorum Codicum."

51. Turretin, *Institutio*, II.xi.11; Heidegger, *Corpus theologiae*, II.c, makes a similar comment —one of the few examples of levity in the orthodox system.

52. Turretin, *Institutio*, II.xi.12; Heidegger, more forcibly than Turretin, denies Massoretic origin to the points, citing Deuteronomy 27:8, in which Moses is ordered by God to write the Law on stone "very clearly": divine clarity necessitates the presence of the vowels (*Corpus theologiae*, II.xlviii). Heidegger simply reiterates the position of the Buxtorfs as his own; but he also acknowledges the opinion of "others" taught neither by Levita nor "apud nos" who make the distinction between the *figura* and the *potestas*: for even if the vowels were not always written they were always a part of Hebrew speech (*Corpus theologiae*, II.xlix); cf. *Formula Consensus Helvetica*, canon 11, summing up the entire argument: "In specie autem Hebraicus Veteris Testamenti Codex, quem ex traditione in Ecclesiae Iudaicae, *cum olim Oracula Dei commisa sunt* (Rom.3.2), accepimus hodieque retinemus, tum quoad consonas, tum quoad vocalia, sive puncta ipsa, sive punctorum saltem potestatem, et tum quoad res, tum quoad verba θεόπνευτος, ut fidei ei vitae nostrae, una cum Codice Novi Testamenti sit Canon unicus et illibatus, ad cuius normam, ceu Lydium lapidum, universae, quae extant Versiones, sive orientales, sive occidentales exigendae, et sic ubi deflectunt, revocandae sunt." Note how the *Formula*, written chiefly by Heidegger, strives toward a more inclusive statement of doctrine than his *Corpus theologiae*: the object of both formulations, more irenically accomplished by the *Formula*, like the object of Turretin's arguments is to take the problem of the origin of the vowel points, whatever its solution, out of hermeneutical debate.

53. Turretin, *Institutio*, II.xi.12.

54. Turretin, *Institutio*, II.xi.13.

55. Turretin, *Institutio*, II.xii.1–3; cf. II.x.5; and Heidegger, *Corpus theologiae*, II.xliii–xlvi. Both writers argue for the faithful and accurate transmission of the text and value highly the work of the Massoretes. This is far more subtle than earlier solutions, like Owen's denunciation of the Massoretes and attempted logical proof of the priority of the Hebrew and the antiquity of the vowels; see his A *Vindication of the Purity and Integrity of the Hebrew and Greek Texts*, in *Works* vol. 16, pp. 381–388.

56. Turretin, *Institutio*, II.xii.10: "Si non adstricti sumus ad lectionem hodiernum Textus Hebraici, sed vera lectio authentica petenda est partim ex collatione veterum Versionum, partim ex nostromet judicio et facultate στοχαστικη, ut nullus alius alius Canon lectionis authenticae sit, quam commodior sensus qui nobis ita videtur; Constitutio lectionis authenticae erit humani arbitrii, et rationis opus, non Spiritus S."

57. Turretin, *Institutio*, II.xii.4: "Sed longe alia est recepta et communis in Ecclesiis nostris sententia; Non alium scilicet agnoscendum esse Codicem praeter Hebraicum hodiernum pro Authentico, ad quem ceu Lydium lapidem Versiones omnes tam veteres quam recentiores exigendae sint, et sicubi ab eo deflectunt corrigendae sint; non vero ex illis ipsum esse emendandum. Quamvis vero Codices varios inter se conferri posse ac debere censeant, ut variae

lectiones, quae descriptorum vel librariorum incuria oriri potuerunt discernantur, et menda quae in his vel illis Codicibus occurrunt corrigantur."

58. Turretin, *Institutio*, II.xii.13; cf. II.xi.8–10; Heidegger, *Corpus theologiae* II.xlvii.

59. After the long battle to establish the correct text *quoad verba* as well as *quoad res*, the orthodox still recognize that "Scriptura non in verbis, sed in verborum sensu consistit" (Heidegger, *Corpus theologiae*, margin at II.lxxviii) and "Non ergo Scriptura in characteribus et signis, seu cortice literarum ac syllabarum, sed in revelatione per externa haec organa facta, verbi scripti significatione, hoc est vero ac genuino *sensu*, ex mente Dei authoris, ceu medulla et essentia sua, consistit. Absque hoc enim est Scriptura non Verbum Dei, sed verborum tantum strepitus et ἄδηλος φωνὴ *incerta vox* est, *qualem si tuba dederit, nemo ad bellum accenditur*, I Cor. XIV.8."

60. Leonhardus Rijssenius, *Summa theologiae didactico-elencticae* (Bern, 1690; Frankfurt and Leipzig, 1731), II.xix, controversia, objectio 1 et resp. N.B., the *editio princeps* appears to be the 1690 Bern edition, reissued in Bern in 1702, and published also in Edinburgh in 1692; other versions of the work, entitled *Compendium theologiae didactico-elencticae* appeared in Amsterdam in 1695 and Utrecht, Leiden, and Amsterdam in 1731.

61. Johannes Marckius, *Compendium theologiae christianae didactico-elencticum* (Amsterdam, 1690), II.viii; Pettus van Mastricht, *Theoretico-practica theologia* (Utrecht, 1724), II.ii.41: what Mastricht here discusses is the purity of the text against the contrary allegations of "Mohammedans" and "Papists"—and he simply states that the Massorah is not corrupt.

10. Henry Ainsworth and the Development of Protestant Exegesis

1. Daniel Neal, *The History of the Puritans; or, Protestant Nonconformists; from the Reformation in 1517 to the Revolution in 1688*, new edition, 5 vols. (London: W. Baynes and Son, 1822), vol. 2, pp. 41–42.

2. William E. A. Axon and Ernest Axon, "Henry Ainsworth, the Puritan Commentator," in *Transactions of the Lancashire and Cheshire Antiquarian Society*, 6 (1888), pp. 42–57; and William E. A. Axon, "Ainsworth, Henry" s.v. in *Dictionary of National Biography*; also see the memoir in *Two Treatises by Henry Ainsworth* (Edinburgh, 1789); John David Finley, *A Comparison of the Concepts of Jean Calvin and Henry Ainsworth on the Church* (M.A. thesis, Northeast Missouri State University, 1973); Michael E. Moody, "A Man of a Thousand: the Reputation and Character of Henry Ainsworth, 1569–70 to 1622," in *Huntington Library Quarterly*, 45/3 (1982), pp. 200–214; and idem, "The Apostasy of Henry Ainsworth: A Case-Study in Early Separatist Historiography," in *Proceedings of the American Philosophical Society*, 131/1 (1987), pp. 15–31; also note Frederick J. Powicke, *Henry Barrow, Separatist (1550?–1593) and the Exiled Church of Amsterdam (1593–1622)* (London: James Clarke, 1900), pp. 232–315, passim; Marshall M. Knappen, *Tudor Puritanism: A Chapter in the History of Idealism* (Chicago: University of Chicago Press, 1939), pp. 314, 330; William Haller, *The Rise of Puritanism: Or, the Way to the New Jerusalem as Set Forth in Pulpit and Press from Thomas Cartwright to John Lilburne and John Milton, 1570–1643* (New York: Columbia University Press, 1938; repr. New York: Harper & Row, 1957), pp. 187–262; and Michael E. Moody, *A Critical Edition of George Johnson's* A Discourse of Some Troubles and Excommunications in the Banished English Church at Amsterdam, 1603 (Ph.D. dissertation, Claremont Graduate School, 1979).

3. Frederick W. Farrar, *History of Interpretation* (1886; repr. Grand Rapids, MI: Baker Book House, 1961), p. 33.

4. Ludwig Diestel, *Geschichte des Alten Testamentes in der christlichen Kirche* (Jena: Mauke, 1869), p. 637: N.B., the Cartwright noted by Diestel is undoubtedly not the famous Thomas Cartwright, teacher of William Perkins and other notable Puritan divines, but Christopher Cartwright, whose *Electa thargumico-rabbinica; sive Annotationes in Genesin* (London, 1648) and

Electa thargumico-rabbinica; sive Annotationes in Exodum (London, 1658) were eventually inserted in the reissued *Critici Sacri* of 1698.

5. Cf. Moody, "The Apostasy of Henry Ainsworth," p. 16. The older sources, including Axon's essay in the Dictionary of National Biography give 1571, but Moody succeeded in finding Ainsworth's baptismal record, from the previous year.

6. William Whitaker, *A Disputation on Holy Scripture, against the Papists, especially Bellarmine and Stapleton*, trans. and ed. by William Fitzgerald (Cambridge: Cambridge University Press, 1849).

7. Moody, "The Apostasy of Henry Ainsworth," p. 16.

8. Cf. John Venn, *A Biographical History of Gonville and Caius College, 1349–1897*, 4 vols. in 5 (Cambridge: Cambridge University Press, 1897), vol. 1, p. 132.

9. On separatism, see Knappen, *Tudor Puritanism*, pp. 303–316; Haller, *The Rise of Puritanism*, pp. 173–194; Stephen J. Brachlow, "More Light on John Robinson and the Separatist Tradition," in *Fides et Historia*, 13 (1980), pp. 6–22; idem, "John Robinson and the Lure of Separatism in Pre-Revolutionary England," in *Church History*, 50 (1981), pp. 288–301; and Timothy George, *John Robinson and the English Separatist Tradition* (Macon, GA: Mercer University Press, 1982).

10. Cf. the discussion in Timothy George, "Predestination in a Separatist Context, the Case of John Robinson," *Sixteenth Century Journal*, 15/1 (1984), pp. 73–85.

11. Powicke, *Henry Barrow*, pp. 238–239; for a discussion of the place of women in the English Separatist church, see Richard L. Greaves, "The Role of Women in Early English Nonconformity," in *Church History*, 52/3 (1983), pp. 299–311.

12. Henry Ainsworth, *An Animadversion to Mr. Richard Clyftons Advertisement* (Amsterdam, 1613), p. 134.

13. Powicke, *Henry Barrow*, p. 256.

14. Axon, "Ainsworth, Henry," p. 192; cf. Powicke, *Henry Barrow*, pp. 256–257.

15. Henry Ainsworth, *The Trying Out of the Truth: Begunn and Prosequuted in Certayn Letters or Passages between Iohn Aynsworth and Henry Aynsworth; the one pleading for, the other against the present religion of the Church of Rome* (London, 1615), cf. the title page: "The chief things here handled, are. 1. Of Gods word and scriptures, whither they be a sufficient rule of our faith. 2. Of the Scriptures expounded by the Church; and of unwritten traditions. 3. Of the Church of Rome, whither it be the true Catholike Church, and her sentence to be received, as the sertayn truth."

16. Ainsworth, *The Trying Out of the Truth*, p. 3.

17. Ainsworth, *The Trying Out of the Truth*, pp. 87, 93, 95.

18. Axon, "Ainsworth, Henry," p. 194.

19. Cf. Neal, *History of the Puritans*, II, p. 41 with Henry M. Dexter, *Congregationalism of the Last Three Hundred Years* (New York: Harper & Brothers, 1880), p. 345.

20. John Paget, *An Arrow Against the Separation of the Brownists* (Amsterdam, 1618), pp. 91–92; on Paget's probable reliability, see Moody, "The Apostasy of Henry Ainsworth," pp. 22–28.

21. Neal, *History of the Puritans*, vol. 2, p. 43; cf. the slightly different account in Benjamin Brook, *The Lives of the Puritans: Containing a Biographical Account of those Divines who Distinguished themselves in the Cause of Religious Liberty, from the Reformation under Queen Elizabeth, to the Act of uniformity, in 1662*, 3 vols. (London: James Black, 1813), vol. 2, p. 299.

22. Neal, *History of the Puritans*, vol. 2, p. 42.

23. Neal, *History of the Puritans*, vol. 2, p. 42, note; cf. Brook, Lives of the Puritans, vol. 2, p. 299.

24. Powicke, Henry *Barrow*, p. 258.

25. Henry Ainsworth, *A Seasonable Discourse, or, A Censure upon a Dialogue of the Anabaptists* (London, 1623).

26. Axon, "Henry Ainsworth, the Puritan Commentator," pp. 54–55.

27. H[enry] A[insworth], *The Book of Psalmes: Englished both in Prose and Metre. With Annotations, opening the words and sentences, by conference with other scriptures* (Amsterdam, 1612), preface, fol. *2 recto.

28. Ainsworth, *Psalmes*, preface, fol. *2 recto.

29. Ainsworth, *Psalmes*, p. 5.

30. Ainsworth, *Psalmes*, p. 22.

31. Cf. W. Schwarz, *Principles and Problems of Biblical Translation: Some Reformation controversies and their Background* (Cambridge: Cambridge University Press, 1955), pp. 84–85.

32. Ainsworth, *Psalmes*, preface, fol. *2 recto.

33. Schwarz, *Principles and Problems*, pp. 46, 61–91: note Schwarz's useful distinction (p. 46) between "the traditional view" of translation, which accepts "the whole tradition in its historical development"; "the philological view," which accepts "the oldest tradition only, later development being rejected"; and "the inspirational view," which embodies "the complete denial of any authoritative tradition."

34. On Reuchlin's interest in Jewish exegesis, see Schwarz, *Principles and Problems*, pp. 77–85.

35. Ainsworth, *Psalmes*, preface, fol. *2 recto.

36. *The Holy Scriptures of the Olde and Newe Testamente; with the Apocrypha: faithfully Translated from the Hebrue and Greke* by Miles Coverdale, sometime Lord Bishop of Exeter (Zürich, 1535; repr. London: Samuel Bagster, 1838), in loc.

37. *The Bible and Holy Scriptures conteyned in the Olde and Newe Testament. Translated according to the Ebrue and Greke, and conferred with the best translations in diuers languages. With moste profitable annotations upon all the hard places* (Geneva, 1560; facsimile edition, Madison: University of Wisconsin Press, 1969), in loc.

38. *The Holy Bible, conteyning the Olde Testament and the Newe. Authorized and appointed to be read in churches* (London, 1591), in. loc.

39. Ainsworth, *Psalmes*, p. 324.

40. Geneva is identical except that it offers "cruel man" instead of "violent man."

41. Ainsworth, *Psalmes*, p. 328.

42. Ainsworth, *Psalmes*, p. 10.

43. Ainsworth, *Psalmes*, p. 130.

44. Ainsworth, *Psalmes*, p. 25.

45. Ainsworth, *Psalmes*, pp. 46, 52, 119.

46. Cf. Richard A. Muller, "William Perkins and the Protestant Exegetical Tradition: Interpretation, Style and Method in the Commentary on Hebrews 11," in William Perkins, *A Cloud of Faithful Witnesses: Commentary on Hebrews 11*, edited by Gerald T. Sheppard, *Pilgrim Classic Commentaries*, vol. 3 (New York: Pilgrim Press, 1991), pp. 71–94.

47. On the exegetical tendencies of the Federal School, see Diestel, *Geschichte des Alten Testamentes*, pp. 527–534; and Wilhelm Gass, *Geschichte der Protestantischen Dogmatik in ihrem Zusammenhange mit der Theologie überhaupt*, 4 vols. (Berlin: Georg Reimer, 1854–1867), vol. 2, pp. 289–290.

48. Cf. James S. Preus, *From Shadow to Promise: Old Testament Interpretation from Augustine to the Young Luther* (Cambridge, MA: Harvard University Press, 1969), pp. 67–69, 138–142.

49. Cf. Richard A. Muller, "The Hermeneutic of Promise and Fulfillment in Calvin's Exegesis of the Old Testament Prophecies of the Kingdom," in *The Bible in the Sixteenth Century*, edited, with an introduction by David C. Steinmetz (Durham, NC: Duke University Press, 1990), pp. 68–82.

50. David Dickson, *A Commentary on the Psalms*, 3 vols. (1653–1655; reissued in 2 vols., London: Banner of Truth, 1965), vol. 2, pp. 4, 32, 76, 98.

51. Dickson, *A Commentary on the Psalms*, p. 2.

52. Dickson, *A Commentary on the Psalms*, p. xxix.

53. Matthew Henry, *The Exposition of the Old and New Testaments* (1706ff, reissued in 3 vols., London: Fisher, 1840), vol. 2, pp. 142–145 (Ps. 2), 158 (Ps. 8), 173–174 (Ps. 17:8–15), 175 (Ps. 18: 17–19).

54. Henry, *The Exposition of the Old and New Testaments*, vol. 2, pp. 142, 466–467.

55. Henry, *The Exposition of the Old and New Testaments*, vol. 2, pp. 139–140.

56. John Calvin, *Commentary on the Book of Psalms*, trans. James Anderson, 5 vols. (Calvin Translation Society, 1845–1849; repr. Grand Rapids, MI: Baker Book House, 1979), Psalm 18, argument (p. 256).

57. Calvin, *Commentary on Book of the Psalms*, Psalm 18, on the superscription (*CTS Psalms*, I, p. 257).

58. Calvin, *Commentary on Book of the Psalms*, Psalm 20, argument (*CTS Psalms*, I, p. 333).

59. Calvin, *Commentary on the Book of Psalms*, Psalm 2, argument (*CTS Psalms*, I, p. 9).

60. Calvin, *Commentary on the Book of Psalms*, preface (*CTS Psalms*, I, p. xxxvii).

61. Calvin, *Commentary on the Book of Psalms*, preface (*CTS Psalms*, I, p. xxxvii).

62. Calvin, *Commentary on the Book of Psalms*, Psalm 110, argument (*CTS Psalms*, IV, pp. 295-296).

63Calvin, *Commentary on the Book of Psalms*, Psalm 110:4 (*CTS Psalms*, IV, p. 304).

64. Cf. John Calvin, *Commentaries on the First Book of Moses called Genesis*, trans. John King, 2 vols. (Calvin Translation Society, 1847–1850; repr. Grand Rapids, MI: Baker Book House, 1979), vol. 1, pp. 386–392; Ainsworth, *Psalmes*, pp. 280–282; Matthew Poole, *A Commentary on the Holy Bible*, 2 vols. (London, 1683–1685; reissued in 3 vols., London: Banner of Truth, 1962), vol. 1, p. 35; II, pp. 171–174; Dickson, *A Commentary on the Psalms*, pp. 295–300; Henry, *Commentary on the Whole Bible*, vol. 1, pp. 56–57; vol. 2, pp. 389–392.

65. Ainsworth, *Psalmes*, fol. *2 verso.

66. Ainsworth, *Psalmes*, fol. *2 verso.

67. Ainsworth, *Psalmes*, p. 4.

68. Ainsworth, *Psalmes*, p. 21, citing Matt. 19:29; Luke 18:29; Mark 10:29 and then Matt 21:15, 16; Mark 11:18. N.B., Ainsworth's versification counts the superscription as verse 1: for the cited verses, Calvin and the King James Version give 1 and 2, 5 and 6.

69. Calvin, *Commentary on the Book of Psalms*, Psalm 8 (*CTS Psalms*, vol. 1, pp. 99–106).

70. Cf. Henry, Commentary on the Whole Bible, vol. 2, p. 158.

71. Ainsworth, *Psalmes*, p. 21.

72. Ainsworth, *Psalmes*, p. 21.

73. Ainsworth, *Psalmes*, p. 22.

74. Ainsworth, *Psalmes*, p. 48.

75. Ainsworth, *Psalms*, p. 342.

76. Cf. Ainsworth's doctrinal exposition in *The Trying Out of the Truth*, pp. 156–182, passim, with Ainsworth, *A Defense of the Holy Scriptures, Worship, and Ministrie, used in the Christian Churches separated from Antichrist* (Amsterdam: Giles Thorp, 1609), pp. 23–45.

77. Cf. Gerald T. Sheppard, "Between Reformation and Modern Commentary: The Perception of the Scope of Biblical Books," in William Perkins, *A Commentary on Galatians*, ed. Sheppard, pp. 42–66.

78. Whitaker, *A Disputation*, V.ii (p. 404); cf. Maccovius, Loci communes, cap. vii (pp. 50–51); and note Charles K. Cannon, "William Whitaker's *Disputatio de Sacra Scriptura*: A Sixteenth-Century Theory of Allegory," in *Huntington Library Quarterly*, 25 (1962), pp. 129–138; and Victor Harris, "Allegory to Analogy in the Interpretation of Scripture," in *Philological Quarterly*, 45 (1966), pp. 1–23.

79. Whitaker, *Disputation*, V.ii (p. 409).

80. Cf. Muller, "The Hermeneutic of Promise and Fulfillment," pp. 76–79, 81–82; with Brevard S. Childs, "The Sensus Literalis of Scripture: An Ancient and Modern Problem," in *Beiträge zur alttestamentlichen Theologie*, ed. Donner, Hanhart, and Smend (Göttingen: Vandenhoeck & Ruprecht, 1977), pp. 80–93.

81. E.g., Andrew Willet, *Hexapla in Genesin* (Cambridge, 1605; second ed., enlarged, 1608); Hexapla in Exodum (London, 1608); *Hexapla in Leviticum* (London, 1631); *Hexapla in Danielem* (Cambridge, 1610); and *Hexapla: That is, a Six Fold Commentarie upon the Epistle to the Romans* (Cambridge, 1620).

82. Thus, e.g., Andrew Willet, *Hexapla in Genesin & Exodum: that is, A sixfold commentary upon the two first Bookes of Moses . . . wherein these translations are compared together: 1. The Chalde. 2. The Septuagint. 3. The vulgar latine. 4. Pagnine. 5. Montanus. 6. Iunius. 7. Vatablus. 8. The great english Bible. 9. The Geneva edition. And 10. The Hebrew originall. Together with a sixfold use of every Chapter, shewing 1. The Method or Argument: 2. The divers readings: 3. The explanation of difficult places and doubtfull places: 4. The places of doctrine: 5. Places of confutation: 6. Morall observations*, fourth edition (London, 1633), pp. 16, 18; cf. the extended description of Willet's method in Muller, *Post-Reformation Reformed Dogmatics*, vol. 2, pp. 513–514, and Peter William van Kleek, *Hermeneutics and Theology in the Seventeenth Century: The Contribution of Andrew Willet* (Th.M. thesis, Calvin Theological Seminary, 1998).

83. H[enry] A[insworth], *Annotations upon the first book of Moses, called Genesis* (Amsterdam, 1616); also Henry Ainsworth, *Annotations upon the Second Book of Moses, called Exodus* (Amsterdam, 1617).

84. Willet, *Hexapla in Genesin*, p. 137.

85. Cf. Willet, *Hexapla in Genesin*, p. 137 with Pseudo-Augustine, *Quaestiones Veteris et Novi Testamenti*, ch. 109 (on Melchizedek), in *PL* 35, cols. 2324–2330, and *De Haeresibus ad QuodvultDeum liber unus*, cap. 34 (on the Melchizedekians), in *PL* 42, col. 31; Willet was correct in his judgment of the *Quaestiones*, but mistaken in his estimate of Augustine's comments on the Melchizedekians, a heretical sect of the second century.

86. Willet, *Hexapla in Genesin*, p. 137.

87. Calvin, *Commentaries on the First Book of Moses*, 14:18 (*CTS Genesis*, I, p. 388).

88. Willet, *Hexapla in Genesin*, p. 137.

89. Willet, *Hexapla in Genesin*, p. 137.

90. Cf. Calvin, *Commentaries on the First Book of Moses*, 14:18 (*CTS Genesis*, I, p. 387) with Poole, *A Commentary*, vol. 1, p. 35; vol. 3, pp. 836–837; Henry, *Commentary on the Whole Bible*, vol. 1, pp. 56–57; vol. 3, p. 1257: Poole and Henry, the latter referring to "the most received opinion," assume that Melchizedek was a Canaanite king who, despite the paganism of his neighbors, had continued to worship the true God. Poole finds his definitive argument in the fact that Shem did have a known genealogy while Henry, looking back to Calvin, finds his answer in the absence of any account that Shem had migrated to Canaan.

91. Willet, *Hexapla in Genesin*, pp. 137–138; the citation of Syracides is to Ben Sirach, i.e., Ecclesiasticus 49:16.

92. Willet, *Hexapla in Genesin*, p. 138.

93. Willet, *Hexapla in Genesin*, p. 138.

94. Ainsworth, *Annotations upon the Book of . . . Genesis*, in loc.

95. Cf. Ainsworth, *Annotations upon the Book of . . . Genesis*, in loc. with Willet, *Hexapla in Genesin*, p. 139.

96. Willet, *Hexapla in Genesin*, p. 142.

97. Willet, *Hexapla in Genesin*, p. 143.

98. Ainsworth, *Annotations upon the Book of . . . Genesis*, in loc., verse 18.

99. Ainsworth, *Annotations upon the Book of . . . Genesis*, in loc., verse 18.

100. Ainsworth, *Annotations upon the Book of . . . Genesis*, in loc., verses 18 and 19; cf.

Ainsworth, Psalmes, p. 281, where the Psalm, particularly vv. 2–3, is understood christologically, but the reference to Melchizedek is directed primarily toward the character of priesthood.

101. Cf. *Annotations upon all the Books of the Old and New Testament, wherein the Text is Explained, Doubts Resolved, Scriptures Parallelled, and Various Readings observed.* By the Joynt-Labour of certain Learned Divines . . . (London, 1645), in loc.: "Most of the Jewish Rabbins and many learned Christians take this *Melchizedek* to be *Shem*; and for the time of their living it is probable enough, for Melchizedek lived seventie yeares after Abrahams coming into Canaan: but other learned, both Jewish and Christian Writers, conceive that he was a Prince, and Priest of another kindred from that of Abraham, Heb. 7.6. extraordinarily raised up by God of the Canaanites, and brought in without mention of parents, Originall, or end, without any predecessour, or successour in the Priesthood, as a Type of the Royall, and eternall Priesthood of Christ, Heb. 7. vers. 17, 21. which cannot be said of *Shem* whose Genealogie is set downe in Scripture." But note Cartwright, *Annotations in Genesin*, p. 118, in which only the rabbinic identification of Melchizedek as Shem is noted and without comment.

102. Willet, *Hexapla in Genesin*, p. 139.

103. Cf. Moshe Goshen-Gottstein, "Foundations of Biblical Philology in the Seventeenth Century: Christian and Jewish Dimensions," in *Jewish Thought in the Seventeenth Century*, ed. Isadore Twersky and Bernard Septimus (Cambridge, MA: Harvard University Press, 1987), pp. 77–94, with Diestel, *Geschichte des Alten Testamentes*, pp. 443–450.

104. See, e.g., John Bowman, "A Seventeenth Century Bill of 'Rights' for Jews," in *Jewish Quarterly Review*, 39 (1949), pp. 379–395; James Parkes, "Jewish-Christian Relations in England," in V. D. Lipman, ed., *Three Centuries of Anglo-Jewish History* (Cambridge: W. Heffer, 1961), pp. 149–167.

11. The Covenant of Works and the Stability of Divine Law

1. Westminster Confession, I.6, in Philip Schaff, *The Creeds of Christendom, with a History and Critical Notes*, 3 vols., sixth edition (New York, 1931; repr. Grand Rapids, MI: Baker Book House, 1983), vol. 3, p. 603.

2. See Ernest F. Kevan, *The Grace of Law: A Study in Puritan Theology* (1964; repr. Grand Rapids, MI: Baker Book House, 1976), pp. 111–112.

3. Wilhelmus à Brakel, *ΛΟΓΙΚΗ ΛΑΤΡΕΙΑ, dat is Redelijke Godsdienst in welken de goddelijke Waarheden van het Genade-Verbond worden verklaard . . . alsmede de Bedeeling des Verbonds in het O. en N.T. en de Ontmoeting der Kerk in het N. T. vertoond in eene Verklaring van de Openbaringen aan Johannes*, 3 parts (Dordrecht, 1700; second printing, Leiden: D. Donner, 1893–1894), I, xii.1 (p. 292). I have consulted the translation, *The Christian's Reasonable Service in which Divine Truths concerning the Covenant of Grace are Expounded, Defended against Opposing Parties, and their Practice Advocated*, 4 vols., translated by Bartel Elshout, with a biographical sketch by W. Fieret and an essay on the "Dutch Second Reformation" by Joel Beeke (Ligonier, PA: Soli Deo Gloria Publications, 1992–1995), vol. 1, p. 355.

4. Herman Witsius, *De oeconomia foederum Dei cum hominibus* (Leeuwaarden, 1685); trans. as *The Oeconomy of the Covenants between God and Man*, 3 vols. (London, 1763; second edition, revised and corrected, 1775), "A Pacific Address," in vol. 1, p. 43; cf. e.g., ibid., I.ii.13–15; iii.9–10; iv.4–7. I have followed the translation where possible, making emendations from the Latin text; quotations from Scripture follow the *Statenvertaling* and the Authorized Version, in order to provide a language terminologically conformable to the older theology.

5. Cf. George Park Fisher, "The Augustinian and Federal Theories of Original Sin Compared," in *Discussions in History and Theology* (New York: Scribner, 1880), pp. 355–409; N. Diemer, *Het Scheppingsverbond met Adam bij de Theologen der 16e, 17e en 18e Eeuw in Zwitserland, Duitschland, Nederland en Engeland* (Kampen: J. H. Kok, 1935); Mark W. Karlberg, *The Mosaic*

Covenant and the Concept of Works in Reformed Hermeneutics: A Historical-Critical Analysis with Particular Attention to Early Covenant Eschatology (Ph.D. dissertation, Westminster Theological Seminary, 1980); idem, "Reformed Interpretation of the Mosaic Covenant," in *The Westminster Theological Journal*, 43 (Fall 1980), pp. 1-57; Peter Alan Lillback, "Ursinus Development of the Covenant of Creation: A Debt to Melanchthon or Calvin," in *Westminster Theological Journal*, 43 (1981), pp. 247-288; Michael McGiffert, "From Moses to Adam: the Making of the Covenant of Works," in *Sixteenth Century Journal*, 19/2 (1988), pp. 131-155.

6. Emanuel von Korff, *Die Anfänge der Föderaltheologie und ihre erste Ausgestaltung in Zürich und Holland* (Bonn, 1908); G. Möller, "Föderalismus und Geschichtsbetrachtung im XVII. und XVIII. Jahrhundert," in *Zeitschrift für Kirchengeschichte*, 50 (1931), pp. 393-440; Leonard Trinterud, "The Origins of Puritanism," in *Church History*, 20 (1951), pp. 37-57; Perry Miller, "The Marrow of Puritan Divinity," in *Errand into the Wilderness* (Cambridge, MA: Harvard University Press, 1956), pp. 48-98; idem, *The New England Mind*, 2 vols. (Cambridge, MA: Harvard University Press, 1939-53; repr. Boston: Beacon, 1961); Carl Hutter, *Der Gottesbund in der Heilslehre der Zürcher Theologen Johann Heinrich Heidegger* (Gossau: Pallottiner-Verlag, 1955); Charles S. McCoy, *The Covenant Theology of Johannes Cocceius* (Ph.D. Dissertation, Yale University, 1956); idem, "Johannes Cocceius: Federal Theologian," in *Scottish Journal of Theology*, 16 (1963), pp. 352-370; and idem, *History, Humanity, and Federalism in the Theology and Ethics of Johannes Cocceius* (Philadelphia: Center for the Study of Federalism, Temple University, 1980); Jens Moeller, "The Beginnings of Puritan Covenant Theology," in *Journal of Ecclesiastical History*, 14 (1963), pp. 46-67; Richard Greaves, "The Origins and Early Development of English Covenant Thought," in *The Historian*, 21 (1968), pp. 21-35; J. Wayne Baker, *Heinrich Bullinger and the Covenant: The Other Reformed Tradition* (Athens: Ohio University Press, 1980); Lyle D. Bierma, *The Covenant Theology of Caspar Olevian* (Ph.D. dissertation, Duke University, 1980); idem, "Federal Theology in the Sixteenth Century: Two Traditions?" in *Westminster Theological Journal*, 45 (1983), pp. 304-321; idem, "Covenant or Covenants in the Theology of Olevianus," in *Calvin Theological Journal*, 22 (1987), pp. 228-250; and idem, "The Role of Covenant Theology in Early Reformed Orthodoxy," in *Sixteenth Century Journal*, 21/3 (1990), pp. 453-462; Derk Visser, "The Covenant in Zacharias Ursinus," in *Sixteenth Century Journal*, 18 (1987), pp. 531-544; John Von Rohr, *The Covenant of Grace in Puritan Thought* (Atlanta: Scholars Press, 1986); Geerhardus Vos, "The Doctrine of the Covenant in Reformed Theology," in *Redemptive History and Biblical Interpretation: The Shorter Writings of Geerhardus Vos*, ed. Richard B. Gaffin (Philippsburg, NJ: Presbyterian and Reformed Publishing Co., 1980), pp. 234-267; David N. J. Poole, *The History of the Covenant Concept from the Bible to Johannes Cloppenburg "De Foedere Dei"* (San Francisco: Mellen Research University Press, 1992).

7. Everett H. Emerson, "Calvin and Covenant Theology," in *Church History*, 25 (June 1956), pp. 136-144; Anthony Hoekema, "Calvin's Doctrine of the Covenant of Grace," in *Reformed Review*, 15 (1962), pp. 1-12; idem, "The Covenant of Grace in Calvin's Teaching," in *Calvin Theological Journal*, 2 (1967), pp. 133-161; Lyle D. Bierma, "Federal Theology in the Sixteenth Century: Two Traditions?" in *Westminster Theological Journal*, 45 (1983), pp. 304-321.

8. Robert W. A. Letham, "The *Foedus Operum*: Some Factors Accounting for its Development," in *Sixteenth Century Journal*, 14 (1983), pp. 457-467; David A. Weir, *The Origins of the Federal Theology in Sixteenth-Century Reformation Thought* (Oxford: Clarendon Press, 1990); and see the reviews of Weir by Lyle D. Bierma in *Calvin Theological Journal*, 26 (1991), pp. 483-485, and by Richard A. Muller in *The Journal of Religion*, 72 (1992), pp. 597-598.

9. Peter Allan Lillback, *The Binding of God: Calvin's Role in the Development of Covenant Theology* (Grand Rapids, MI: Baker Book House, 2001).

10. Cf. Kevan, *The Grace of Law*, pp. 167-249; John Von Rohr, "Covenant and Assurance in Early English Puritanism," in *Church History*, 34 (1965), pp. 195-203; idem, *The Covenant*

of Grace in Puritan Thought (Atlanta: Scholars Press, 1986), pp. 53–85, et passim; Richard A. Muller, "Covenant and Conscience in English Reformed Theology: Three Variations on a Seventeenth Century Theme," in *Westminster Theological Journal*, XLII/2 (1980), pp. 308–334.

11. Michael McGiffert, "Grace and Works: the Rise and Division of Covenant Divinity in Elizabethan Puritanism," in *Harvard Theological Review*, 75/4 (1982), pp. 463–502; "From Moses to Adam: the Making of the Covenant of Works," in *Sixteenth Century Journal*, 19/2 (1988), pp. 131–155.

12. Holmes Rolston III, *John Calvin versus the Westminster Confession* (Richmond, VA: John Knox, 1972); idem, "Responsible Man in Reformed Theology: Calvin Versus the *Westminster Confession*," in *Scottish Journal of Theology*, 23 (1970), pp. 129–156; James B. Torrance, "Strengths and Weaknesses of the Westminster Theology," in *The Westminster Confession*, ed. Alisdair Heron (1982), pp. 40–53; idem, "Covenant or Contract? A Study of the Theological Background or Worship in Seventeenth-Century Scotland," in *Scottish Journal of Theology*, 23 (1970), pp. 51–76; idem, "Calvin and Puritanism in England and Scotland – Some Basic Concepts in the Development of 'Federal Theology,'" in *Calvinus Reformator* (Potchefstroom: Potchefstroom University for Christian Higher Education, 1982), pp. 264–77; David N. J. Poole, *The History of the Covenant Concept from the Bible to Johannes Cloppenburg "De Foedere Dei"* (San Francisco: Mellen Research University Press, 1992); cf. my review of Poole in *Calvin Theological Journal*, 28/1 (1993), pp. 217–218.

13. The standard work on Witsius's life and thought remains J. van Genderen, *Herman Witsius: Bijdrage tot de kennis der gereformeerde theologie* (The Hague: Guido de Bres, 1953); note also van Genderen's essay, "Herman Witsius (1636–1708)," in T. Brienen, ed., *De Nadere Reformatie: Beschrijving van haar voornaamste vertegenwoordigers* (The Hague: Boekencentrum, 1986), pp. 193–218, and idem, "Wilhelmus à Brakel (1635–1711)," in ibid., pp. 165–191; on Brakel, also see F. J. Los, *Wilhelmus à Brakel* (Leiden: Groen en Zoon, 1892) and W. Fieret, "Wilhelmus à Brakel," in Brakel, *Reasonable Service*, I, pp. xxxi–lxxxi. The essay by Fieret is an excerpt from his *Theodorus à Brakel, Wilhelmus à Brakel en Sara Nevius* (Houten: Den Hertog, 1988). The two theologians are well paired, inasmuch as both were students of Voetius at Utrecht and granting that Brakel most probably read and followed Witsius's *De oeconomia foederum* at many points in his exposition of the covenants. Both, in addition, represent the normative form of Reformed federalism fashioned in the wake of debate over Cocceius's doctrine.

14. Cf. Muller, *Post-Reformation Reformed Dogmatics*, vol. 2, pp. 507–519.

15. Chapters 9 and 10 in this volume offer some context for this generalization. Also see Erwin R. Gane, "The Exegetical Methods of Some Sixteenth-Century Anglican Preachers: Latimer, Jewel, Hooker, and Andrews," in *Andrews University Seminary Studies*, 17 (1979), pp. 23–38, 169–188, and idem., "The Exegetical Methods of Some Sixteenth-Century Puritan Preachers: Hooper, Cartwright, and Perkins," in *Andrews University Seminary Studies*, 19 (1981), pp. 21–36, 99–114; and Richard A. Muller, "William Perkins and the Protestant Exegetical Tradition: Interpretation, Style and Method in the Commentary on Hebrews 11," in William Perkins, *A Cloud of Faithful Witnesses: Commentary on Hebrews 11*, edited by Gerald T. Sheppard, *Pilgrim Classic Commentaries*, vol. 3 (New York: Pilgrim Press, 1990), pp. 71–94.

16. See, further, D. Kroneman, *Verbond en testament bij Johannes Cocceijus en bij Herman Witsius: een vergelijkend oderzoek* (MA thesis, Utrecht University, 1987).

17. Witsius, *De oeconomia foederum*, I.i.2; cf. the similar discussion in Brakel, *Redelijke Godsdienst*, I.xvi.1.

18. Brakel, *Redelijke Godsdienst*, I.xvi.1 (*Reasonable Service*, I, p. 427).

19. Witsius, *De oeconomia foederum*, I.i.3.

20. Witsius, *De oeconomia foederum*, I.i.3.

21. Witsius, *De oeconomia foederum*, I.i.4, citing Buddaeus, *In comment. ling. Graec.* (for discussion of Isocrates, Aeschines, and Demosthenes) and Hebrews 9:15.

22. Witsius, *De oeconomia foederum*, I.i.4.
23. Witsius, *De oeconomia foederum*, I.iv.
24. Cf. Poole, *History of the Covenant*, pp. 11, 168, 253–255, et passim.
25. Witsius, *De oeconomia foederum*, I.i.5, citing Grotius, *Annotationes* on Matt. 26:28, Bochart, *Hierozoicon*, II.xxxiii (p. 325), and Owen, *Theologoumena*, III.i.[8].
26. Witsius, *De oeconomia foederum*, I.i.6.
27. Witsius, *De oeconomia foederum*, I.i.7.
28. Perkins, Ames, Maccovius, Mastricht, and other heirs of this tradition typically defined theology as a *scientia* or *sapientia* directed toward the attainment of ultimate happiness or blessedness: see the discussion in Muller, *Post-Reformation Reformed Dogmatics*, vol. 1, pp. 334–337, 342–344.
29. Witsius, *De oeconomia foederum*, I.i.9.
30. Witsius, *De oeconomia foederum*, I.i.12, 14.
31. Witsius, *De oeconomia foederum*, I.i.10.
32. Witsius, *De oeconomia foederum*, I.i.11.
33. Brakel, *Redelijke Godsdienst*, I.xii.4–5 (*Reasonable Service*, vol. 1, pp. 356–358).
34. Witsius, *De oeconomia foederum*, I.i.12, citing Deut. 29:12 and Neh. 10:29; cf. Brakel, *Redelijke Godsdienst*, I.xii.11; xvi.6–7, 12–13 (*Reasonable Service*, vol. 1, pp. 363–64, 431–32, 434).
35. Witsius, *De oeconomia foederum*, I.i.13, citing also Exodus 24:8, ". . . the blood of the covenant, which the Lord hath made with you"; cf. Brakel, *Redelijke Godsdienst*, I.xii.11.
36. Witsius, *De oeconomia foederum*, I.i.14.
37. Witsius, *De oeconomia foederum*, I.i.15, citing Romans 3:27; 10:5, 11.
38. Witsius, *De oeconomia foederum*, I.i.15, citing Romans 4:1–5; cf. Brakel, *Redelijke Godsdienst*, I.xii.2; xvi.3
39. Cf. Trinterud, "The Origins of Puritanism," pp. 37–57; Moeller,"The Beginnings of Puritan Covenant Theology," pp. 46–67; Greaves, "The Origins and Early Development of English Covenant Thought," pp. 21–35; Baker, *Heinrich Bullinger and the Covenant*, pp. 165, 200–207; and Poole, *History of the Covenant*, pp. 114–123, 164–168, et passim.
40. Cf. Bierma, "Federal Theology in the Sixteenth Century", pp. 304–321, with Richard A. Muller, *Christ and the Decree: Christology and Predestination in Reformed Theology from Calvin to Perkins* (Durham, NC: Labyrinth Press, 1986; Grand Rapids, MI: Baker Book House, 1988), pp. 40–41.
41. Contra Baker, *Heinrich Bullinger and the Covenant*, pp. 199–200, 205–207.
42. Cf. Heinrich Heppe, *Geschichte des Pietismus und der Mystik in der reformirten Kirche namentlich der Niederlande* (Leiden, 1879), pp. 208–211, with idem, *Die Dogmatik des deutschen Protestantismus im sechzehnten Jahrhundert*, 3 vols. (Gotha, 1857), pp. 145–146, and with Lillback, "Ursinus' Development of the Covenant of Creation," pp. 247–248, 254–255.
43. Wolfgang Musculus, *Loci communes* (Basel, 1563), *locus* xiv (pp. 231–232); Andreas Hyperius, *Methodi theologiae, sive praecipuorum christianae religionis locorum communium, libri tres* (Basel, 1567), pp. 12–14; Ursinus, *Summa theologiae*, qq. 10–19, in August Lang, *Der Heidelberger Katechismus und vier verwandte Katechismen . . . mit einer historisch-theologischen Einleitung* (Leipzig: Deichert, 1907), pp. 153–156.
44. Cf. Heppe, *Geschichte des Pietismus und Mystik*, pp. 205–211, with Schrenk, *Gottesreich und Bund*, pp. 40–44, 50–51, 55–59.
45. See Susan E. Schreiner, *The Theater of His Glory: Nature and the Natural Order in the Thought of John Calvin* (Durham, NC: Labyrinth Press, 1991), especially pp. 22–28, 77–79, 87–90, and note the error in the arguments of Rolston ("Responsible Man in Reformed Theology," pp. 139–142) and Torrance ("Calvin and Puritanism in England and Scotland," pp. 271–272), who insist on a radical priority of grace over law and consequently on attributing the order to an act of grace; cf. the similar strictures in Poole, *History of the Covenant*, p. 255.

46. Bierma, review of Weir, *The Origins of the Federal Theology*, in *Calvin Theological Journal*, 26 (1991), p. 484.

47. Lillback, "Ursinus' Development of the Covenant of Creation," pp. 274–86.

48. Letham, "The *Foedus Operum*: Some Factors Accounting for its Development," pp. 462–63.

49. Cf. Calvin, *Institutes*, II.viii.1; IV.xx.16 with idem, *Commentary on Genesis*, 2:16, in loc. (CTS, vol. 1, pp. 125–126).

50. Ursinus, *Summa theologiae*, qq. 10–19; and see the analysis in Lyle D. Bierma, "Law and Grace in Ursinus Doctrine of the Natural Covenant," in Trueman and Clark, eds., *Protestant Scholasticism*, pp. 96–110.

51. Cf. George Park Fisher, "The Augustinian and Federal Theories of Original Sin Compared," pp. 355–409.

52. Cf. Johannes Cocceius, *Summa theologiae ex Scriptura repetita*, in *Opera omnia theologica, exegetica, didactica, polemica, philologica*, 12 vols. (Amsterdam, 1701–1706), vol. 7: VII.xxxi.1 with Franz Burman, *Synopsis theologiae et speciatim oeconomiae foederum Dei* (Geneva, 1678), II.ii.vi; Johannes Marckius, *Compendium theologiae christianae didactico-elencticum* (Groningen, 1686), XIV.xiv; Benedict Pictet, *Theologia christiana ex puris ss. literarum fontibus hausta* (Geneva, 1696), IV.vii.1; Salomon van Til, *Theologiae utriusque compendium cum naturalis tum revelatae* (Leiden, 1719), II.ii (p. 81); Daniel Wyttenbach, *Tentamen theologiae dogmaticae methodo scientifica pertractatae*, 3 vols. (Frankfurt, 1747–1749), VII, §792.

53. Contra Weir, *Origins*, pp. 14–15.

54. Cf. Witsius, *De oeconomia foederum*, I.ii.15-iii.8 with Brakel, *Redelijke Godsdienst*, I.xii.1–14 (*Reasonable Service*, I, pp. 355–367)and note Cocceius, *Summa theol.*, VIII.xxxi.1; see Muller, *Post-Reformation Reformed Dogmatics*, vol. 2, pp. 434–439 for a discussion of the interpretation of Hosea 6:7. It is simply not to the point to note "that nowhere in Scripture is a covenant with Adam mentioned" (Poole, *History of the Covenant*, p. 254), granting that this imposes a standard of "proof texting" on the seventeenth century that was not then held and ignores the character of the interpretive process.

55. Witsius, *De oeconomia foederum*, I.iii.6, ad fin.

56. Brakel, *Redelijke Godsdienst*, I.xii.5/3 (*Reasonable Service*, vol. 1, p. 358).

57. Brakel, *Redelijke Godsdienst*, I.xii.5/3 (*Reasonable Service*, I, pp. 357–358); cf. Witsius, *De oeconomia foederum*, I.iii.2–8.

58. Witsius, *De oeconomia foederum*, I.iii.2.

59. Witsius, *De oeconomia foederum*, I.iii.2.

60. Kevan, *Grace of Law*, pp. 112–113.

61. Cf. the discussion in Seeberg, *History*, II, pp. 114–118; with Diemer, *Het Scheppingsverbond*, pp. 7–8.

62. See the critique of their approach in Karlberg, "Reformed Interpretation of the Mosaic Covenant," pp. 13–16. It also must be noted that Rolston, who examines Calvin's discussions of the prelapsarian condition of Adam and of the problem of sin as a perversion of "order" at length in the hope of finding there an "order of grace," had to admit that "Calvin does not use that term" ("Responsible Man in Reformed Theology," p. 139; cf. *John Calvin Versus the Westminster Confession*, pp. 23–24): Calvin clearly indicates the goodness of God and the divine intention to order the world for "the comfort and happiness of men" and argues that human beings ought to respect "the law of their creation" (cf. Calvin, *Commentary on the Book of Psalms*, 8:6, in loc. [CTS *Psalms*, vol. 1, p. 106] with idem, *Institutes*, I.iii.3), but he arguably avoids the term "grace" inasmuch as he typically uses the term quite strictly to be the divine response to sin. In a broader sense, grace also can indicate the divine gift of original righteousness and of the right ordering of reason, will, and affections in subjection to God (cf. Thomas Aquinas, *Summa theologiae*, Ia, q. 95, a. 1). In this sense Calvin—and the federal theologians as well—

assume grace before the Fall (cf. Calvin, *Institutes*, I.xv.1–3 with idem, *Commentary on Genesis*, 2:9 [CTS, I, pp. 116–18]): this is precisely the issue of the scholastic doctrine of the *donum superadditum*.

63. Witsius, *De oeconomia foederum*, I.ii.7; cf. Brakel, *Redelijke Godsdienst*, I.xiii.9; cf. xi.10 (*Reasonable Service*, I, pp. 374–375; cf. pp. 336–341).

64. Witsius, *De oeconomia foederum*, I.ii.13; cf. Brakel, *Redelijke Godsdienst*, I.xiii.11.

65. Cf. Thomas Aquinas, *Summa theologiae*, Ia, q. 95, a.1; Ia, IIae, q. 109, a. 2–3, with Heiko A. Oberman, *The Harvest of Medieval Theology: Gabriel Biel and Late Medieval Nominalism*, revised edition (Grand Rapids, MI: Eerdmans, 1967), pp. 128–145 and idem, "*Facientibus Quod in se est Deus non Denegat Gratiam*: Robert Holcot O.P. and the Beginnings of Luther's Theology," in Heiko A. Oberman, *The Dawn of the Reformation: Essays in Late Medieval and Early Reformation Thought* (Edinburgh: T. & T. Clark, 1986), pp. 84–103.

66. Witsius, *De oeconomia foederum*, I.iii.5; cf. Brakel, *Redelijke Godsdienst*, I.xii.6/2 (*Reasonable Service*, vol. 1, p. 358, obj. 2).

67. Witsius, *De oeconomia foederum*, I.iii.6, citing James 1:25; cf. Brakel, *Redelijke Godsdienst*, I.xii.6 (*Reasonable Service*, vol. 1, pp. 358–359).

68. Witsius, *De oeconomia foederum*, I.iii.6; Brakel, *Redelijke Godsdienst*, I.xii.6–7 (*Reasonable Service*, vol. 1, p. 358); cf. Calvin, *Institutes*, II.i.4 and Karlberg, "Reformed Interpretation of the Mosaic Covenant," p. 16.

69. Witsius, *De oeconomia foederum*, I.iii.6, citing 1 John 4:18.

70. Brakel, *Redelijke Godsdienst*, I.xii.7 (*Reasonable Service*, vol. 1, p. 359); Witsius, *De oeconomia foederum*, I.iii.7.

71. Witsius, *De oeconomia foederum*, I.viii.30, citing Romans 5:12; Brakel, *Redelijke Godsdienst*, I.xii.2 (*Reasonable Service*, vol. 1, p. 355).

72. Witsius, *De oeconomia foederum*, I.viii.31; II.v.2, 11; cf. Brakel, *Redelijke Godsdienst*, I.xvii.24 (*Reasonable Service*, vol. 1, p. 482).

73. Witsius, *De oeconomia foederum*, I.ix.21; cf. Brakel, *Redelijke Godsdienst*, I.xiii.11 (*Reasonable Service*, vol. 1, p. 376).

74. Witsius, *De oeconomia foederum*, II.v.6.

75. Witsius, *De oeconomia foederum*, I.iv.7.

76. Witsius, *De oeconomia foederum*, I.iv.7, citing Galatians 3:11–12.

77. Brakel, *Redelijke Godsdienst*, I.xii.11/3, 4 (*Reasonable Service*, vol. 1, p. 361).

78. Brakel, *Redelijke Godsdienst*, I.xii.9/6 (*Reasonable Service*, vol. 1, p. 363).

79. Witsius, *De oeconomia foederum*, I.ix.20.

80. Witsius, *De oeconomia foederum*, I.ix.17; cf. I.v.20; and see Brakel, *Redelijke Godsdienst*, I.xiii.10–11 (*Reasonable Service*, vol. 1, pp. 375–377).

81. Calvin, *Institutes*, II.viii.5.

82. Witsius, *De oeconomia foederum*, I.xi.23.

83. Brakel, *Redelijke Godsdienst*, I.xii.9/3 (*Reasonable Service*, vol. 1, p. 361).

84. Witsius, *De oeconomia foederum*, II.ii-iv; Brakel, *Redelijke Godsdienst*, I.vii.1–20 (*Reasonable Service*, vol. 1, pp. 251–263).

85. See Johannes Cocceius, *Summa doctrinae de foedere et testamento Dei*, v; cf. idem, *Summa theologiae, locus* XIV, *cap*. 34–35; Schrenk, *Gottesreich und Bund*, pp. 91–93; and cf. Richard A. Muller, "The Spirit and the Covenant: John Gill's Critique of the *Pactum Salutis*," in *Foundations: A Baptist Journal of History and Theology*, 24/1 (Jan. 1981), pp. 5–6, and idem, *Christ and the Decree*, pp. 151–152, 161–162, 166.

86. Witsius, *De oeconomia foederum*, II.ii.1.

87. Brakel, *Redelijke Godsdienst*, I.xiii.9, citing 1 Pet. 1:20; cf. I.vii.2–4, 11 (*Reasonable Service*, vol. 1, p. 374; cf. ibid., pp. 252–253, 256–257).

88. Witsius, *De oeconomia foederum*, II.i.4.

89. Note that this is a problem typical of the Torrances' (i.e., T. F. and J. B.) approach to language—namely, the assumption that the meaning of a term is determined by its linguistic root rather than by its actual usage: see the critique of T. F. Torrance in James Barr, *The Semantics of Biblical Language* (Oxford: Oxford University Press, 1961), pp. 188–194, et passim. Note also that, in the specific case of J. B. Torrance's claim that the use of *foedus* for *berith* and *diatheke* imported a legalism, implying a contract rather than a covenant, the claim entirely overlooks two fundamental linguistic points. First, the Latin word itself, although it has the legal or political significance of a contract, also has a broader sense of covenant, treaty, or stipulation—which latter correspond precisely to the meanings of *berith*. Second, it overlooks the vernacular usage of the era, whether in translations of the Bible or in theological treatises, in which, in the actual usage of the theologians criticized by Torrance, *foedus* corresponds not to contract but in fact to "covenant," *verbond*, and like terms.

Index